getting
things
done
on your
PC

getting
things
done
on your
PC

LONDON, NEW YORK, MUNICH, MELBOURNE, DELHI

EDITOR Richard Gilbert
SENIOR ART EDITOR Sarah Cowley
DTP DESIGNER Rajen Shah
PRODUCTION CONTROLLER Sarah Sherlock

MANAGING EDITOR Adèle Hayward
SENIOR MANAGING ART EDITOR Marianne Markham
CATEGORY PUBLISHER Stephanie Jackson

Produced for Dorling Kindersley Limited by
Design Revolution Limited, Queens Park Villa,
30 West Drive, Brighton, East Sussex BN2 0QW
EDITORIAL DIRECTOR Ian Whitelaw
SENIOR DESIGNER Andrew Easton
PROJECT EDITOR John Watson

First published in Great Britain in 2002
by Dorling Kindersley Limited,
80 Strand, London WC2R 0RL

A Penguin Company

2 4 6 8 10 9 7 5 3 1

Copyright © 2002 Dorling Kindersley Limited
Text copyright © 2002 Dorling Kindersley Limited

Screen grabs from Microsoft® Windows® Me, Word 2000,
Excel 2000, Internet Explorer and Outlook Express
used by permission of Microsoft Corporation.

A CIP catalogue record for this book is available from the British Library.

ISBN 0-7513-4645-4

Colour reproduced by Colourscan
Printed and bound by Graphicom

For our complete catalogue visit
www.dk.com

ABOUT THIS BOOK

Getting Things Done On Your PC is an easy-to-follow guide to
creating documents and spreadsheets, exploring the internet,
using email, and operating your scanner and printer.

T HIS BOOK WILL HELP YOU TO GET
the most out of your computer,
whether you are a complete novice
or an experienced user approaching
Windows for the first time or looking at
programs you have never investigated. In
a series of eight sections, *Getting Things
Done On Your PC* takes you through using
Windows, Word, Excel, and the internet, as
well as making the most of your printer,
scanner, and computer.

Each section is divided into chapters that
deal with specific topics, and within each
chapter you will find subsections that cover
self-contained procedures. Each of these
procedures builds on the knowledge that
you will have accumulated by working
through the previous chapters.

The chapters and subsections use a step-
by-step approach, and almost every step is
accompanied by an illustration showing

how your screen should look at that stage.
The book contains several other features
that make it easier to absorb the quantity of
information that is provided. Cross-
references are shown within the text as left-
or right-hand page icons: ⏴ and ⏵. The
page number within the icon and the
reference are shown at the foot of the page.

As well as the step-by-step sections, there
are boxes that explain the meaning of
unfamiliar terms and abbreviations, and
give additional information to take your
knowledge beyond that provided on the
rest of the page. Finally, at the back, you
will find a glossary explaining new terms,
and a comprehensive index.

For further information on computer
software and digital technology, see the
wide range of titles available in the *DK
Essential Computers* series.

CONTENTS

USING WINDOWS

MANAGING YOUR FILES

USING WORD

DESIGNING DOCUMENTS

USING WINDOWS

BEGINNING TO USE A COMPUTER FOR the first time is inevitably difficult. There is no other gadget that you can compare with a computer, nor one that can have provided you with any experience to draw on. This section will help to introduce you to the computer. We start by advising you on how to use the keyboard and the mouse, and then show you what the different elements of the opening screen mean when you turn on your computer. The two basic elements of windows and their menus are covered, which naturally lead into how to start using a few of the programs that are provided with Windows Me. Using these programs, you will learn how to create and save files, and we also tell you how to organize them. Installing software is considered, and finally, for your relaxation, we show you how to play games on your PC.

KEYBOARD & MOUSE

Your computer's central processing unit, or CPU, allows you to create and manipulate text, images, and numerical data, but without a keyboard and a mouse it is practically useless.

INPUTTING AND MANIPULATING

In order for a computer to fulfil its purpose, it needs information, and the main method of inputting the necessary data is by means of the keyboard, which enables you to key in text and figures. The purpose of the mouse is to help you access the programs on your computer, to use the menus and options that each program offers, and to edit and move words, images, numbers, and graphics within programs. Your keyboard and mouse are your most useful tools.

TYPEWRITER PLUS
● The layout of the alphabet keys on a computer keyboard ⌐ is essentially the same as that on a standard typewriter, with the addition of function keys that tell the computer program to carry out specific commands. An "extended" keyboard also has extra keys at the right-hand side, commonly referred to as calculator, or number pad, keys.

THE MOUSE

A mouse is basically a pointing device that is attached to your PC via a cable and moves the cursor across the screen. The most common type has two buttons on the top, and clicking these allows the user to open documents, drag and drop items on the computer desktop or between applications, and access program menus. In addition, some mice have a wheel situated between the buttons, and this can be used to scroll up and down through documents and web pages on the internet.

MOUSE BASICS

As you move the mouse across a flat surface (a mouse mat is best), the speed and direction of the movement are transmitted to the computer by rollers connected to sensors. Clicking or rolling the mouse wheel also sends instructions to the PC. In this way, the movement of a cursor on the computer screen is controlled by the mouse.

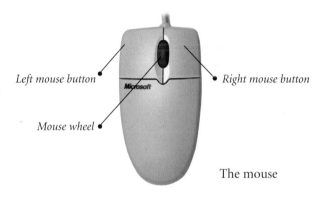

Left mouse button

Right mouse button

Mouse wheel

The mouse

LEFT CLICK
- The click of the left mouse button is probably the most common task performed with a mouse.
- Clicking once or twice with this button on an application's "icon" for instance, will open that application. Clicking and holding down the left mouse button on an item, such as a folder, will allow you to drag that item to a another folder on your computer. When you let go of the left mouse button, the item is released. This use of the mouse is called "drag and drop."

RIGHT CLICK
- Clicking on the right mouse button, particularly on a file, usually launches a pop-up menu, which offers extra options or functions related to that file. Right-clicking on the Windows Me desktop, for instance, allows you to arrange icons, create new folders and icons, and alter the properties of your PC.

MOUSE WHEEL
- The mouse wheel is extremely useful when working on the internet, as it allows you to scroll up and down individual pages using the wheel or, by clicking on the wheel, to change the cursor into a directional tool that will cause the page to move up or down on your screen.

After clicking on the mouse wheel, the cursor can be used to scroll down through the web page

TUNING YOUR MOUSE

The way your mouse behaves on screen can be adjusted to suit the way you work. For example, the speed that you have to double-click in order to open a file can be changed, and so can the speed at which the pointer travels across the screen when you move the mouse. Follow the steps below, and experiment with the settings.

MOUSE PROPERTIES

● First click on the **Start** menu in the bottom left-hand corner of your screen.
● Go to **Settings** in the pop-up menu, choose **Control Panel**, and double-click on the **Mouse** icon. The **Mouse Properties** dialog box opens.
● The **Buttons** tab enables you to change the mouse from right-handed to left-handed, and to change the double-click speed.
● Clicking on the **Pointer Options** tab allows you to change the pointer speed.

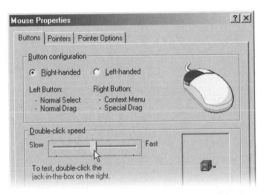

ADJUSTING KEYBOARD SETTINGS

Various aspects of the way the keyboard operates can also be controlled from within the **Control Panel**. Instead of double-clicking on the **Mouse** icon, choose **Keyboard** instead. The **Keyboard Properties** dialog box opens. Under the **Speed** tab you can alter the time you need to hold down a key before it starts to repeat that letter on screen, and you can set the rate at which repeat letters then appear on the screen.

THE KEYBOARD

DISCOVERING THE KEYBOARD LAYOUT

● One of the biggest challenges with your first PC is simply finding the right keys on the keyboard. So before going any further we will briefly look at the layout. In addition to the alphabet, number, and punctuation keys, the PC keyboard also has special keys that provide shortcuts to actions within the various programs. These are described below.

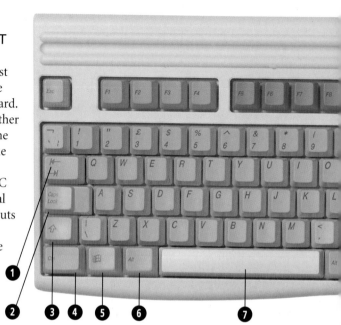

THE KEYBOARD LAYOUT

❶ Tab Key
This key moves the insertion point (the position in which typed letters appear) to an indented position on the page.

❷ Caps Lock
When this key has been pressed, all typed letters will be capital, or upper-case, letters.

❸ Shift Key
To type upper case letters and special symbols, hold down the shift key and press the letter key.

❹ Control Key
In combination with letter keys, the control key allows you to carry out various tasks, such as copying and pasting in Word.

❺ Windows Key
Press and release this to bring up the Windows Start menu.

❻ Alt Key
Like the Control key, this key can be used in combination with letter keys to carry out various tasks.

❼ Space Bar
Pressing the space bar introduces a letter space when keying in text.

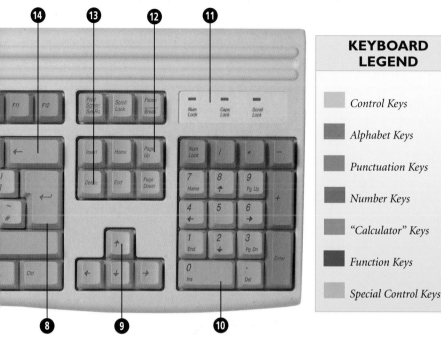

KEYBOARD LEGEND

- Control Keys
- Alphabet Keys
- Punctuation Keys
- Number Keys
- "Calculator" Keys
- Function Keys
- Special Control Keys

THE KEYBOARD LAYOUT

8 Return/Enter
Introduces a paragraph end when working with text, and enters a command when an option is highlighted in a program dialog box.

9 Cursor Keys
These keys move the cursor or insertion point up and down, left and right.

10 Calculator Keys
When the Number Lock key

has been pressed, these can be used to key in numbers, and they also work as the number pad for the Windows calculator

11 Indicator Lights
Lights on this panel show when the Number Lock, Caps Lock, or Scroll Lock are active.

12 Page Up/Page Down
Pressing these keys takes you to the page before, or the page after, the current of the document.

13 Delete Forwards
Deletes the character to the right of the insertion point.

14 Delete
This key deletes a character to the left of the insertion point, and will also delete any highlighted element.

WINDOWS ME

Windows Me has been developed with the home PC user in mind, and with this latest offering, Microsoft is aiming to make the PC an even better environment in which to work.

WHAT IS WINDOWS ME?

Windows Me is an operating system – the backbone of your day-to-day computing environment. Windows Me has simplified the PC experience by removing some irritations of earlier versions of Windows and introducing improvements of its own.

RECOGNIZE ME?

In the early 1990s, Microsoft released its first version of Windows, known as Windows 3.x (the "x" stood for the different version numbers). This was a great leap forward from the old operating system, known as MS-DOS. In 1995, Windows 95 was released, which was a smaller step forward than 3.x. Three years later, Windows 98 appeared, and was an even smaller step forward than the 95 version. The release of Windows Millennium Edition (Me) is an even smaller advance, but it's still an improvement on its immediate predecessor.

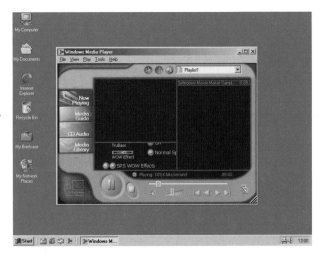

Technically Speaking...
Windows is a Graphical User Interface (GUI), which means that instead of typing commands into your computer as MS-DOS required, you use a mouse to point and click to issue instructions to the machine.

FEATURES OF WINDOWS ME FOR EXPERIENCED USERS

● MEDIA PLAYER

Media Player can access digital media on the internet, from movies to radio stations. You can also download and play MP3 files. A database called Media Library lets you organize MP3 files, audio, WAVs, and video files into one source. You can also copy CDs to your hard disk in Windows Media Audio format.

● MOVIE MAKER

Movie Maker captures video off a camcorder, VCR, or webcam and lets you edit the footage before saving it as a movie. Connect your camera to your PC then click on the record button. Movie Maker imports your video and automatically breaks it into compressed clips for easier management and manipulation. Digital photos for slide shows can be imported, and background music and narration can be added. You are likely to need additional hardware, such as a video capture card to transfer the video from your camcorder or VCR.

● HOME NETWORKING

Windows Me features Universal Plug and Play, which enables devices to be connected and to share resources. Connecting PCs used to be complicated, but with the Windows Me Home Networking Wizard, creating a home network is easy. It is also possible to connect digital music players, digital cameras and camcorders, and wireless devices over a network. For example, a clock radio and a thermostat could communicate over the network to turn on the heating before the alarm goes off in the morning.

● AUTOUPDATE

AutoUpdate allows the latest enhancements to Windows Me to be downloaded automatically. When you are online, AutoUpdate uses the occasions when the modem is inactive to download updates. When an update is fully downloaded, AutoUpdate informs you and provides an opportunity to install the update. AutoUpdate is easily configurable and provides a convenient way to keep your computer system current.

● SYSTEM FILE PROTECTION

System File Protection (SFP) prevents problems before they occur by stopping the accidental or unauthorized overwriting of system files and helps keep the system stable. For example, a new application may try to overwrite a system file with an older or an altered file, which can affect the system's stability. SFP does not allow any correct system files to be overwritten.

● SYSTEM RESTORE

The System Restore feature enables the computer's system to be returned easily to its previous settings. For example, if a newly installed application is causing problems, the computer can be returned to its preinstallation settings. Users can choose a date as a restore point, such as the point before the new installation, or one of the predefined system checkpoints.

THE WINDOWS ME DESKTOP

When you first start your computer, the Windows Me desktop appears. It is from this location that every action that you carry out on your computer begins. From here, you can launch programs, search for documents, surf the internet, and play games. The desktop is also a place where you can keep all your letters, documents, photographs, and much more. The desktop is also highly customizable.

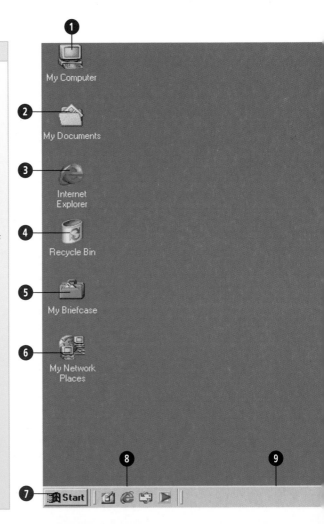

FEATURES KEY

❶ My Computer
The My Computer window displays all the folders, documents, and programs on your computer.

❷ My Documents
The My Documents folder is a place to store any files you need. For example, you may create other folders within it, separating your graphics files from your text documents.

❸ Internet Explorer
If your computer is set up correctly, then double-clicking this icon 📄 will connect you to the internet.

❹ Recycle Bin
The Recycle Bin 📄 is where you place items that you want to delete.

❺ My Briefcase
My Briefcase allows you to carry work between two computers, and makes sure that the files are up-to-date on both hard disk drives.

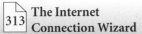

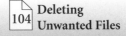

313 **The Internet Connection Wizard**

104 **Deleting Unwanted Files**

STARTUP PROBLEMS?

When you turn on your PC, it should go through a procedure known as booting up. If this fails to happen, or if the computer fails to start up as it should, carry out these checks. First make sure that the power cable is plugged in and that the power is turned on. Second, check there isn't a floppy disk in the floppy disk drive. Third, check all interconnecting cabling from the PC.

FEATURES KEY

6 My Network Places
This tool links your computer to any others that are on the same network.

7 Start Button
The Start button provides a tree structure of shortcuts to the document folders, files, and programs stored on the computer.

8 The Quick Launch Toolbar
Add or remove applications to access them easily.

9 Taskbar
The Taskbar gives quick access to programs and documents that are open on your desktop.

10 System Tray
The System Tray contains the icons of special utilities.

11 The Desktop
The Windows Me desktop is where you work. Programs open here, and you can store files for as long as you need.

EXPLORING ME

Now that we have seen the Windows Me desktop, it's time to explore your surroundings further and discover what the taskbar does, as well as the different menus and help screens.

USING THE TASKBAR

The taskbar is a panel initially located at the foot of the screen. It contains the **Start** button, from where programs can be launched, the Quick Launch bar, the System tray, and the buttons for all your open files, programs, and windows.

NAVIGATING BETWEEN WINDOWS

● As you use, experiment, and play with Windows Me, you will find that you can easily have many different applications and windows open at the same time, and that your screen may resemble the example on the right.

All the documents and windows that are active have a corresponding button on the taskbar ●

● Clicking on a program button on the taskbar brings the program to the foreground where it is ready to use. Here, we have clicked on the **3D Pinball for Windows** button to open its window.

Note that 3D Pinball for Windows is now in the foreground and active

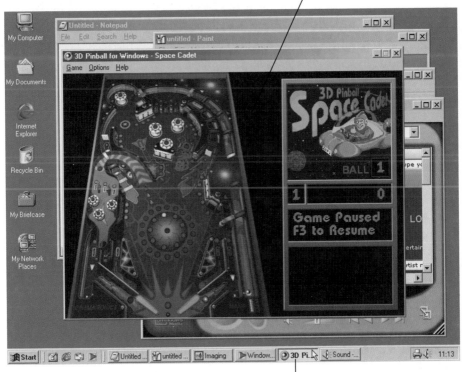

Clicking on a button makes the application active ●

USING THE MOUSE BUTTONS

Generally speaking, the left mouse button is used to activate applications or menu options by clicking once. It is also used for scrolling through windows and menus 🖱, and for dragging and dropping 🖱. If you right-click with the mouse on an object, for instance, the **My Computer** icon on the desktop, a menu of options appears (right). This allows you, among other options, to open, browse, create a shortcut to, rename, and view the properties of that object.

MINIMIZING ALL WINDOWS

● To minimize all windows when you start to lose track of where they all are, right-click on a blank area of the taskbar and click on **Minimize All Windows**.

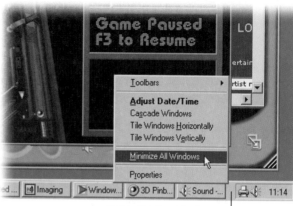

Right click in a blank space ●

RESTORING A WINDOW

● All the applications have been minimized and the desktop is clear. However, any one of the windows can still be accessed through the taskbar by left-clicking on its taskbar button.

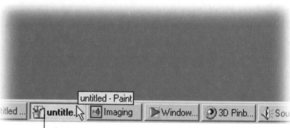

●*Single-click on the application that you wish to use; in this case we have clicked on Paint and the application opens*

MINIMIZING AND MAXIMIZING INDIVIDUAL WINDOWS

❶ Minimize
Clicking on this button minimizes the window. The window is still available by left-clicking on its button on the taskbar.

❷ Maximize
The Maximize button expands the window to fill the whole screen. Once maximized, the button then changes its name to Restore.

❸ Restore
Clicking on the Restore button returns the window to its previous dimensions and location onscreen.

❹ Close
To shut down an application or to close a window, such as Windows Explorer, click the Close button. If you need to save an open file before closing, Windows prompts you.

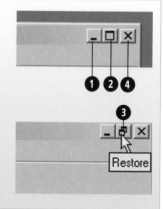

USING THE START MENU

The Windows **Start** button is the main starting point for finding and accessing files and documents, installing and using programs, and changing and customizing the settings on your computer to suit your own requirements. It is also the location from where you can access the **Help** options, and, paradoxically, is the place where can you restart your computer or shut it down at the end of a session.

OPENING THE START MENU

● Place the cursor over the **Start** button and click the left mouse button once.

● The Start menu pops up. Any of the options can be clicked on to select it. When the options that are accompanied by a black, right-pointing arrowhead are clicked on, they display a submenu of further options.

START MENU KEY		
❶ Windows Update *see* p.17	❹ Settings Menu *see* p.26	❼ Run Command *see* p.25
❷ Programs Menu *see* p.24	❺ Search Menu *see* p.27	❽ Log Off Option *To log off as a user*
❸ Documents Menu *see* p.29	❻ Windows Help *see* p.316	❾ Shut Down Option *see* p.29

THE PROGRAMS MENU

The **Programs** menu lists the software, sometimes called "applications," that you use to perform tasks on your computer.

The **Programs** submenu also allows access to further submenus where related applications are grouped together.

PROGRAMS SUBMENU

● When you initially move the cursor over the **Programs** entry in the **Start** menu, the submenu may contain one or two entries.

● The rest of the menu can be seen by clicking on the two down arrowheads.

Windows Me "tidies" items that haven't been used recently by placing them in a subordinate part of the menu

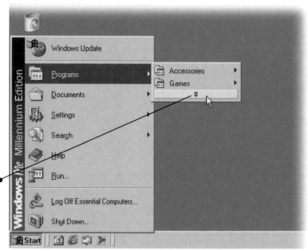

● When the down arrowheads are clicked, they display these hidden, less used, applications.

*The **Online Services** submenu contains connections to the internet*

*Clicking on this option immediately launches **Windows Media Player***

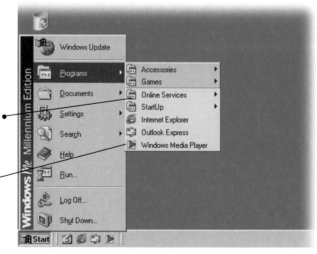

ACCESSORIES

● The **Accessories** menu contains applications that are installed along with Windows Me. They include games, a calculator, and text-editing tools.

● In addition, this menu also contains its own submenus.

The Run Command

An alternative method of launching a program is to click on **Run** in the **Start** menu and type the name of the file that is needed to run the program. This option is generally used by more experienced users of Microsoft Windows.

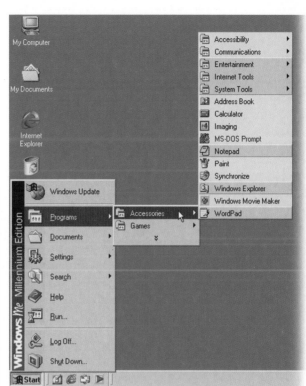

GAMES

● The **Games** submenu contains a selection of simple applications for passing time.

● Not only are there a number of games that can be played on your own, but there are also five that can be played over the internet. With Windows Me, you can now play games from your office against someone sitting on the other side of the world.

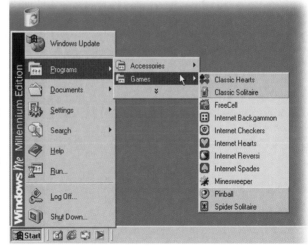

THE SETTINGS MENU

The **Settings** menu contains options that include the opportunity to customize and fine-tune the working of your computer, to connect to another computer, to handle printers, and to select what appears in the taskbar and the **Start** menu.

SETTINGS
● The **Settings** menu has four main options: The **Control Panel, Dial-Up Networking**, the **Printers** folder, and **Taskbar and Start Menu**.

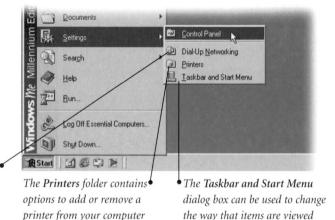

Dial-Up Networking enables you to connect to another computer and to a network by using a modem

*The **Printers** folder contains options to add or remove a printer from your computer*

*The **Taskbar and Start Menu** dialog box can be used to change the way that items are viewed*

THE CONTROL PANEL OPTIONS
● The **Control Panel** has options available to alter many of the settings on your computer. It also has facilities to add and remove hardware and programs, alter the settings for your peripherals and network, and it also includes **Accessibility Options**.

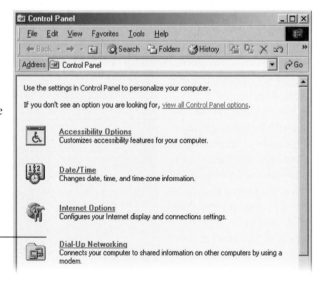

*The **Control Panel** contains many options for customizing your PC*

THE SEARCH MENU

The **Search** menu has three options. The first is to search for files and folders contained on your computer, the second and third options allow you to search for websites and for people – for these latter two options, internet access is needed 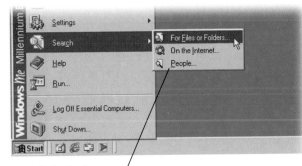.

1 SELECTING FILES OR FOLDERS

● Click once on the **Start** button, select **Search**, move the cursor across to **For Files or Folders** in the submenu, and click once.

*There are also the options to search **On the Internet** and for **People**; you will need your computer to be connected to the internet to use these options*

● The **Search Results** dialog box opens. Click inside the text box below **Search for files or folders named**. Enter as much of the name as you can. In this example, a missing **Letter** is being searched for.
● The next box down, labeled **Containing text**, allows you to enter words contained in the file. The letter we are looking for here has the date **May**, so this is entered into the box. Click the Search Now button and the search will begin. Results are displayed in the right-hand window.

2 SEARCH THE INTERNET

● The second option is to search the internet. Again, click on the Start button, select Search and then On The Internet.

● Your Internet connection opens. The left hand side of the Internet Explorer window contains the search panel. Type in your Search word, or words and click the search button. Results are displayed as links to websites, below the search button.

● Clicking on these results will display that particular website in the right-hand window.

3 SEARCH FOR PEOPLE

● This option allows you to search for people, and/or their email address.

● Once the Find People dialog panel is open, from the drop-down menu, select a search engine, there are several available.

● Either enter your details in the Name and email boxes, or click on the Website button which will take you straight to the homepage of that search engine. This latter method has greater search capabilities.

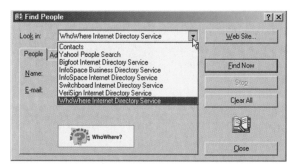

THE DOCUMENTS OPTION

- The **Documents** option on the **Start** menu opens documents that you have been working on recently. Click on the **Start** menu, point to **Documents**, move the cursor over the document that you want to open, and click on it.

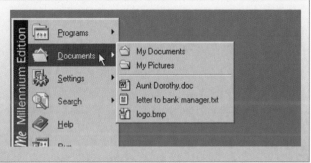

RESTARTING AND SHUTTING DOWN

Turning off a computer is different from switching off the television. There are internal settings that a computer has to maintain, and these have to be recorded before shutdown. However, with Windows Me, shutting down is now much faster.

1 LAUNCHING SHUT DOWN

- Click on the **Start** button and click on **Shut Down**.

2 SELECTING THE RIGHT OPTION

- **Shut down** is the first option on the menu.
- **Restart** is the equivalent of shutting down and starting again.
- **Stand by** puts your computer into a low power-consumption mode.
- When the correct selection is highlighted, click on **OK**.

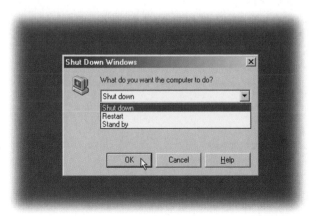

WINDOWS ME PROGRAMS

When you start Windows Me, and take a look around for the first time, you will notice that there are various programs available for use. Let's take a look at a few of them.

NOTEPAD

Notepad is a basic text editor, used mainly for creating, viewing, and editing documents that only contain text, and do not contain any images.

Notepad has some very useful features. Text can be cut, copied, and pasted; and there is also an option to add the date and time if you want to include those details.

1 LAUNCHING NOTEPAD

● The first step in using any program or tool on a computer is to open or "launch" it. There may be "shortcuts" available, but to begin with, using the **Start** button is the simplest method.

● Click on the **Start** button, move to **Programs**, **Accessories**, and then finally to **Notepad**.

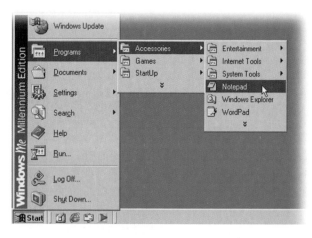

WHAT IS A PROGRAM?

A program allows you to perform a specific task or function on your computer. Programs can also be called "applications," which is a slightly broader term. Programs and applications are also called software. Windows Me is a piece of software that creates a "platform" for other applications.

2 THE NEW DOCUMENT

● A new, blank document screen opens with a blue title bar at the top and a menu bar below it.

● A cursor flashes at the top left of the window and shows where text will appear when you begin typing.

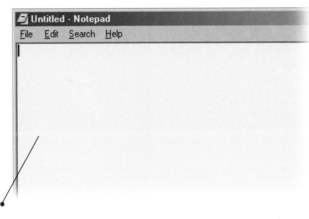

*The **Notepad** main window*

● When you begin typing, the cursor disappears.

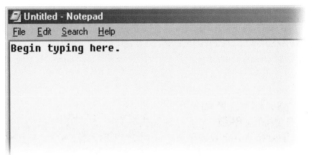

3 SAVING THE DOCUMENT

● Once you have created your first document, you can save it. This allows it to be opened again at any time.

● When you save a file for the first time, Windows asks you to give it a name and select a location where it is to be saved on your hard drive.

● Click on **File** in the Menu bar, and from the drop-down menu click on **Save**.

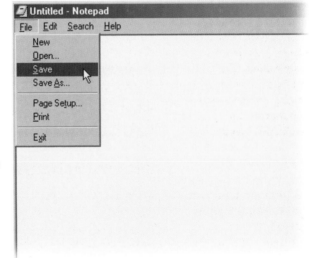

● The **Save As** dialog box opens. By default, Windows directs the file to the **My Documents** folder, which is a useful location for your files when you first start .

● In the **File name** text box, type in a descriptive name for the document.

● Click on the **Save** button. The **Save As** box closes and your document is saved.

4 OPENING AN EXISTING FILE

● At some time, you are likely to need to open a file that you have saved to edit it or print it out. There are two main ways of opening a file.

● The first method is carried out from inside Notepad. Open Notepad as before, then click on **File** in the Menu bar, and click on **Open**.

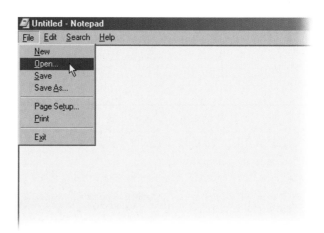

● The **Open** dialog box opens. Notepad makes the assumption, by default, that any documents created previously have been saved to the **My Documents** folder.

● Click on the file that you wish to open (in this case, the **Monday Shopping List.txt**).

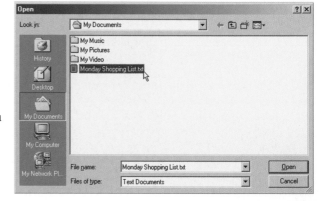

● Now move the cursor down to the **Open** button at the bottom right hand corner and click on it.

● The file will open onscreen and you can make changes and then resave it.

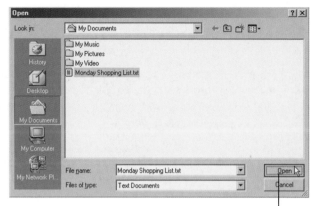

Click on the Open button ●

● The second method of opening an existing file is more direct than the first.

● Select the folder that contains the file you want to open. In this case, it is the **My Documents** folder. Double-click on the folder icon to open its window.

● In the **My Documents** window, double-click on the file that you wish to open. The file automatically opens in the program that was used to create it – in this case, Notepad.

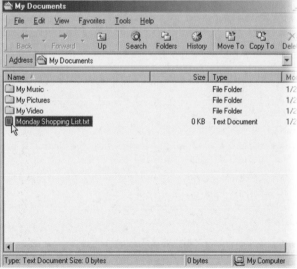

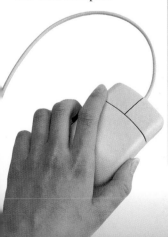

PAINT

Paint is a piece of graphics software that is used to create and work with images. An image you have created can then be pasted into another document, and you can even edit photographs that have been scanned in. Paint also has its own text tool.

LAUNCHING PAINT

● You can launch Paint in the same way that Notepad was launched ⌐. Click on the **Start** button, move up to **Programs**, select **Accessories** from the submenu, and then click on **Paint**.

● A window opens that contains painting tools, a color palette, and the main Paint window.

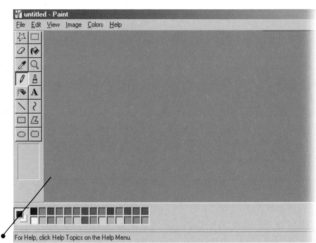

The main Paint window ●

DRAWING WITH PAINT

● Using the **Pencil** tool, we have drawn an outline of a tree, and then with the **Airbrush** tool we have started to color the image.

*The **Pencil** tool* ●

*The **Color palette** from which you can select a color by clicking on it*

30 Launching Notepad

THE FINISHED DRAWING

● Using various shades of colors from the color palette, we have created a reasonable representation of a tree. Further efforts will improve with practice.

THE PAINT TOOLS PALETTE

● There are many tools available in Paint, from a simple line tool to an airbrush. With time and patience, these tools can soon be mastered.

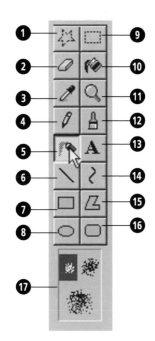

Find Out More...
We have only been able to give an overview of Paint here. The **Help** drop-down menu within the program contains numerous hints and tips for greater creativity.

PAINT TOOLS

❶ Free-Form Select
❷ Eraser/Color Eraser
❸ Pick Color
❹ Pencil
❺ Airbrush
❻ Line
❼ Rectangle
❽ Ellipse
❾ Select
❿ Fill With Color
⓫ Magnifier
⓬ Brush
⓭ Text
⓮ Curve
⓯ Polygon
⓰ Rounded Rectangle
⓱ Airbrush Nozzles

Note: The Airbrush Nozzles Palette only shows when the Airbrush tool is selected.

IMAGING

Windows Imaging is a great application for scanning or importing images and downloading photographs directly from a digital camera. Notes can be added to images and then the whole document can be printed out or emailed.

QUICK AND FUN

- Imaging is very simple to use, and yet it offers countless opportunities for creating documents that you can share with family and friends with its direct email link.
- If you have a scanner connected to your computer, then images can be instantly placed in an imaging document and printed out.
- Text can be added to documents as well as to images in a variety of entertaining ways.
- Documents can be created to your own specifications. You can choose the file type that you require, the level of color needed (whether a single color or millions of colors), decide whether you want to compress your document to save disk space or time while sending by email, and select the resolution and size of your image.

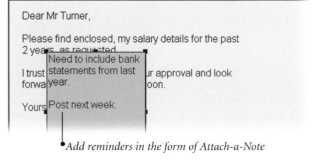

Add reminders in the form of Attach-a-Note

IMAGING TOOLS

1 Annotation Selection
Selects annotation for deleting, moving, or changing

2 Freehand Line
Draw a freehand line, and change its color and width

3 Highlighter
Use this to highlight important areas of text

4 Straight Line
Draw a straight line

5 Hollow Rectangle
Change the width of the rectangle's line and add color

6 Filled Rectangle
Draw a solid rectangle

7 Text
Type and edit text and select different fonts

8 Attach-a-Note
Place a sticky note, change its color and its font style

9 Text From File
Import text from a file

10 Rubber Stamp
Place a rubber stamp effect on your page. You can even create your own designs

WORDPAD

Wordpad takes text editing further than Notepad. With Wordpad, you are able to design and produce colorful documents, and insert graphics (as shown here) or photographs that you may have created or downloaded from the internet. You will see that Wordpad has a far more extensive range of tools than Notepad.

1 ENTERING AND SELECTING TEXT

- Wordpad, like Notepad and Paint, is opened from the **Start** menu, moving to **Programs**, choosing **Accessories**, and then **Wordpad**.
- When you start typing into the document that opens, a font size of 10 points is used automatically. However, the font size can be reduced or enlarged.
- Hold down the mouse button when the cursor is at the end of the line, then drag the cursor over the text to highlight the line.

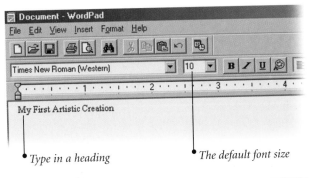

Type in a heading

The default font size

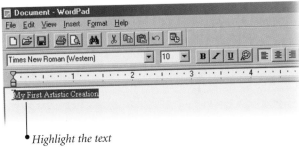

Highlight the text

2 SELECTING THE FONT SIZE

- Click on the down arrow to the right of the Font Size box, and in the drop-down menu click on a larger font size. Here, a font size of 22 is selected.

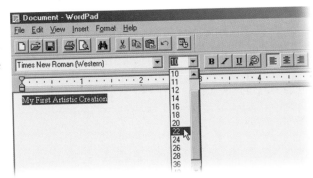

● The text changes to the selected size.
● Click the cursor at the end of the line of text to deselect it, and press [Enter ←] twice.

The cursor is now here ●

3 INSERTING AN OBJECT
● Click on **Insert** in the Menu bar and click on **Object** in the drop-down menu that appears.

Click on Object ●

4 BROWSING FOR AN IMAGE
● The **Insert Object** dialog box opens. As the image to be inserted is in a file, click on the **Create from File** radio button.

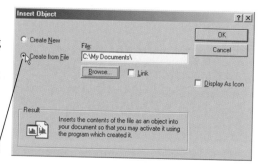

Click on Create from File ●

● The contents of the dialog box change to show a text field where the names of folders and files can be displayed.
● Click on the **Browse** button to navigate to the location of the graphic.

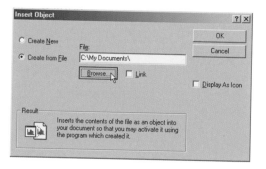

5 OPENING MY PICTURES

● The **Browse** dialog box opens. The image of the tree, which was created using Paint, is stored in the **My Pictures** folder.
● Double-click on that folder to open it.

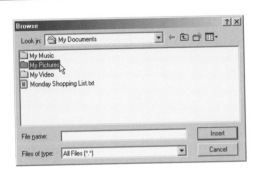

6 SELECTING THE IMAGE

● The tree is the only image contained in the **My Pictures** folder.
● Click on the image and then on the **Insert** button.

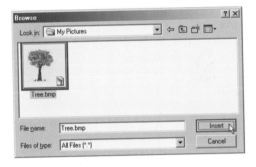

7 INSERTING THE SELECTION

● The filename is shown in the text field, and you can now click on **OK**.

8 THE INSERTED GRAPHIC

● The picture is inserted into the document below the heading.
● The techniques shown here can be used for a variety of different purposes in different documents – from letterheads to greeting cards.

My First Artistic Creation

35 **The Finished Drawing**

INSTALLING SOFTWARE

Having Windows Me installed on your computer means that you have a great many new and exciting programs to explore and play with. However, the time will come when you will want to develop and expand your computing and gaming horizons. This means that you will want to start to installing software.

WHERE CAN YOU OBTAIN SOFTWARE?

There are many ways to source software, and thousands of applications are available – from the latest games to a program to help redesign your backyard.

Where you look for software depends on what you want. Large graphics-creation programs are available from computer stores and an immense range of mail-order websites. Computer utilities are available as downloads or from CDs on the covers of computer magazines.

Websites are a useful source of free software.

WHAT DIFFERENT FORMS OF SOFTWARE ARE AVAILABLE?

The bulk of the software you will install is the commercially available form that you install on one computer and make one backup copy □. Another form of software is shareware, which you can try before paying a fee to use it. After a trial period, you are then asked to pay a registration fee, which is less than you would pay for commercial software, and which funds the author to support the software, update it, and develop new programs. In some cases, you may receive updates and manuals.

A NOTE OF CAUTION

Installing software is far from being a completely safe operation. New programs can have the tendency to want to work in parts of your computer where other programs are working, which can lead to conflicts. Programs might also try to install themselves in the system tray at the right-hand end of the taskbar, which should be reserved for programs that need to be running all the time, such as antivirus software. The most important precaution you can take is to monitor each installation closely. Read what each window says, and if it's unclear or unwanted, just click on the "No" option.

45 The Problem of Software Piracy

INSTALLING FROM A CD

For this example, a piece of software is going to be installed from a CD-ROM that was supplied with a popular home computing magazine. These discs can contain fully functional programs or trial versions with a limited life.

1 AUTORUN FEATURE

● Most CDs that are free with magazines have an autorun feature that automatically opens the CD-ROM when it is placed in the drive.
● A screen appears that usually lists the software available and advertisements for other products.

2 CHOOSING YOUR SOFTWARE

● Choose the program that you want to install. In this case, we are going to install the latest version of WinZip, which is a file-archive and compression utility.
● After clicking on the **Install Software** button, the setup begins.

Install Software

WHAT IS FILE COMPRESSION?

WinZip – as we have mentioned – is a file compression and archiving utility. File compression is a method of making files smaller in size, and therefore saving disk space, without losing quality or data, which is vital for files you want to archive. WinZip is probably the most common program used for this function. A trial version of WinZip can be downloaded from the internet from its own website: **http:// www.winzip.com**.

- The **WinZip Setup** window appears.
- Click on the **Setup** button to continue.

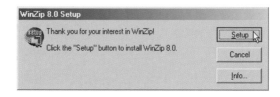

3 CHOOSING A LOCATION

- Programs usually install themselves in a location that they select, and to which you can agree by clicking on **OK**.

- A screen appears, providing information on the software you are about to install.
- After reading the information, click on **Next** to continue.

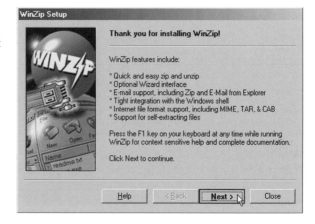

4 LICENSE AGREEMENT

- The License Agreement is where the lawyers briefly take over from the programmers. Some applications present you with the whole agreement. WinZip's option is simpler where you can simply click on **Yes** to agree.

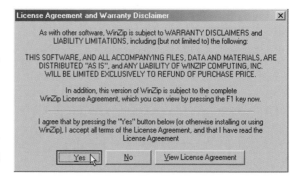

5 CONTINUING INSTALLING

● You are offered the opportunity to print or view useful information about the installation and the use of WinZip.

● Click **Next** to continue with the installation.

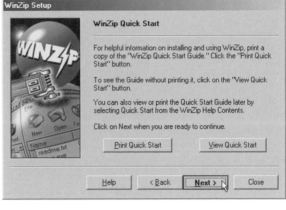

● WinZip has almost completed its installation. It now needs to know which type of WinZip you wish to start with. In this example, we have chosen to start with WinZip Classic. Read the text on the dialog box carefully and make your own choice.

We have chosen to start with WinZip Classic

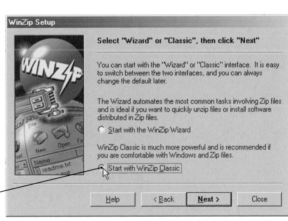

● When you are given the choice, click in the circle (known as a "radio button") next to **Start with WinZip Classic**. Don't be deterred by the fact that this is recommended for people already familiar with Zip files – you will not be performing any tasks within the program yet.

● Click on **Next**.

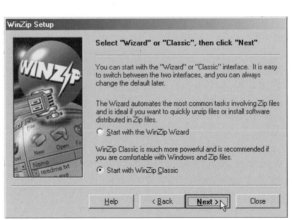

● Click in the radio button next to **Express setup (recommended)**.
● Click on the **Next** button.

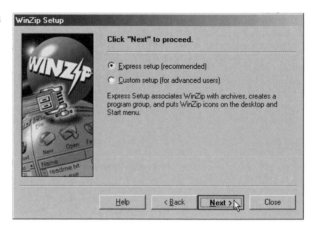

● Once the installation process is complete, click on the **Finish** button.

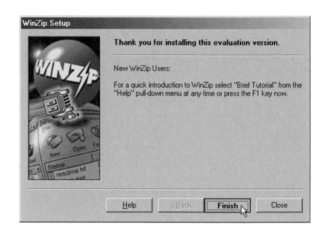

6 CLOSING WINZIP

● You can now close the the program by clicking on the **Close** button.
● In future, WinZip will automatically expand compressed files when you download them to your computer.

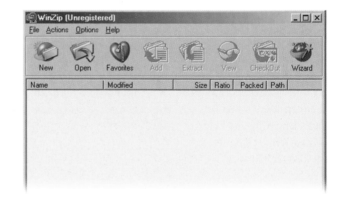

● As well as installing the software on your computer, other changes have been made. A shortcut to WinZip has automatically been placed on the desktop.

● In addition, the **Start** menu now also contains a shortcut to WinZip.

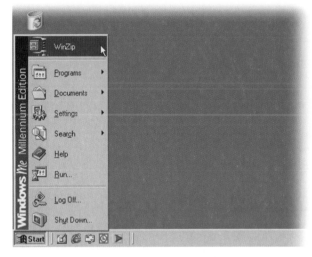

THE PROBLEM OF SOFTWARE PIRACY

● The ease with which computer software can be copied from computer to computer makes it very tempting to copy programs for friends. However, when you buy a program, you are buying a license to install the program only on one computer and to make a backup copy for archiving purposes only. Any use of computer software beyond those activities is illegal.

● In the US, the Copyright Act gives the copyright owner the exclusive rights to reproduce the work and distribute copies. Buying software does not include the purchase of those legal rights of reproduction and distribution as well.

● In addition to being illegal, software piracy is very risky. The computer from which the software is copied may contain a virus that is also copied. The version may not be fully functional, and it will not have manuals or technical support. Neither is there access to patches, upgrades, or innovations. Piracy also deprives the software manufacturers of their legitimate earnings.

FUN AND GAMES

As you do your day's work, or complete that letter to the bank manager, Windows Me can offer some light relief, whether for playing CDs, listening to internet radio, or watching movies.

THE MULTIMEDIA EXPERIENCE

Possibly the biggest change between Windows Me and previous Windows versions is the collection of facilities contained in Windows Me for managing digital media files. Here we look at Windows Media Player for Windows Me, which encompasses all the latest audio/visual technology in one package, including playing a music CD. We look at customizing Media Player and using the visualizer. We also examine the Explorer radio bar and playing Me games.

LAUNCHING MEDIA PLAYER
● You can use Media Player to play audio CDs, video/ animation files, and also to control items such as the CD-ROM drive.
● Media Player can be accessed from the **Start** menu or the Quick Launch section of the taskbar.
● Note that when nothing is playing on Media Player, some of the options and buttons are inaccessible.

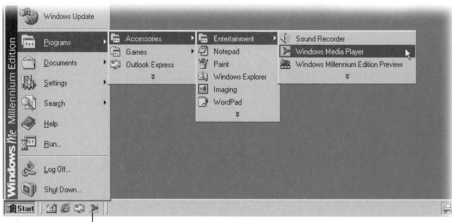

•*Windows Media Player Quick Launch icon*

THE MEDIA PLAYER WINDOW

To enjoy Windows Media Player, you will need a sound card, a modem, and speakers attached to your computer. Most modern computers include all these items as standard, but if you have an older PC, you may have to purchase one of these.

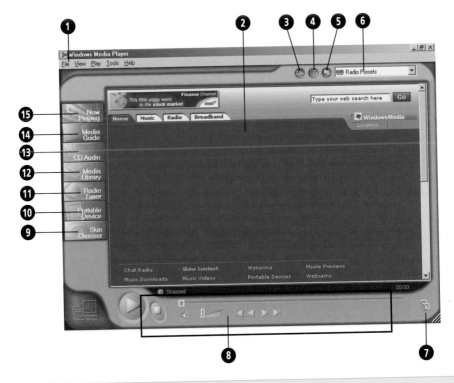

MEDIA PLAYER TOOLS

❶ Drop-down Menus
❷ Main Visual Window
❸ Hide/Show Equalizer & Settings *Only operable if Now Playing button is selected.*
❹ Hide/Show Playlist *Only operable if Now Playing button is selected.*

❺ Shuffle
❻ Audio Selector
❼ Compact/Full Mode *Reduce/enlarge the size of Media Player.*
❽ Audio/Video Controls *Not operable when there is no audio available.*

❾ Skin Chooser
❿ Portable Device
⓫ Radio Tuner
⓬ Media Library
⓭ CD Audio
⓮ Media Guide
⓯ Now Playing

PLAYING A MUSIC CD

When you insert an audio CD into the CD-ROM drive on your computer, Media Player automatically detects it and starts playing immediately. When an audio CD starts playing, some visual changes occur in Media Player.

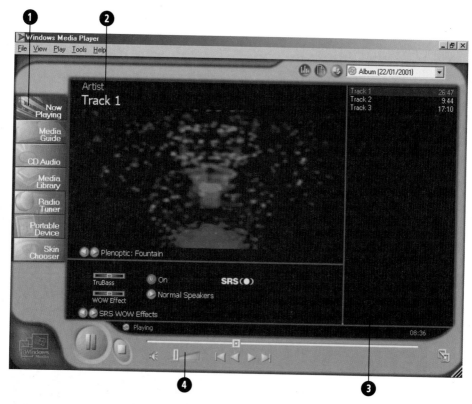

MEDIA PLAYER TOOLS

❶ **Now Playing Button**
The Now Playing button becomes highlighted when an audio CD is inserted.

❷ **Main Visual Window**
The main visual window

contains a "visualization" of colored patterns, which move in response to the music. It may also show the artist and title.

❸ **Track Details Window**
The right-hand window has the

track listing of artist, album, and track information including track times, if known.

❹ **Audio/Visual Controls**
All of the Audio/visual controls are now displayed.

WHAT ELSE CAN MEDIA PLAYER DO?

THE MUSIC MACHINE

Not only can Media Player play your CDs, it can also store the songs on your computer in Windows Media Format. This makes the files very small and means they take up very little hard disk space. In addition, if you are connected to the internet, Media Player will automatically find and retrieve the name of the artist, the title of the album, and track listings for every song that you have recorded on your PC. However, if you are not connected to the internet, you can manually enter the information. Once you have built up a collection of music, Media Player allows you to build up customized playlists that can be any length you choose. Media Player can also play and store MP3 and WAV files.

MEDIA GUIDE

With Media Guide, it is possible to download music, videos, and movie trailers via the website: **WindowsMedia.com**.

RADIO

Now you can listen to the immense variety of radio stations available from around the world with Media Player. You can choose between AM, FM, or internet-only radio.

CUSTOMIZING MEDIA PLAYER

Even the experience of playing a music CD can be heightened by personalizing the way that Windows Media Player looks onscreen. You can change the size of the player, dress it up in an elaborate or a fun skin to change its appearance, and even select a visualization effect to suit the music or your mood.

CHANGING THE APPEARANCE

● You can alter the way that Media Player looks by changing its skin. The Player has to be displayed in full mode to do this.
● Click on the **Skin Chooser** button.

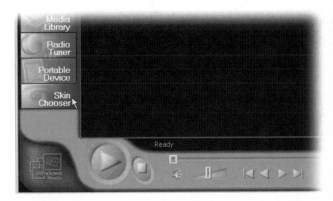

● The skin selector window opens. On the right-hand side of the window, there is an image of the skin that you are using at the moment; in this case, it is the **Default Media Player** skin. In the left-hand window, there is a list of the optional skins that are supplied with Media Player.

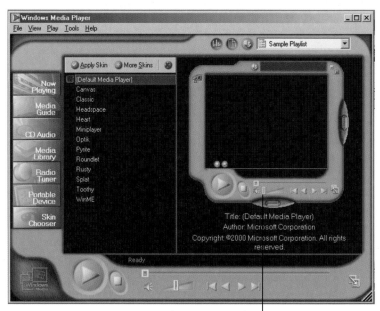

The preview window ●

● Clicking on each of the skin names displays a preview of the design in the right-hand window.
● Click through each of the names in turn until you find a skin that you like the look of.

Weird and wonderful, this skin is called Headspace ●

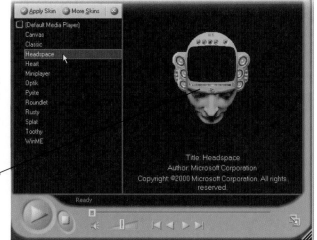

MORE SKINS

● If you don't like any of the optional skins that come with Media Player, **windowsmedia.com** has an immense selection of alternatives that you can browse through.

● Begin by clicking on the **More Skins** button at the top of the main Skin Chooser window.

● Your internet connection opens the **windowsmedia. com** website at the first skins page. Here you can browse through page after page of weird and wonderful skins. You can even find out what is involved in designing a skin yourself.

VISUALIZATIONS

Visualizations in Media Player provide a relaxing series of light shows that respond to and accompany the rhythms of the music as it plays. There are many visualizations to choose from, and they are grouped according to specific themes.

● When a CD is playing, the visualization starts, whether the player is in full or compact mode. Some skins do not have the facility to accommodate visualization, particularly in compact mode.

By clicking on the left and right arrows, you can scroll through the many visualization effects in Windows Media Player

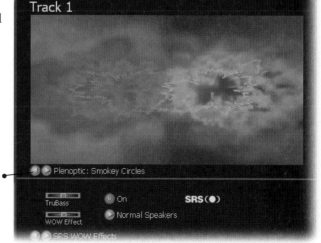

EXPLORER RADIO BAR

As well as internet-only radio stations, many national and local stations broadcast live over the internet. These will run in the background while you browse the web. Internet Explorer's Radio Guide provides links to hundreds of radio stations.

1 LOCATING THE TOOLBAR
● In the Internet Explorer window, the **Radio** toolbar can be accessed by choosing **Toolbars** from the **View** menu and then **Radio** from the drop-down menu.

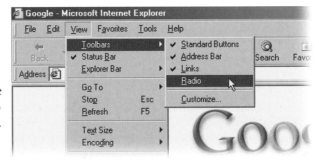

2 LOCATING THE GUIDE
● On the **Radio** toolbar, click on **Radio Stations**, and choose **Radio Station Guide** at the foot of the drop-down menu.

3 LOCATING THE STATIONS
● Radio stations are found by selecting a category, including **Format**, and then from subdivisions within that category.

There are many radio stations available to suit all music tastes

WINDOWS ME GAMES

Windows Me is designed to make playing games easier and faster, so after figuring out your finances or writing a letter to Aunt Dorothy, take it easy and have some fun, either playing a game solo or online against opponents anywhere in the world.

1 PLAY ON THE INTERNET

● To launch a game on the internet, begin by clicking on the **Start** button, then move to **Programs,** and then to **Games.**

● From the collection that is available in the **Games** submenu, we'll choose to play a game of **Internet Checkers.**

2 CONNECT TO THE INTERNET

● The first time that you play across the internet, the **Zone.com** dialog box opens onscreen.

● You can click in the **Show this every time** check box to deselect it if you don't want to see this box each time you start to play online.

● When you're ready, click on the **Play** button.

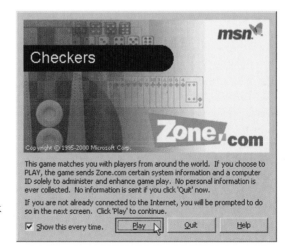

3 CONNECT TO GAMES SERVER

● A message tells you that an attempt is being made to connect you to the games server, which is at **Zone.com**.

4 STARTING THE GAME

● Now you are launched straight into the fray, pitting your wits against an opponent who could be thousands of miles away.

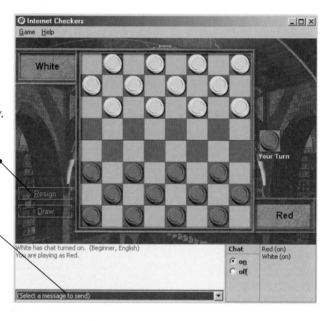

If you decide after a while that you just cannot win, you could always tactfully resign

*If you have the **Chat** button turned on, you can talk to your opponent by selecting a remark from the **Select a message to send** drop-down menu*

5 EXCHANGING MESSAGES

● Don't worry if you are playing someone whose language you do not understand as the message that you send from your computer will be translated at their end into their language and vice versa.

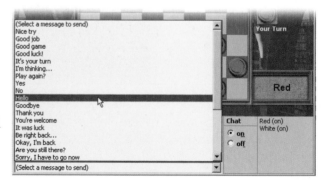

6 PLAYING ANOTHER GAME

● If you lose your game dismally, as we did here, either of the players can suggest another game, or the program offers you an opportunity to play another game against a new opponent.

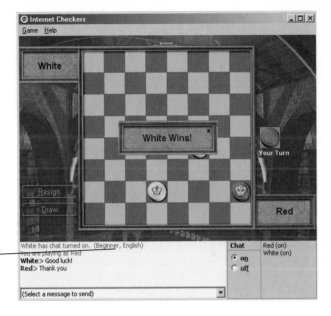

The language spoken by your opponent is given here

3D PINBALL SPACE CADET

● If you prefer a more fast-paced and immediate style of gaming, **3D Pinball Space Cadet** is worth trying – it's an exciting electronic version of a classic arcade pinball machine.

● The menu bar contains options to customize the game, and you can even listen to music or sound effects while you play.

GAMING ZONE

Microsoft's Gaming Zone, at **http://zone.msn.com**, has a **Game Index** link that lists all the games currently being played; one visit showed 110 games. Click on a game to see a list of games rooms and the total numbers playing.

MANAGING YOUR FILES

WHETHER YOU ARE A COMPLETE beginner or are already using Windows Me at a basic level, the ability to manage the documents on your computer efficiently is essential. This section explains in simple terms how to view the files on your computer, navigate through the many levels of folders on your hard disk, set up a personal filing system, and maintain the good organization of your documents in the future.

By working your way through the section from the beginning and following the tasks in sequence, you will achieve a thorough understanding of the principles involved in managing your files. At the same time, the tasks that you complete will prepare your computer for the next time you come to save new documents. Afterwards, you can return to the individual tasks and use them as a quick-reference guide.

VIEWING YOUR FILES

Managing files is easy once you are familiar with how they appear on your computer. There are many different ways to view files, and you can adopt a preference that suits you.

LOOKING INSIDE MY COMPUTER

All of the programs and files on your computer are stored on the hard disk: **Local Disk (C:)**. This is located in the **My** Computer icon – the main "entrance" into your PC. Here you will also find access to the floppy disk and CD-ROM drives.

OPENING MY COMPUTER

● Position your cursor over the **My Computer** icon in the top left corner of the Windows desktop.
● Double-click the left mouse button and the **My Computer** window opens. Note that the taskbar now displays a button for the open window ⬀.

Clicking on this taskbar button will return you to the window at any time

20 **Using the Taskbar**

The floppy disk drive

Your computer's hard disk, where the programs and files on your computer are stored

The CD-ROM drive

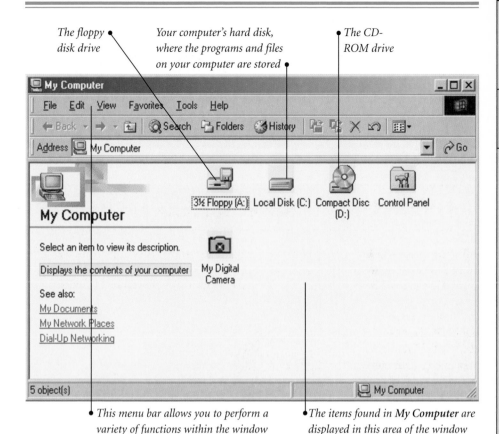

This menu bar allows you to perform a variety of functions within the window

*The items found in **My Computer** are displayed in this area of the window*

MINIMIZING, MAXIMIZING, AND CLOSING A WINDOW

The three buttons in the top right of an open window control how it appears onscreen. Clicking on the minimize button (–) makes the window disappear, but you will see a button remain on the taskbar. The maximize button (□) makes the window fill the

screen. You can click on it again to restore the window to its original size. The (X) button closes the window.

RESIZING A WINDOW

You can make a window larger or smaller by clicking in the bottom right corner and dragging the window to a new size.

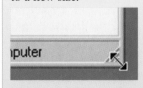

VIEWING FILES IN WINDOWS

The default setting for Windows Me is to display the contents of open windows as large icons, showing nothing more than the name of the file and an icon to indicate its file type ⬜. However, there are many ways to organize and view items within windows by changing the appearance of files, and by arranging them in a particular order.

1 SELECTING AUTO ARRANGE

● A window's contents displayed as large icons can often appear disordered, but you can arrange a window's contents by using **Auto Arrange**.

● Folders created in the **My Documents** folder may display their contents in this disorganized way, so open this window by double-clicking on its icon.

● With a "messy" folder open, select **Arrange Icons** from the **View** menu and choose **Auto Arrange** from the submenu.

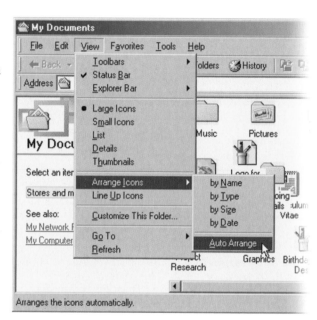

2 THE CONTENTS REARRANGED

● The menu closes and the icons rearrange themselves neatly within the window. With the **Auto Arrange** feature left on, the icons always automatically align themselves with one another when you resize a window or add new folders.

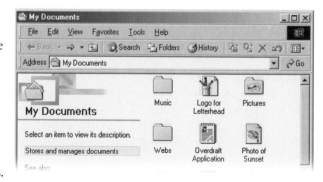

71 **File Name Extensions and File Icons**

3 ARRANGING IN OTHER WAYS

● As well as arranging icons automatically, it is also possible to arrange the icons by **Name**, **Type**, **Size**, or **Date** – just as you can by sorting files in **Details** mode ⬋.

● Experiment by using the same procedure as **Auto Arrange**, but select one of the other options under **Arrange Icons** option in the **View** menu.

● In this example the items are arranged by their size.

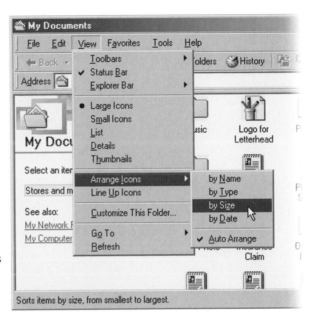

Menu options...

Wherever relevant, the steps in this section show you how to select options from the menus found at the top of open windows. Often, many of these functions are also available by clicking on the right mouse button within a window, or by using a keyboard shortcut. By experimenting, you will become more familiar with your computer and develop methods of performing these tasks with which you feel most comfortable.

LINING UP THE CONTENTS OF A WINDOW

Under the **View** menu you will also see an option called **Line Up Icons**. This performs the same action as arranging the icons, but not in any order. This option aligns the icons into columns and rows by moving them slightly from their current positions.

4 VIEWING AS SMALL ICONS

- Next, we are going to look at changing the appearance of the information that is displayed in a window.
- Return to the **My Computer** window 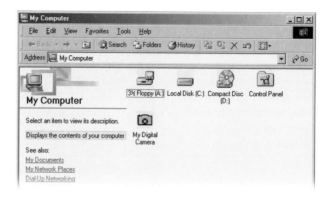. Its contents are currently displayed as large icons.

- Click on **View** in the menu bar, and in the drop-down menu you will see that the current option – **Large Icons** – is indicated as being selected by a black circle, known as a bullet.
- Place the mouse cursor over the **Small Icons** option and click once.

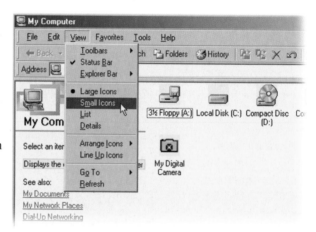

- The icons in the window change to the smaller size and realign themselves into tighter columns.

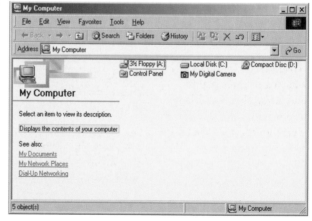

5 VIEWING AS A LIST

● Display the **View** menu again, but this time select **List** from the options.

● The contents retain their small icons, but now appear as a list arranged vertically in the window.

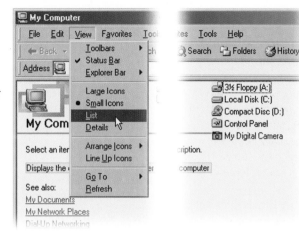

6 VIEWING DETAILS

● Now select **Details** from the **View** menu.

● When you select this option, certain information appears alongside the icons such as **Type** and **Total Size**.

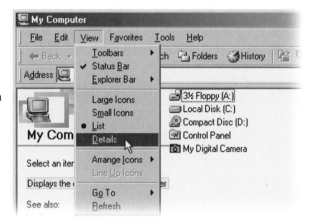

● Later, when you start to view windows containing individual files and folders in this way, you will also see their modification date.

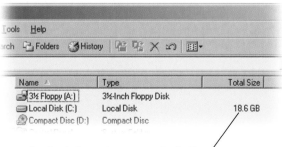

Further information appears in the list ●

ORGANIZING A WINDOW'S CONTENTS

When you view the contents of a window in **Details** 🗋 mode, you will see that a series of small boxes appears along the top of the open window containing headings for each category of information shown. By clicking on these headings you can reorganize the contents of the window into different lists according to different criteria.

1 ORGANIZING FILES BY NAME

● To explore the different ways of organizing your files in **Details** mode, double-click on **Local Disk (C:)**. Here, you will be able see the effect of reorganizing the files and folders that are listed.

● When the **Local Disk (C:)** window opens, display the **View** menu and select **Details**.

● Windows Me automatically sorts the items listed under the **Name** heading into alphabetical order. Folders are always shown at the top of the list, with individual files listed below.

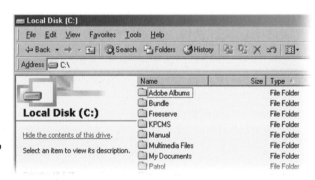

● By clicking once on the **Name** heading box, you can view the items in reverse alphabetical order, which also places the folders in the window after the list of individual files.

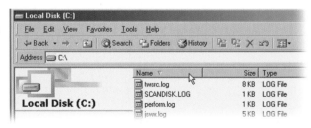

2 ORGANIZING FILES BY SIZE

● You can view items listed by size by clicking on the **Size** heading box at the top.

● The files are listed with the smallest shown at the top, folders are again grouped at the top.

● Click again on the **Size** heading box if you want to view the files listed in reverse size order.

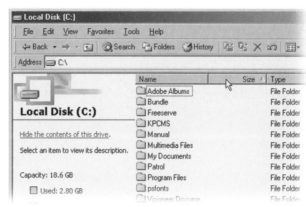

3 ORGANIZING FILES BY TYPE

● Click on the **Type** heading box.

● The items in the window are grouped according to their different types, which are listed alphabetically.

● As before, you can click again on the heading box to view the groups in reverse alphabetical order.

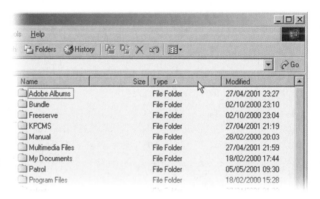

4 ORGANIZING FILES BY DATE

● Click on the **Modified** heading box.

● The files and folders are reordered so that the oldest items are shown at the top of the list.

● If you want to view the newest files, click again on the heading box. The date order of the list is reversed.

VIEWING FILES IN WINDOWS EXPLORER

The last few pages have shown you the basic methods for viewing files within open windows. However, Windows ME has an additional tool, Windows Explorer, which provides you with another means of viewing and managing your files. It allows you to do all the same things that you would do by using Windows conventionally, but also shows you exactly where a file is saved by guiding you visually through the hierarchy of folders on your computer's hard disk.

1 LAUNCHING EXPLORER

● To launch Windows Explorer, click once on the **Start** button in the bottom left corner of the taskbar ⏏.
● Choose **Programs** from the pop-up menu, followed by **Accessories**. Then select **Windows Explorer** from the submenu that appears at the side.

● Either release the mouse button, or left-click, and Windows Explorer opens.
● By default, the window displays the contents of the **My Documents** folder.

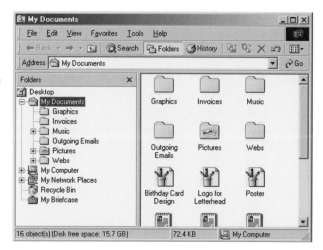

● To make the window fill the screen, click on the **Maximize** button.

RESIZING THE WINDOW PANELS

If the folders displayed in the left-hand panel are obscured, place the cursor over the gray vertical bar that divides the two parts of the window. The cursor changes to a double-headed arrow. Hold down the mouse button and drag the bar to the right. When the left-hand panel is sufficiently large to reveal the list of folders, release the mouse button.

59 **Minimizing, Maximizing, and Closing a Window**

NAVIGATING WITH EXPLORER

When you first launch Windows Explorer, a diagram is displayed in the left-hand panel listing items that branch from the **Desktop** – the top level of your computer. You will see that **My Documents** is automatically highlighted in the list because this is where the majority of the folders and files that you would usually access are stored. The folders that the disk contains are listed below its name. As the disk is highlighted, its contents appear automatically in the panel to the right. Note that individual files are not shown in the list to the left, but they do appear along with the folders in the main panel. By following the connecting lines in the diagram, you can see that **Pictures** is stored in **My Documents,** which, in turn, can be found on the **Desktop.**

• Many options appear as buttons in a menu bar

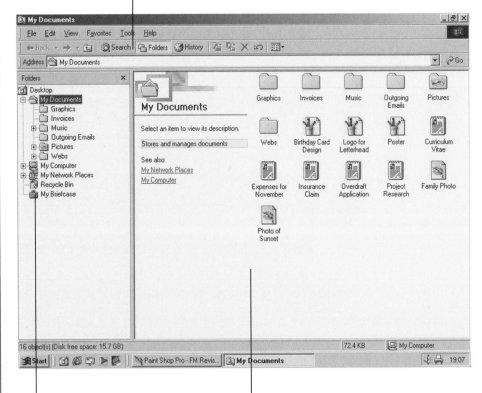

• The left-hand panel displays a diagram showing the hierarchy of all the drives and folders on your computer

• When a folder or drive in the left-hand diagram is highlighted, the files and folders it contains appear in the panel to the right

WHY USE WINDOWS EXPLORER?

It is purely personal preference whether you want to use Windows Explorer to manage your files. With Explorer, you can perform all the operations – copying 🗋, renaming 🗋, and deleting 🗋 – that you might carry out across open windows. The main advantage of using Windows Explorer is the ability to navigate your way through the entire contents of your computer within a single open window. This avoids constantly opening and closing different windows, or having a number of windows open at the same time.

FOLDERS WITHIN FOLDERS

In the diagram, you will see that many folders have a small square next to them containing either a plus symbol (+) or a minus symbol (–). This is a quick way of seeing whether a folder contains other folders that aren't currently displayed. A plus sign (+) next to a folder means that it contains other folders (known as subfolders), but they are not presently displayed in the diagram. A minus symbol (–) next to a folder shows that it is open and other folders it contains are listed in the diagram. If there is no symbol next to a folder, there are no other folders inside it. This does not necessarily mean that the folder is empty, as it could still contain individual files.

3 REVEALING THE SUBFOLDERS

● Position the cursor over one of the squares in the diagram that contains a plus symbol (+) and left-click once.

● A new list of folders appears underneath, branching from the folder you selected, and the plus symbol (+) changes to a minus symbol (–).

4 REVEAL FOLDER CONTENTS

● To see all the files that the folder contains, click once on the folder that you just clicked next to.

● The folder becomes highlighted and its contents are displayed in the main right-hand panel.

The contents of the folder are displayed in this panel

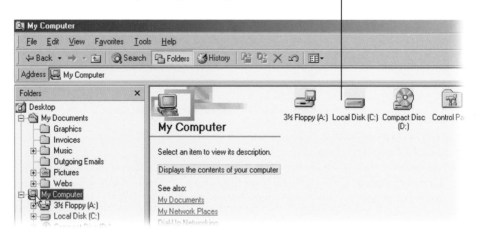

5 HIDING THE SUBFOLDERS

● Place the cursor over the square that now contains a minus symbol (–) and left-click once.

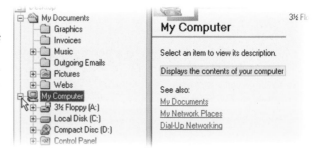

● The folders that stem from your selected folder disappear, and the symbol in the square becomes a plus sign (+) again.

FILE NAME EXTENSIONS AND FILE ICONS

Whenever you save a file, three letters are added to the name, which indicate its file type. This is known as a file name extension, but it isn't always visible. In addition, the file is also given a graphic symbol called an icon – which is always visible – so you can instantly recognize the file type, or the program used to create it.

VIEWING THE FILE EXTENSIONS

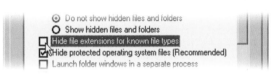

● Open a window that contains some of your files and select **Folder Options** from the **Tools** menu. Under the **View** tab, click in the square next to **Hide file extensions for known file types** to remove the check mark. When you click on **OK**, the extensions appear after the file names.

My Documents

Select an item to view its description.

Stores and manages documents

See also:

Logo for Letterhead....

Poster.bmp

Curriculum Vitae.doc

<table>
<tr><td>

FILE NAME EXTENSIONS

Here are some common extensions that you may see following the names of files that you save:

.doc   Word/WordPad document

.xls   Excel spreadsheet

.txt   Text document

.psp   Paint Shop Pro image file

.tif   Tagged Image File Format

.png   Portable Network Graphic file

</td><td>

COMMON FILE ICONS

Files are given a unique icon depending on the program they were created in. These icons provide you with a simple way of distinguishing text files from graphics files, and so on.

 A document created in WordPad

 A graphics file created in Paint

 A document created in Microsoft Word

 A spreadsheet created in Microsoft Excel

 An image file created in Paint Shop Pro

 The standard Windows icon

</td></tr>
</table>

OPENING AND SAVING

These two operations are among the first that you will carry out on your computer. However simple they may seem, saving your files correctly is a crucial part of good file management.

OPENING FILES FROM A WINDOW

A common way of opening documents is first to open the program used to create it, and then select **Open** from the **File** menu. However, a simpler way to open a file is to locate it on your computer (using the navigation techniques described in the previous chapter) and open it directly from the folder window containing the file.

1 SELECTING A FILE TO OPEN
● Open the window of the folder containing the file that you wish to open.
● Click once on the file icon to highlight it.

2 OPENING THE FILE
● Click on **File** in the Menu bar at the top of the window and select **Open** from the drop-down menu.
● The program that was used to create the file launches automatically, and the file you selected opens onscreen.

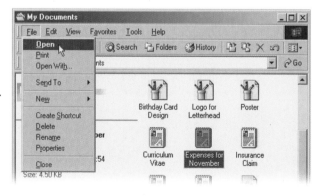

OPENING A RECENT FILE

Windows Me contains a feature that allows most programs to add files to a list of up to 15 files in the **Start** menu. These are the files that you have been working on most recently. This feature provides a quick and easy way of opening a recent file.

1 OPENING FROM THE START MENU

● Click once on the **Start** button in the bottom left corner of the taskbar ⌐.
● Choose **Documents** from the pop-up menu. You will see that your most recent files are listed in the submenu that appears.
● Highlight a file and release the mouse button.
● As before, the program launches and your chosen file opens.

The most recent files that you have been working on appear in this list

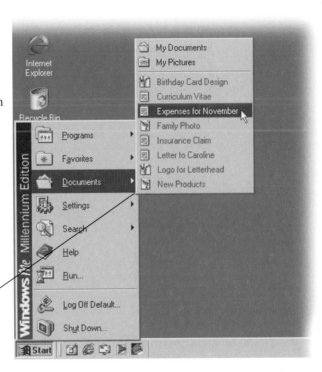

OPENING FILES THE QUICK WAY

Once you gain confidence in handling files within their windows, the easiest, and by far the quickest, way to open them is by simply double-clicking on the file icon. Within an open window, double-click on the file icon (there is no need to highlight it first by selecting it). The program launches and the file opens to be worked on.

20 | **Using the Taskbar**

SAVING A FILE TO MY DOCUMENTS

Although saving is a very simple process, it is not without its pitfalls. If you don't have logical locations on your computer to save your files, you can soon create filing havoc on your computer's hard disk. The next few steps show the default location of your files when you save them, and how you can modify that location.

1 CREATING A NEW DOCUMENT

● Before you can familiarize yourself with saving files, you first need to create a new document with which to experiment. If the document from the previous task is open, then close it and create a new file.

● In the example shown below, we are using a new document created in WordPad ⬜, which is a simple word processing program that comes with Windows Me. It can be found in the **Start** menu under **Programs** and then under **Accessories**.

Wordpad
37

2 SELECTING SAVE AS

● With the new WordPad document open, click on **File** in the Menu bar and select **Save As** from the drop-down menu.

3 SELECTING THE LOCATION

● The **Save As** dialog box opens. At the top there is a text box with the words **Save in** written alongside. This is where you select the location in which to save your document.

● The current location shown in the box is **My Documents**. Your computer automatically selects this location when you open a program and select **Save** or **Save As** for the first time.

● Any other folders that are also contained in this location are displayed in the window. Although you can choose to save the document loose in **My Documents**, try placing it into one of the existing folders by double-clicking on the folder's icon. If there are no folders, you can create a new one in which the document can be saved 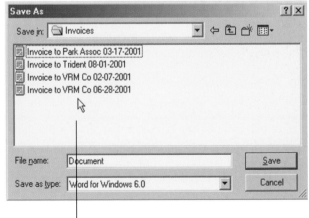.

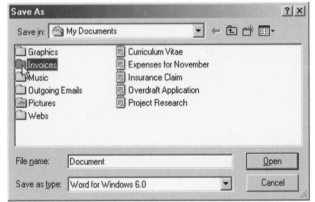

● Double-clicking on a folder displays its contents in the window, and selects it as the new location

83 **Creating New Folders as You Save**

4 NAMING THE DOCUMENT

● Click in the **File name** text box at the start of the default name (**Document**). The cursor changes to a blinking insertion bar.

● Hold down the mouse button and drag the insertion bar over the name to highlight it.

● Type in the new name.

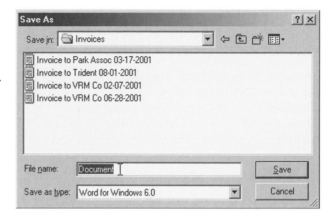

5 SAVING THE DOCUMENT

● Click on the **Save** button and your document is saved to your preferred location.

● Close the program and check that the file has been saved to the correct location by opening the folder window containing your document.

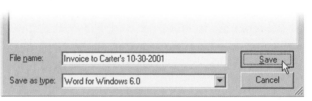

The file has been saved in your chosen location

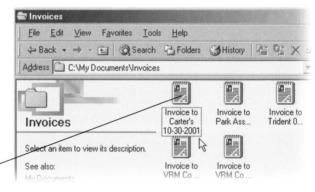

I Can't See the My Documents Folder on the Desktop…

If for any reason the **My Documents** folder doesn't appear on your desktop,

then it can be found within **My Computer** ⌐. Double-click on the **My Computer** icon on the desktop to view its contents. The main drives of your computer

(the floppy disk drive, the hard disk, and the CD-ROM drive) appear in the list. Double-click on **Local Disk (C:)** and you will see the **My Documents** folder.

CHANGING THE FILE TYPE

When you save a file for the first time, the program that you are running saves the document as a specific file type 🗋, usually a basic format recognized only by that particular program. However, it is possible to change the file type of the document you are saving so that it can be recognized by other software packages or a different computer operating system (such as the Apple Macintosh system, for example).

1 OPEN THE SAVE AS DIALOG BOX

● Save a file through the **Save As** dialog box as usual 🗋, choosing its location and giving the document a name. Before you save, click on the arrow next to the **Save as type** box to see a list of file type options.

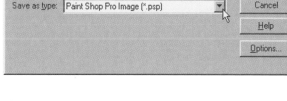

2 SELECTING THE FILE TYPE

● In this example we are going to save a Paint Shop Pro image file as a TIFF (**Tagged Image File Format**).
● Highlight this option in the list and click on **Save**.

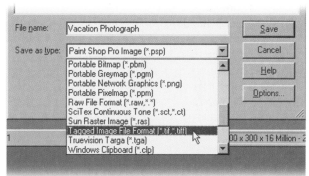

SELECTING A FILE TYPE FOR TEXT DOCUMENTS

The most common format for transferring text documents is **Text Only**. Although this format is widely recognized, be aware that it will remove the formatting (indents, text styling, etc) from your document, and strip it down to simple unformatted text. Because of this, it makes more sense to save your text documents in a standard format, then make a copy (saved as **Text Only**) to use for file transfer.

YOUR FILING SYSTEM

The key to good file management is not only understanding where files on your computer are stored – you also need to develop your own system for saving files in organized folders.

BETTER FILE MANAGEMENT

You can, if you want, save your documents loose within the **My Documents** folder. However, as you create more files, the folder will soon become very full and disorganized, and you will begin to lose track of what each file contains. This can be time-consuming and frustrating when you want to return to documents. The next few pages take you through all the steps involved in setting up a filing system.

KEEPING IT ORGANIZED

You will be surprised by just how many files you create as you begin to use your computer's potential. In addition to simple word processing and spreadsheets, you may also want to create graphics and pictures by using image-based software. If you are connected to the internet, you will want to save emails, as well as files that you download, for future reference. Not only will you be doing all these things as a home user, you may also be creating documents that are work-related. If you have two or three family members using the PC for their own purposes, you will soon begin to understand why good file management is essential.

From searching the world wide web to juggling home finances, from drawing images to business matters, all the files you create need to be stored sensibly.

DESIGNING YOUR NEW FILING SYSTEM

It is essential to start using a logical system for saving your files as soon as possible. It is easy to overlook this in your haste to "play" with your new PC, but it will be a long and arduous task to return and organize all those files later. Before creating a filing system on the computer, begin by planning it on paper.

1 WHO WILL BE USING YOUR PC?

● First, make a list of all the people who will be using your computer. In the case of a home PC, this is likely to be the members of your household.

● These people become first-level entries in your new filing system.

● Even if you are the only person using your computer, still put your name at the top of the list.

My new filing system
Gary
Melanie
- Work:
- Personal Projects: Digital Photograph
- Internet:
- Home Finances:
Expenses, Invoicing
My Web Site, Do
Bank Account

2 WHAT WILL THEY BE USING IT FOR?

● Each person that uses your PC will do so for a variety of reasons.

● Against each user's name, list the categories of the different types of work that they are likely to undertake. These might include work, personal projects, home finances, college, etc. You may have to repeat some of the categories, for example, most of the users will have their own personal projects.

● These categories become second-level entries in the system.

3 LIST SPECIFIC PROJECTS

● Next to each category, make a third-level list of more specific projects or jobs relevant to the particular category.

● The entries in this third level will eventually become folders to contain all the text documents, graphics, emails, and other files that are associated with a particular job or project.

● This level will constantly expand, but begin by listing as many specific projects as possible that are already on your computer.

YOUR FINAL DESIGN

This is a modified illustration, based on how Windows Explorer might represent your new filing system, showing the levels in your design as folders. Later, we will be creating all the folders shown in the diagram on your computer. These folders will form the basis of your filing system.

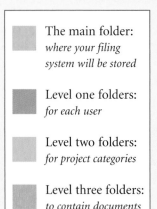

The main folder:
where your filing system will be stored

Level one folders:
for each user

Level two folders:
for project categories

Level three folders:
to contain documents

Just the beginning...

Remember that this is just the starting point for your new filing system. Over time, you will need to modify your use of folders, indeed you will certainly have to create many more levels of subfolders to store individual projects. Where you choose to save your files is not set in stone, and you can easily modify your system later by moving files and folders to new locations 🗋.

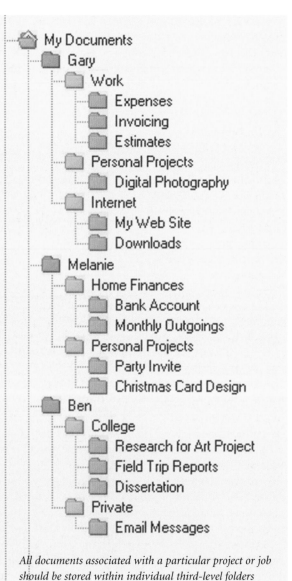

All documents associated with a particular project or job should be stored within individual third-level folders

CREATING NEW FOLDERS

A folder on your computer should be used to store files that are associated with one another. This means that all your documents are kept in logical groups and are easy to find. In order to create your filing system, you will need to make a number of new folders on your PC, in which you can place your files. You can create as many folders and subfolders as you wish, and you should develop the habit of creating a new folder for each new job or project that you undertake.

1 OPENING MY DOCUMENTS

● We are going to use the existing folder, **My Documents**, as the location for housing your new filing system.

● Double-click on the **My Documents** icon on the desktop.

● The **My Documents** window opens. There are some standard folders that will already exist in this location, including **Pictures, Music,** and **Webs.**

● If you are not using your computer for the first time, there are also likely to be some other existing files, and possibly folders, saved in the **My Documents** folder as well. These will have to be organized into your new filing system, but for now we are going to put them all out of the way into one folder so that you can return and sort through them later.

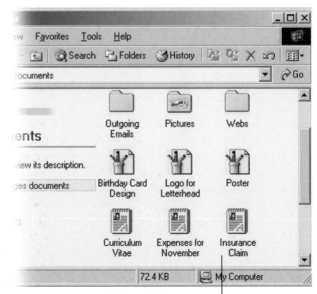

*Your **My Documents** folder is likely to contain a number of disorganized files and folders*

2 CREATING A NEW FOLDER

● Within the window of the **My Documents** folder, click on the **File** menu. Select **New**, followed by **Folder** at the top of the submenu.

● A new folder appears in the **My Documents** window.

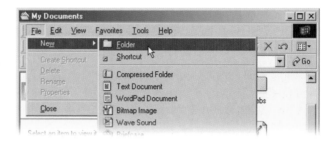

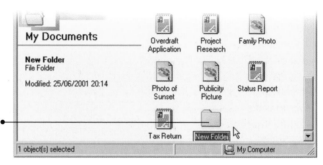

The new folder ●

3 NAMING THE NEW FOLDER

● With the new folder highlighted, type in a new name, **Files to sort**. Press the Enter key and deselect the folder by clicking once in any blank area of the window.

● You have now created a new folder that is ready to be used to store all those disorganized files.

● To keep the window neat while you create your new filing system, we are going to place the files and folders, currently saved in **My Documents**, into the new folder.

4 PUT AWAY YOUR EXISTING FILES

● Click on an existing file and keep the mouse button held down. The file becomes highlighted.

● Move the file into the new folder by dragging the icon over the folder and releasing the mouse button. The file is now placed in the folder.

● Repeat this process for each of the files and folders in the window. If there are a number of items to move, refer to the section dealing with making multiple selections ⌐. You can leave the standard folders – **Pictures, Music,** and **Webs** – where they are.

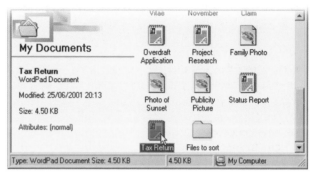

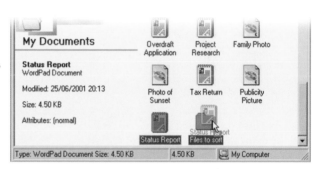

CREATING NEW FOLDERS AS YOU SAVE

Another way to make new folders is to create them at the same time as saving a document. You will find this a useful feature once your new filing system is in place because you can create folders for new projects as you save documents, rather than preparing them in advance. When you select **Save As**, to save a document for the first time ⌐, select a location for your file as normal, but do not click on **Save** immediately. Instead, click once on the **Create New Folder** button – a new folder appears in the list. The folder's name is automatically highlighted so that you have the opportunity to give it a more specific name. Once you have typed in the folder's new name, double-click on it to select the folder, then name the new document by typing it into the **File Name** box. When you click on the **Save** button, the document is saved into your new folder.

Create New Folder button ●

90 | **Selecting Your Files**

74 | **Saving a File to My Documents**

CREATING YOUR NEW FILING SYSTEM

We are now going to continue creating new folders within **My Documents** to set up the filing system you designed on page 79. The following steps also show you how to create folders within folders, which are known as subfolders.

1 CREATING YOUR MAIN FOLDERS

● Other than the standard folders, there should now only be one folder currently in view in the **My Documents** window, named **Files to sort**, which contains all the files and folders that were already saved in this location. Make sure that it is not selected by clicking on any blank area in the window.

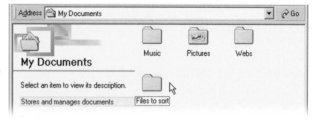

● Click on **File** in the Menu bar. Select **New** from the top of the drop-down menu, and **Folder** from the submenu.

● Give the new folder the name of one of your computer users from the top level of your design, in this case – **Gary**.

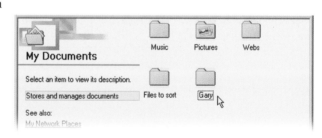

● Continue to create new folders for each of the users, naming each of the folders as you create them.

2 CREATE A USER'S SUBFOLDERS

● We are now going to place a series of folders within the user's main folder, corresponding to the second level in the design.

● Select a user's folder by double-clicking on its icon in the window. A new window opens to reveal the contents of that particular folder which, of course, is currently empty. Any folders that you now create are saved directly into that user's folder.

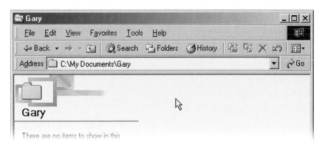

● Create a folder in the new window in the usual way and give it a category name, in this case – **Work**.

● Make new folders for each of the categories listed underneath this particular user in the second level of your design.

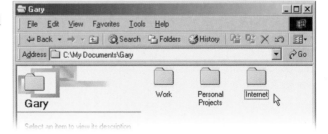

3 FURTHER SUBFOLDERS

● Before repeating the above process for each of the other users, first complete the filing system for your currently selected user. In the same way as shown in step 2, you need to create further subfolders within the category folders you have just made. These will correspond to the third level in your design.

● Double-click on a category folder to view its contents.

● In the new window, create new folders for each of the third-level entries under the currently selected category.

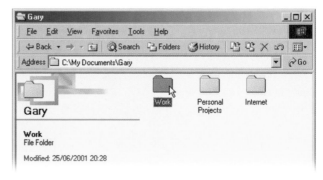

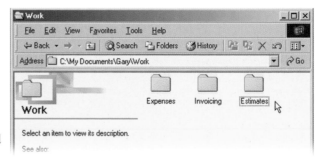

4 MOVING TO THE NEXT CATEGORY

● To create third-level folders in the remaining second-level categories, you will need to return to view the contents of your current user in level one.

● Keep clicking on the **Back** button in the menu bar until you return to the window that displays the folders for each second-level category.

● Double-click on the next category to open its window.

● Create the third-level folders for this category.
● Repeat step four for each second-level category.

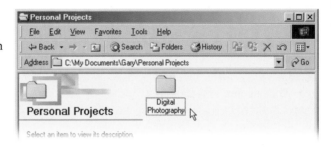

5 MOVING TO THE NEXT USER

● Having completed the filing system for one user, you need to repeat the process for each of the others. Remember that the window will currently display the contents of a second-level subfolder for your first user.
● Return to your first level of folders by clicking on the **Back** button.
● Repeat steps 2 to 5 for each of the people listed in the design of your filing system.

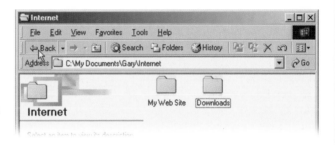

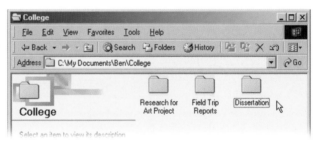

See your filing system in all its glory...
Remember that once you have completed your filing system, you can check its complete structure by viewing it through Windows Explorer 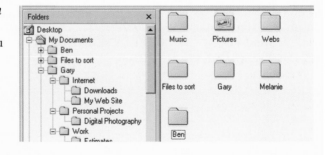.

CREATING A SHORTCUT TO A FOLDER

If there is a particular folder, or folders, in your filing system that you need to access regularly, then it may be worth creating a shortcut on the desktop. A shortcut made from a folder acts as a direct link taking you directly to an open window for that particular folder, instead of having to "drill down" through many levels of folders to reach it. With this in mind, a shortcut can become a valuable time-saving device if your chosen folder is buried within many levels of subfolders.

1 CHOOSING THE FOLDER
● Open the window that contains the folder you wish to create a shortcut to.
● Click once on your chosen folder so that it is highlighted.

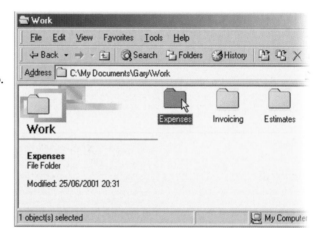

2 CREATING THE SHORTCUT
● Click on **File** in the menu bar at the top of the open window. In the drop-down menu, click once on **Send To**, then click on **Desktop (create shortcut)** in the submenu.

Selecting this option instead creates a shortcut in the same location

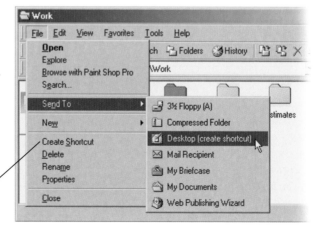

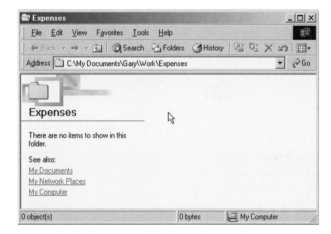

3 YOUR SHORTCUT IS CREATED

● Close the window and the shortcut that you created appears on the desktop. Shortcuts are distinguished by a small arrow in the bottom left-hand corner of the icon.

This arrow indicates that the folder is a shortcut

4 OPENING FROM A SHORTCUT

● To open the folder linked to the shortcut, simply double-click on the shortcut's folder icon.

● The window for that specific folder opens immediately.

SHORTCUTS FOR FILES AND PROGRAMS

You can create shortcuts for individual files and programs in the same way as folders. Be careful about this though. You may have just created a thoroughly efficient filing system on your computer, but creating too many shortcuts can very quickly make an unusable mess of your desktop!

MOVING AND COPYING

**An important part of organizing your files is the ability
to move and copy your documents between different
locations within your filing system.**

SELECTING YOUR FILES

Moving and copying both use simple "drag and drop" techniques that involve picking up a file, or folder, from one open window and placing it into another. For this to happen, you need first to select the files that you want to move. You can select individual files, or several at a time. To become familiar with the different methods of selecting, we are going to organize all the files that you stored under **Files to sort** earlier in the book ◩. If you don't have some old files to organize, the following steps are equally as relevant for selecting and moving files in the future.

1 SELECTING A SINGLE FILE

● Open the window to display the contents of the **Files to sort** folder.
● Within this window you should see a variety of files and folders, as shown here.
● To select a file, click once on its icon in the window. The file becomes highlighted to show that it is now selected.

2 SELECTING GROUPS OF FILES

● You can continue to select further files that are positioned next to your currently selected file.

● With the file still selected, place the cursor over the next file to be selected.

● Hold down the ⬆ Shift key and now, when you click on your second file, both are highlighted.

● Holding down the ⬆ Shift key can also be used to select files in a block by clicking on two files that occupy the opposite corners of a grid.

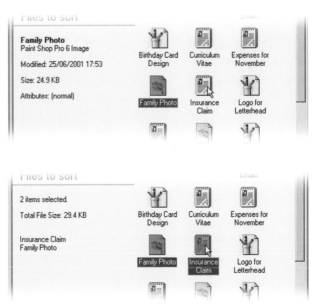

3 SELECTING UNGROUPED FILES

● You can select several files from the window, even if they are not positioned next to one another.

● Click on any empty area of the window to deselect any highlighted files.

● Select your first file, as described in step 1.

● Hold down the Ctrl key and click on a second file anywhere in the window, both files become highlighted.

● Keep the Ctrl key held down to select further files.

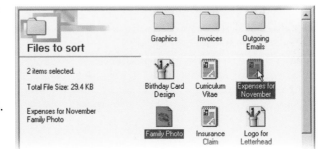

4 SELECTING ALL FILES

● To select all the items in an open window, click on **Edit** in the menu bar. Choose **Select All** from the drop-down menu.

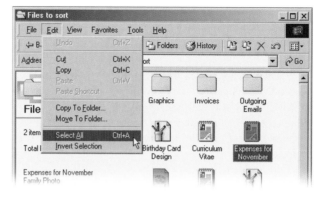

● When you release the mouse button, the menu closes and the entire contents of the window are highlighted.

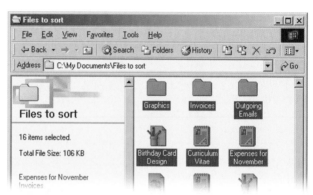

5 DESELECTING FILES

● To deselect a single file from this group of selected files, hold down the Ctrl key.
● Click on the file that you would like to deselect. You will see that it is no longer highlighted.
● Keep the Ctrl key held down to deselect further files.

INVERTING A SELECTION

You can reverse which files are selected and deselected by choosing **Invert Selection** from the **Edit** menu within the window. When you select this option every file that is currently highlighted will become deselected and the files that are deselected become highlighted.

MOVING FILES BETWEEN LOCATIONS

We are now going to use the selection methods described in the previous task to move your existing files into your new filing system. When you move a file, it means that the place where that file is saved on your computer changes from one location to another. This is different from copying , where the file that you copy and move can result in copies being stored in any number of locations.

1 CHOOSING THE FILES TO MOVE

● Open the window of the **Files to sort** folder to display its contents.
● Decide which file(s) you are going to move first, for example, all files that are connected by belonging to one of the users.
● In this case, we are going to move all the photo-graphic files that belong to Gary into the relevant folder in the filing system.

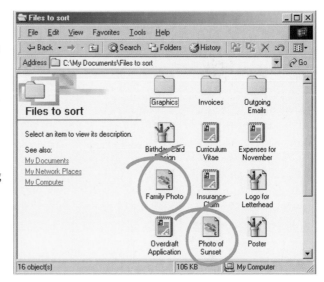

2 CHOOSING THE NEW LOCATION

● Select the files that are to be moved.
● Click on the **Edit** in the menu bar and select **Move To Folder**.

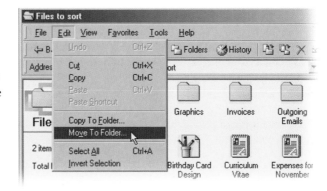

79 Designing Your New Filing System

95 Copying Files to Other Locations

- The **Browse For Folder** window opens.
- Before you move a file, you need to decide where you want to move it to. The files that we have chosen belong in the new folder called **Digital Photography**, found within Gary's own set of folders.
- Navigate to this folder using the techniques shown on pages 66–70 , and click on the folder to select it.
- Click on the **OK** button.

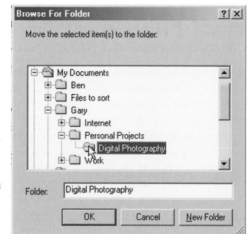

3 **VIEWING THE MOVED FILES**
- The files will move from one location to the other.
- You can check this by opening the window for the new location. The files will be visible in the window.

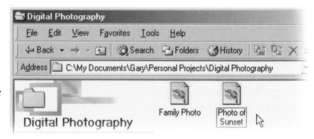

BEWARE OF WHAT YOU MOVE

Although moving your own files around your computer is a simple task, don't be tempted to start "organizing" other aspects of your computer's hard drive. To make everything work properly, the operating system "knows" where important system files are stored, and uses these to launch the programs that you run on your computer. If you inadvertently move files that the computer requires, you can expect a time-consuming, and possibly expensive, process to fix it. This is why it is safest to restrict all your file management to the **My Documents** folder.

Continue sorting...
Check your computer for files that may have been accidentally saved to other locations on your hard drive and move these into your filing system as well.

COPYING FILES TO OTHER LOCATIONS

The process of copying files is similar to moving them – however, the original file remains in place and a duplicate file appears in a new location. Probably the main reason for copying files to different locations on your computer is to create backups in case anything goes wrong with your original file. Remember though, copying is not like making a shortcut ⬒ – when you make a copy, both files become independent of one another, whereas a shortcut is a link to the original. This means that changes made to the original file are not reflected in the copy until you overwrite it with a new copy. For more information on backups, see page 114.

1 CHOOSING THE FILE TO COPY

● Let's assume that you already have a file saved on your computer that needs to be located in two different folders within your new filing system. During your reorganiz-ation, the file will have been moved into one of the relevant folders.

● Open the window containing the file you wish to copy and select it.

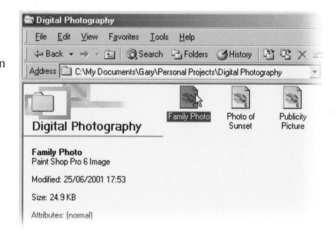

2 COPYING THE FILE

● Select **Copy To Folder** from the **Edit** menu.

┌──┐
│88│ **Creating a Shortcut**
└──┘ **to a Folder**

● The **Browse For Folder** window opens.
● Navigate to the folder into which you would like to place the duplicate file, and click on the folder once to select it.
● Click on the **OK** button.

● A copy of the file is placed in the new location, leaving the original file in place.

USING DRAG AND DROP

Another way to move or copy files and folders between locations is by "dragging and dropping" them between two or more open windows. In order to do this you must first change the default Windows Me settings so that different folder contents open in independent windows, rather than opening in the same one.

1 CHANGING THE SETTINGS
● With the **My Documents** window open, select **Folder Options** from the **Tools** menu. The **Folder Options** window opens.

• Within the **Browse Folders** section, click once in the radio button next to **Open each folder in its own window**, so that a bullet appears in it.

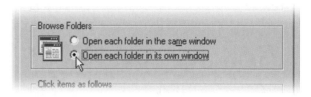

• Click on the **OK** button.

• Now, when you double click on folder icons their contents are displayed in separate windows.

• As before, select the files that you wish to move and, while keeping the left mouse button pressed down, drag the files from one window to the other.

• To copy files between locations – rather than moving them – hold down the Ctrl key as you release the mouse button.

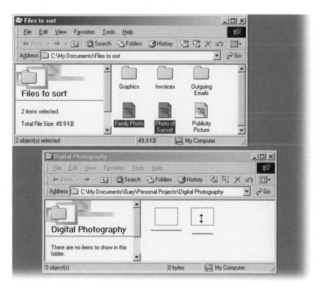

AN ALTERNATIVE WAY OF MOVING AND COPYING

Instead of using the Ctrl key to ensure that you are copying rather than moving, you can also make the choice from a menu. Drag a file into a second location using the technique described, regardless of whether you would like to make a copy or not. As you drag the file from one window to another, hold down the right-hand mouse button rather than the left. When you release the mouse button, a pop-up menu appears from which you can select either **Copy Here** or **Move Here**. It is purely personal preference, but you may want to adopt this technique until you are confident about using

keyboard commands to perform certain tasks. Note also that you can create a shortcut within your chosen location by using this method.

COPYING FILES TO A FLOPPY DISK

So far we have only made copies of files to different locations on the same hard disk. This is fine for making temporary back-ups, or if you need to use the same file for several projects, but what happens if your whole computer should develop some kind of fault that prevents you from accessing your files? Having copies on a floppy disk will mean that you still have access to those files. Or you may want to take a file to work so that you can continue working on it. Perhaps you want to give someone else a copy of one of your files. These are all good reasons why you may want to copy files to an external device – commonly a floppy disk.

1 INSERTING A DISK

● Insert a formatted floppy disk into the computer's disk drive with the metal edge facing forward and the circular metal disc on the underside. Push the disk in firmly and you will hear it snap into position in the drive.

Storage Capacity...
There are two types of 3½" floppy disk – Double Density, which can store 720KB, and High Density, which can store 1440KB (1.44MB). High Density disks display an HD symbol.

2 SELECTING THE FILES

● Open the window of the folder containing the files that you wish to copy to the floppy disk. Remember, you can change the view of the window to **Details** so that you can check the size of the files and make sure that they will fit on the disk 🗅.
● Select the files 🗅.

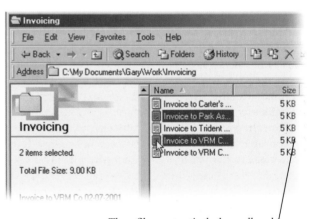

These files are particularly small and will easily fit onto a floppy disk

63 | Viewing Details

90 | Selecting Your Files

3 COPYING THE FILES

● With the files highlighted, click on **File** in the menu bar and select **Send To** from the drop-down menu. You will see that the floppy disk drive appears in the submenu as: 3¹/₂ **Floppy (A:)**. Click once on this option.

● Copies of the files that you selected are placed on the floppy disk.

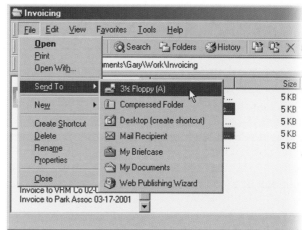

FORMATTING A FLOPPY DISK

When you buy new floppy disks, they are usually preformatted so that you can start to use them immediately. If you insert an unformatted disk into your floppy disk drive, your computer will not be able to recognize the disk and will display an alert message. To format a disk, select the drive 3¹/₂ **Floppy (A:)** from within the **My Computer** window 🗋, and click on **Format** in the **File** menu. Select the relevant options in the **Format** window to format the disk.

VIEWING THE CONTENTS OF A FLOPPY DISK

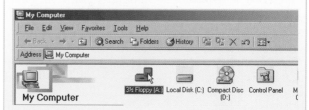

The above steps assume that you are using a new disk with maximum storage capacity. If you want to use a disk that already has files stored on it, you can view the contents of the disk in a window, just like any other drive or folder on your computer. With the floppy disk inserted, double-click on **My Computer** on the desktop. In the window there will be an icon for the floppy disk drive, 3¹/₂ **Floppy (A:)**. Double-click on the icon, and a window appears displaying the contents of the floppy disk currently in the drive. From this window, you can edit or delete the contents of the disk as normal, for example, to create more storage space on the disk.

FINDING YOUR MISPLACED FILES

No matter how well-managed your filing system might be, over time you are bound to misplace some files, or forget what they are called. Because the filing system you have created is housed in one location (the My Documents folder), it is a relatively easy procedure for the computer to search for your misplaced files. To do this, you have to enter a few details about the file, and tell the computer where to look.

1 OPENING THE FIND WINDOW

● Click once on the **Start** button at the left-hand end of the taskbar.
● Select **Search**, and then **For Files or Folders** from the submenu.
● The **Search Results** dialog box appears.

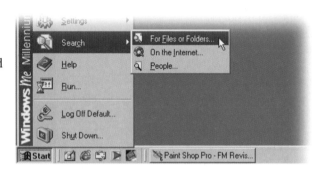

2 ENTERING THE SEARCH DETAILS

● Within the window there are several boxes into which you can enter details about the file you want to find.
● Click inside the text box next to **Search for files or folders named**. Type in a few details about what the file is called. Be as specific as possible – if you know the file name, then enter the complete name into the box. If you can't remember the name exactly, then enter as much as you can. In this example, a missing

invoice is being searched for on the hard drive.
● The next box down, labeled **Containing text**, allows you to enter specific words that you know are contained within the file. So, for example, the invoice we are looking for here has been addressed to **Park Associates**, so this is entered into the box.

3 FINDING THE FILE

● To tell the computer where specifically to search for your file, click on the arrow next to the text box labeled **Look in**. If the filing system has been used as described so far, the file that you are searching for should be contained somewhere in the folder **My Documents**. In the list, click on **My Documents** so that it appears in the box.
● Click on **Search Now**.

4 VIEWING THE RESULTS

● Any files that match your search criteria are displayed in the window.
● Click once on a file to display its description. The details at the top of the **Search Results** panel tell you where the file is located on your computer and give additional information, such as the file size and when it was last modified.
● If you want to open the file immediately, you can easily do so by double-clicking on the file icon.

MAXIMIZING YOUR SEARCH SUCCESS

The more information with which you can provide the computer, the more likely it is that the files you are looking for will be found. To help, you can click on the **Date** and **Advanced** tabs in the **Find** window. Here, you can enter further inform-ation about the date when the file was created, or last modified, as well as its file type and size.

MODIFYING YOUR FILES

Now that all your files are efficiently organized, it is time to examine the different ways in which you can modify them to ensure your filing system is kept in good working order.

RENAMING FILES AND FOLDERS

Over time, as you expand your filing system to include new folders and, certainly, many more files, it will become necessary to rename certain items. Follow the steps below to rename both folders and files.

1 SELECTING THE FILE
● In an open folder window, click once on the file that you wish to rename so that it becomes highlighted (you can only rename one file at a time). Here, we are renaming the file that we copied from one location to another on page 95, so that they clearly become different files.

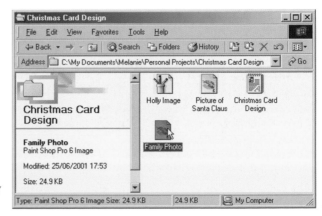

File Names

Windows Me allows you to use up to 255 characters when naming your documents. On one hand this is obviously a benefit, because you can provide a full and concise description of your document. On the other hand, however, Windows will only make the beginning of very long file names visible when you view your documents in certain modes . This can become confusing if you have many files with a similar beginning, so try to differentiate file names as much as possible – using 20 to 30 characters.

2 RENAMING THE FILE

● Click on **File** in the menu bar and select **Rename** from the drop-down menu.

● A box appears around the current file name. If you want to change the name completely, press the Delete key and type in the new name. If you want to modify the name, for example, by adding to it, place the cursor at the point in the name that you want to alter and left-click.

● Rename the file and press the Enter ← key.

● Your file is now renamed.

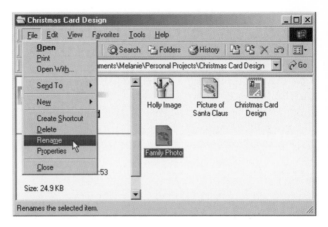

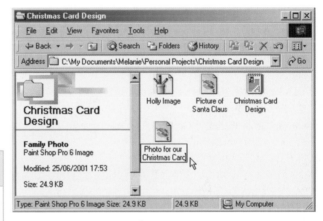

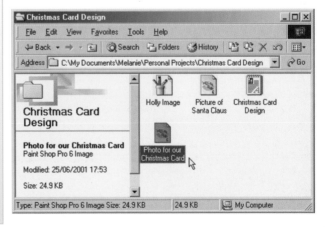

RENAME FILES WITH CAUTION!

Just as you should exercise caution when moving files ☐, the same applies to renaming files. Changing the name of a file or folder that has not been created by you can give you and your computer a big headache when you try to perform certain functions or run applications. Limit any renaming you do to your own filing system.

DELETING UNWANTED FILES

Deleting files from your computer is just like throwing something away – you put it in the wastebasket. Be ruthless when it comes to removing files from your computer, and only keep what you are sure you need. It won't take long for you to accumulate hoards of worthless files, including those that you believe you might *possibly* need later! In practice, you will not return to them, eventually forget what they are, and use up valuable storage space on your computer in the process.

1 SELECTING THE FILE

● In this example we are going to delete the files that are deemed not important enough to keep in the filing system. These are the files that were left in the folder called **Files to sort**. By deleting the folder you are also throwing away all the files that it contains – this saves you having to delete each file one by one.

● In the open window, click once on the folder to be deleted. If necessary, you can also use the selecting techniques ⌐ to delete many files in one process.

2 DELETING THE FILE

● Click on **Delete** in the **File** menu, or press the Delete key.

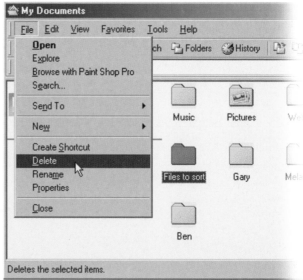

● A box appears onscreen asking you to confirm the deletion. Click on the **Yes** button.

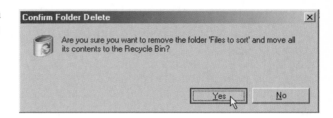

● The folder disappears from the window.
● You can also delete files by either clicking on the red cross in the menu bar (below) or dragging them to the Recycle Bin.

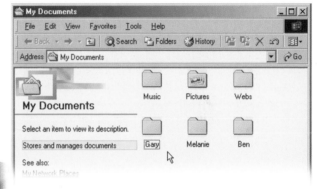

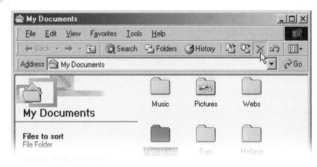

HAVING REGULAR CLEANUPS

An important part of maintaining your filing system is to have a regular review of the files stored there. If there are files that have been forgotten about, then consider whether you really need them. And if you start seeing many updated versions of the same file appearing in your folders, then you can be even more ruthless.

MANAGING THE RECYCLE BIN

Rather than deleting files immediately, the computer really moves them into the **Recycle Bin** positioned on the desktop. From this location you can restore files, so there's no problem if you suddenly realize you have made a mistake by performing the deletion. Files are only deleted permanently when you empty the **Recycle Bin**.

1 VIEWING THE BIN'S CONTENTS
● Position the cursor over the **Recycle Bin** icon on the desktop, and double-click. Notice that the icon for the bin shows that there are files contained inside it. The **Recycle Bin** window opens and displays the files you have thrown away since the bin was last emptied.

2 RESTORING YOUR DELETED FILES
● All is not lost if you place a file in the **Recycle Bin** that you later decide you need – as long as you haven't yet emptied the Bin.
● Highlight the folder that you deleted in the previous task. By selecting the folder, the entire contents of that folder are also selected.
● Click on the **Restore** button on the left-hand side of the window or select **Restore** from the **File** menu.
● The folder disappears from the window. It has been restored to the location from which you deleted it.

3 THROWING AWAY DELETED FILES

● For this task, delete the **Files to sort** folder again so that we can now dispose of it permanently.

● In the **Recycle Bin** window, click on the **Empty Recycle Bin** button on the left-hand side of the window or select **Empty Recycle Bin** from the **File** menu.

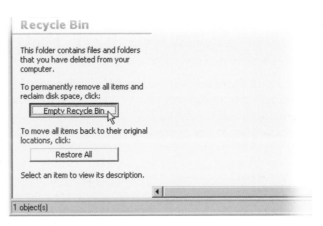

● A box appears onscreen asking you to confirm the deletion. You cannot be selective about the files that you permanently remove – clicking on the **Yes** button deletes all the files displayed in the window.

● The contents of the window vanish, and the icon for the **Recycle Bin** shows that it is now empty.

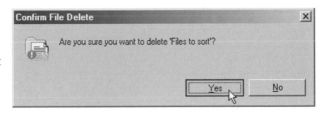

● *No documents are shown in the bin, indicating that the Recycle Bin is empty*

Too nervous to bin those files?

If you really can't bear to dispose of certain files then store them on some form of external device, such as a floppy disk. At least you won't be using up your hard disk space – and the files will be available, just in case!

EMPTYING THE RECYCLE BIN

You should empty the **Recycle Bin** frequently so that you do not clog up your computer's hard disk with unwanted files. However, before doing so, remember that this is your last chance to save any files from permanent deletion from your computer. Once you have emptied the **Recycle Bin**, the lost files cannot be restored.

VIEWING FILE PROPERTIES

Identical features, known as "properties," are assigned to every new file that you create on your computer, and they make the file function in certain ways. By changing a file's properties you can control the operations that can be carried out on it.

These changes include locking a file so that no modifications can be made to it (**Read-only**), hiding the file to make it invisible to others (**Hidden**), and "tagging" a file so that it is selected and backed-up automatically by your computer (**Archive**).

1 SELECTING THE FILE

● Select any file in an open folder window so that it becomes highlighted.

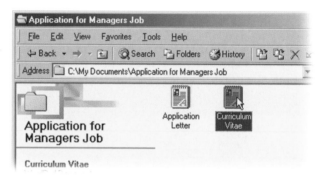

2 OPEN THE FILE PROPERTIES BOX

● Click on **File** in the menu bar and select **Properties** from the drop-down menu.

● The **Properties** of the file appear in a dialog box.

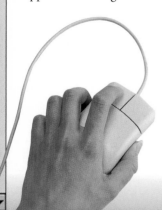

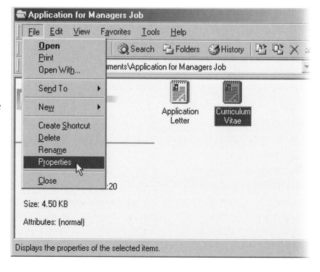

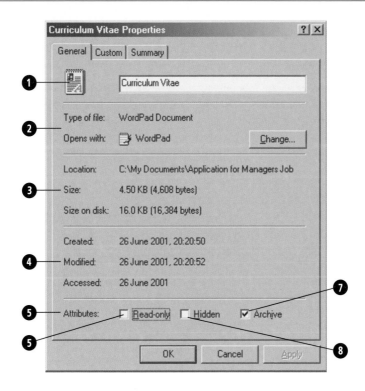

THE FILE PROPERTIES BOX

1 *The top part of the box displays the name of the file, along with an icon* ◻ *to indicate which program it was created in.*

2 *Here you can see what type of file it is and which program is assigned to open it (in this case, the file is a WordPad document called* **Curriculum Vitae***). You can modify which program opens*

the file by clicking on the **Change…** *button.*

3 *The location where the file is saved and its size (in this case, shown in kilobytes and bytes) is specified in this part of the box.*

4 *This area tells you when the file was created and when it was last modified and last accessed.*

5 *The attributes in this part of the box can be modified by clicking in the check boxes.*

6 *Click on the* **Read-only** *option to lock your files. You will be able to open the document, but not modify or delete it.*

7 *When the* **Archive** *box is checked, the file will be included in an automated backup.*

8 *Selecting the* **Hidden** *option makes files invisible on your computer* ◻.

71 **File Name Extensions and File Icons**

110 **Creating Hidden Files**

CREATING HIDDEN FILES

A hidden file remains where it is on your computer, but becomes invisible. In other words, you cannot see an icon for the file within a folder window, or its file name in an **Open** menu. This is a basic form of security because another user will not immediately be aware that the file exists. Beware though – it is a relatively simple process to display the file by anyone who knows how to make it accessible.

1 SELECTING THE HIDDEN OPTION

● Before you perform this operation, make a note of the file name because you won't be able to see it while the file is hidden.

● Open the **Properties** box ☐ for the file you that you want to hide.

● Click in the check box next to **Hidden** so that a check mark appears.

● Click on **OK** and close the **Properties** box.

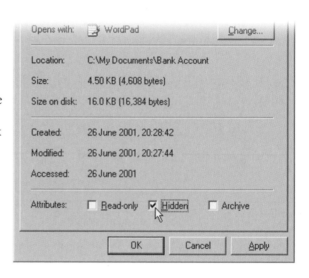

2 HIDING THE FILE

● Your file only becomes hidden once you have changed the **View** options for the folder window that it appears in.

● Open the window to display the contents of the folder where your hidden file is located.

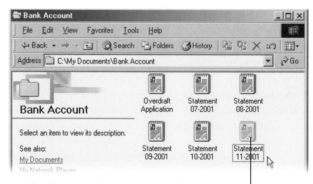

*The file is grayed-out to indicate that the **Hidden** property is applied, but it is still visible in the window*

108 Viewing File Properties

● The file to which you applied the **Hidden** property may still be visible in the folder window. If it is, click on **Tools** in the menu bar, followed by **Folder Options** from the drop-down menu.

● When the **Folder Options** dialog box opens, click on the **View** tab.

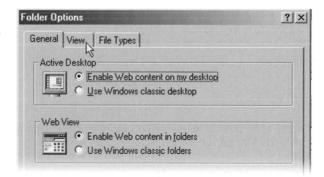

● Click on the radio button next to **Do not show hidden files and folders** so that a bullet appears in the button.
● Click on the **OK** button. Now, when you view the contents of the window, your hidden file will be invisible.

3 HIDING THE STATUS BAR

● Although the file is now hidden, if the **Status Bar** is visible it will show that the file exists in the location.

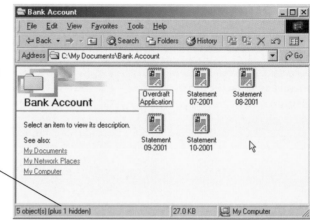

*The **Status Bar** shows there is one hidden file in the location* ●

● To hide the **Status Bar** click on **View** and select **Status Bar** from the drop-down menu.

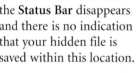

● When the menu closes the **Status Bar** disappears and there is no indication that your hidden file is saved within this location.

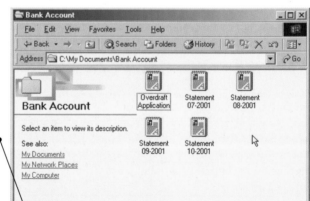

*The **Status Bar**, and the information that it contained, are no longer visible* ●

4 OPENING A HIDDEN FILE

● Launch the program in which you want to open your hidden file.
● Select **Open** from the **File** drop-down menu.

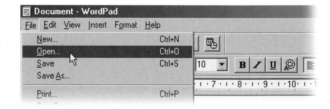

- The **Open** dialog box appears.
- Select the location of your file in the **Look in** box, then type the name of your file into the **File name** text box.
- Click on the **Open** button.
- Your hidden document now appears onscreen.

Enter the name of the file here •

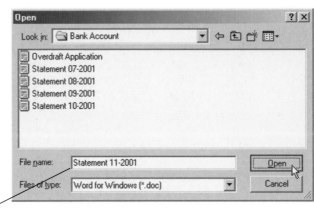

5 VIEWING HIDDEN FILES

- To make hidden files visible again, reopen the **Folder Options** box via the **Tools** menu, and click once in the radio button next to **Show hidden files and folders** so that a bullet appears.
- Click on the **OK** button to close the **Folder Options** box. Any hidden files now reappear in the window. Be aware, however, that anyone else can also follow this procedure.

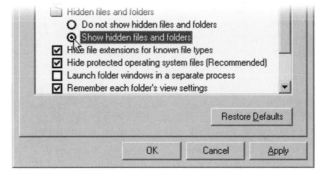

The file reappears • *in the window*

BACKING UP YOUR FILES

Now that your filing system is in place and you are managing your files effectively, it is time to consider safeguarding your work against accidental loss.

WHY BACK UP YOUR FILES?

Think for a moment about all the work that is stored on your computer. It represents a huge commitment of not only your money, but more importantly, your time. If your computer should fail, or is stolen, it will be virtually impossible for you to recreate the documents that were stored on your hard drive. For this reason, creating back ups on a regular basis is crucial. This simply involves copying files from one location to another that is separate from the computer itself.

PERMANENT ARCHIVES

The principle reason for backing up your files is to insure that you have access to them should anything happen to your computer or to the original files. However, the situation may also arise when it becomes very difficult or even impossible to store any more files on your computer. You may have used up your hard disk space, or the volume of files and folders on your hard drive becomes too unwieldy to manage. The only option left may be to remove files from your computer and store them on an external device. Good practice is to remove documents from your filing system as you finish with them. This

means that there is always maximum storage capacity on your computer, and the backing up process takes minutes rather than hours.

Microsoft Backup
See the final section of this book for detailed information on using Microsoft Backup to automate the backing up procedure.

CREATING A COMPRESSED ARCHIVE

Unless you are regularly transferring large files to and from your computer, you may not have any device available to you apart from a floppy disk drive. If this is the case, you will need to maximize the amount of space available so that you can fit as many files as possible. File compression enables you to store many times the normal amount of files on a floppy disk by compacting them into a single "archive."

USING WINZIP

Probably the most commonly used file compression software for Windows is WinZip. If you wish, you can download a free evaluation version of this software from the internet and use it for a limited time before you have to purchase the full copy.

Visit **www.winzip.com** to download the program

and follow the onscreen instructions to install it onto your computer. You will be asked a few questions in order to set up WinZip. When you are given the option, choose to run WinZip Classic – this is the simplest means of creating a basic archive file for these purposes.

WinZip has many more features than those shown

below and, to appreciate its potential fully, you should treat the following steps as an introduction only. File compression is also very useful for transferring files between computers, especially if you are sending attachments by email. You can experiment with the program to see what best suits your archiving needs.

1 **CREATING A NEW ARCHIVE**
- Once the Winzip setup is complete, the WinZip window opens.
- Before you start, insert a floppy disk into your computer.
- Click on the **New** button at the top of the window to create a new archive.

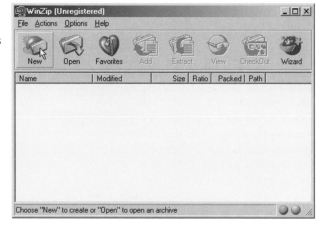

98 **Copying Files to a Floppy Disk**

2 CHOOSING THE LOCATION

● The **New Archive** dialog box opens.

● In the **Create** box, choose a location in which the archive is to be saved. In this case you can select the floppy disk directly by highlighting 3¹/₂ **Floppy (A:)**.

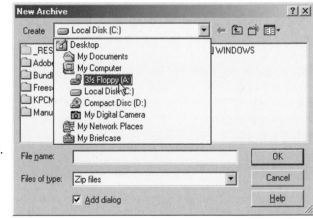

3 NAMING THE ARCHIVE

● It makes sense to create separate archive files that correspond with the names of the folders you use in your filing system.

● Decide which files you are going to archive first, and give the archive the same name as the folder where they currently reside.

● Click on the **OK** button.

4 SELECTING THE FILES

● The **Add** dialog box opens. Select the location where the files are currently saved, and highlight them in the main window.

● Once the files are selected, click on the **Add** button.

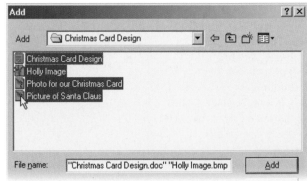

5 THE ARCHIVE IS CREATED

● The WinZip window displays the contents of your archive file, which has now been saved onto your floppy disk.

● Close the window.

● It is now safe for you to delete the original files from your computer.

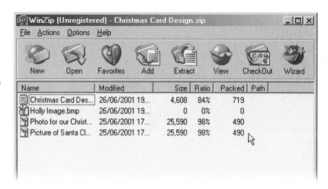

6 OPENING FROM AN ARCHIVE

● You can open the archive file by double-clicking on its icon. Then, whenever you want to open one of your archived files, simply double-click on it in the WinZip window.

● To restore files to your computer, click on the **Extract** button at the top of the window. You can then select the individual files you want to restore from the archive to your PC.

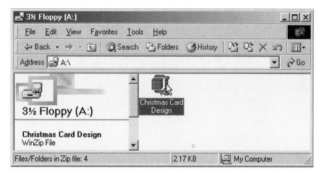

Label your disks... File management doesn't stop there! Remember to label your floppy disks clearly to keep track of where your files are saved.

COMPARING FILE SIZES

You can see how much space you have saved by comparing the file properties ⌐ of the original folder with those of the archive file. The original files created a 54.4KB folder, whereas the archive is 2.17KB.

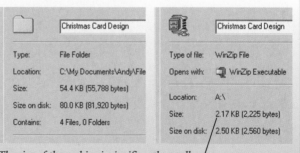

The size of the archive is significantly smaller ●

USING WORD

WORD'S ESSENTIAL FEATURES are presented in separate chapters within this section. The tasks that are covered include launching this word-processing program on your PC, understanding the Word window and the toolbars, keying in text, and changing its appearance. This section also shows you how to save your documents and organize them in folders, print them, improve them using Word's tools, templates, and wizards, and how to carry out a mail merge.

MICROSOFT WORD

Microsoft Word has been around for well over a decade and, with each new release, adds to its reputation as the world's leading word-processing program.

WHAT CAN WORD DO?

The features contained in Word make it one of the most flexible word-processing programs available. Word can be used to write anything from shopping lists to large publications that contain, in addition to the main text, illustrations and graphics, charts, tables and graphs, captions, headers and footers, cross references, footnotes, indexes, and glossaries – all of which are easily managed by Word. Word can check spelling and grammar, check text readability, search and replace text, import data, sort data, perform calculations, and provide templates for many types of documents from memos to web pages. The comprehensive and versatile design, formatting, and layout options in Word make it ideal for desktop publishing on almost any scale. In short, there's very little that Word cannot do.

WHAT IS A WORD DOCUMENT?

In its simplest form, a Word document is a sequence of characters that exists in a computer's memory. Using Word, a document can be edited, added to, and given a variety of layouts. Once the document has been created, there are a large number of actions that can be carried out, such as saving, printing, or sending the document as an email.

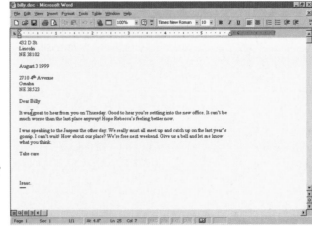

LAUNCHING WORD

Word launches just like any other program running in Windows. With the Windows desktop onscreen, you can launch Word as the only program running, or you can run Word alongside other software to exchange data with other applications.

1 LAUNCHING BY THE START MENU

● Place the mouse cursor over the **Start** button on the taskbar and click with the left mouse button.

● Move the cursor up the pop-up menu until **Programs** is highlighted. A submenu of programs appears to the right.

● Move the cursor down the menu to **Microsoft Word** and left-click again. (If **Microsoft Word** is missing from the **Programs** menu, it may be under **Microsoft Office**.)

● The Microsoft Word window opens ⌐|.

2 LAUNCHING BY A SHORTCUT

● You may already have a Word icon onscreen, which is a shortcut to launching Word. If so, double-click on the icon.

● The Microsoft Word window opens ⌐|.

THE WORD WINDOW

At first, Word's document window may look like a space shuttle computer display. However, you'll soon discover that similar commands and actions are neatly grouped together. This "like-with-like" layout helps you quickly understand where you should be looking on the window for what you want. Click and play while you read this.

THE WORD WINDOW

1 Title bar
2 Menu bar
Contains the main menus.
3 Standard toolbar
Buttons for frequent actions.
4 Formatting toolbar
Main layout options.
5 Tab selector
Clicking selects type of tab.
6 Left-indent buttons
Used to set left indents.
7 Ruler
Displays margins and tabs.
8 Right-indent button
Used to set right indent.
9 Insertion point
Shows where typing appears.
10 Text area
Area for document text.
11 Split box
Creates two text panes.
12 Scroll-up arrow
Moves up the document.
13 Scroll-bar box
Moves text up or down.
14 Vertical scroll bar
Used to move through text.

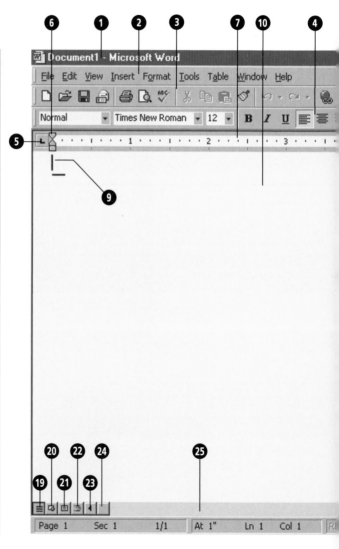

126 Insertion Point

144 Indenting the Address

TOOLBAR LAYOUT

If Word doesn't show the Formatting toolbar below the Standard toolbar, first place the cursor over the Formatting toolbar "handle." When the four-headed arrow appears, (right) hold down the mouse button and "drag" the toolbar into position.

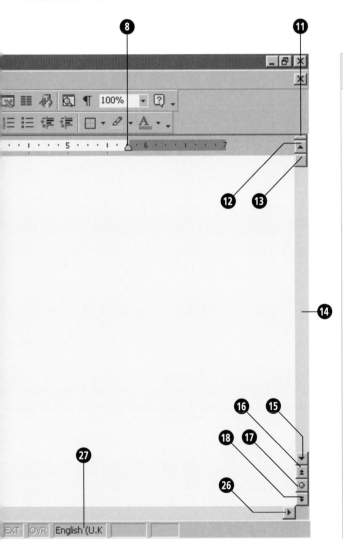

THE WORD WINDOW

15 Scroll-down arrow
Moves down the document.
16 Page-up button
Shows previous page of text.
17 Select browse object
Opens browse options menu.
18 Page-down button
Displays next page of text.
19 Normal view
Default document view.
20 Web layout view
Web-browser page view.
21 Page layout view
Printed-page view of text.
22 Outline view
Shows document's structure.
23 Left-scroll arrow
Shows the text to the left.
24 Scroll-bar box
Moves text horizontally.
25 Horizontal scroll bar
To view wide documents.
26 Right-scroll arrow
Shows the text to the right.
27 Language
Spelling, thesaurus, and proofing settings.

THE WORD TOOLBARS

Word provides a range of toolbars where numerous commands and actions are available. The principal toolbars are the Standard toolbar and the Formatting toolbar, which contain the most frequently used features of Word. There are also more than 20 other toolbars available for display. Click on **Tools** in the Menu bar, move the cursor down to **Customize**, and click the mouse button. The **Customize** dialog box opens. Click the **Toolbars** tab to view the variety of toolbars available.

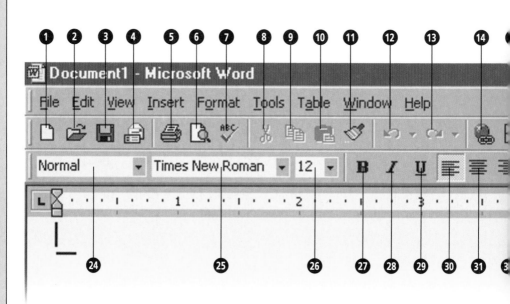

THE STANDARD TOOLBAR

❶ New document
❷ Open folder or file
❸ Save
❹ Email
❺ Print
❻ Print preview
❼ Spelling and grammar
❽ Cut text
❾ Copy text
❿ Paste text
⓫ Format painter
⓬ Undo action(s)
⓭ Redo action(s)
⓮ Insert hyperlink
⓯ Tables and borders
⓰ Insert table
⓱ Insert Excel worksheet
⓲ Columns
⓳ Drawing toolbar
⓴ Document map
㉑ Show/hide formatting marks
㉒ Zoom view of text
㉓ Microsoft Word help

129 Formatting Marks

160 Print Preview

163 Printing Quickly

CUSTOMIZING A TOOLBAR

To add a **Close** button to a toolbar, click on the **Commands** tab of the **Customize** box (see left). Place the cursor over the **Close** icon, hold down the mouse button, drag the icon to the toolbar, and release the mouse button.

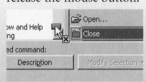

ScreenTips
It isn't necessary to memorize all these buttons. Roll the cursor over a button, wait for a second, and a ScreenTip appears telling you the function of the button.

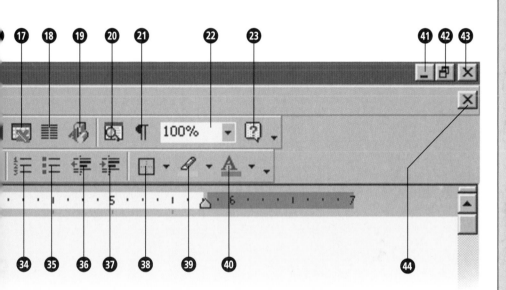

THE FORMATTING TOOLBAR

- ㉔ Style selector
- ㉕ Font selector
- ㉖ Font size selector
- ㉗ Bold
- ㉘ Italic
- ㉙ Underline
- ㉚ Left-aligned text
- ㉛ Centered text
- ㉜ Right-aligned text
- ㉝ Justified text
- ㉞ Numbered list
- ㉟ Bulleted list
- ㊱ Decrease indent
- ㊲ Increase indent
- ㊳ Outside border
- ㊴ Highlight color
- ㊵ Font color
- ㊶ Minimize Word
- ㊷ Restore Word
- ㊸ Close Word
- ㊹ Close document

149 **Quick Ways to Align Text**

150 **Font and Font Size**

150 **Quick Ways to Format Fonts**

YOUR FIRST LETTER

Microsoft Word makes the process of writing a letter and printing it out easier than ever. This chapter takes you through the few simple steps involved in creating your first letter.

TYPING THE LETTER

The first image on your screen when you start Microsoft Word is a blank area with a blinking cursor, surrounded by buttons and symbols that may mean nothing to you. Don't worry about them for now. To begin with, the only thing you need to concentrate on is to start writing your letter on that blank screen.

1 BEGINNING TYPING

• Type the first line of your address. As you type, the insertion point moves with your text. Don't worry about mistakes – they are easily corrected ⌐.

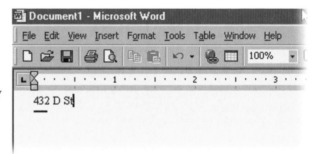

2 STARTING A NEW LINE

• Press the [Enter ↵] button.
• The insertion point has now moved to the beginning of a new line.

Insertion point •

INSERTION POINT

This is a blinking upright line that precedes your text as you type. If you are ever unsure about where your typing will appear on the page, check where the insertion point is.

[128] **Correcting Errors as You Type**

3 COMPLETING THE ADDRESS

● Finish typing your address, pressing Enter ← at the end of each line.
● At the end of the last address line, press Enter ← twice to leave a line space.

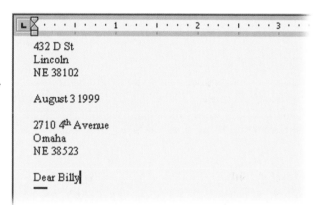

```
432 D St
Lincoln
NE 38102
```

4 STARTING THE LETTER

● Now type the date, leave another line space, then type the recipient's address.
● Leave two lines (by pressing Enter ← three times) and type your greeting.

```
432 D St
Lincoln
NE 38102

August 3 1999

2710 4th Avenue
Omaha
NE 38523

Dear Billy
```

5 CREATING PARAGRAPHS

● Leave another line and start your first paragraph. When typing paragraphs in Word, just keep typing until the end of the paragraph, and only then press Enter ←. At the end of each line, Word "wraps" your text round to start a new line.
● To start a new paragraph, press Enter ← to end the first paragraph, and press Enter ← again to leave a line space. You are ready to start the new paragraph.

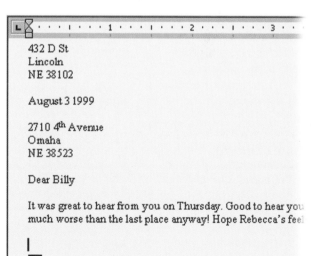

```
432 D St
Lincoln
NE 38102

August 3 1999

2710 4th Avenue
Omaha
NE 38523

Dear Billy

It was great to hear from you on Thursday. Good to hear you
much worse than the last place anyway! Hope Rebecca's feel
```

6 FINISHING THE LETTER

● If your letter is longer than can fit on the screen, Word moves the text up as you type. If you need to go back to it, simply hold down the ↑ arrow key. The insertion point moves up the text to the top of your letter.

● Type a farewell after the last paragraph. Press Enter↵ a few times to leave room for your signature. Then type your name.

● You have now typed your first letter using Word.

CORRECTING ERRORS AS YOU TYPE

1 REMOVING THE ERROR

● You have misspelled a word as you are typing.

● To remove the misspelled word, first press the Backspace (← Bksp) key. This removes text one letter at a time to the left of the insertion point.

● Keep tapping ← Bksp until the word is gone.

Dear Billy

It was great to hear from you on Thursday. Good to hear you
much worse than the last place anyway! Hope Rebecca's feel

I was speaking to the Jaspers the other day. We really must
gossip. How aubot|

Dear Billy

It was great to hear from you on Thursday. Good to hear you
much worse than the last place anyway! Hope Rebecca's feel

I was speaking to the Jaspers the other day. We really must
gossip. How|

2 REPLACING THE ERROR

● Now type the word again. Remember to leave a space before it – `← Bksp` also removes spaces and line spaces if they are immediately to the left of the insertion point.

● You have corrected the error and you can carry on typing your letter.

Dear Billy

It was great to hear from you on Thursday. Good to hear you much worse than the last place anyway! Hope Rebecca's fee

I was speaking to the Jaspers the other day. We really must a gossip. How about|

FORMATTING MARKS

Word uses invisible markers (called formatting marks) within your text to mark the spaces between words, and where you have decided to leave line spaces. Formatting marks do not appear on paper when you print out. Initially you don't see them on your screen, which makes the text on the screen appear exactly how it will print out. However, you may want to see the formatting marks so that you can see double spaces and control where you want the line spaces to be placed. To see the formatting marks, click on the small, down-arrow button in the middle of your toolbar. A menu drops down. Click on the button with the paragraph mark. You are now able to see the formatting marks. Click the button again when you want to turn off the formatting marks. You won't need to drop down the menu again – after the first use, Word adds the button to your toolbar.

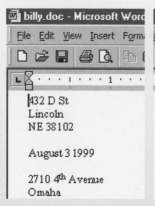

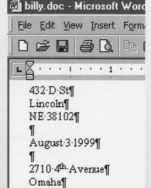

CORRECTING ERRORS FROM EARLIER IN THE TEXT

It is inevitable that errors are made as you type, such as misspellings and duplicate words. If you notice an error higher up in your letter than where you are currently typing, you can move the insertion point back to the error and easily correct it.

1 MOVING TO THE ERROR

- The misspelled word is higher in the text than the insertion point. You may be familiar with using the mouse to relocate the insertion point, but you may be less familiar with using the arrow keys.

It was great to hear from you on Thursday. Good to hear you much worse than the last place anyway! Hope Rebecca's fee

I was spaeking to the Jaspers the other day. We really must a gossip. How about our place? We're free next weekend. Giv think|

- Move the insertion point up to the line containing the error by using the ⬆ arrow key.
- Use the ⬅ and ➡ arrow keys until you've placed the insertion point at the end of the misspelled word.

It was great to hear from you on Thursday. Good to hear you much worse than the last place anyway! Hope Rebecca's fee

I was spaeking|to the Jaspers the other day. We really must a gossip. How about our place? We're free next weekend. Giv think.

2 CORRECTING THE ERROR

- Remove the misspelled word and type it in with the correct spelling.
- You have now corrected the error. Use the ⬇ arrow key to return the insertion point to where you left off. You can now continue with your typing.

It was great to hear from you on Thursday. Good to hear you much worse than the last place anyway! Hope Rebecca's fee

I was speaking|to the Jaspers the other day. We really must a gossip. How about our place? We're free next weekend. Giv think.

ADDING WORDS IN THE MIDDLE OF THE TEXT

Word makes it easy for you to change your text at any time while writing your letter. If you decide to add something further, or suddenly realize that an important point has been left out, you can type it in by first using the insertion point.

1 POSITIONING THE INSERTION POINT

● Move the insertion point to the place in the text where you want to add words. Use the arrow keys on your keyboard again for further practice. Remember, you can only move to where text has already been typed.

Insertion point ●

Omaha
NE 38523

Dear Billy

It was great to hear from you on Thursday. Good to hear you much worse than the last place anyway! Hope Rebecca's fee

I was speaking to the Jaspers the other day. We really must a gossip. How about our place? We're free next weekend. Giv think.

Take care

Isaac.

2 ADDING THE WORDS

● Start typing the new text. If the insertion point is in the middle of a paragraph, you'll notice that Word automatically moves text along to accommodate what you are adding.
● Use the arrow keys to return to the place where you left off typing.

Omaha
NE 38523

Dear Billy

It was great to hear from you on Thursday. Good to hear you much worse than the last place anyway! Hope Rebecca's fee

I was speaking to the Jaspers the other day. We really must a gossip. I can't wait! How about our place? We're free next w what you think.

Take care

MANIPULATING PARAGRAPHS

Paragraphs organize your text, help with the sense of your document, and make your document more readable. With Word, it's easy to create a new paragraph when another is needed, and to combine them when two paragraphs aren't required.

1 SPLITTING A PARAGRAPH

● To split a paragraph into two, move the insertion point to the start of the sentence that will begin the new second paragraph. Then press Enter ⏎ twice. You now have two paragraphs.

I was speaking to the Jaspers the other day. We really must a gossip. I can't wait! How about our place? We're free next w what you think.

Take care

I was speaking to the Jaspers the other day. We really must a gossip. I can't wait!

How about our place? We're free next weekend. Give us a b

Take care

2 COMBINING PARAGRAPHS

● If you want to join two paragraphs together to make one, place the insertion point at the beginning of the second paragraph. Then press ← Bksp twice to remove the line spaces. Your two paragraphs now form one larger paragraph.

It was great to hear from you on Thursday. Good to hear you're settling into the new office. It c much worse than the last place anyway! Hope Rebecca's feeling better now.

I was speaking to the Jaspers the other day. We really must all meet up and catch up on the last gossip. I can't wait! How about our place? We're free next weekend. Give us a bell and let me k what you think.

Take care

3 PARAGRAPH MARKS

● Pressing the [Enter ←] key ends a paragraph and inserts a paragraph mark. You can see these marks by turning on the formatting marks ⬚. Deleting the line space between paragraphs is just a matter of deleting the paragraph mark just like any other character.

> It was great to hear from you on Thursday. Good to hear you're settling into the new office. It c
> much worse than the last place anyway! Hope Rebecca's feeling better now. I was speaking to
> Jaspers the other day. We really must all meet up and catch up on the last year's gossip. I can't
> wait! How about our place? We're free next weekend. Give us a bell and let me know what you
>
> Take care

USING WORD TO START A NEW PAGE

If you want to begin a new page, before the text has reached the end of the current page, you can use Word to split the page into two.

Move the insertion point to the position in your letter where you want the new page to start. Hold down the [Ctrl] key and press [Enter ←]. Word inserts a "manual" page break. You can delete this page break by placing the insertion point at the top left of the second page and pressing [← Bksp].

> Dear Billy
>
> It was great to hear from you on Thursday. Good to hear you're settling into the new office. I
> much worse than the last place anyway! Hope Rebecca's feeling better now.
>
> I was speaking to the Jaspers the other day. We really must all meet up and catch up on the l
> gossip. I can't wait! How about our place? We're free next weekend. Give us a bell and let m
> what you think.

> Dear Billy
>
> It was great to hear from you on Thursday. Good to hear you're settling into the new office. I
> much worse than the last place anyway! Hope Rebecca's feeling better now.
> --------------------------------Page Break--------------------------------
> I was speaking to the Jaspers the other day. We really must all meet up and catch up on the l
> gossip. I can't wait! How about our place? We're free next weekend. Give us a bell and let m
> what you think.

129 **Formatting Marks**

SAVING YOUR LETTER

Now that your letter is finished and correct, you should save it as a file on your computer's hard disk so that if you need to find it later, or make changes after you have printed it out, you will be able to bring it back up on the screen.

1 SAVING THE FILE

● Move your mouse pointer over the word **File** in the Menu bar at the top of the screen and left-click to display its menu. Move the mouse pointer down and click on **Save**.

● The **Save As** dialog box pops up in the middle of your screen. In this box you are able to give your letter a file name and decide where you want to save it on the hard disk.

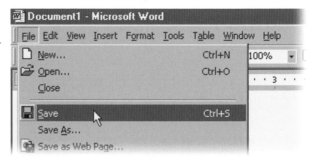

2 NAMING AND SAVING

● Choose a file name that identifies the letter for you and type it into the **File name** box.

● Select a folder in the **Save in** box and click on the **Save** button. The dialog box closes and your letter is saved to disk.

PRINTING YOUR LETTER

1 CHOOSING TO PRINT

● Click on the **File** menu. The **File** menu drops down.
● This time choose **Print** from the **File** menu by clicking once on **Print**.

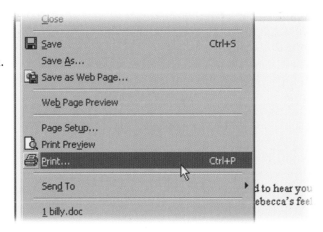

2 PRINTING YOUR LETTER

● The **Print** dialog box pops up. Don't worry about any of the features here at this stage. Just make sure that the printer is plugged into the computer and is switched on.
● Click on the **OK** button at the bottom of the dialog box and your letter begins to print.

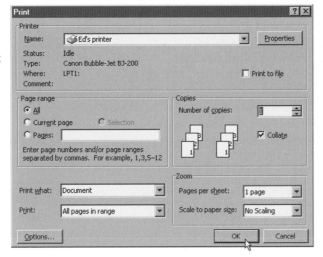

Well done...
You have now typed, corrected, saved, and printed your first letter using Word. These simple steps have shown you the basic process that you use to create a letter with Microsoft Word. Now we go into more detail and explore each step of the process in detail.

WORKING WITH TEXT

This chapter deals with methods of working with text: moving around text, shifting text from one place to another, deleting text, and copying text.

MOVING AROUND YOUR TEXT

There are many different ways to move around and see different parts of your letter. Here are some techniques to move through your letter that make use of either the mouse or the different actions that are available through the keyboard.

1 GET TO THE START OF THE LETTER

● The insertion point is midway through or at the end of the letter.
● Hold down the `Ctrl` key and press the `Home` key on your keyboard.
● The screen now shows the top of the letter. The insertion point is at the very beginning of the text.

The insertion point ●
moves to the start
of the letter

Dear Billy

It was great to hear from you on Thursday. Good to hear you
much worse than the last place anyway! Hope Rebecca's fee

I was speaking to the Jaspers the other day. We really must a
gossip. I can't wait! How about our place? We're free next w
what you think.

Take care

432 D St
Lincoln
NE 38102

August 3 1999

2710 4th Avenue
Omaha
NE 38523

Dear Billy

2 GET TO THE END OF THE TEXT

● Hold down the Ctrl key and press the End key on your keyboard.

● The screen now shows the foot of the letter. The insertion point is at the very end of the text.

> I was speaking to the Jaspers the other day. We really must a‍ gossip. I can't wait! How about our place? We're free next w‍ what you think.
>
> Take care
>
> Isaac|

3 SCROLLING THROUGH TEXT

● If you can't see the part of the letter you want, position the mouse cursor over the sliding box in the scroll bar.

Hold down the left mouse button and move the box up and down the bar to scroll through the text.

● Alternatively, use the buttons at the top and

bottom of the scroll bar. Click on them to scroll the text up and down.

● Stop when the section of the text appears that you want to work on.

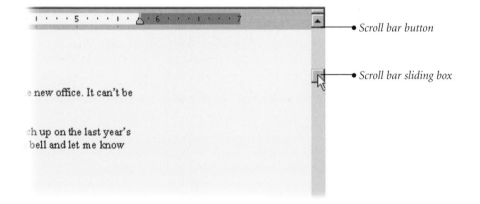

● Scroll bar button

● Scroll bar sliding box

> e new office. It can't be
>
> ch up on the last year's
> bell and let me know

MOVING AROUND WITHOUT THE MOUSE

If you want to move quickly around your letter without using the mouse, you can use the PgUp and PgDn keys on your keyboard to move up or down your letter one screen at a time. This method moves the insertion point directly. You can use the arrow keys to place the insertion point in the exact position in the text where you need to make your changes.

4 CLICKING ON TEXT

● Move the mouse pointer to the exact point in the text where you want the insertion point to go.

● Left-click once. The insertion point appears.

Dear Billy

It was great to hear from you on Thursday. Good to hear you much worse than the last place anyway! Hope Rebecca's feel

I was speaking to the Jaspers the other day. We really must a gossip. I can't wait! How about our place? We're free next w what you think.

Take care

SELECTING TEXT

Before Word can carry out any changes that you want to make, you first need to tell Word what parts of the text you want it to work on. This is done by selecting text, which is one of the most frequently used operations when using Word.

1 USING THE KEYBOARD

● Move the insertion point to the start of the text you want to select.

● Hold down the ⇧ Shift key and press the → arrow key. This has the effect of creating a block of selected text one letter at a time.

It was great to hear from you on Thursday. Good to hear you much worse than the last place anyway! Hope Rebecca's feel

I was speaking to the Jaspers the other day. We really must a gossip. I can't wait! How about our place? We're free next w what you think.

Take care

It was great to hear from you on Thursday. Good to hear you much worse than the last place anyway! Hope Rebecca's feel

I was speaking to the Jaspers the other day. We really must a gossip. I can't wait! How about our place? We're free next w what you think.

Take care

● If the block you want to select extends over more than one line, keep the ⇧Shift key held down, and press the ↓ key to select whole lines at a time. Then use the ← and → keys to choose the end of the block. Don't release the ⇧Shift key until you have selected the entire block of text that you want.

Dear Billy

It was great to hear from you on Thursday. Good to hear you
much worse than the last place anyway! Hope Rebecca's fee

I was speaking to the Jaspers the other day. We really must a
gossip. I can't wait! How about our place? We're free next w
what you think.

Take care

Vanishing Point

You will notice that when you have selected and highlighted a block of text, there is no longer an insertion point in your Word window. What has happened is that the block of selected text becomes one very large insertion point. It is important to be careful here because if you press any character key on the keyboard while your block is selected, your entire block will vanish and be replaced by whatever you type.

2 USING THE MOUSE

● Move the mouse pointer to the precise point where you want to start your selected block of text.
● Hold down the left mouse button and move the mouse pointer to the position that marks the end of the block that you want.
● Release the mouse button. Your block of text is now selected.
● If you make a mistake, simply click outside the selection and go through the process again.

Dear Billy

It was great to hear from you on Thursday. Good to hear you
much worse than the last place anyway! Hope Rebecca's fee

I was speaking to the Jaspers the other day. We really must a
gossip. I can't wait! How about our place? We're free next w
what you think.

Dear Billy

It was great to hear from you on Thursday. Good to hear you
much worse than the last place anyway! Hope Rebecca's fee

I was speaking to the Jaspers the other day. We really must a
gossip. I can't wait! How about our place? We're free next w
what you think.

3 SELECTING ALL THE TEXT

● Click on **Edit** on the menu bar. The **Edit** menu drops down.

● Now click on **Select All** in the **Edit** menu.

● The whole of your letter is now selected.

● Alternatively, you can move the mouse cursor to the left of your text where it changes from pointing left to pointing to the right. Hold down the [Ctrl] key and click on the left mouse button. The whole of your text is now selected.

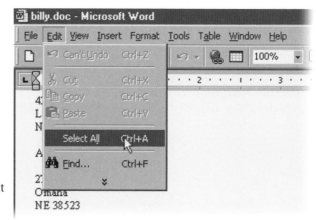

4 SELECTING LINES AT A TIME

Selecting blocks of text by lines can save time. Move the mouse pointer to the left of the first line that you want to select. Hold down the left mouse button and move the mouse pointer to the last line of your chosen block. Release the mouse button and the block is selected.

2710 4th Avenue
Omaha
NE 38523

Dear Billy

It was great to hear from you on Thursday. Good to hear you much worse than the last place anyway! Hope Rebecca's feel

I was speaking to the Jaspers the other day. We really must a gossip. I can't wait! How about our place? We're free next w what you think.

Take care

MOVING TEXT – CUT AND PASTE

You can move whole blocks of text either within your document or between documents when using Word. The easiest way to do this is by "cutting" selected blocks of text from your letter and "pasting" them back into a different place.

1 CUTTING TEXT

- Select a block of text ⌐.
- Click on **Edit** on the menu bar. The **Edit** menu drops down.
- Click on **Cut** in the **Edit** menu. Your block of text will disappear, but it is not lost. The rest of the text will move back into place around it.

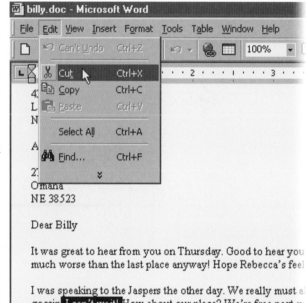

Block of text to be cut •

Cutting has removed the text •

2 PASTING TEXT

● Position the insertion point where you want the text to reappear.
● Click on **Edit** in the Menu bar, then on **Paste** in the drop down menu.
● The text is pasted back into your letter exactly where you want it.

COPYING TEXT

You may want to copy a block of text to a new location while leaving the original block in its old position. Simply go through the cut and paste procedures detailed on these pages, but when you come to cut the text, select **Copy** instead of **Cut** on the **Edit** menu. The block will stay where it is, but you will be able to paste copies of it whenever you want.

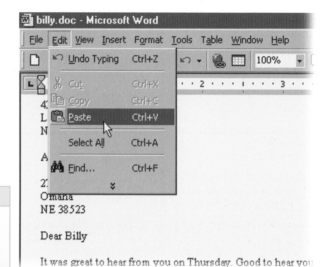

Dear Billy

It was great to hear from you on Thursday. Good to hear you much worse than the last place anyway! Hope Rebecca's fee

I was speaking to the Jaspers the other day. We really must gossip. How about our place? We're free next weekend. Giv think

Take care

MOVING TEXT – DRAG AND DROP

This method is a quicker way of moving text around and uses only the mouse. Once you've told Word what part of the text you want to move, you can then "drag" it to the position where you want to move it, and "drop" it into place.

1 SELECTING THE TEXT

● Select a block of text using one of the methods that you have already learned ⬚.

Dear Billy

It was great to hear from you on Thursday. Good to hear you much worse than the last place anyway! Hope Rebecca's fee

I was speaking to the Jaspers the other day. We really must gossip. How about our place? We're free next weekend. Giv think. I can't wait!

Take care

2 MOVING THE TEXT

● Place the mouse cursor over the block of selected text. Hold down the left mouse button and move, or "drag," the mouse cursor to the position in your letter where you want the text to appear. Don't release the mouse button until the mouse pointer is in exactly the right place.

● Now release the mouse button and the text appears in the new location.

Dear Billy

It was great to hear from you on Thursday. Good to hear you much worse than the last place anyway! Hope Rebecca's fee

I was speaking to the Jaspers the other day. We really must gossip. How about our place? We're free next weekend. Giv think. I can't wait!

Take care

Dear Billy

It was great to hear from you on Thursday. Good to hear you much worse than the last place anyway! Hope Rebecca's fee

I was speaking to the Jaspers the other day. We really must gossip. We're free next weekend. How about our place? Giv think. I can't wait!

Take care

⬚ 138 **Selecting Text**

CHANGING THE LAYOUT

In this chapter we deal with how to lay your text out on the page in the way you want it. The most common layout changes that you'll be making are indenting and aligning.

INDENTING THE ADDRESS

1 SELECTING YOUR ADDRESS

● Using either the mouse or the keyboard, select the lines of your address as a block of text ⌐.

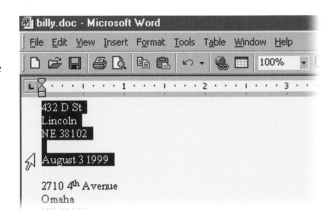

2 CHANGING THE INDENT

● Directly above the text on the screen is a numbered line. This is the ruler.

● Move your mouse pointer to the small symbol called the left indent marker shown at right.

● Click on the box at the base of the left indent marker, and hold down the left mouse button.

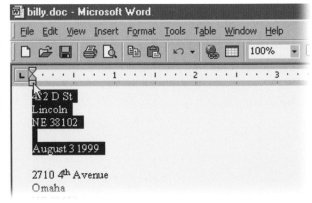

138 Selecting Text

● Drag the left indent marker, by using the box, across the ruler however far you want your address to be indented.

● Now release the mouse button. Your address has moved across the screen.

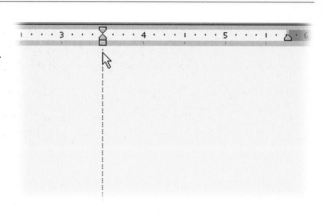

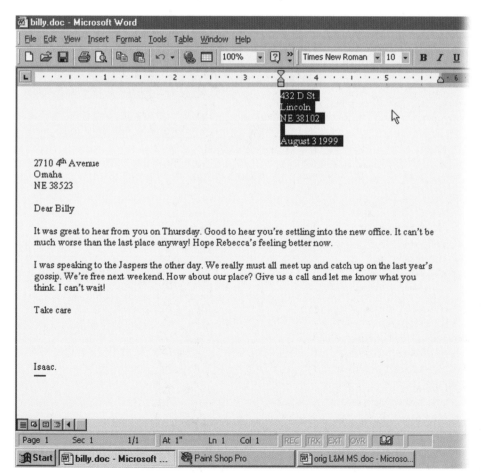

INDENTING PARAGRAPHS

You may want to make each of your paragraphs begin a little further into the page than the main text (a "first line indent"). Or you may want the body of text indented except for the lines beginning each paragraph (a "hanging indent"). These steps take you through how to do each of these procedures.

1 SELECT THE PARAGRAPHS

● Select only the paragraphs of text in your letter and not the addresses, date, greeting, and sign-off.

2710 4ᵗʰ Avenue
Omaha
NE 38523

Dear Billy

It was great to hear from you on Thursday. Good to hear you much worse than the last place anyway! Hope Rebecca's feel

I was speaking to the Jaspers the other day. We really must a gossip. We're free next weekend. How about our place? Giv think. I can't wait!

Take care

2 FIRST LINE INDENT

● Move your mouse pointer over the left indent marker on the ruler.
● When the pointer is on the top part of the left indent marker, hold down the left mouse button.
● Drag the pointer along the ruler to however far in you want the indent.

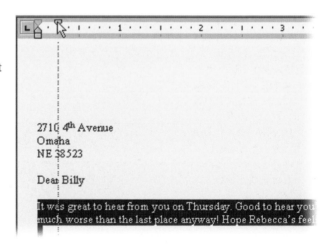

2710 4ᵗʰ Avenue
Omaha
NE 38523

Dear Billy

It was great to hear from you on Thursday. Good to hear you much worse than the last place anyway! Hope Rebecca's feel

● Release the mouse button. The first lines of each of your paragraphs are now indented.

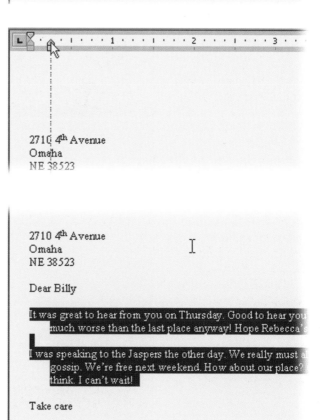

3 HANGING INDENT

● For a hanging indent, go through Step 1 (opposite) to select the text.

● Now, move the mouse pointer until it is over the left indent marker ⌐.

● Position the pointer over the middle part of the left indent marker, (avoiding the other two parts of the left indent marker may need some practice).

● Hold down the left mouse button and drag the pointer over to the right as far as you want the paragraphs to be indented.

● Release the mouse button. Your paragraphs are now formatted with a hanging indent.

ALIGNMENT

At the moment all your text except for your address is aligned to the left – the left side is straight while the right is ragged, like text created with a typewriter. Word can make the right side straight as well, like text in a book (this is called "justified text"). Other possibilities include aligning your text to the right, which leaves the left side ragged, or centering the text exactly down the middle of the page.

1 JUSTIFIED TEXT

● Select the text you want to realign.
● Drop down the **Format** menu from the menu bar at the top of the screen.
● Click on **Paragraph** in the Format menu and the **Paragraph** dialog box opens onscreen.
● Click on the drop-down button next to the **Alignment** option. A small menu will drop down.
● Click on the word **Justified** in this menu.
● Click on **OK** and the dialog box closes.

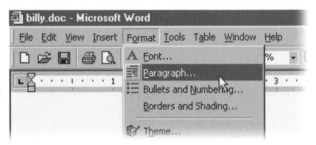

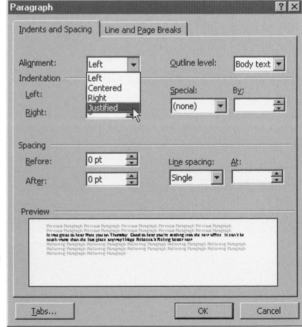

● Your text is now justified with the left- and right-hand sides both straight.

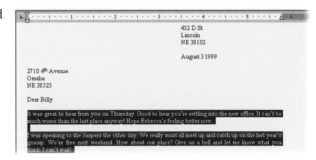

2 RIGHT-ALIGNED TEXT

● Follow Step 1 (opposite) until you get to the **Alignment** drop-down menu in the **Paragraph** dialog box.

● This time click on **Right** and then on **OK**.

● Your text has been aligned to the right.

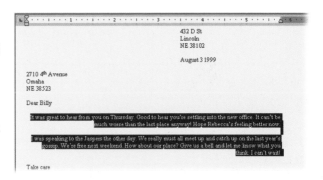

3 CENTERED TEXT

● Follow Step 1 until you get to the **Alignment** drop-down menu in the **Paragraph** dialog box.

● Click on **Center** this time, then on **OK**.

● Your text has been centered on the page.

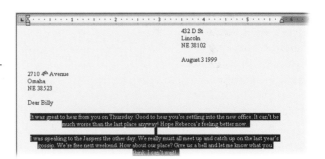

QUICK WAYS TO ALIGN TEXT

 You are also able to realign text by using the alignment buttons (shown at left) on the toolbar at the top of the screen. First select the text and click on the button you need. From left to right, the buttons mean: left-align, center, right-align, and justify.

APPEARANCE

Your letter now looks better than it did before. However, there are many other tweaks and touches that can transform your text to just the way you want it to appear.

FONT AND FONT SIZE

The font is the kind of lettering that Word uses to display your text. You may wish to use different fonts in different kinds of letter: a stern, professional-looking font for business letters, and a lighter, friendlier font for your personal letters. You may also wish either to increase or decrease the size of the font that you use.

1 THE FONT DIALOG BOX
- Select all the text in the document ⌁.
- Drop down the **Format** menu from the menu bar.
- Choose **Font** in the **Format** menu. The **Font** dialog box opens.

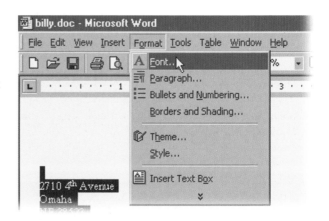

QUICK WAYS TO FORMAT FONTS

You may have noticed that the font, font size, and the buttons for bold, italic, and underline are included in the Formatting toolbar (just above the ruler). To format fonts without using the **Font** dialog box, you can select the text and use these tools to format it. The font and font size are drop-down menus. The font style buttons (shown left) click in or out to show if, say, Bold is on or off in a selected block of text.

2 CHANGING THE FONT

● The **Font** menu is displayed under the **Font** tab in the **Font** dialog box. Scroll up and down it using the scroll bar at the side of the menu. Your text is probably in Times New Roman at the moment.

● As you click on different fonts, the appearance of the selected font is shown in the **Preview** box in the **Font** dialog box.

● Keep scrolling through the fonts until you find one you want to use.

Preview Box •

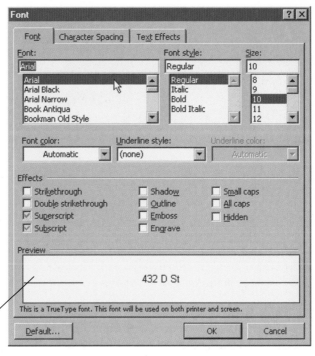

3 CHANGING THE FONT SIZE

● Now check the **Size** menu at top right of the **Font** dialog box.

● The font size is probably set to 10. This is quite small. Try clicking on **12** or any font size you want – 10 and 12 are the most often used in plain text.

● The **Preview** box will show the new font in its new size.

4 APPLYING YOUR CHANGES

● When you are satisfied with the font and font size, click on the **OK** button.
● The **Font** dialog box will close. Your text is now formatted in the new font and font size.

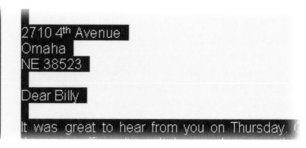

FONT STYLE

In addition to the regular font, there are three other font styles – bold, italic, and underline – that can be used to emphasize individual words, phrases, or any other block of text. They can also be used in combination for extra effect.

1 MAKING YOUR TEXT BOLD

● Select the text you want to make bold.
● Open the **Font** dialog box from the **Format** menu.
● In the **Font style** menu click on **Bold**.
● Click **OK** to close the **Font** dialog box.
● Your selected text now appears in bold.

Dear Billy

It was great to hear from you on Thursday. the new office. It can't be much worse tha Rebecca's feeling better now.

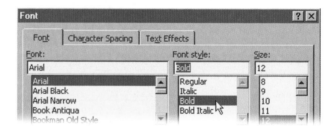

Dear Billy

Bold text ●——— It was **great** to hear from you on Thursday. the new office. It can't be much worse tha Rebecca's feeling better now.

2 MAKING YOUR TEXT ITALIC

● Follow Step 1 (opposite), but click on **Italic** in the **Font Style** menu of the **Font** dialog box.
● Click **OK** to close the **Font** dialog box.
● Your selected text is now displayed in italics.

Dear Billy

It was great to hear from you on Thursday. (the new office. It can't be much worse tha Rebecca's feeling better now.

I was speaking to the Jaspers the other day catch up on the last year's gossip. We're fre place? Give us a call and let me know what you

Take care

Italicized text ●

3 UNDERLINING YOUR TEXT

● Select the text and open the **Font** dialog box in the usual way.
● Drop down the **Underline style** menu (below the **Font** menu in the dialog box).
● There are many underline options, but the most useful is **Single** – a single line under the selected text. An alternative is **Words only** – each word is underlined, but not the spaces separating them. Click on your choice.
● Click **OK** to close the **Font** dialog box.
● The selection is now emphasized by underlining.

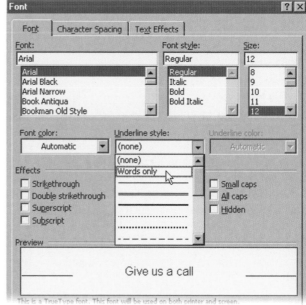

I was speaking to the Jaspers the other day catch up on the last year's gossip. We're fre place? Give us a call and let me know what you

Take care

Words only ●
underlined text

LINE SPACING

You may want to increase the spacing between the lines of your letter – some find it easier to read. For example, double line spacing creates a space the height of one line between each line of the text. Other options are also available.

1 SELECT THE ENTIRE LETTER
● Click on **Format** on the menu bar to drop down the **Format** menu.
● Click on **Paragraph** from the **Format** menu to open the **Paragraph** dialog box.

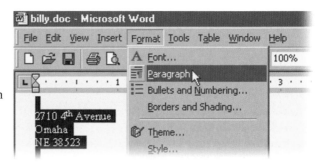

2 LINE SPACING SELECTION
● Click the small down arrow on the right of the **Line spacing** box. The **Line spacing** menu drops down.
● Choose **Double** line spacing from the menu.

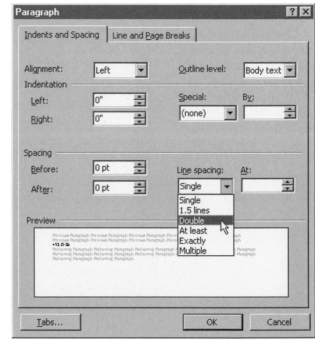

● Click on the **OK** button. Your selected text now appears with the chosen line spacing.

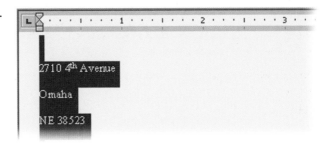

3 MULTIPLE LINE SPACING

You are not limited only to single, 1.5, and double line spacing when using Word.

● Select part of your text and click the down arrow in the **Line spacing** box. The **Line spacing** menu drops down.

● Click on **Multiple** at the foot of the menu.

● In the **At** box the figure **3** appears. Three-line spacing is the default selection for multiple line spacing. If you want a different number, highlight the 3, type the number of line spaces, and click on **OK**.

● The lines of your selected text are now separated by your chosen line spacing.

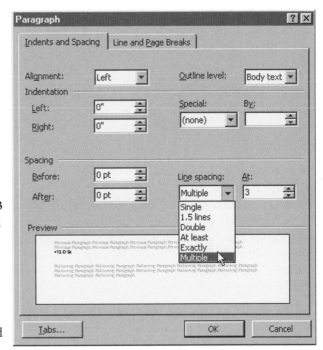

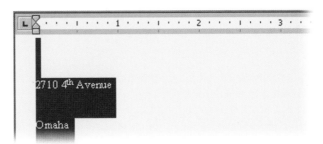

STORING YOUR LETTERS

It is usually essential to save your letters on your hard disk so that you can refer to them at a later date. This chapter provides an overview of how to store and recall your text.

WORKING WITH FILES

A file is what we call any piece of data that is stored on a computer's hard disk. This could be a spreadsheet, a program, or your letter that you have created using Word. Not only can you store (save) your documents when you have completed them, it is important that you also save your files as you work, especially if they are long and you have put a lot of work into them. If your computer suddenly crashes, you could lose everything you have done since you last saved your work.

1 CREATING A NEW FILE
● When you open Word, a new file is automatically created in which you can begin typing.
● You may want to create other new files later on. Drop down the **File** menu and click on **New**.
● Click on **Blank Document** to select it and click on **OK**.

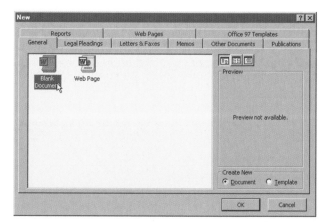

2 SAVING A FILE
● Drop down the **File** menu from the menu bar. Click on **Save**.

● If the file has already been saved, the **Save** command will simply save the new version and you may continue typing. If you are saving the file for the first time, the **Save As** dialog box appears and you can assign the document a name and a location.

3 OPENING A FILE

● Drop down the **File** menu from the menu bar. Click on **Open**. The **Open** dialog box appears.

● The **Open** dialog box shows the files you have already saved. Click on the file you want and then click on **Open**.

● The file opens and you may begin working on it.

4 CLOSING A FILE

● You usually close a document when you have finished working on it. Drop down the **File** menu and click on **Close**.

● If you have not saved your text, or if you have changed it since you last saved, you are asked if you want to save the file.

● Click on **Yes** if you have forgotten to save your work. Click on **No** if you're absolutely sure that you don't want to save either the document or the changes you have made since you last saved. If in doubt, click on **Cancel** and return to the document.

5 SAVING THE FILE TO FLOPPY DISK

● Click on **Save As** in the **File** menu to open the **Save As** dialog box.

● Drop down the **Save in** menu in the dialog box.

● Click on **3½ Floppy (A:)** in the **Save in** menu.

● Click **OK** and your file is saved to the floppy disk.

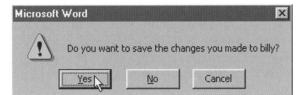

WORKING WITH FOLDERS

As you create more files, your hard disk may begin to look cluttered. When you want to open a file, you may not be able to find it because the list of files is so long.

The way to avoid this is to use folders, which can be given names, such as Personal and Finance, so that you know where to store and find your files.

1 CREATE A NEW FOLDER

● When you want to save a document in a new folder, begin by dropping down the **File** menu and click on **Save As**. The **Save As** dialog box appears.

● Click on the button showing a sparkling folder – this is the **Create New Folder** button.

● The **New Folder** dialog box opens. Type in a name for your new folder and click the **OK** button.

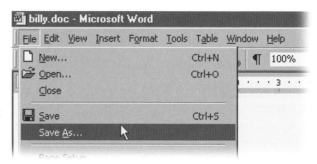

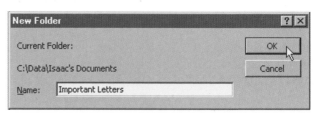

- The **New Folder** dialog box closes. The **Save As** dialog box reappears, this time showing your new, and empty, folder.

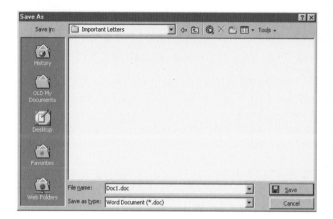

2 SAVING INTO YOUR FOLDER

- Type a name for your file in the **File** name text box and click on **Save**. The **Save As** dialog box closes and your file has been saved in the new folder.

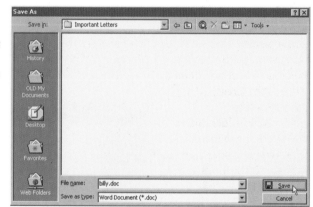

3 MOVING WITHIN FOLDERS

- To open the folder containing the current folder, click on the folder icon that contains the right-angled arrow in the **Save As** dialog box – this icon is also in the **Open** dialog box.

So many folders...
You can have as many folders as you want within a single folder, but again, this may become unwieldy. So it might be better to split your folders according to type. You could have a Work folder with a Customer folder and a Supplier folder to divide two different kinds of letters; and a Personal folder with a Friends folder and a Family folder within it. You can of course further subdivide. Utility is the key – create folders only when you think they'll be helpful.

PRINTING

You will want your letter to appear on paper looking as neat as possible. Word has features that let you preview the printout of your letter, make improvements, and finally print your letter.

PRINT PREVIEW

Print Preview lets you see how the printed version of your letter will appear. This is done by showing each page as a scaled-down version of the specified paper size – usually 8½ x 11. The changes you can make in Print Preview include adjusting the margins, but it's not possible to edit the text when previewing. You can preview one page at a time or view several pages at once. Seeing more than one page lets you compare how they look and see how your changes affect your letter.

1 PREVIEW YOUR TEXT

● Open a file that you want to print out.

● Go to the top of the text with the insertion point ⌐.

● Click on **File** in the Menu bar and click on **Print Preview** in the **File** drop-down menu.

● Your screen now shows a print preview of your letter.

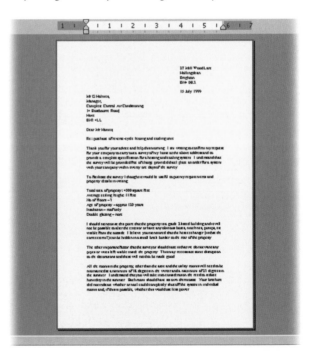

Insertion Point

2 SHOWING MULTIPLE PAGES

● If your letter has more than one page, you may want to see them all on one screen. Look at the Print Preview toolbar (now the only toolbar at the top of the screen). There is a rounded box containing four small rectangles (shown at right). This is the **Multiple Pages** icon.

● Click on the **Multiple Pages** icon, a menu of gray pages appears.

● Move the mouse pointer over the menu to choose

how many pages you want to view. In the example shown, **1 x 2 Pages** is selected. The first number is the number of rows in which your pages appear, the second number is the number of pages to be shown. The maximum is 3 x 8, which is selected by holding down the left mouse button and moving the mouse pointer right.

● Release the mouse button over the required display.

● You can now see how your letter will appear on the printed page.

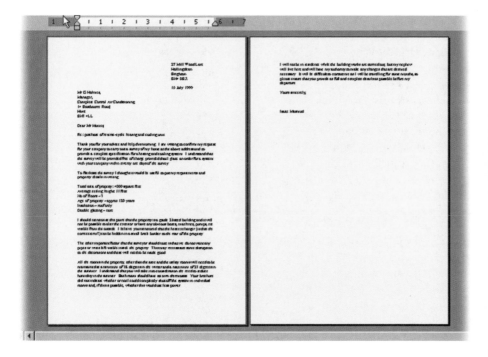

3 PAGE SETUP

● You may want to improve the look of your letter. Perhaps there is not enough room between the text and the edge of the paper. Or maybe a couple of lines spill onto a new page that could fit on the previous page. Both these problems can be solved by changing the margins.

● Begin by dropping down the **File** menu and click on **Page Setup**.

● The **Page Setup** dialog box appears.

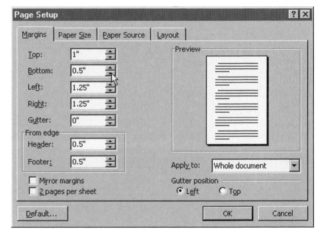

4 CHANGING THE MARGINS

● There are four boxes in the **Page Setup** dialog box to control the top, bottom, left, and right margins.

● You can increase or decrease the margins by increments of one-tenth of an inch by clicking the up and down arrow buttons to the right of each margin control box. Or click inside a box to enter a size.

● When you have selected the margin sizes, click the **OK** box to see your results.

● When you are satisfied with your changes, click on **Close** in the Print Preview toolbar to return to the normal view of your letter.

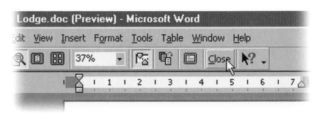

PRINTING YOUR LETTER

The actual process of printing out your letter is very simple. The Print Preview feature makes it unnecessary to print a number of draft versions of your letter because you now know how it will appear on the page. All that is left to do now is to use the very simple **Print** command to produce a hard copy of your letter.

1 THE PRINT DIALOG BOX

● Drop down the **File** menu and click on **Print** to open the **Print** dialog box.
● You can print selected pages of your letter if you want. Enter the numbers of the pages into the **Pages** box under **Page range**.
● You can also print more than one copy of your letter. Enter the number you want into the **Number of copies** box at the right of the **Print** dialog box.
● Check that your printer is connected to your computer and that it is switched on.
● Click on **OK** and your letter begins to be printed.

Enter the number of copies required ●——

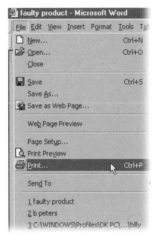

PRINTING QUICKLY

In the majority of cases, you will not need to "customize" the printing of your document because you will need only one copy of your letter. Click on the printer icon in the toolbar at the top of the screen. Your letter is printed without using the **Print** dialog box.

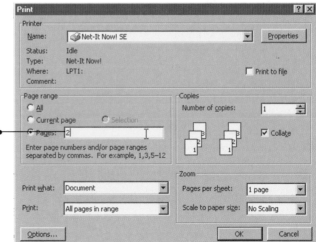

LET WORD HELP

Word has many helpful features including a spelling checker, a grammar checker, a thesaurus, templates on which to base your documents, and wizards that produce customized documents.

SPELLING CHECKER

However good your letter looks on paper, it can be let down by typing errors. Even if your spelling is impeccable, it is inevitable that some incorrect keystrokes are made.

Word can check your spelling for you as you type, or you can have Word check the spelling of your whole document when you've finished writing it.

1 CHECKING AS YOU TYPE

● Try typing a deliberate mistake into your letter.
● A wavy red line appears below the incorrect word.
● Move the mouse pointer over the word containing the error and click with the right mouse button (right click). A pop-up menu appears near the word.
● Word lists alternative words that you could have intended to type instead of the mistake. Left-click on the correct word.

Dear Margaret

Thanks for your leter

Thanks for your leter

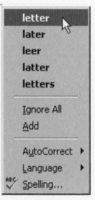

letter
later
leer
latter
letters

Ignore All
Add

AutoCorrect ▶
Language ▶
Spelling...

- The mistake is replaced by the correct word and the pop-up closes.

Dear Margaret

Thanks for your letter

2 ADDING WORDS

- Now type something that is correct but obscure and which the spelling checker is unlikely to recognize, such as a foreign word or an unusual name.
- The word, though not a mistake, is underlined by the wavy red line.
- Right-click the word. The menu drops down.
- Click on **Add**. The spelling checker adds the word to its dictionary and will no longer underline the word as a "mistake."
- The wavy red line disappears because the spelling is now accepted as being correct.

Dear Margaret

Thanks for your letter. I've made some calls to but so far no luck. C'est la vie.

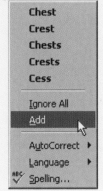

Thanks for your letter. I've made some calls to but so far no luck. C'est la vie.

> Chest
> Crest
> Chests
> Crests
> Cess
> Ignore All
> Add
> AutoCorrect ▶
> Language ▶
> ✓ Spelling...

Dear Margaret

Thanks for your letter. I've made some calls to but so far no luck. C'est la vie.

GRAMMAR CHECKER

Word's automatic grammar checker works very much like the spelling checker. The obvious difference is that Word marks what it believes to be grammatical errors with a wavy green line, not a red line. The grammar checker cannot offer perfect advice due to the complexities of English. So accept its suggestions carefully.

CORRECTING GRAMMAR

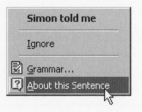

- Word has detected a clumsy sentence structure.
- Right-click the sentence and a menu pops up.
- Choose the suggestion or click on **About this Sentence** to have the problem explained. Click on **Ignore** if you think the grammar checker is itself making a mistake.
- If you click on **About this Sentence**, the office assistant, which can be switched on by using the **Help** menu, pops up and explains what Word thinks is the problem.
- Click with the mouse button away from the advice to close the panel.

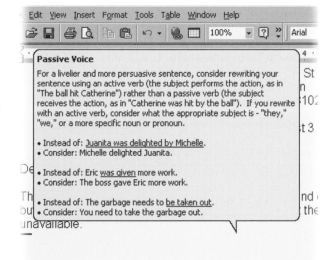

● Right-click the sentence again to display the pop up menu and click on the suggested correction.

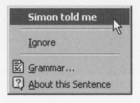

The grammar of the sentence has been revised

THESAURUS

You may want to find an alternative word to express what you mean. The thesaurus feature in Word lists possible words in the same way as the paper-based thesaurus except that it works directly on the word for which you require a synonym.

SYNONYMS

● Place the insertion point in the word for which you want to find a synonym.

● Drop down the **Tools** menu from the menu bar. Click on **Language**.

● A submenu appears, click on **Thesaurus**.

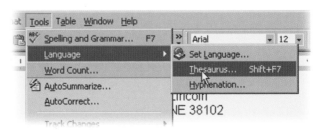

- The **Thesaurus** dialog box opens. The list of available synonyms are listed in the right-hand panel of the dialog box.
- Click on a synonym. It appears in the **Replace with Synonym** box.
- Click on the **Replace** button.
- The word is replaced with the synonym.

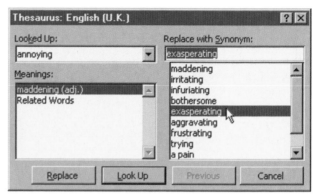

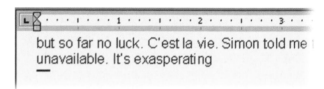

CHECKING AFTER YOU HAVE FINISHED TYPING

Some people find that having Word checking their spelling and grammar as they type is distracting and intrusive.

If you would prefer not to have the wavy red and green underlines appearing below your text, you can turn these functions off.

1 TURNING OFF CHECKING

- To turn off the spelling checker while you type, drop down the **Tools** menu from the toolbar.
- Click on **Options** and the **Options** dialog box opens on-screen.

● There are a number of tabs at the top of the **Options** dialog box for altering different aspects of Word. Click on the **Spelling & Grammar** tab to display the available options under **Spelling** and **Grammar**.

● Click once in the **Check spelling as you type** tick box. The tick disappears.

● Click on the **OK** button. Word will now no longer check your spelling as you type. You can still, however, check the spelling of all the text in one pass, after you have finished typing.

● If you wish to stop Word checking the grammar, click once in the **Check grammar as you type** tick box. The tick disappears and the grammar checker is turned off.

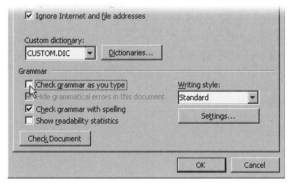

2 CHECKING THE DOCUMENT

● Drop down the **Tools** menu from the menu bar.

● Click on **Spelling and Grammar** from the **Tools** menu. Word will work through your document with the **Spelling and Grammar** dialog box, prompting you at every error that is found.

● If you want to accept a suggested spelling, click on the correct one from the **Suggestions** box and click on the **Change** button.

● If you want to correct the error yourself, click inside the **Not in Dictionary** box and position the insertion point over the error. Make the text correction yourself by using the keyboard and click on the **Change** button.

● If you don't think that there is an error, click on the **Ignore** button.

● Word moves on to the next error in your text until it can find no more and the information box appears telling you that the check is complete. Click on **OK**.

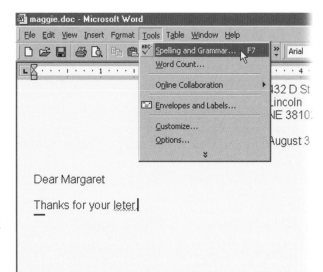

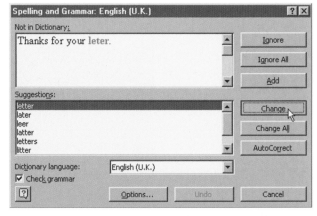

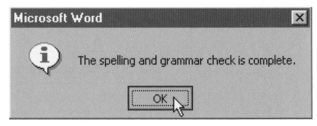

TEMPLATES

Usually when you come to create a new file, either you work from the blank file that Word creates when it is launched, or you create a new blank file by choosing the **Blank Document** option from the New dialog box. This time, you can save yourself some of the work involved in laying out a document by creating a preformatted letter and filling in the blanks. As an example of this, follow the steps below to create a letter using the **Elegant Letter** template.

1 CREATE A NEW FILE

● Drop down the **File** menu and click on **New**.
● In the **New** dialog box click on the **Letters & Faxes** tab and click on the icon labeled **Elegant Letter**.
● Click on **OK**.

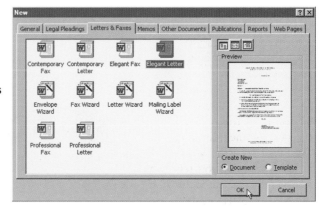

2 FILLING IN THE BLANKS

● Your new file will now be open on the screen.
● Click on the box at the top of the letter marked **Click here and type in company name**. The box itself is not printed out - it's only to show you the boundaries of where you can type.

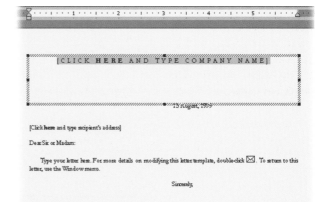

● Click on the line of text that reads **Click here and type recipient's address.** You can begin typing the recipient's address – the line of text vanishes when you begin typing.

13 Augu:

[Click **here** and type recipient's address]

Dear Sir or Madam:

    Type your letter here. For more details on modifying this letter letter, use the Window menu.

Sincerely,

● Using the insertion point or the mouse pointer, select the text of the paragraph that is already in place and begin typing. The old text disappears as you begin to start typing.

13 Augu:

[Click **here** and type recipient's address]

Dear Sir or Madam:

Type your letter here. For more details on modifying this letter letter, use the Window menu.

Sincerely,

● Add your name and job title over the lines of text at the end of the letter. Just click in these lines to select them, and start typing.

Sincerely,

[Click **here** and type your name]
[Click **here** and type job title]

● Your address goes at the foot of the Elegant Letter. Scroll down the page and add your address into the address box.

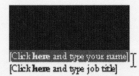

[STREET ADDRESS] · [CITY/STATE] · [ZIP/POSTAL CODE]
PHONE· [PHONE NUMBER] · FAX· [FAX NUMBER]

● You have now created a letter using the Elegant Letter template.

WIZARDS

Wizards are a simple way of producing formatted letters quickly. There is no need to type names and addresses directly into the letter – Word uses dialog boxes for you to supply the information and then adds this to the letter. You can create the same letter using the Letter Wizard that you did using the template.

1 STARTING THE WIZARD

● Drop down the **File** menu and click on **New** as usual.
● Click the **Letters & Faxes** tab and click on the icon marked **Letter Wizard**.
● Click on the **OK** button.
● A small dialog box appears along with the office assistant.
● Click on **Send one letter**.

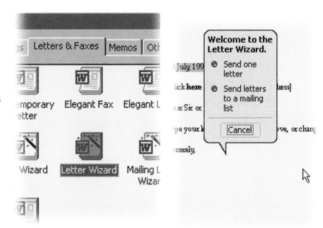

2 LETTER FORMAT

● The **Letter Wizard** dialog box opens. There are four steps in the Letter Wizard – the first is **Letter Format**.
● Drop down the **Choose a page design** menu and choose the one you want. You will notice that **Elegant Letter**, the template we used earlier in this section, is one of the designs.
● Drop down the **Choose a letter style** menu and choose from **Full Block** (no indents), **Modified Block** (some indenting), or **Semi-Block** (full, with stylish first line indents).
● Click on the **Next** button to go to the next section.

3 RECIPIENT'S INFORMATION

● The **Letter Wizard** dialog box now shows the **Recipient Info** step.

● Enter the recipient's name and address in the relevant text boxes.

● Choose a salutation from the drop-down menu under **Salutation**, or type in your own.

● Click on the **Next** button.

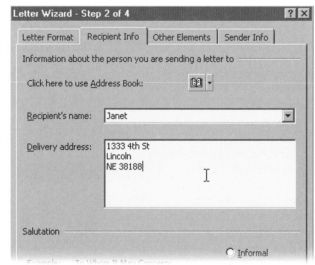

4 OTHER ELEMENTS

● The **Letter Wizard** dialog box now shows the **Other Elements** step.

● If you want to include a reference line, click on the check box to the left of **Reference line**. A tick will appear in the box. You can now drop down the **Reference line** menu and use the available options.

● Do the same for any other features you want: **Mailing instructions**, **Attention**, **Subject**.

● If you wish to send a courtesy copy, insert the details into the boxes at the foot of the dialog box.

● Click on the **Next** button.

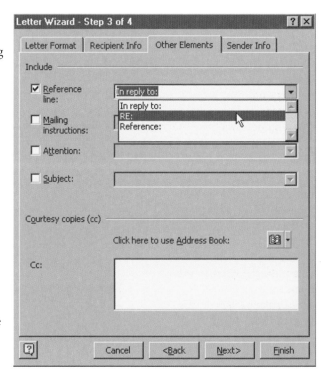

5 SENDER INFORMATION

● The last step of the **Letter Wizard** dialog box is the **Sender Info** step.

● Type your name into the Sender's name box.

● Type your address into the **Return address** box.

● Select a closing from the **Complimentary closing** drop-down menu – or type your own into the box.

● Click on **Finish** to allow the Letter Wizard to create your document.

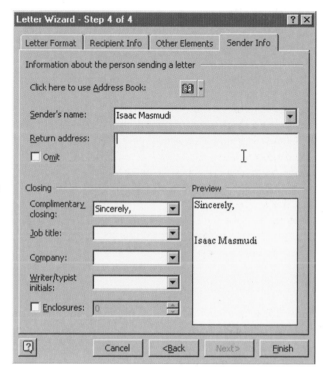

6 START TYPING

● The **Letter Wizard** dialog box vanishes. The office assistant appears and asks you if you want to do any more to your letter.

● Make a selection or click on **Cancel**.

● Your letter is ready. Everything is in place except the paragraphs of main text.

● Start typing as with the Elegant Letter template.

MAIL MERGE

Mail merge is a way of sending personalized letters to a number of people. Although more often used by business, mail merge is useful for telling people about the large events in our lives.

MAIN DOCUMENTS AND DATA SOURCES

So far you have only been working with letters to individual recipients. You may however wish to create a letter to be sent to a number of people – for instance, to notify all your friends that you have moved. You could produce a letter addressed to one person, print it out, change the recipient's name and address, print out the new letter to the next person, and so on. This would however be a very tedious and time-consuming process. To save you this trouble you can use a feature called Mail Merge. This allows you to create a standard letter and a list of names and addresses. The letter and the list are then merged to create personalized letters to everyone in the list. The standard letter is called a Main Document – the list is called a Data Source. Let's start by creating a Main Document from scratch.

1 **CREATE A MAIN DOCUMENT**
● Drop down the **Tools** menu and click on the **Mail Merge** option.

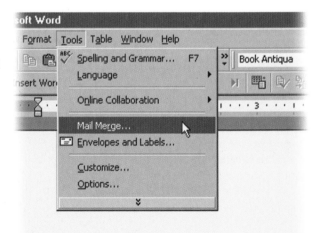

- The **Mail Merge Helper** dialog box opens.
- Click on the **Create** button under **Main document**.
- A menu drops down. Click on **Form Letters** at the top of the menu.
- A dialog box opens. Click on **New Main Document**.
- A blank document will appear under the **Mail Merge Helper** dialog box. This is your Main Document.

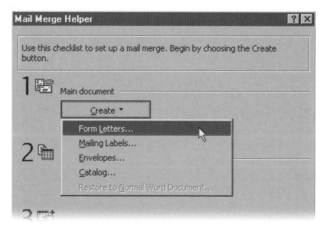

2 CREATE A DATA SOURCE

- Before working on your new Master Document, you need to create a structure for your data. You need a Data Source to do this.
- Click on the **Get Data** button under **Data Source** in the **Mail Merge Helper** dialog box.
- Click on **Create Data Source** in the menu.

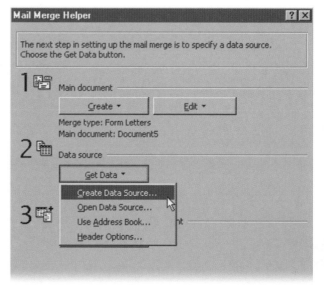

- The **Create Data Source** dialog box opens.
- The list shows the fields (see Fields and Records below) that are going to make up the Data Source.
- You won't need all the fields. You can remove the fields with the **Remove Field Name** button. Add new ones by typing a new field name into the **Field name** box and clicking on **Add Field Name**.
- Remove all the fields except Address1, Address2, City, and PostalCode.
- Now type **Name** into the **Field name** box. Click on the **Add Field Name** button. You have created a new field called **Name**.
- Your list of fields should appear as shown at right.
- Now click on **OK**.

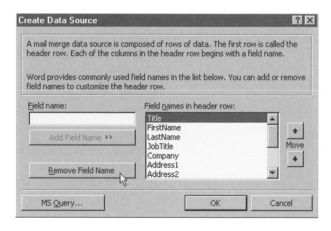

FIELDS AND RECORDS

Each kind of data in the Master Document that is attached to the Data Source (such as the recipient's names, or each line of their addresses) is called a field. Fields are what link the Master Document to the Data Source. The actual data in the fields – such as in the Name field: James, Mr., Doncaster, Mum & Dad – are called records.

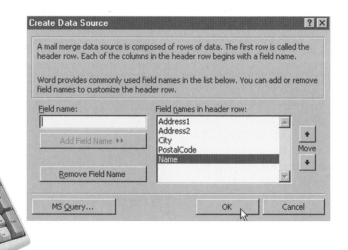

● The **Save As** dialog box opens. Type **List** in the **File Name** box and click the **Save** button.

● You have now created a Data Source.

● A dialog box will appear. Click on **Edit Data Source**.

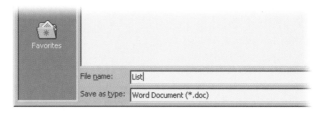

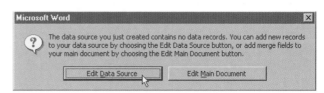

3 ENTER RECORDS

● The **Data Form** dialog box opens and you can edit the Data Source.

● Type the name and address of your first recipient into the boxes in the dialog box.

● When you have finished with the first recipient, move to a fresh record by clicking the **Add New** button. The field boxes empty and you are ready to type in a new record.

● Add as many records as you want. You can go back to your old records and correct them with the buttons at the foot of the dialog box.

● When you have finished entering all the records that you wish to include, click on **OK**.

4 INSERT MERGE FIELDS

● The **Data Form** dialog box closes. You will now see the Main Document.

● Type in your own address and the date.

● Instead of typing the first line of the recipient's address, click on the **Insert Merge Field** button on the Mail Merge toolbar at the top of the screen.

● A menu drops down. Click on Address1.

● The field will appear in the letter as <<**Address1**>>. Don't worry, it won't print out like this – it is a way of showing you the structure of your Main Document before it is merged with the Data Source.

● Add the remainder of the address by entering one line in each field.

● Type **Dear**, leave a space, and add the Name field from the **Insert Merge Field** drop-down menu.

● Finish your letter in the normal way.

5 READY TO MERGE

● Check your Main Document. It should look something like the document shown at right.

● To make sure you are ready to print your mail merge, click on the **View Merged Data** button on the Mail Merge toolbar at the top of the screen.

● This shows your letter as it will go out to each person. The arrow buttons on the Mail Merge toolbar allow you to move through different records.

«Address1»
«Address2»
«City»
«PostalCode»

Dear «Name»,

Just a quick note to let you kno
the launch of Masmudi Enterp

We would love to see you ther
come.

Many thanks

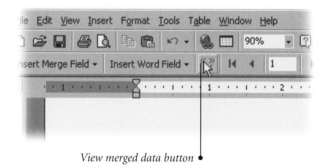

View merged data button ●

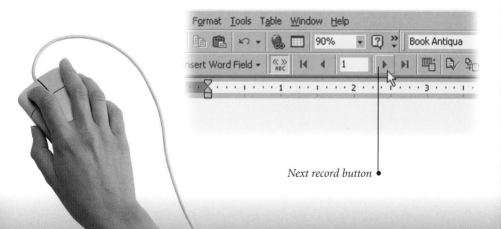

Next record button ●

6 CHECK YOUR MAIL MERGE

● With the **View Merged Data** button down (it will stay down until you click it again – don't try to hold it down with the mouse), you will be able to see the different versions of the same letter that are going out to different recipients.

7654 32nd St
Lincoln
NE 38122

Dear James,

● Each letter displays the same basic text, but the details of the individual recipient's are different.

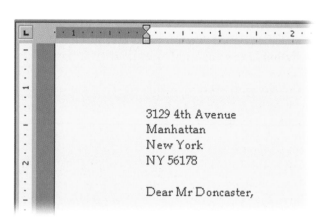

3129 4th Avenue
Manhattan
New York
NY 56178

Dear Mr Doncaster,

● When you have finished viewing, click on the **View Merged Data** button again to return to normal view of the Main Document.

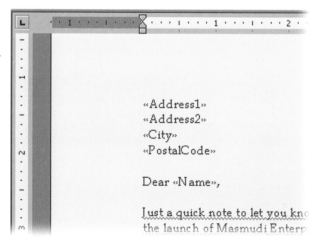

«Address1»
«Address2»
«City»
«PostalCode»

Dear «Name»,

Just a quick note to let you kn
the launch of Masmudi Enterp

7 PRINT MERGE

- You are now ready to print out your mail merge.
- Drop down the **Tools** menu and click on **Mail Merge** to bring up the **Mail Merge Helper** dialog box.
- Click the **Merge** button in the **Mail Merge Helper** dialog box. The **Merge** dialog box opens.
- Drop down the **Merge to** menu with the small down arrow box at the side of the **Merge to** box.
- Click on **Printer**.
- The **Merge to** box now contains the word **Printer**.
- Click on **Merge**. The **Print** dialog box opens.
- Click on **OK**.
- All copies of the letter, each personalized for the individual recipient, will now be printed.

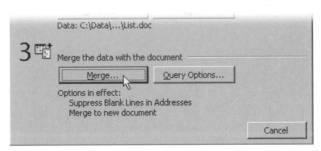

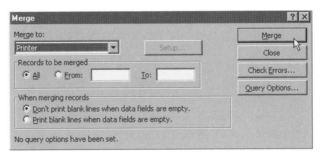

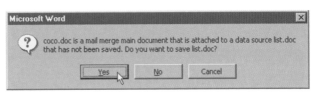

8 SAVING THE FILES

Once you have finished with your mail merge, close down the file as normal (click on **Close** from the **File** menu). You will be prompted with a dialog box asking you if you want to save the changes to your Data Source. Click on **Yes** to save your current data. Then, if you have made any changes to the Main Document, you will be asked if you want to save the changes, as normal. Click on **Yes** if you want to keep the changes.

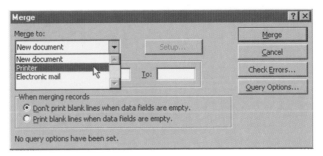

DESIGNING DOCUMENTS

I N THIS SECTION WE CONCENTRATE on the facilities that Word offers to help you design more interesting and professional text documents than those produced by simply using the default settings that Word provides. These facilities include font selection, customizing and manipulating paragraphs, adding colored borders and backgrounds, using tabs, columns, and lists, and creating your own style sheets to save time and effort.

WORKING WITH FONTS

There are several different levels of formatting and styling available in Word. This chapter looks at changing the font, resizing it, and changing the spacing and color of the letters.

CHANGING THE FONT

The default font in Microsoft Word is Times New Roman, which is one of the most popular fonts. There are many other fonts available and, while you can use as many fonts as you wish in a document, it is better to use no more than three in any one section. Increasing the number of fonts can have the effect of fragmenting the text and making it look messy, and certain fonts do not look good together.

THE CHOSEN VIEW

Throughout this book it is recommended that you work in Print Layout view, as many of the effects used are only displayed in this view of a document. To do this, click on **View** in the Menu bar and select **Print Layout,** or click on the **Page Layout View** button at the bottom of the screen ◻.

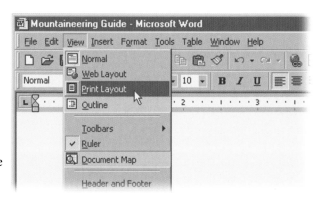

A VARIETY OF FONTS

In the examples of styling and formatting text that are used throughout this book, the text is displayed in a variety of fonts. While Microsoft Word includes a range of the most commonly used fonts, you may not have all the fonts shown here. This will not affect your ability to work your way through the examples, but you will need to choose alternative fonts. An almost limitless number of fonts can be bought from stores or over the internet.

1 CREATING THE TEXT

- In the example used here, we are writing a document for a mountaineering company that offers guided expeditions and more.
- Begin by typing their contact details in a new document, and press `Enter ↵` at the end of each line with an extra `Enter ↵` after the zip code.
- You'll see that when the email address is typed in, Word recognizes it for what it is and automatically shows it in blue.

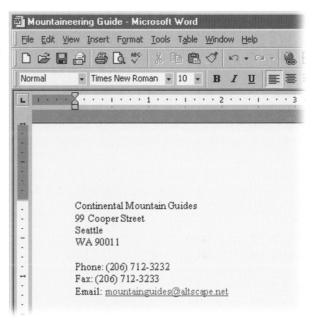

2 SELECTING A NEW FONT

- Although this text is perfectly clear, it lacks any impact. The first change that you can make is to use different fonts to emphasize the different parts of the company's details.
- Highlight the company name, click on **Format** in the Menu bar, and click on **Font** at the top of the drop-down menu.

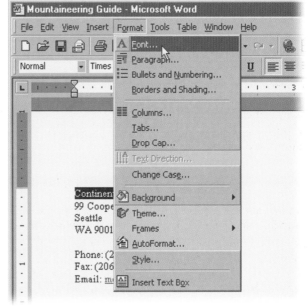

● The **Font** dialog box now opens. In the **Font** selection menu, use the scroll bar to move to another font (we have chosen Charlesworth, which has only upper-case letters). The **Preview** panel at the foot of the dialog box shows how the text will appear in your document. Click on **OK**.

● For the rest of the contact details, except for the email address, we are going to use another font. Highlight the text to be selected, open the **Font** dialog box again, and choose another font (we selected BankGothic Md BT). Now click on **OK**.

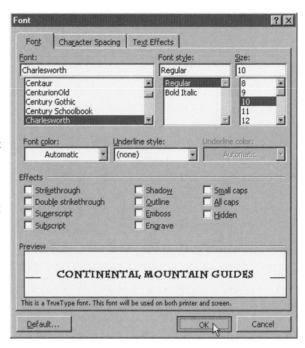

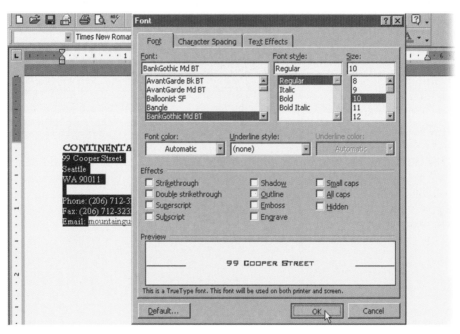

● The fonts have now been changed, and the company name, company address, and email address are each in a different font, which distinguishes the various elements from each other.

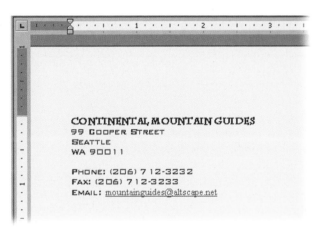

CONTINENTAL MOUNTAIN GUIDES
99 COOPER STREET
SEATTLE
WA 90011

PHONE: (206) 712-3232
FAX: (206) 712-3233
EMAIL: mountainguides@altscape.net

CHANGING THE FONT SIZE

Word's default font size of ten points (a point is one seventy-second of an inch) is fine for the bulk of the text that you are likely to produce, but different parts of your document, such as headings, can benefit from being in a larger font size.

USING THE FONT SIZE SELECTOR BOX

● With the text that you wish to resize already highlighted (in this case the company name), click on the Font size selector box ☐ in the Formatting toolbar, scroll to **16** (meaning 16 point), and click on it. The lettering of the selected text is now larger.

Selected font size ●

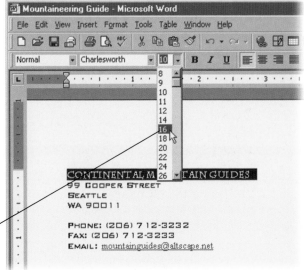

㉖ Font Size Selector

● Highlight the next three lines of the address and follow the same sequence to change the font size to 14 pt, and then do the same to change the final three lines to 12 pt. Your text should now appear as shown in this example.

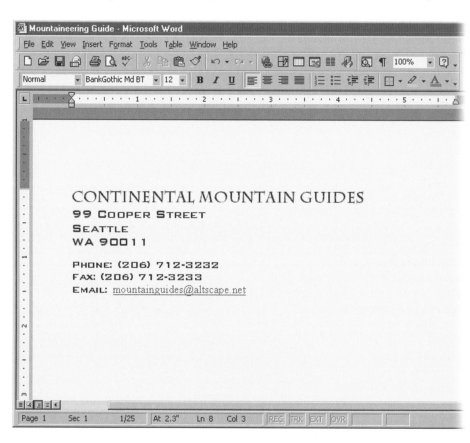

FONT STYLES

You will see that, as well as offering a choice of fonts, the **Font** dialog box also has a **Font style** panel. Choosing different options in this panel will enable you to turn the font from its normal, or regular, form to italic, bold, or italic bold type, providing that all these variations are available in the particular font that you are using. These options can be used to emphasize parts of your text.

●*Alternative font styles*

CHANGING THE FONT EFFECT

As well as bold, italic, and underline, there are a number of effects available in Word that you can use to change the appearance of your text. For example, shadowed, outlined, embossed, and engraved effects can all be used. Once you have followed this example, try out the other effects, some of which can be very useful.

EMBOSSING TEXT

● Begin by highlighting the company name in the address and open the **Font** dialog box, and click on the **Font** tab at the top of the dialog box.

● In the center of the **Effects** section of the **Font** dialog box, you'll see check boxes for **Shadow**, **Outline**, **Emboss**, and **Engrave** effects. Click in the check box next to **Emboss** and then click on **OK**.

● Click anywhere on your page to remove the highlighting, and the embossed effect on the lettering becomes visible.

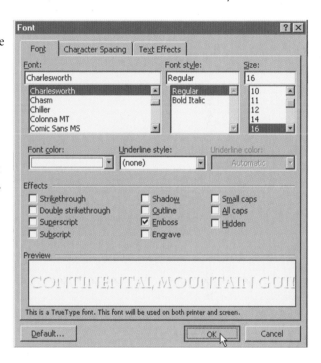

Selecting a New Font

CHANGING THE LETTER SPACING

Changing the amount of space between individual letters can also be used to emphasize important parts of the text.

In this example, we will space out the letters of the company name to give it greater weight on the page.

INCREASING THE LETTER SPACING

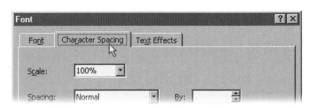

- Highlight the company name again, open the **Font** dialog box ⬆, and click on the **Character Spacing** tab.
- In the **Spacing** box, click on the arrow next to **Normal** and select **Expanded**. In the **By** box, enter the figure **3**, meaning 3 pt, and click on **OK**.

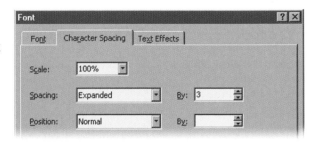

- Click on the company name again to see how the name now extends across the page.

CONTINENTAL MOUNTAIN GUIDES
99 COOPER STREET
SEATTLE
WA 90011

PHONE: (206) 712-3232
FAX: (206) 712-3233
EMAIL: mountainguides@altscape.net

CHANGING THE FONT COLOR

With the increasing availability, and falling cost, of color printers, using some of the color options in Word offers a simple and effective way of making selected text stand out. Bear in mind that it's best not to combine too wide a range of colors.

1 SELECTING THE COLOR PALETTE

● Although the snowy-whiteness of the embossed text is appropriate for the company's business, it's a little pale. To change the font color, highlight the company name and then open the **Font** dialog box.

● Click the arrow to the right of the **Font color** selection box and the color palette will appear.

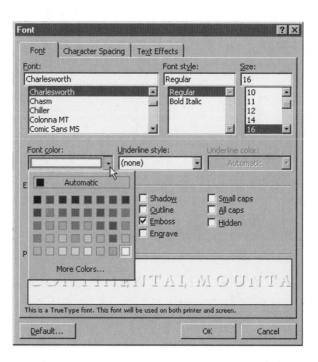

2 CHOOSING THE COLOR

● Move the mouse cursor down to **Blue** and click once. This color has now been selected for the text.

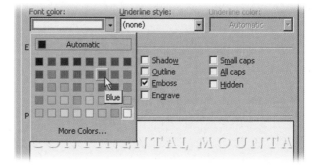

● The text in the **Preview** window now shows you the effect of the color change. If you are happy with this color, click on **OK**.

● Click anywhere on your page to remove the highlighting and reveal the text in the new color.

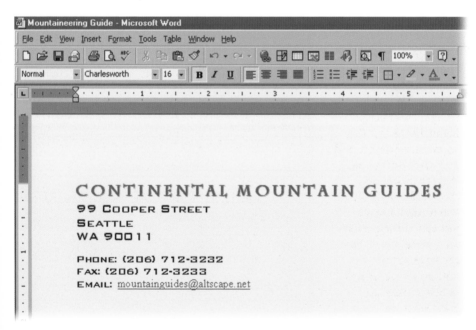

3 CHOOSING FURTHER COLORS

● As Word automatically colors the email address in blue, the contact details above the email address can also have their own colors. Try changing the **Phone** details to orange and the **Fax** line to sea green to achieve the effect shown in the example here.

Lines of text stand out from each other ●

Bold, Italic, and Underline

The quickest way to change your text by using these effects is to highlight the text that you want to change and then click on one of these three buttons ⌐ in the Formatting toolbar. You're not limited to just one of these effects for a piece of text. You can have text that is bold and italic, as well as being underlined, if that's what you want.

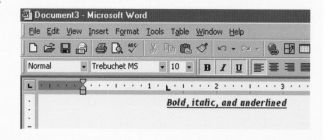

125 ❷❼ Bold, ❷❽ Italic, ❷❾ Underline

STYLING PARAGRAPHS

As far as Word is concerned, a paragraph is any piece of text that ends with a paragraph mark, so the styling shown here can be applied to a single letter or to several pages of text.

ALIGNING PARAGRAPHS

There are four possible ways to align paragraphs in Word: left-aligned, centered, right-aligned, and justified. Left-alignment is the default paragraph alignment in Word. Each line of a paragraph starts against the left margin, and the line endings are "ragged" in the way a typewriter would produce them. Centered alignment has the effect of centering each line of a paragraph on the mid-point between the margins. Right-alignment has the effect of aligning the right-hand end of each line up against the right-hand margin leaving the start of each line ragged, and justified alignment produces a straight edge at both the beginning and the end of each line by adding spaces to make every line of text the same length.

1 SELECTING THE TEXT

● The company's details are going to be the heading of the guide, and a heading frequently benefits from having its own alignment, in order to distinguish it from the text on the rest of the page. Begin by highlighting all of the company's details.

CONTINENTAL MOUNTAIN GUIDES
99 COOPER STREET
SEATTLE
WA 90011

PHONE: (206) 712-3232
FAX: (206) 712-3233
EMAIL: mountainguides@altscape.net

2 ALIGNING TEXT TO THE RIGHT

- First we'll see how right-aligning affects the appearance, so click on the **Align Right** button in the Formatting toolbar.
- Click off the highlighted text to see the effect.
- Although the shorter lines are obviously right-aligned, the company name has hardly moved because it almost fills the width of the page, and it sticks out way beyond the other lines.

CONTINENTAL MOUNTAIN GUIDES

99 COOPER STREET
SEATTLE
WA 90011

PHONE: (206) 712-3232
FAX: (206) 712-3233
EMAIL: mountainguides@altscape.net

3 CENTERING THE TEXT

- The start of the company name looks as if it's out on a limb, so the whole heading would look better if it were centered.
- Highlight the company details again and click on the **Center** button in the Formatting toolbar.
- Click off the highlighted text to see how the separate lines of the company's details now all appear to be part of a single unit.

CONTINENTAL MOUNTAIN GUIDES

99 COOPER STREET
SEATTLE
WA 90011

PHONE: (206) 712-3232
FAX: (206) 712-3233
EMAIL: mountainguides@altscape.net

125 ❷ Right-Aligned Text

125 ❶ Centered Text

INSERTING A DROPPED CAPITAL

First paragraphs can be made more noticeable by starting them with a large initial capital letter that drops down more than one line. This dropped capital letter is familiarly known as a "drop cap", and it is easily achieved in Word.

WHAT WE DO

Continental Mountain Guides has built up a fine reputation that now extends beyond the climbing community following two heavily publicized rescues that we were fortunate enough to be called to carry out. The expeditions we lead are always safe and successful, and one enthusiastic climber suggested out motto should be: "We ain't lost one yet." But as we never intend to, the suggestion was put to one side. We offer many climbing opportunities for the absolute beginner and to the climbing professional who might need our specialized knowledge of specific mountaineering regions. Guides join our staff when they have at least ten year's of climbing. And they have to demonstrate to us that they are dedicated to climbing and to sharing that passion.

1 SELECTING THE DROP CAP BOX

● The Mountaineering Guide has an introductory section with a heading that has been formatted in BankGothic Md BT 16 pt, and a paragraph formatted in Trebuchet MS 10 pt. This paragraph would be more interesting if it began with a drop cap.

● Place the cursor over the paragraph and click to position the insertion point within it. Go to **Format** in the Menu bar and select **Drop Cap**. The **Drop Cap** dialog box opens.

● Click on **Dropped** in the **Position** options.

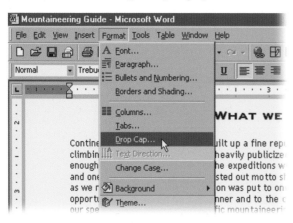

2 CHOOSING THE SIZE

● The **Lines to drop** box shows the default number of lines for the capital letter to drop is 3. This is too large a drop cap for a short paragraph, so change the figure to 2 and click on **OK**.

● The drop cap is shown surrounded by a frame.

● Click elsewhere on the document and the altered paragraph, with its new dropped capital, appears as it will on the printed page.

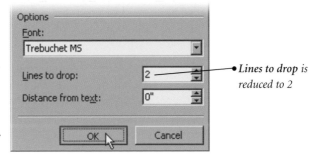

Lines to drop is reduced to 2

3 CREATING JUSTIFIED TEXT

● Finally, this paragraph would sit better with the company details above it if it were justified.

● Highlight the text and click on the **Justify** button in the Formatting toolbar.

● Both the beginnings and endings of the lines of the paragraph now align, and the start of the document is beginning to look tidier.

WHAT WE DO

Continental Mountain Guides has built up a fine reputation that now extends beyond the climbing community following two heavily publicized rescues that we were fortunate enough to be called to carry out. The expeditions we lead are always safe and successful, and one enthusiastic climber suggested out motto should be: "We ain't lost one yet." But as we never intend to, the suggestion was put to one side. We offer many climbing opportunities for the absolute beginner and to the climbing professional who might need our specialized knowledge of specific mountaineering regions. Guides join our staff when they have at least ten year's of climbing. And they have to demonstrate to us that they are dedicated to climbing and to sharing that passion.

❸❸ **Justified Text**

ADDING SPACE BETWEEN PARAGRAPHS

Creating space between paragraphs can improve the look of your document. This can be done by simply inserting a number of paragraph returns (Enter⏎). However, there is a better way of choosing precisely the amount of space you wish to insert.

1 SELECTING THE PARAGRAPH

● In a section of the Mountaineering Guide on seminars and expeditions, paragraphs are separated by paragraph marks (you can make these visible using the Standard toolbar ⛶).

● A better method of separating paragraphs, particularly when a large amount of space is required between them, is to select manually how much space there should be.

Extra paragraph returns
add a fixed amount of space

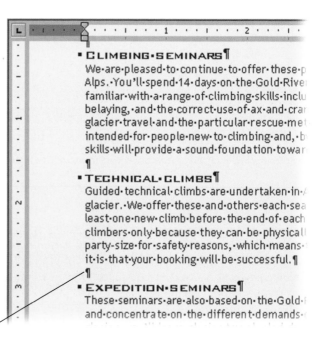

● First delete the paragraph marks separating the paragraphs, and highlight the first paragraph. Then click on **Format** in the Menu bar and choose **Paragraph** from the menu.

㉑ Show/Hide Formatting Marks

2 DEFINING THE SPACE

● The **Paragraph** dialog box opens. In the **Spacing** section, click on the up arrow in the **After** panel. The entry now reads **6 pt** and the **Preview** panel shows the increased space following the paragraph. Click on **OK**.

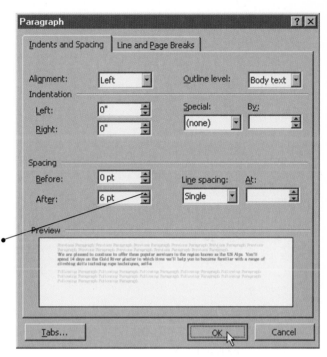

Up arrow increases the spacing after paragraph ●

● The paragraph is now separated from the following paragraph by a 6 pt space without an extra Enter ◄┘ being inserted.

*Using the **Paragraph** formatting menu, this space can be made exactly the size you want it* ●

CLIMBING·SEMINARS¶
We·are·pleased·to·con tinue· to·offer· these·p
Alps.·You'll·spend·14·days·on·the·Gold·Rive
familiar·with·a·range·of·climbing·skills·inclu
belaying,·and·the·correct·use·of·ax·and·cra ·
glacier·travel·and·the·particular·rescue·me
intended·for·people·new·to·climbing·and, ·b
skills·will·provide·a·sound·foundation·towar

TECHNICAL·CLIMBS¶
Guided· technical· climbs·are·undertaken·in·
glacier.·We·offer·these·and·others·each·sea
least·one·new·climb·before· the·end·of·each
climbers·only·be cause·they·can·be·physicall
party·size·for·safety·reasons,·which·means·
it·is·that·your·booking·will·be·successful. ¶

EXPEDITION·SEMINARS¶
These·seminars·are·also·based·on·the·Gold·
and·concentrate·on·the·different·demands·

CHANGING THE INDENT

In printing terms, a "displayed" paragraph is one where the beginning and ends of the lines are indented compared to the paragraphs before and after it, producing a narrower column of text. This has the effect of emphasizing the paragraph.

SETTING THE LEFT INDENT

● Highlight the first paragraph, about climbing seminars, and place the mouse cursor over the **Left Indent** box on the ruler.

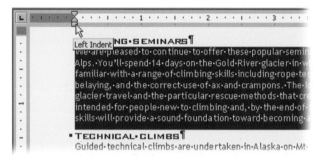

● Holding the mouse button down, drag the cursor to the right until the left indent box and the two indent arrows are over the quarter-inch mark, and release the mouse button. The left-hand edge of the paragraph is now indented.

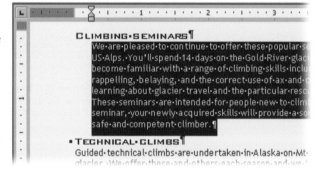

SETTING THE RIGHT INDENT

● Now place the mouse cursor over the right-hand indent arrow, hold down the mouse button, and drag the mouse cursor to the 5.5-inch position on the ruler and release the mouse button to set the indent.

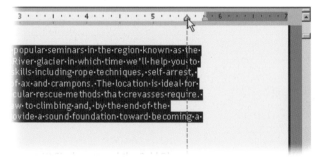

● The right-hand line endings of the paragraph are now indented.

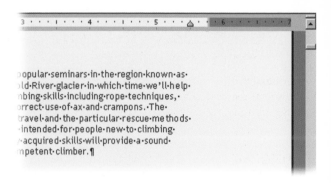

opular·seminars·in·the·region·known·as·
ld·River·glacier·in·which·time·we'll·help·
nbing·skills·including·rope·techniques,·
orrect·use·of·ax·and·crampons.·The·
travel·and·the·particular·rescue·methods·
·intended·for·people·new·to·climbing·
·acquired·skills·will·provide·a·sound·
npetent·climber. ¶

ADDING A BORDER

Word allows you to emphasize a selected paragraph by adding a border in a range of styles and colors. We are going to create a border around the outside of the selected text, but there are other options available in the **Outside Border** menu.

1 OPENING THE BORDER MENU
● Highlight the paragraph and click on the **Outside Border** button in the Formatting toolbar.

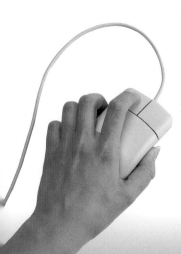

2 SELECTING OUTSIDE BORDER

● A menu of border selections appears. Click on the **Outside Border** option.

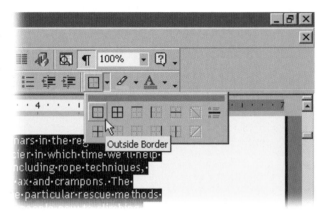

● The paragraph is now enclosed within a border.

CLIMBING·SEMINARS¶

We·are·pleased·to·continue·to·offer·these·popular·seminars·in·the·region·known·as·
the·US·Alps.·You'll·spend·14·days·on·the·Gold·River·glacier·in·which·time·we'll·help·
you·to·become·familiar·with·a·range·of·climbing·skills·including·rope·techniques,·
self-arrest,·rappelling,·belaying,·and·the·correct·use·of·ax·and·crampons.··The·
location·is·ideal·for·learning·about·glacier·travel·and·the·particular·rescue·methods·
that·crevasses·require.··These·seminars·are·intended·for·people·new·to·climbing·
and,·by·the·end·of·the·seminar,·your·newly·acquired·skills·will·provide·a·sound·
foundation·toward·becoming·a·safe·and·competent·climber.¶

TECHNICAL·CLIMBS ¶

3 CHANGING THE BORDER STYLE

● With the text within the border highlighted, go to the **Format** menu and click on **Borders and Shading**.

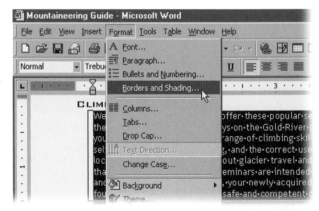

● The **Borders and Shading** dialog box opens. Click on the **Borders** tab if it is not already at the front. In the **Style** panel, click on the down arrow and select one of the selection of borders by clicking on it. Click on **OK**.

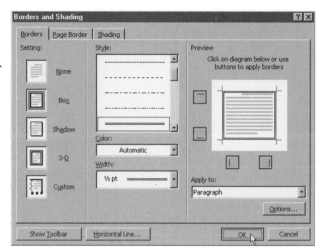

● The border around the paragraph changes to the selected style.

CLIMBING·SEMINARS¶

We·are·pleased·to·con tinue·to·offer·these·popular·seminars·in·the·region·known·as· the·US·Alps.·You'll·spend·14·days·on·the·Gold·River·glacier·in·which·time·we'll·help· you·to·become·familiar·with·a·range·of·climbing·skills·including·rope·techniques,· self-arrest,·rappelling,·belaying,·and·the·correct·use·of·ax·and·crampons.·The· location·is·ideal·for·learning·about·glacier·travel·and·the·particular·rescue·methods· that·crevasses·require.·These·seminars·are·intended·for·people·new·to·climbing· and,·by·the·end·of·the·seminar,·your·newly·acquired·skills·will·provide·a·sound· foundation·toward·becoming·a·safe·and·competent·climber.¶

TECHNICAL·CLIMBS¶
Guided·technical·climbs·are·undertaken·in·Alaska·on·Mt·Stephenson·and·the·Gold·River· glacier.·We·offer·these·and·others·each·season·and·we·have·been·successful·in·adding·at·

RESIZING BORDERS MANUALLY

There are two ways in which you can change the distance between the text and the border that encloses it. If you open the **Borders and Shading** dialog box you will see an **Options** button that allows the precise adjustment of the distance between the text and the border. An alternative method is simply to place the cursor against one of the sides of the border, hold down the mouse button, and drag the edge of the border to a new position.

4 ADDING COLOR TO THE BORDER

- With the text within the border highlighted, go to the Format menu and click on **Borders and Shading**. Click in the **Color** box to display the color palette.

- Move the mouse cursor down and click on **Tan**.

- Click on **OK** and the border is now colored.

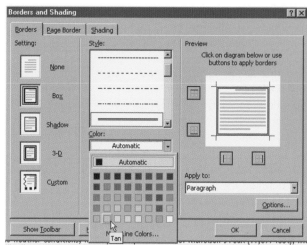

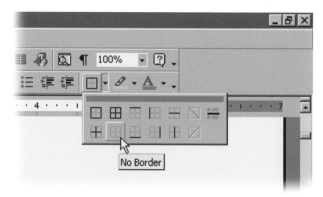

CLIMBING·SEMINARS¶

We·are·pleased·to·continue·to·offer·these·popular·seminars·in·the·region·known·as·the·US·Alps.·You'll·spend·14·days·on·the·Gold·River·glacier·in·which·time·we'll·help·you·to·become·familiar·with·a·range·of·climbing·skills·including·rope·techniques,·self-arrest,·rappelling,·belaying,·and·the·correct·use·of·ax·and·crampons.·The·location·is·ideal·for·learning·about·glacier·travel·and·the·particular·rescue·methods·that·crevasses·require.·These·seminars·are·intended·for·people·new·to·climbing·and,·by·the·end·of·the·seminar,·your·newly·acquired·skills·will·provide·a·sound·foundation·toward·becoming·a·safe·and·competent·climber.¶

TECHNICAL·CLIMBS¶

REMOVING A BORDER

- With the text within the border highlighted, click on the **Outside Border** button in the Formatting toolbar. The menu of border selections appears.
- Move the cursor over the **No Border** option and click to remove the border.

SHADING A PARAGRAPH

Whether or not a paragraph has been given a border, the text can be made to stand out by shading or coloring the background. Even if you don't have a color printer, this method can be used to choose a shade of gray, which can be effective.

1 SELECTING THE DIALOG BOX

● Highlight the paragraph, go to the Format menu in the toolbar and click on **Borders and Shading**. Now click on the **Shading** tab in the **Borders and Shading** dialog box to bring it to the foreground.

2 CHOOSING A COLOR

● Click on **Light Green** on the bottom row of the color palette, and the preview panel shows what this will look like.

● Click on **OK**, and the paragraph is now colored.

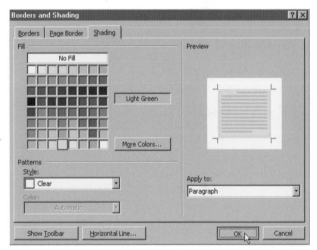

CLIMBING·SEMINARS¶

We·are·pleased·to·con tinue·to·offer·these·popular·seminars·in·the·region·known·as· the·US·Alps.·You'll·spend·14·days·on·the·Gold·River·glacier·in·which·time·we'll·help· you·to·become·familiar·with·a·range·of·climbing·skills·including·rope·techniques,· self·arrest,·rappelling,·belaying,·and·the·correct·use·of·ax·and·crampons.·The· location·is·ideal·for·learning·about·glacier·travel·and·the·particular·rescue·methods· that·crevasses·require.·These·seminars·are·intended·for·people·new·to·climbing· and,·by·the·end·of·the·seminar,·your·newly·acquired·skills·will·provide·a·sound· foundation·toward·becoming·a·safe·and·competent·climber.¶

TECHNICAL·CLIMBS¶

Guided·technical·climbs·are·undertaken·in·Alaska·on·Mt·Stephenson·and·the·Gold·River· glacier.·We·offer·these·and·others·each·season·and·we·have·been·successful·in·adding·at·

REMOVING SHADING FROM A PARAGRAPH

If you wish to remove shading that you have already created, follow these steps. With the paragraph highlighted, open the **Borders and Shading** dialog box via the Format menu, and choose **Shading**. Now click in the **No Fill** box above the color palette, click **OK**, and the shading is removed.

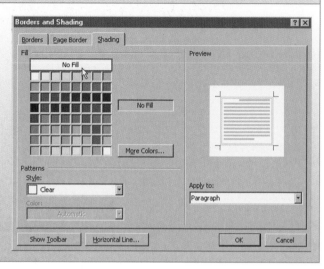

ALIGNING THE TEXT

● When text is within a rectangular border, it can look better being justified ⌐. Highlight the paragraph and click on the **Justify** button in the Formatting toolbar. The text now fits neatly within the border.

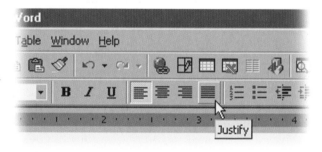

CLIMBING·SEMINARS¶

We·are·pleased·to·continue·to·offer·these·popular·seminars·in·the·region·known·as·the·US·Alps.·You'll·spend·14·days·on·the·Gold·River·glacier·in·which·time·we'll·help·you·to·become·familiar·with·a·range·of·climbing·skills·including·rope·techniques,·self-arrest,·rappelling,·belaying,·and·the·correct·use·of·ax·and·crampons.·The·location·is·ideal·for·learning·about·glacier·travel·and·the·particular·rescue·methods·that·crevasses·require.·These·seminars·are·intended·for·people·new·to·climbing·and,·by·the·end·of·the·seminar,·your·newly·acquired·skills·will·provide·a·sound·foundation·toward·becoming·a·safe·and·competent·climber.¶

TECHNICAL·CLIMBS¶

Aligning Paragraphs
196

USING FORMAT PAINTER

Once you've decided on a paragraph format that you want to apply to other paragraphs, you can apply the style by using a feature of Word known as **Format Painter**, rather than going through each individual step again for each paragraph.

1 SELECTING THE FORMAT TO COPY

● Select the paragraph whose format you wish to apply to another paragraph. Make sure that the paragraph mark is also selected. Click on the **Format Painter** button on the Standard toolbar.

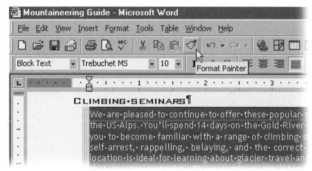

2 SELECTING THE NEW PARAGRAPH

● The cursor changes to a paintbrush icon. Move to the paragraph that is to be formatted in the same way as the selected paragraph.
● Click on the paragraph.

● All the formatting that has been done, including adding space, indenting the paragraph, adding a colored border and shading, and justifying the text, will be applied instantly to the chosen paragraph.

Formatting has been applied ●

MULTIPLE PAINTING

If you want to apply the same format to more than one paragraph by using **Format Painter**, double-click on the **Format Painter** button when you select it. You can then format as many paragraphs with the chosen format as you want by clicking in each one. When you've finished applying the format, either click on the **Format Painter** button to deselect or press the [Esc] key.

⓫ **Format Painter**

LISTS AND COLUMNS

Some data looks neater and more readable when presented as a list or in a column. In this chapter we look at the list and column options available in Word, and how to use them.

USING NUMBERED LISTS

Displaying items line by line, each new entry starting with a number, is probably the most common form of list. Text that has already been typed in can be turned into a list, and Word also has the facility to create a list automatically as you type.

1 **SELECT BULLETS AND NUMBERING**
- Type in a list of items, starting a new line each time. Now highlight the list, go to the **Format** menu in the toolbar, and select **Bullets and Numbering**.

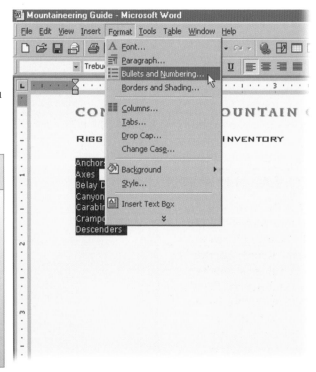

AUTOMATIC NUMBERING

Word detects when you are manually creating a numbered list. If you type a line of text that begins with a **1** followed by a space, when you press the Enter ↵ key, Word automatically begins the new line with a **2** and inserts a tab.

2 CHOOSING THE OPTION

● The **Bullets and Numbering** dialog box opens. Click on the **Numbered** tab to view the numbering options.

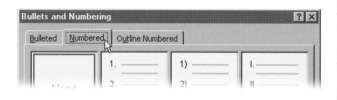

● Select the numbering style immediately to the right of the **None** box by clicking on that box. The chosen box is highlighted by a blue rectangle. Now click on **OK**.

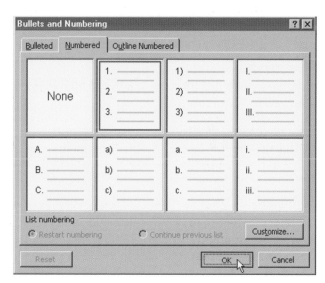

● The list of items is now numbered.

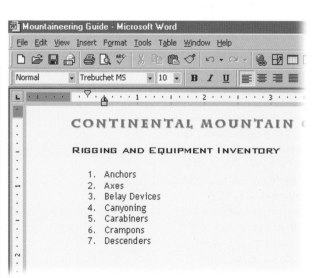

SWITCHING OFF THE NUMBERING

Word's automatic numbering feature can be annoying when you don't want to number every line. To remove a number, press the ←Bksp backspace key once to delete the number, and again to remove the indent.

CHANGING THE INDENTS

As you have seen on the previous page, when you turn a list into a numbered list, Word automatically indents it. To remove the indent, or indent the list further, follow these steps. This method also works for other kinds of lists and for normal text.

1 SELECTING THE LIST

● If the list is not already highlighted, begin by doing so. Don't worry if the numbers themselves aren't highlighted. This is because Word treats them differently from regular text.

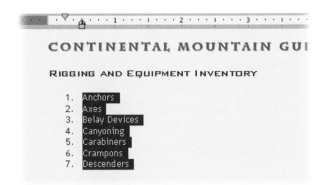

2 CHANGING THE INDENT

● Move the cursor up to the Formatting toolbar and click on the **Decrease Indent** button.

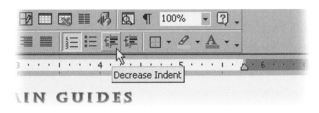

● The whole list moves to the left, aligning with the text above it.
● If you want to increase, rather than decrease, the indent, click on the **Increase Indent** button, which is to the right of the **Decrease Indent** button.

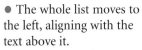

36 Decrease Indent
125

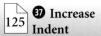
37 Increase Indent
125

BULLETED LISTS

Even when the lines in a list do not need to be numbered, you may still wish to emphasize the entries. Word offers a range of bulleted lists suited to different purposes. For example, you might use check marks for a list of completed tasks.

1 SELECTING THE LIST
● Begin by highlighting the list that you wish to bullet.
● Select **Bullets and Numbering** from the **Format** menu in the toolbar ⌐.

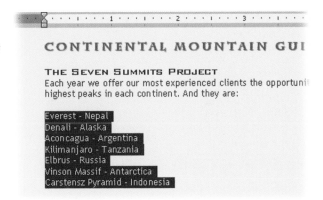

2 SELECTING THE BULLETED TAB
● In the **Bullets and Numbering** menu, click on the **Bulleted** tab to bring it to the front.

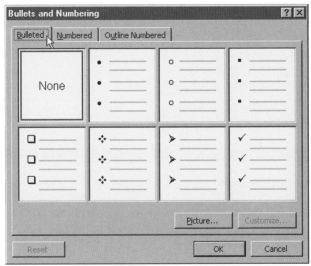

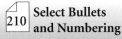

210 **Select Bullets and Numbering**

3 SELECTING THE BULLET STYLE

- There are several bullet styles that you can use, but in this example we are selecting the option next to **None**. Now click on **OK**.

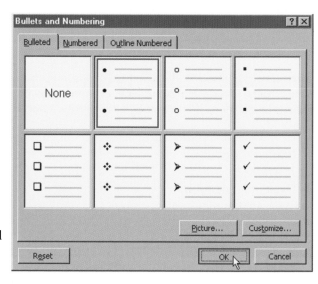

- The list now has a bullet at the start of each line, and you can change the indent, if you want to, as before.

PICTURE BULLETS

Word offers a very wide range of picture bullets. Click on **Picture** in the **Bulleted** tab of the **Bullets and Numbering** dialog box. A palette menu opens, and you can select a particular combination of shape and color from the variety available.

CONTINENTAL MOUNTAIN GUI

THE SEVEN SUMMITS PROJECT
Each year we offer our most experienced clients the opportuni
highest peaks in each continent. And they are:

- Everest - Nepal
- Denali - Alaska
- Aconcagua - Argentina
- Kilimanjaro - Tanzania
- Elbrus - Russia
- Vinson Massif - Antarctica
- Carstensz Pyramid - Indonesia

QUICK LISTS

If you are happy with the default style of numbering or bullet size, there is a quick way to produce a numbered or bulleted list. Once you have typed in the list of items, highlight the list, and then click on either the **Numbering** button or the **Bullets** button in the Formatting toolbar.

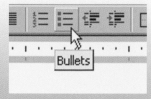

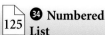

125 ❸❹ **Numbered List**

125 ❸❺ **Bulleted List**

CREATING A TABBED LIST

Microsoft Word includes the facility to set out text or figures in neat tables, but for small amounts of information it can often be easier to create columns by turning the entries into a tabbed list, using the **Tabs** menu to format the page.

1 INSERTING TABS BETWEEN ITEMS

● Type a list of items and press the Tab↹ key between each item on each line. With the Formatting Marks turned on, the tab mark (the right-pointing arrow) shows where each tab has been inserted.

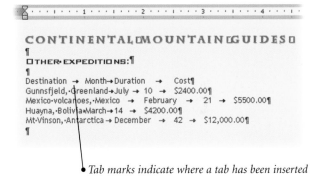

Tab marks indicate where a tab has been inserted

2 BRINGING UP THE TABS DIALOG BOX

● Take a look at the list and decide which is the longest left-hand entry. In this case it is the Mexican entry, at just over 1.5 inches wide.
● Ignoring the line of headings for the moment, highlight the rest of the list.
● Click on **Format** in the Menu bar, and choose **Tabs**.

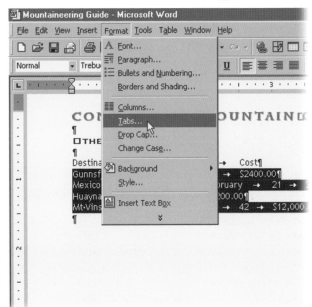

3 SETTING A TAB STOP POSITION

● The **Tabs** dialog box opens. Given the length of the Mexico destination, we are going to set the first column at 2 inches, so in the **Tab stop position** box type **2**. Now click on **Set**, and then click on **OK**.

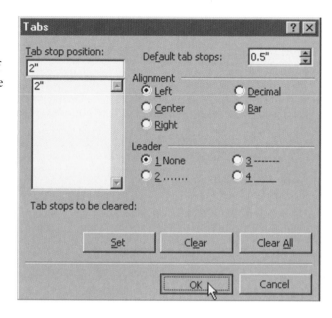

● A tab stop appears in the ruler at the 2-inch position, and the months are now lined up in a column.

4 SETTING THE NEXT TAB STOP

● With the list still highlighted, follow the same steps to set another tab at 3 inches. The numbers of the duration are now lined up.

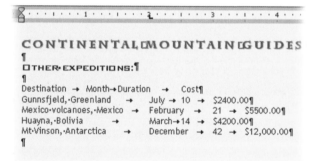

5 SETTING A DECIMAL TAB

● So far we've only used a left tab, that is, the items are lined up down their left-hand side. The cost figures would look better lined up down their right-hand side, so we will use a decimal tab.

● With the list highlighted, open the **Tabs** dialog box again. Set a tab at 4 inches and click on the **Decimal** radio button.

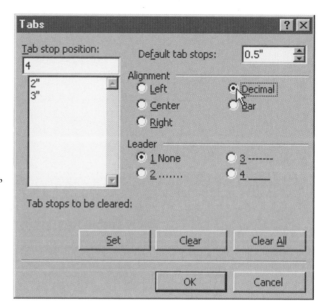

● Click on **Set** and then on **OK**. A decimal tab stop appears on the ruler, and the prices are now aligned down the decimal point at the 4-inch position.

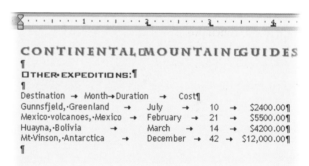

CONTINENTAL MOUNTAIN GUIDES
¶
OTHER·EXPEDITIONS:¶
¶
Destination → Month→Duration → Cost¶
Gunnsfjeld,·Greenland → July → 10 → $2400.00¶
Mexico·volcanoes,·Mexico → February → 21 → $5500.00¶
Huayna,·Bolivia → March → 14 → $4200.00¶
Mt·Vinson,·Antarctica → December → 42 → $12,000.00¶
¶

REMOVING A TAB SETTING FROM THE RULER

A quick way to remove a tab setting is first to highlight the text that contains the tab. Place the mouse cursor on the ruler tab setting that you want to remove, and hold the mouse button down. The vertical alignment line appears, but all you need to do is to drag the tab symbol down off the ruler and release the mouse button. The tab disappears.

Setting Tabs by the Ruler

As is the case with many of the functions in Microsoft® Word, there is more than one way of setting tabs. Using the ruler provides a more visual method than the **Tabs** dialog box, and allows you to make quick adjustments until you are satisfied.

1 SETTING THE FIRST TAB IN THE RULER

- The headings above the list still need aligning over their respective columns. Highlight that line and click on the ruler at the 2-inch mark. A left tab appears on the ruler.

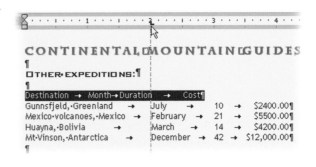

- The **Destination** heading remains aligned to the left, but the **Month** heading now lines up with the months below it.

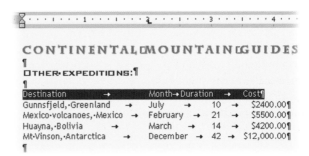

2 SELECTING A CENTER TAB

- With the line of headings still highlighted, click on the **Left Tab** symbol at the left-hand end of the ruler. The symbol for a **Center Tab** appears. This tab has the effect of centering text on the tab.

3 SETTING THE CENTER TAB

● Click on the ruler at the 3-inch mark. A center tab is set and the word **Duration** is almost centered above the list of days.

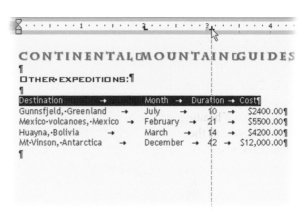

4 FINE TUNING THE SETTING

● The word **Duration** is slightly to the left of center, so move the cursor up to the ruler, place it over the center tab, and hold down the mouse button. A dotted vertical alignment line now appears down the screen. Move the cursor slightly to the right until this line falls exactly between the digits.

● Release the mouse button, and the heading is now precisely centered over the column of numbers.

5 SELECTING A RIGHT TAB

● Finally, click through the options of the tab button at the left-hand end of the ruler until the **Right Tab** symbol appears.

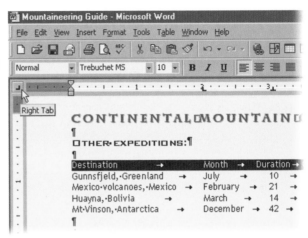

6 SETTING THE RIGHT TAB

● Click on the ruler at about the 4.2-inch mark. The end of the word **Cost** is now aligned with the trailing zeroes of the amounts in the column.

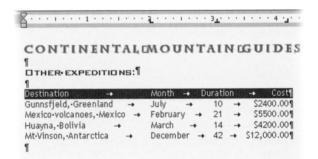

7 CHECKING THE EFFECT

● The right tab lines up the right-hand end of the text. To see the effect, change **Cost** to **Cost/person**. The words move to the left as you type, and the end of "person" is aligned with the zeroes. The effect is clearer with the formatting marks turned off 🔲.

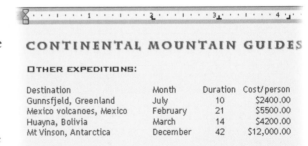

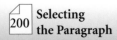
**Selecting
the Paragraph**

8 ADDING LEADERS BETWEEN ITEMS

● One way of making it easier to read across tabbed columns is to add a leader between each one.

● Highlight the list of destinations and click on **Tabs** in the **Format** menu. The **Tabs** dialog box opens. Click on the radio button next to **2.......**, and then click on **Set**.

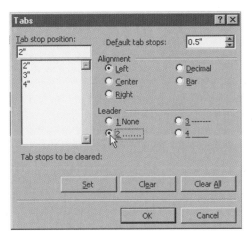

● Now highlight **3"** in the **Tab stop position:** list of tabs, click on the radio button next to **2.......** again, and then click on **Set**.

● Repeat this process for the 4" tab position and click on **OK**. The list of expeditions now has rows of leaders to make the list more readable.

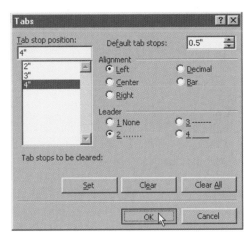

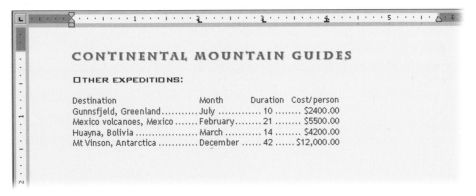

CONTINENTAL MOUNTAIN GUIDES

OTHER EXPEDITIONS:

Destination	Month	Duration	Cost/person
Gunnsfjeld, Greenland	July	10	$2400.00
Mexico volcanoes, Mexico	February	21	$5500.00
Huayna, Bolivia	March	14	$4200.00
Mt Vinson, Antarctica	December	42	$12,000.00

USING MULTIPLE COLUMNS

We have looked at ways of turning lists into columns, but there are times when continuous text benefits from being set in columns, too. This can give the page a newspaper like appearance, and can be useful in newsletters and pamphlets.

1 CHOOSING THE COLUMNS OPTION

● In this example, the Mountain Guides brochure includes a section on rented accommodation, which we are going to set in columns.

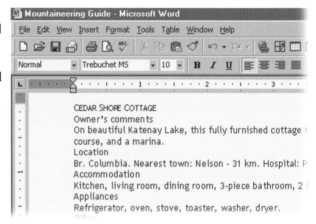

● Begin by highlighting the text that you want to be laid out in columns.
● Then click on **Format** in the Menu bar and choose **Columns** from the drop-down menu.

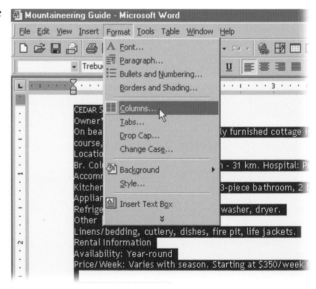

2 SET THE NUMBER OF COLUMNS

● The **Columns** dialog box opens. Click on box **Three** in the **Presets** section of the dialog box to select three columns, and click on **OK**.
● The preview panel shows how the text will look.

● Click on **OK**, and the selected text is now set out in three columns, with the default space of 0.5 inches between them.

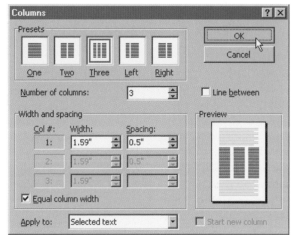

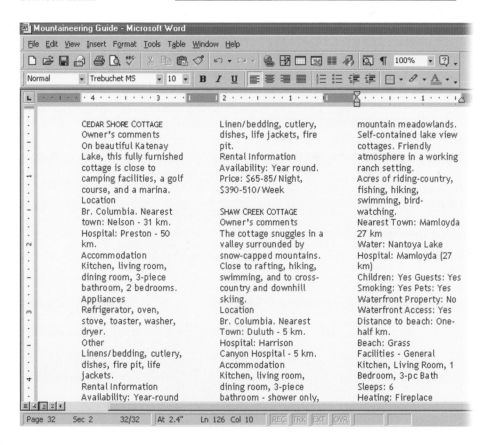

3 INSERTING COLUMN BREAKS

● The information would be clearer if each column began with a new entry. This can be done by using column breaks.

● Place the cursor at the point in the text where you would like to start a new column, click on **Insert** in the Menu bar, and choose **Break** from the menu.

● The **Break** dialog box opens. Click on the radio button next to **Column break** and click on **OK**.

● By using this method, each column can begin with a new entry.

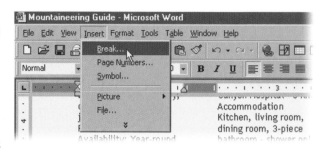

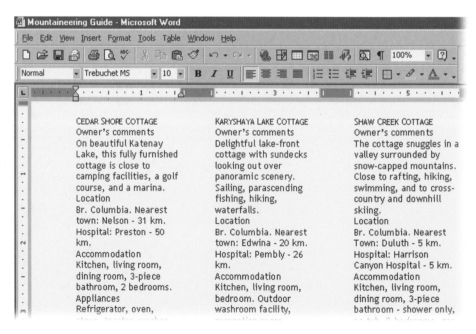

CEDAR SHORE COTTAGE
Owner's comments
On beautiful Katenay Lake, this fully furnished cottage is close to camping facilities, a golf course, and a marina.
Location
Br. Columbia. Nearest town: Nelson - 31 km.
Hospital: Preston - 50 km.
Accommodation
Kitchen, living room, dining room, 3-piece bathroom, 2 bedrooms.
Appliances
Refrigerator, oven,

KARYSHAYA LAKE COTTAGE
Owner's comments
Delightful lake-front cottage with sundecks looking out over panoramic scenery.
Sailing, parascending fishing, hiking, waterfalls.
Location
Br. Columbia. Nearest town: Edwina - 20 km.
Hospital: Pembly - 26 km.
Accommodation
Kitchen, living room, bedroom. Outdoor washroom facility,

SHAW CREEK COTTAGE
Owner's comments
The cottage snuggles in a valley surrounded by snow-capped mountains. Close to rafting, hiking, swimming, and to cross-country and downhill skiing.
Location
Br. Columbia. Nearest Town: Duluth - 5 km.
Hospital: Harrison Canyon Hospital - 5 km.
Accommodation
Kitchen, living room, dining room, 3-piece bathroom - shower only,

4 INSERTING VERTICAL LINES

- Rather than having blank spaces between columns, you can insert a vertical line between them. Place the cursor anywhere in the columns, open the **Columns** dialog box 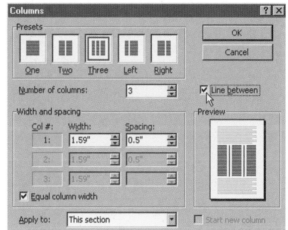, and click in the **Line between** check box.
- Click on **OK** and the columns are now separated by a vertical line, which helps lead the eye in the same way that we saw earlier with tab leaders 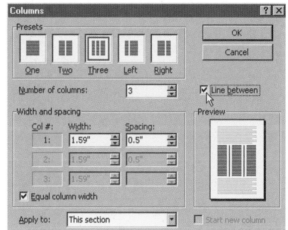.

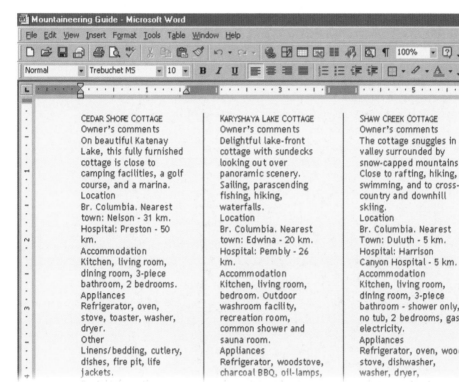

CEDAR SHORE COTTAGE
Owner's comments
On beautiful Katenay Lake, this fully furnished cottage is close to camping facilities, a golf course, and a marina.
Location
Br. Columbia. Nearest town: Nelson - 31 km. Hospital: Preston - 50 km.
Accommodation
Kitchen, living room, dining room, 3-piece bathroom, 2 bedrooms.
Appliances
Refrigerator, oven, stove, toaster, washer, dryer.
Other
Linens/bedding, cutlery, dishes, fire pit, life jackets.

KARYSHAYA LAKE COTTAGE
Owner's comments
Delightful lake-front cottage with sundecks looking out over panoramic scenery. Sailing, parascending fishing, hiking, waterfalls.
Location
Br. Columbia. Nearest town: Edwina - 20 km. Hospital: Pembly - 26 km.
Accommodation
Kitchen, living room, bedroom. Outdoor washroom facility, recreation room, common shower and sauna room.
Appliances
Refrigerator, woodstove, charcoal BBQ, oil-lamps,

SHAW CREEK COTTAGE
Owner's comments
The cottage snuggles in a valley surrounded by snow-capped mountains. Close to rafting, hiking, swimming, and to cross-country and downhill skiing.
Location
Br. Columbia. Nearest Town: Duluth - 5 km. Hospital: Harrison Canyon Hospital - 5 km.
Accommodation
Kitchen, living room, dining room, 3-piece bathroom - shower only, no tub, 2 bedrooms, gas, electricity.
Appliances
Refrigerator, oven, wood stove, dishwasher, washer, dryer,

222 Choosing the Columns Option

221 Adding Leaders Between Items

USING STYLE SHEETS

This chapter deals with style sheets, a feature of Word that enables you to define many aspects of the style of each kind of text and apply the defined styles throughout your document.

THE POWER OF THE STYLE SHEET

Style sheets are one of the most powerful – and least understood – features of Word. Each style sheet is a list of formatting instructions, or styles, that can be applied to text. Every document is based on a style sheet. When you open a new document by clicking on the **New Blank Document** button in the Standard toolbar, Word automatically bases it on the normal style sheet, which is why the word **Normal** appears in the **Style** box at the end of the Formatting toolbar.

DEFINING FEATURES
A style sheet can define many features of a section of text. These include the font, and its size, color, and effects; the shape of a paragraph as determined by indents, spacing, and how page breaks are controlled; the position and alignment of tabs; what borders and shading are used, if any; and how bullets and numbering are styled. The smallest unit to which a style sheet can be applied is a paragraph, which need only be one line that ends with a paragraph mark.

CHOOSING ELEMENTS
To apply styles sensibly to a document, first identify the various parts of the text that play different roles. For example in a book, the title, the table of contents, main text, captions, and index all play different roles, and can all be styled differently. The styles can be set in separate style sheets and applied.

SAVING TIME
Once a style sheet has been created, any changes that you make to that sheet are automatically applied to all parts of your document that are based on that style.

CEDAR SHORE COTTAGE

Owner's comments
On beautiful Katenay Lake, this fully furnished cottage is close to camping facilities, a golf course, and a marina.

Location
Br. Columbia. Nearest town: Nelson - 31 km. Hospital: Preston - 50 km.

Accommodation
Kitchen, living room, dining room, 3-piece

Styled text •

Using a style sheet, a defined font, type size, and indent has been applied to every instance of this kind of text each time it appears in the document.

CREATING A NEW STYLE SHEET

Style sheets come into their own when applied to a document in which the information falls into various categories, and in which these categories are used repeatedly. In the example below, each entry in the directory contains the same categories of information, such as **Owner's comments**, **Location**, and **Accommodation**.

1 SELECTING THE TEXT

● The list of cabins and their details has all been formatted in Trebuchet 10 pt. Now, new styles are going to be designed for each part of the details of the properties, starting with the name of the property.

● Highlight the name of the first property and click on **Format** in the Menu bar. Now click on **Style** in the drop-down menu.

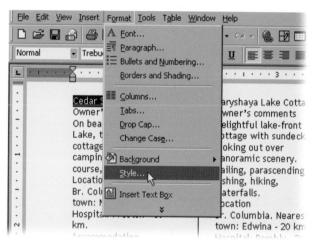

2 OPENING A NEW STYLE OPTION

● The **Style** dialog box opens. Click on **New** to create a new style for the property name. The text that you have highlighted can be seen in the preview box, and this will show the effects of any changes that you make to its style.

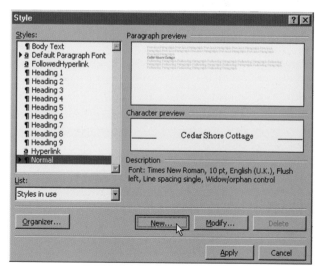

3 NAMING THE STYLE

● The **New Style** dialog box now opens. The first task is to give a name to the new style that we are creating, so type **Property Name** in the **Name** box. A descriptive name like this will help you to know which style to choose when you are styling text at a later date.

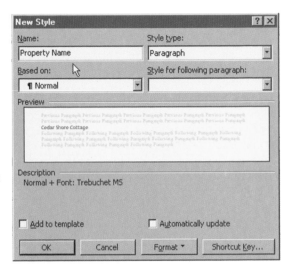

4 CHOOSING THE FONT

● Now click on **Format** at the bottom of the **New Style** dialog box, and click on **Font** in the pop-up menu that appears.

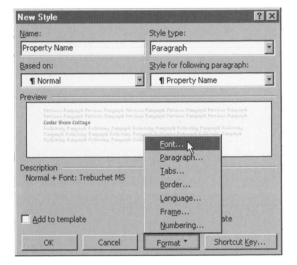

● The **Font** dialog box opens. This box offers you a range of possibilities for changing the appearance of the font, including the font itself, its style (Italic etc.), and its size.

● In the **Font** selection box choose **BankGothic Md BT**, and you will see that the text is now shown in this font in the preview panel.

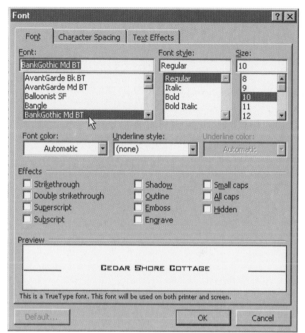

5 CHANGING THE FONT SIZE

● In the **Size** selection box choose **14**. Again, the text in the preview panel now reflects this change.

- BankGothic Md BT is an upper-case only font, that is, it does not use lower-case letters. However, if you are using a font that is upper- and lower-case, click the **Small caps** check box of the **Effects** section. This has the effect of turning all the lower-case letters into small capital letters.
- Click on **OK**.

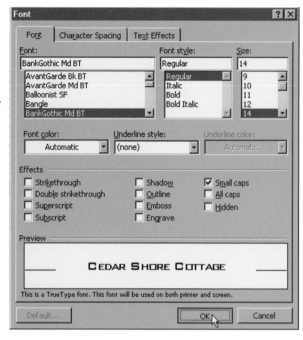

6 INTRODUCING SPACE AFTER

- The appearance of the text on the page would be improved if there were a small space between the name and the text that follows it.
- Click on **Format** in the **New Style** dialog box and then click on **Paragraph** in the pop-up menu.

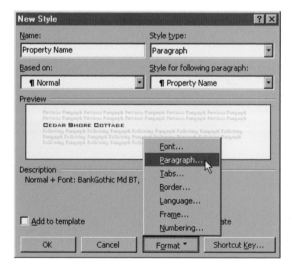

● The **Paragraph** dialog box opens. In the **Spacing** section, click once on the up arrow to the right of the **After** box. The figure of **6 pt** appears in the panel, meaning that a 6 point space will be inserted after the property name.

● Click on **OK** to close the **Paragraph** dialog box.

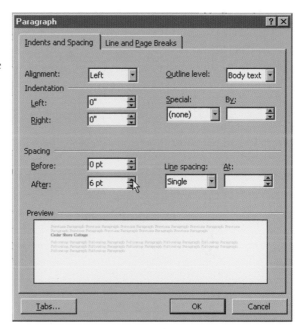

● The **New Style** dialog box now reappears. In the **Description** box the new formatting that has been chosen is shown.

● Click on **OK** to close the **New Style** dialog box and save this new style.

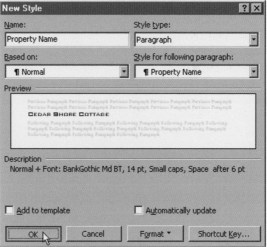

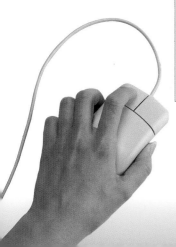

7 APPLYING THE NEW STYLE

● Click on **Apply** in the Style box, which is now visible again.

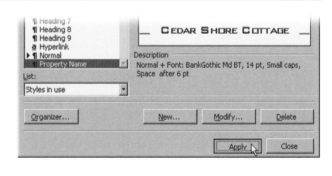

● The new style is now applied to the name of the property.

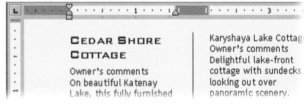

8 CREATING ANOTHER STYLE

● The details of each property are divided into sections, and a style is needed for the section heads. Highlight the words **Owner's comments**. Choose **Style** from the **Format** menu and click on **New** to open the **New Style** dialog box. Call this style **Section Head**.

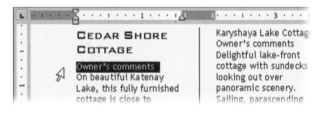

● Click on **Format** and again click on **Font** to open the **Font** dialog box.
● Choose **Californian FB** as the font and choose **Bold** in the **Font style** box. Click on **OK**.

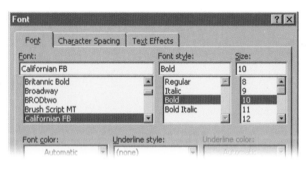

● The **New Style** dialog box reappears. Click on **Format**, select **Paragraph** to open the **Paragraph** dialog box, and in the **Spacing After** box type **2**. This will introduce a small space after the heading. Click on **OK** to close the **Paragraph** dialog box.

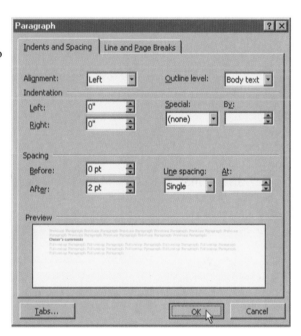

● Click on **OK** in the **New Style** dialog box and click on **Apply** in the **Style** dialog box. The section heading now has the required style.

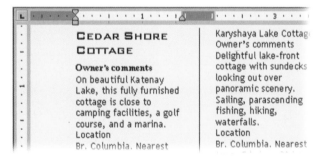

9 STYLING THE MAIN TEXT

● The text of each section needs its own style. Click in the paragraph below the newly styled **Owner's comments**, select **Style** from the **Format** menu, click on **New** to open the **New Style** dialog box, and call this style **Section Details**.

● Click on **Format** and select **Font** to open the **Font** dialog box. This time choose **Trebuchet MS** and make it **9** pt. Click on **OK** to return to the **New Style** box.

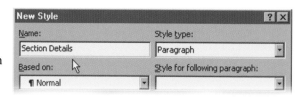

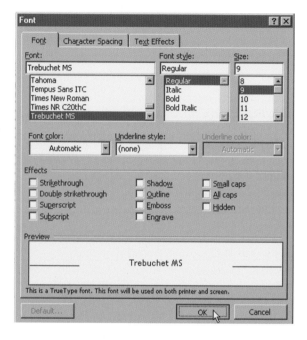

INDENTING THE TEXT

● The text will stand out more if it is indented. From the **Format** pop-up menu choose **Paragraph** and in the **Indentation** section of the **Paragraph** dialog box click on the up arrow of the **Left** box. The figure of **0.1"** appears. Click on **OK**.

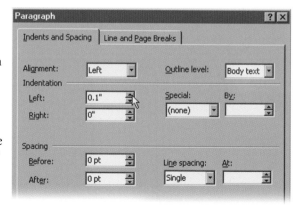

● Click **OK** again in the **New Style** box, click on **Apply**, and the text that appears, in the chosen font, is indented.

APPLYING YOUR STYLE SHEETS

● Highlight the name of the second property at the top of the second column.

● Click on the down arrow to the right of the **Style** selection box and move the cursor down to **Property Name**. (The other styles in the **Style** menu shown here may not be identical to the list in your **Style** menu.)

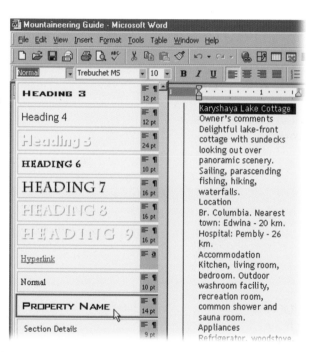

● Click on **Property Name** and that style is applied to the second property name.

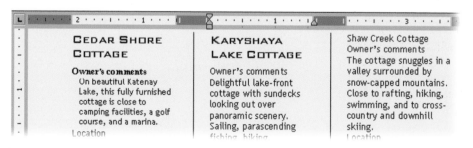

- Highlight **Owner's comments** beneath it and select the **Section Head** style.

- Click on **Section Head** and the style is applied to the heading.

Text now changes to Section Head style •

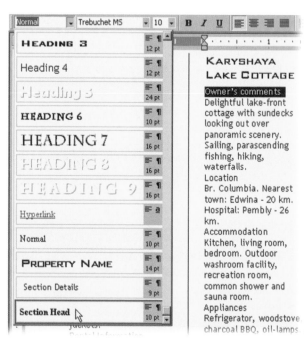

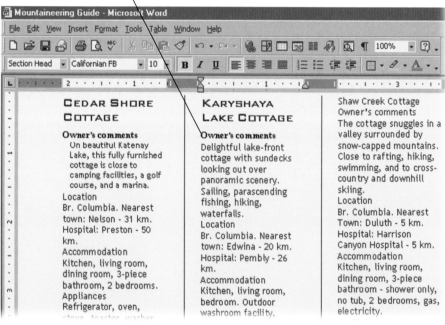

● Highlight the text beneath that heading and select **Section Details** from the style list. Click on this panel and the style is applied to the text.

● Follow these steps to apply the style sheets to all the text throughout your document.

Text now changes to Section Details style

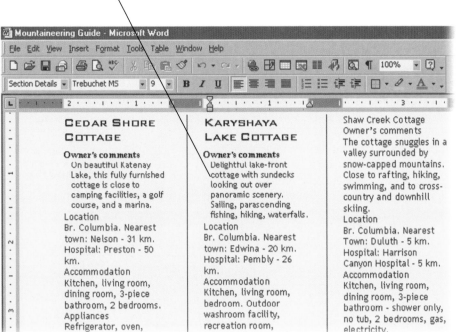

USING FORMAT PAINTER
TO APPLY STYLES

We have seen how to create style sheets and apply them to all the text throughout a document, but this last process can be laborious if the text is extensive. Luckily, Word offers a solution – Format Painter enables you to do the job much faster.

1 STYLING THE PROPERTY NAME

● Highlight the property name at the top of the second column and make sure that you include the paragraph mark because this contains all the style details for the paragraph. (You can turn on the Formatting Marks to ensure that the paragraph mark is highlighted ⌐.)

● Click on the **Format Painter** icon in the Standard toolbar ⌐.

● Your cursor now has a paintbrush icon next to it. Go to the property name at the top of the third column and highlight it.

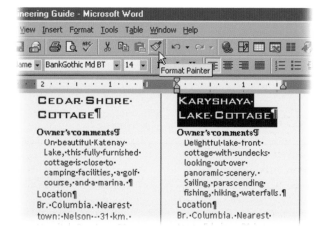

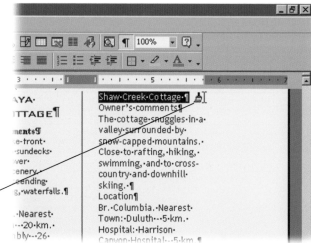

Paintbrush icon ●

124 ㉑ **Show/Hide Formatting Marks**

124 ⑪ **Format Painter**

- Release the mouse button, and the text is now styled in the selected style.

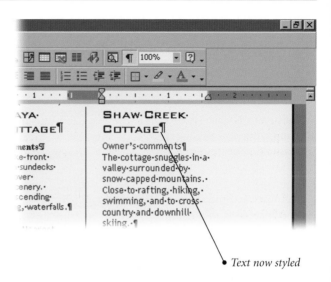

● *Text now styled*

2 STYLING THE SECTION HEAD

- Select **Owner's comments** near the top of the first paragraph and double-click on the **Format Painter** button. You can now "paint" all the section heads in the text with the **Section Head** style 🖺. Press the [Esc] key, or click on the **Format Painter** button again when you have produced this result.

Styled Section Head ●

3 STYLING THE SECTION DETAILS

● Finally, highlight the first paragraph in the first column that has been formatted with the **Section Details** style, double-click on the **Format Painter** button and apply the style to all the remaining unstyled paragraphs.

● The document should now look like the one below, with all text in the chosen styles.

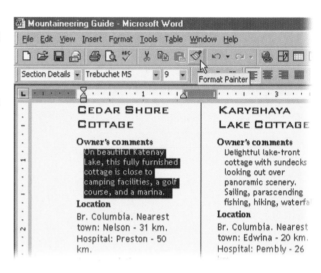

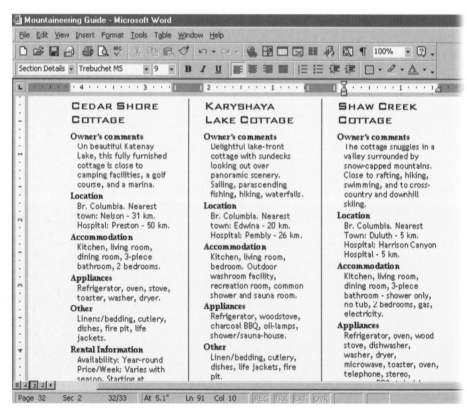

MAKING ONE STYLE FOLLOW ANOTHER

Once you have decided that one style is always to be followed by a second particular style, you can instruct Word always to follow the first style with the second. Begin by clicking on **Format** in the Menu bar and selecting **Style** to open the **Style** dialog box.

1 SELECTING THE FIRST STYLE

● In the **Style** dialog box, select the first of the two styles, in this case **Section Head**, and click on **Modify**.

Chosen style ●

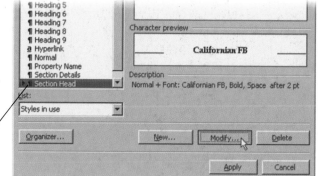

2 SELECTING THE SECOND STYLE

● The **Modify Style** dialog box opens. The first style, **Section Head**, appears in the **Name** box. Click on the down arrow to the right of the **Style for following paragraph** box to drop down the list of styles.
● Click on the style that is to follow the first style, in this case **Section Details**.

3 SAVING THE CHANGES

● **Section Details** appears in the **Style for following paragraph** box.

● Click on **OK**, and the **Modify Style** dialog box closes. Now click on **Close** in the **Style** dialog box to complete the changes.

● On each occasion now when **Section Head** is used as a style and the Enter ← key is pressed, the following text will be formatted with the **Section Details** style.

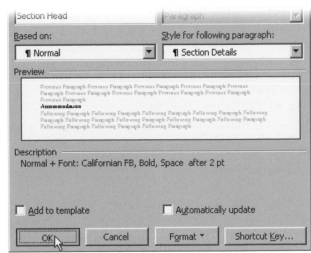

STYLING FROM A TEXT SELECTION

So far we have created styles by choosing each of the features for the style through the **Style** dialog box. An alternative method is to begin by formatting a paragraph with all the style features that you want to be in a style sheet.

1 FORMATTING THE TEXT

● In this example, the following formatting has been applied to the text:
Font: *Gill Sans Ultra Bold*
Font size: *16 pt*
Font color: *Red*
Space after: *12 pt*
Border setting: *Shadow*
Border style: *Thin-thick*
Border color: *Tan*
Shading: *Light Yellow*
Text: *Centered*
Right indent: *3.77 inches*

2 FROM A FORMAT TO A STYLE

● Highlight the text that you have formatted, click on **Format** in the Menu bar, select **Style** to open the **Style** box, and click on **New** near the foot of the dialog box to open the **New Style** dialog box. Word has picked up the formatting specifications of the selected text and almost all of them are shown in the **Description** section of this dialog box. Certain elements are not shown only because the **Description** box is too small to contain them all. Enter a name for the new style (here the name **Redeye** has been chosen). Click on **OK** to close the **New Style** dialog box.

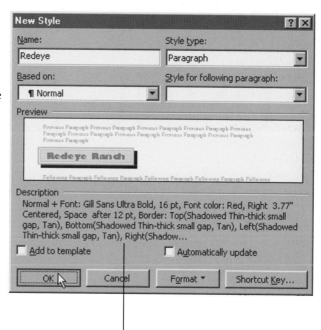

Formatting specifications ●

3 MAKING THE STYLE AVAILABLE

● The **Style** dialog box reappears with the new style listed in the **Style** menu to the left. To close the dialog box, just click on **Apply** even though the text already contains the required formatting. This style is now available to be applied quickly to any chosen text.

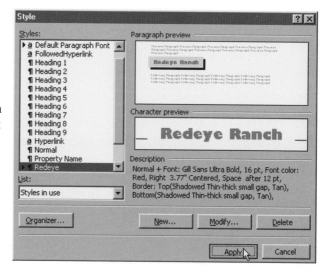

USING EXCEL

THE ESSENTIAL FEATURES of Excel are presented in this section in separate chapters to allow easy understanding of their functions. Before you can do anything sophisticated with Excel, you need to know how to enter data correctly into worksheet cells. You also need to know how to change or correct this data; how to copy and move data within the worksheet; and how to insert, clear, and delete cells. The majority of this section consists of instructions for performing these essential, simple tasks. Some basic examples run through the book, and it may be difficult to keep track of these if you skip any sections. Please note that these examples are designed to illustrate various specific techniques, and do not necessarily reflect typical worksheet uses or design.

MICROSOFT EXCEL

Excel belongs to the group of computer applications known as spreadsheets, and the first spreadsheet program started the process of making computers an indispensable business tool.

WHAT CAN EXCEL DO?

Storing spreadsheet data is only the beginning as far as Excel is concerned. The wide range of features it contains let you manipulate and present your data in almost any way you choose. Excel can be an accounts program; it can be used as a sophisticated calculator capable of utilizing complex mathematical formulas; it can also be a diary, a scheduler, and more. Used in combination with Microsoft Word, Excel's database features make creating mailing lists and personalized letters very easy. Excel's presentation facilities use color, borders, and different fonts to emphasize data. A variety of charts is available, which can be selected to suit the kind of data being presented. For storing, manipulating, and presenting data, Microsoft Excel offers an unrivaled range of possibilities.

WHAT IS A WORKSHEET?

At the heart of Excel is a two-dimensional grid of data storage spaces called a worksheet (right). This is where you input the data that you want to store, manipulate, or analyze. The individual spaces are called worksheet cells. To begin with, all the cells are empty. As you put data into the cells, you build and develop the individual worksheets.

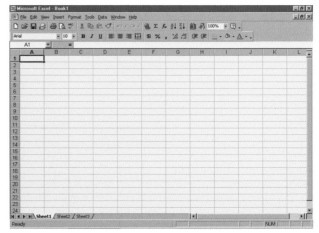

LAUNCHING EXCEL

Approaching a new program for the first time can be a daunting experience because you don't know what to expect. However, new programs are learned one step at a time and the first step is the simple one of launching Excel from your desktop.

1 LAUNCHING WITH THE START MENU

So, let's get going. First you need to launch Excel.

● If you are running Windows, click on the **Start** button at bottom left, and then choose **Programs** from the pop-up list. **Microsoft Excel** should appear in the submenu to the right (or it may be within a Microsoft Office Program group). Highlight the Excel bar and click with the mouse.

● The Excel window appears on screen.

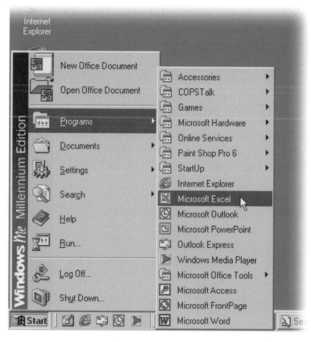

2 LAUNCHING WITH A SHORTCUT

● If there is already a shortcut to Excel on your Desktop, just double-click on the shortcut icon.

● The Excel window appears on screen.

THE EXCEL WINDOW

Soon after you launch Microsoft Excel, a window called **Microsoft Excel – Book1** appears. At the center of the window is a worksheet – a grid of blank rectangular cells. Letters and numbers label the columns and rows of the grid. Each cell has an address (such as E3), which is the column and row in which it is found.

THE EXCEL WINDOW

❶ Title bar
Title of the active workbook.

❷ Menu bar
Contains the main menus for frequently used commands.

❸ Formula bar ⌐
What you enter in the active cell also appears here.

❹ Standard toolbar
These buttons carry out frequently used actions.

❺ Formatting toolbar
Options for changing data presentation.

❻ Column header buttons
Click on the header button to select the whole column.

❼ Row header buttons ⌐
Click on the row header to select the entire row.

❽ Active cell ⌐
Whatever you type appears in the active cell.

❾ Worksheet tabs
Workbooks contain work-sheets – click to select one.

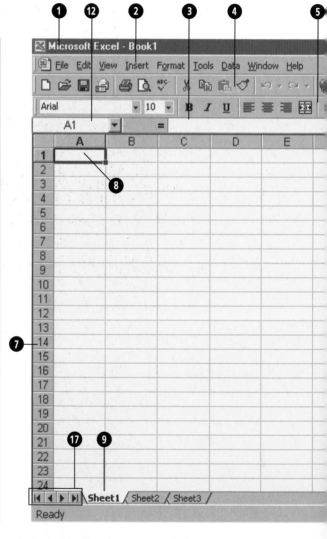

256 | **Selecting Worksheet Cells**

258 | **Selecting a Single Row**

270 | **Formulas and Calculations**

TOOLBAR LAYOUT

If Excel doesn't show the Formatting toolbar below the Standard toolbar, first place the cursor over the Formatting toolbar "handle." When the four-headed arrow appears, (right) hold down the mouse button and "drag" the toolbar into position.

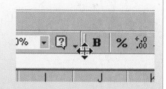

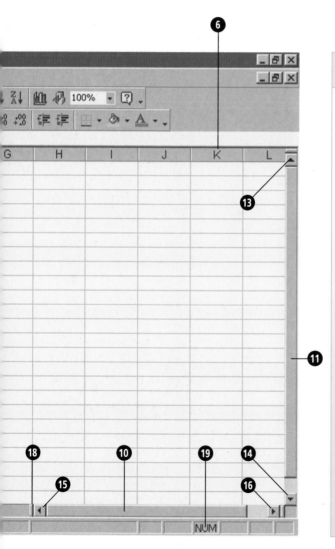

THE EXCEL WINDOW

❿ Horizontal scroll bar
To scroll horizontally through the worksheet.

⓫ Vertical scroll bar
To scroll vertically through the worksheet.

⓬ Name box
Gives the address of the active cell.

⓭ Scroll-up arrow
Move up the worksheet.

⓮ Scroll-down arrow
Move down the worksheet.

⓯ Left-scroll arrow
Scrolls the sheet to the left.

⓰ Right-scroll arrow
Scrolls the sheet to the right.

⓱ Tab scrolling buttons
Scroll through the sheets if they cannot all be displayed.

⓲ Tab split box
Click and drag to show tabs or to increase the scroll bar.

⓳ NUM lock
Shows that the numeric keypad on the right of the keyboard is on.

THE TWO MAIN EXCEL TOOLBARS

Many of the actions, or commands, that you want to perform on data can be carried out by clicking on toolbar buttons. When you launch Excel, the Standard toolbar and the Formatting toolbar are the usual toolbars displayed. They contain buttons whose actions are described below. The Standard toolbar contains buttons for actions as diverse as opening a new workbook or undoing an action. The Formatting toolbar contains buttons for changing the worksheet's appearance.

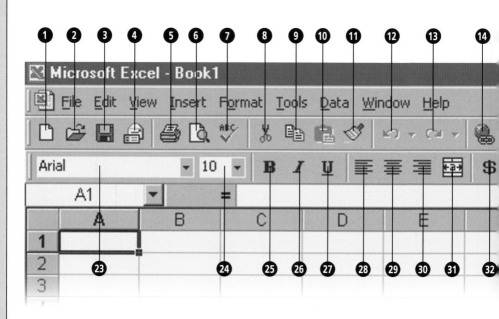

BUTTON FUNCTIONS

❶ New workbook
❷ Open file
❸ Save workbook
❹ Email workbook/sheet
❺ Print
❻ Print preview
❼ Spelling checker
❽ Cut
❾ Copy
❿ Paste
⓫ Format painter
⓬ Undo action(s)
⓭ Redo action(s)
⓮ Insert hyperlink
⓯ AutoSum
⓰ Paste function
⓱ Sort ascending
⓲ Sort descending
⓳ Chart wizard
⓴ Drawing toolbar
㉑ Zoom view
㉒ Help
㉓ Font selector
㉔ Font size selector

254 Opening a New Workbook

281 Copying and Pasting

296 Checking Spelling

CUSTOMIZING A TOOLBAR

Click the arrow at far right of the Formatting toolbar then on the arrow on the **Add or Remove Buttons** box that appears. A drop-down menu opens from which you can add or remove toolbar buttons.

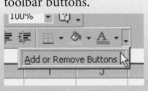

ScreenTips

It isn't necessary to memorize all these buttons. Roll the cursor over a button, wait for a second, and a ScreenTip appears telling you the function of the button.

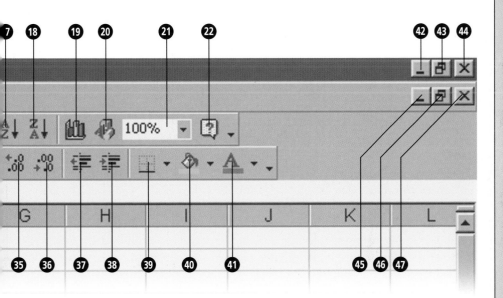

BUTTON FUNCTIONS

- **25** Bold
- **26** Italic
- **27** Underline
- **28** Align left
- **29** Center
- **30** Align right
- **31** Merge and center
- **32** Currency style
- **33** Percent style
- **34** Comma style
- **35** Increase decimals
- **36** Decrease decimals
- **37** Decrease indent
- **38** Increase indent
- **39** Add/remove borders
- **40** Fill color
- **41** Font color
- **42** Minimize Excel
- **43** Restore Excel
- **44** Close Excel
- **45** Minimize worksheet
- **46** Restore worksheet
- **47** Close worksheet

265 **Entering Decimals**

274 **Adding a Border**

275 **Highlighting Information**

NAMING, SAVING, AND FINDING WORKBOOKS

Anything you create using Microsoft Excel is stored on your computer as a file called a workbook. A workbook contains one or more separate worksheets. When you first start up Excel, you are presented with an unused workbook called Book1. This contains from 3 to 10 blank worksheets, depending on the version of Excel. The blank worksheets are initially called Sheet1, Sheet2, and so on.

1 RENAMING A WORKSHEET

● You can switch between worksheets by clicking on the tabs at the bottom of the workbook window. To begin with, the worksheets are all blank.

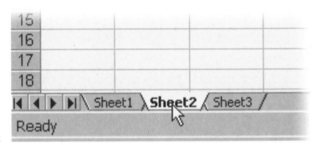

● Once you put data into a worksheet, you should give the worksheet a short name to indicate what it contains. Because all worksheets start with a default name (such as **Sheet1**), you are actually renaming the worksheet. Here's how to do it.

● Double-click on the existing name, so that it becomes highlighted.

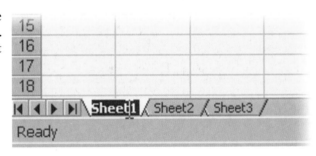

● Type the new name and press Enter ↵.

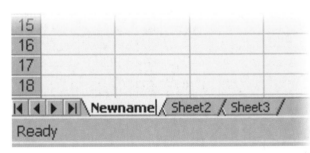

2 SAVING AND NAMING

● You should save your work frequently. Saving means copying to your computer's hard disk. When you save in Excel, you save the whole workbook containing the worksheet(s) that you have been developing.

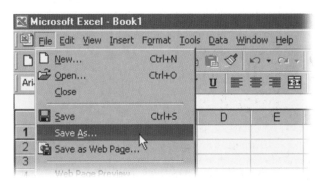

● The first time you save a workbook, you should name it (actually rename it) at the same time.

● Choose **Save As** from the **File** menu.

● The **Save As** dialog box appears. Your workbook will be saved in the folder displayed in the **Save in** box. In this instance, just accept the displayed folder. Remember the name of the folder in which you've saved the workbook.

● In the **File name** box, type the name you would like to give your workbook (Excel will automatically add the extension **.xls**). Then click on the **Save** button.

● On subsequent occasions when you want to save the workbook, just click the **Save** button on the Standard toolbar.

3 CLOSING A WORKBOOK

● Click the close button at top right.

● If you have made any changes since your last save, a box appears asking whether you want to save changes. Click **Yes** (or **No** if you do not wish to save any changes you've made).

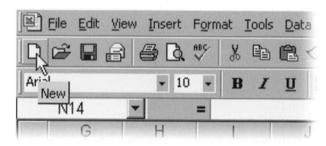

4 OPENING A NEW WORKBOOK

● Just click the new workbook button on the Standard toolbar.

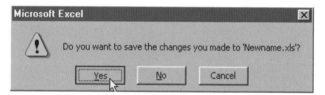

5 OPEN A SAVED WORKBOOK

● Click the **Open** button on the Standard toolbar

● In the **Open** dialog box, click on the workbook you want to open.

● Click on the **Open** button at the bottom right of the box.

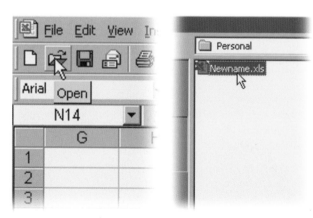

6 FIND A SAVED WORKBOOK

● After you have been using Excel for some time, there will be occasions when you cannot find the workbook you want. Excel contains its own find file facility to help you when this happens.

● To find a workbook, begin by clicking on **Open** in the **File** menu, click on **Tools** at top right in the **Open** dialog box and choose **Find**.

● The **Find** dialog box opens. Drop down the **Look in** menu and select the area to search – in this case, the folder called **My documents**. Click in the **Search subfolders** check box if necessary, and click on **Find now**.

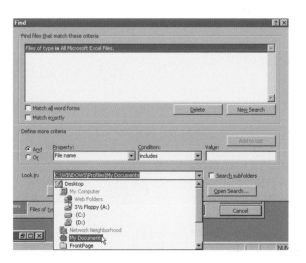

● The **Open** window reappears with the list of Excel workbooks found.

ENTERING DATA

The Excel program is based on the worksheet – a grid of individual boxes, or "cells," into which you enter data. You can then manipulate that data in various ways.

SELECTING WORKSHEET CELLS

Before performing any operation in Excel – for example, typing data into cells, coloring cells, or deleting them – you need to choose which cells you are going to perform the action on. This process is called cell selection and is a fundamental Excel skill. You can select a single cell, a block of cells, a horizontal row or vertical column, or several rows or columns at the same time. You can also select several groups of cells. When a group of cells is selected, they will appear in black, except for one cell, the "active cell" (see box below), which remains white. Try practicing these techniques following the instructions below.

1 SELECTING A SINGLE CELL

● Move the mouse pointer over your chosen cell and click the left mouse button.
● The thick black border that now appears around the cell indicates that it is selected, and this is now the active cell.

Active cell

ACTIVE CELLS

The significance of the active cell is that once you have made a selection, anything you type will appear only in the active cell. Other actions that you perform after selection (such as coloring cells or deleting them) will apply to all the cells in the selected area.

WHY SELECT MULTIPLE CELLS?

You select multiple cells most often to perform "block" activities such as formatting 🗋, inserting new columns, rows, and cells 🗋, clearing cells, or duplicating existing data 🗋 from a single cell to several cells. New data can be typed into cells only one cell at a time (in the outlined or "active" cell), but it sometimes saves time to select all the cells into which you are going to enter data before you start typing. You can easily move the active cell around in the selected area one cell at a time using the [Tab↹] key.

2 SELECTING A BLOCK OF CELLS

● A block can range from a few adjacent cells in a single row or column to a large rectangular area.
● Click on a cell at one end (or at one corner) of the block you wish to select.
● Hold down the [⇧ Shift] key, and then click on the cell at the opposite end (or corner) of the block.

Active cell

3 SELECTING A SINGLE COLUMN

● Click on the column header button at the top of your chosen column.

Column header button ●

	Simple Formatting		Copying Data by Filling		Inserting New Columns, Rows, and Cells
273		276		286	

4 SELECTING A SINGLE ROW

● Click on the row header button to the left of your chosen row. This row will then be highlighted.

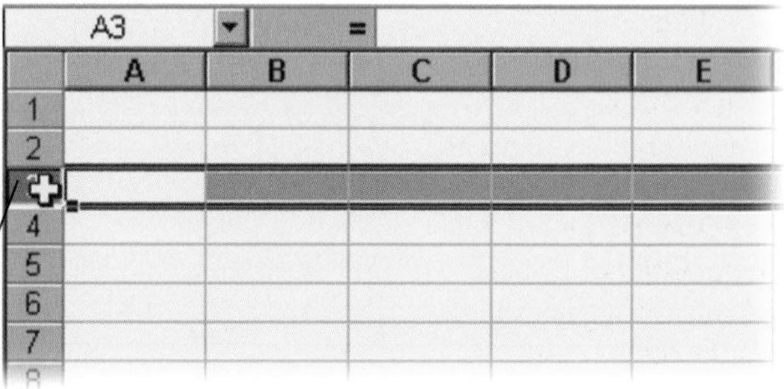

Row header button

5 SELECTING ROWS OR COLUMNS

● While holding down the left-hand mouse button, drag the mouse pointer across the header buttons for the columns or rows you wish to include, and then release the button.

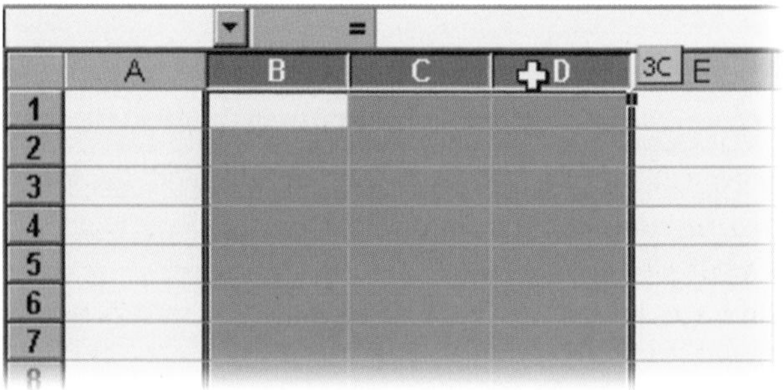

6 SELECTING SEVERAL BLOCKS

● Select the first cell or block, hold down the Ctrl key, select the next cell or block, then select a third cell or block, and so on. Release the Ctrl key only when you have completed your selections.

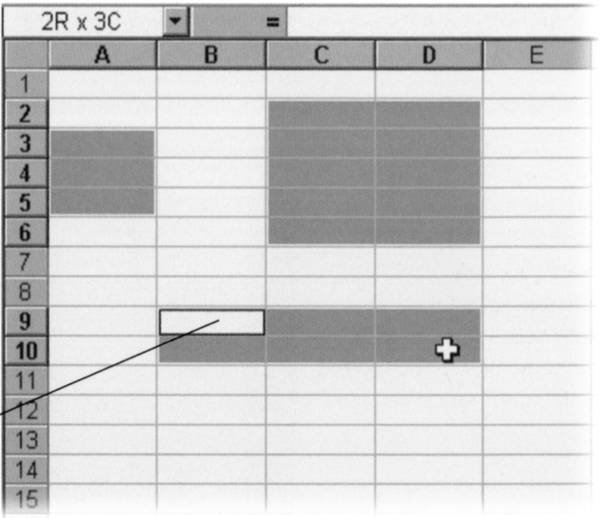

Active cell

7 SELECTING ALL THE WORKSHEET

- Click on the top left corner of the border of the worksheet. This is called the **Select All** button. The whole of the worksheet will now be highlighted, and the top left cell is the active cell.

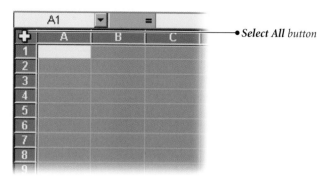

• *Select All button*

ENTERING TEXT

There are three categories of data that you can put into a worksheet – text, numbers, and formulas. Worksheets usually take a tabular form, and text is used most often as labels for the table's rows and columns. It makes sense to enter these text labels first, in order to provide a structure for the numerical data and formulas. To learn the techniques for entering data, you may find it helpful to follow a worked example. The example given here involves creating a sales worksheet for a small business, Fantasy Ices, that makes ice cream products. Alternatively, you can use the same methods for any worksheet you choose. To follow the example, open a new workbook and save it as **fantasyices.xls** ☐. Rename Sheet1 in the workbook **Sales** ☐.

1 SELECT THE FIRST CELL FOR TEXT

Click on cell A2 to select this cell. Cell A2 is now the active cell and anything you type on the keyboard will appear in this cell. Note that **A2** appears in the name box to the top left of the worksheet.

• *Name box*

• *Active cell*

253 **Saving and Naming**

252 **Renaming a worksheet**

2 TYPING IN THE TEXT

For the worked example, type the word **Product**. Note that a flashing bar, called the insertion point, stays just to the right of the last letter you typed, marking where the next letter you type will appear. Don't worry for now if you make typing mistakes.

Insertion point

Oops... typing error

If you mistype a letter, press the ← Bksp key on your keyboard to delete the last letter you typed. If you want to start data entry into a cell from scratch, press the Esc key. Even if you have completed entering data, it's easy to change data later ⌐.

3 COMPLETE THE ENTRY

● Once you have typed your text, press Enter ↵. This completes the data entry into the cell, and the active cell now moves down a single cell to A3.

4 LABELS FOR ROW HEADINGS

● Into cell A3, type **Twizzlesticks** – this is the company's biggest product. Press Enter ↵.
● Repeat the process by typing **Chokky bars**, **Orange sorbet**, and **Raspberry surprise** into cells A4, A5, and A6. These are the company's other three products. Press Enter ↵ after typing each of these text labels.

⬜ Changing
292 Cell Contents

5 COLUMN HEADING TEXT

● Now add some further text labels as column headers for the numerical data you are going to enter into the worksheet.

● Select cells B2 to D2 (see page 256 to remind yourself how to select). Type **Sales (boxes)**, which appears in the active cell, B2.

● Complete the entry by pressing the [Tab↹] key. This time, the active cell moves one cell to the right.

● Type **Price ($)** into C2, press the [Tab↹] key, and type **Sales Revenue** into D2.

B2	▼	✗ ✓ =	Sales (boxes	
	A	B	C	D	E
1					
2	Product	Sales (boxes			
3	Twizzlesticks				
4	Chokky bars				
5	Orange sorbet				✛
6	Raspberry surprise				
7					

	▼	✗ ✓ =	Price ($)	
	A	B	C	D	E
1					
2	Product	Sales (box	Price ($)		
3	Twizzlesticks				
4	Chokky bars				
5	Orange sorbet				
6	Raspberry surprise				
7					
8					

Overflowing text

When you type a long text label into a cell, it may appear to overflow into the next cell on the right – and when you type into that next cell, your long text label appears to have been cut off. Don't worry – it's easy to fix. There are several ways of adjusting the width of columns so that all the text fits 🖿.

TEXT ALIGNMENT

Note that Excel will automatically start any text label at the left-hand end of the cell (the text is said to be ranged left) whereas numerical values are ranged right. Excel classifies anything typed into a cell as text unless it specifically recognizes it as a numerical value. You can change the alignment of data in a cell using toolbar buttons 🖿.

| 263 | **Adjust the Column Widths** | | 250 | **The Two Main Excel Toolbars** |

6 ADD FURTHER TEXT LABELS

- Select cell C7 and type **Total Revenue**. Press [Enter ←] when finished.
- Select cell B10 and type **Last Updated**. Press [Enter ←], type **Date** into cell B11, press [Enter ←], and type **Time** into the B12 cell.
- Select cell A14 and type **Proportion of our products that are**. Press [Enter ←] and type the text labels shown at bottom right into cells A15 to A17. When you type **Ice milk** in cell A17, Excel may suggest that you want to enter the label **Ice cream** in this cell. Ignore this and just keep typing.

C7	▼	✗ ✓ =	Total Revenue	
	A	B	C	D	E
1					
2	Product	Sales (box	Price ($)	Sales Revenue	
3	Twizzlesticks				
4	Chokky bars				
5	Orange sorbet				
6	Raspberry surprise				
7			Total Revenue		
8					
9					
10					
11					

A17	▼	✗ ✓ =	Ice milk	
	A	B	C	D	E
1					
2	Product	Sales (box	Price ($)	Sales Revenue	
3	Twizzlesticks				
4	Chokky bars				
5	Orange sorbet				
6	Raspberry surprise				
7			Total Revenue		
8					
9					
10		Last Updated			
11		Date			

9					
10		Last Updated			
11		Date			
12		Time			
13					
14	Proportion of our products that are				
15	Ice cream				
16	Sorbets				
17	Ice milk				
18					
19					
20					
21					

COMPLETION KEYS

There are various keyboard methods for completing the entry of data into a cell. In addition to the [Enter ←] and [Tab ⇆] keys (which move the active cell down or to the right, respectively, on completing the entry), you can use the cursor arrow keys for moving the active cell in various directions as you complete an entry.

7 ADJUST THE COLUMN WIDTHS

● There are some quick methods for adjusting the widths of columns to fit cell data. For this example:

● Move the mouse pointer over the line that divides column headers A and B. The pointer should form a bar with arrows pointing to either side.

Mouse pointer

● Press down on the left mouse button, and drag the mouse pointer to the right. A dotted vertical line shows the position of the new column divider. Release the mouse button when it is to the right of the words **Raspberry surprise** in cell A6, and the column widens to that extent.

● With the mouse pointer on the line that divides column headers B and C, double-click the mouse. This method automatically widens column B to display the longest line of text in that column. Now widen columns C and D.

AUTOCOMPLETE

You will often need to enter the same text label more than once into a worksheet. If Excel detects that you have started typing a text label for the second time into the same column, the handy Autocomplete feature supplies the text for you, highlighted in black. To accept the autocompleted text, press Enter↵ (or Tab⇆). To ignore it, just carry on typing.

ENTERING NUMBERS

Numerical values include integers (whole numbers), decimal numbers (such as 3.25), fractions, monetary amounts, percentages, dates, and times. Excel applies various rules to detect whether a string of characters typed into a cell constitute a numerical value and, if so, what types (integer, date, time etc). If Excel recognizes the typed-in expression as a numerical value, it will align it ranged right in the cell. Excel can perform a calculation on the contents of a cell only if it has been entered and recognized as a numerical value.

1 ENTERING WHOLE NUMBERS

● Just click on the cell that you wish to hold the number and then type.
● In the case of our worked example, click on cell B3 and type in any whole number between 1,000 and 10,000. These are the sales of boxes of Twizzlesticks. You can choose whether or not to type commas in numbers above 1,000. Press [Enter ←] to complete the entry once you have typed your number.
● Now enter further whole numbers (less than 1,000) into cells B4 to B6, pressing [Enter ←] after each entry. These numbers represent the sales of boxes of the company's other products.

B3	▼	X ✓ =	3467	
	A	B	C	
1				
2	Product	Sales (boxes)	Price ($)	Sales
3	Twizzlesticks	3467		
4	Chokky bars			
5	Orange sorbet			
6	Raspberry surprise			
7			Total Revenue	

B6	▼	=	345	
	A	B	C	
1				
2	Product	Sales (boxes)	Price ($)	Sales
3	Twizzlesticks	3467		
4	Chokky bars	893		
5	Orange sorbet	98		
6	Raspberry surprise	345		
7			Total Revenue	

IS IT A NUMBER?

Excel interprets various sorts of expression (not just strings of digits) as numerical values. For example $43, or 43%, or 4.3, or 4,300, or 4.3E+7 (standing for 43,000,000) are all recognized as numerical values. Both −43 and (43) would be recognized as negative or debit numbers.

NUMBER FORMATS

The way in which a number or numerical expression is displayed in a cell is affected by what format that cell has. By default, cells have a "general" number format. When you type any numerical expression into a cell that has this "general" number format, Excel analyzes what type of expression it is and then displays it in an appropriate standard way, usually (though not always exactly) as it is typed. For example, an integer will be displayed as an integer, a date will be given a date format, and so on.

2 ENTERING DECIMALS

● You enter decimal numbers into cells just as you would write them. Simply type a period to represent the decimal point.

● For the worked example, select cell C3 in the Price column, and type a decimal number, such as **6.25**. This is the price of a box of Twizzlesticks, with cents after the decimal point (you'll apply a $ sign later). Press [Enter ⏎].

● A box of Chokky bars is priced at only 74 cents, so enter **0.74** in cell C4 and press [Enter ⏎]. Orange sorbet is a big ticket item at $21.33 a box, so type **21.33** in cell C5.

C3	▾	✕ ✓ =	6.25

	A	B	C	
1				
2	Product	Sales (boxes)	Price ($)	Sale
3	Twizzlesticks	3467	6.25	
4	Chokky bars	893		
5	Orange sorbet	98		
6	Raspberry surprise	345		
7			Total Revenue	
8				
9				

C4	▾	✕ ✓ =	0.74

	A	B	C	
1				
2	Product	Sales (boxes)	Price ($)	Sale
3	Twizzlesticks	3467	6.25	
4	Chokky bars	893	0.74	
5	Orange sorbet	98		
6	Raspberry surprise	345		
7			Total Revenue	
8				
9				
10		Last Updated		
11		Date		
12		Time		

3 ENTERING FRACTIONS

- For fractions, you type the two parts of the fraction divided by a / (forward slash).
- A box of Raspberry surprise ices has the rather curious price tag of $12¾. In cell C6, type the fraction **12 3/4**, i.e., type a 1, a 2, a space, a 3, then a forward slash, and finally a 4. Then press Enter ⏎.

C6	▼ X ✓ =	12 3/4

	A	B	C	
1				
2	Product	Sales (boxes)	Price ($)	Sale
3	Twizzlesticks	3467	6.25	
4	Chokky bars	893	0.74	
5	Orange sorbet	98	21.33	
6	Raspberry surprise	345	12 3/4	
7			Total Revenue	
8				
9				
10		Last Updated		
11		Date		
12		Time		

LONG NUMBERS

If you enter a number that is more than 11 digits long into a cell, it is displayed in abbreviated scientific notation. For example, if you type 3,287,600,000,000, on completing the entry it will be displayed as 3.2876E+12. This means 3.2876×10^{12}. If you want the number to be displayed in full, you must change the format of the cell from general to the number format. To do this, select the cell, choose Cells from the Format menu, click on Number under Category in the Format Cells dialog box, and then click on OK. You may then see a series of ###s in the cell, indicating that your number does not fit in the cell. To fix this, you must widen 🗋 the cell.

ENTERING CURRENCY AND DATES

You can enter monetary amounts into cells by typing the appropriate currency symbol ($ or £) before the number representing the amount. Alternatively it can save time to enter all the amounts without symbols, and then apply the **Currency Style** to all the appropriate cells. A Style is a set of formats (attributes that define how the contents of a cell look or behave). In the case of the Currency Style, this is a very simple set of formats that can be applied with one click of a toolbar button, as you will see. To enter dates and times, you should follow certain conventions to make sure what you type is recorded correctly as a date or time.

263 **Adjust the Column Widths**

1 ENTERING CURRENCY

- In the worked example, you have already entered the product prices in column C. Here's how to apply the Currency Style.
- Select ⌐ cells C3 to C6.
- Click on the Currency Style button on the Formatting toolbar.
- A $ sign is added before each product price.

SINGLE CURRENCY

For Excel to recognize a monetary amount as a number, you are limited to using the currency defined under Regional Settings in your system's Control Panel (normally $ in the US and £ in the UK). If the default symbol is $, typing £35, for example, will not be recognized as a numerical value (but you can change the default if you wish). Cell entries that are not recognized as numerical values cannot be used in Excel calculations.

256 **Selecting Worksheet Cells**

2 ENTERING DATES

● A standard way for entering a date into a cell so that it will be recognized as a date is to type the day, a space, the first three letters of the month, a space, then the year in full.

● Select cell C11, type **7 Jun 2000** and press Enter ⏎ .

● The entry is displayed in the cell as 7-Jun-00, ranged right indicating that it has been recognized as a date.

C11	▼	✕ ✓ =	7 Jun 2000
	A	B	C
1			
2	Product	Sales (boxes)	Price ($)	Sale
3	Twizzlesticks	3467	$ 6.25
4	Chokky bars	893	$ 0.74
5	Orange sorbet	98	$ 21.33
6	Raspberry surprise	345	$ 12.75
7			Total Revenue
8			
9			
10		Last Updated	
11		Date	7 Jun 2000
12		Time	

C12	▼	=	
	A	B	C
1			
2	Product	Sales (boxes)	Price ($)	Sale
3	Twizzlesticks	3467	$ 6.25
4	Chokky bars	893	$ 0.74
5	Orange sorbet	98	$ 21.33
6	Raspberry surprise	345	$ 12.75
7			Total Revenue
8			
9			
10		Last Updated	
11		Date	7-Jun-00
12		Time	
13			

Today's the Day

There is a quick way of entering today's date (as held by your PC's internal clock) into a cell. Select the cell and then press the Ctrl key and ; (semicolon) keys together.

MAKE A DATE!

An alternative way of entering a date is to type the month as a number, the day, then the year, separated by forward slashes, i.e. 6/7/2000 to indicate 7 June 2000. If you were to type June 7 2000, on the other hand, it would not be recognized as a date or, in fact, as any type of numerical expression. Note also that what is displayed in the cells is not always exactly what you typed. Once Excel has recognized what category a numerical value falls into, it sometimes displays it in a standard format for that category rather than showing the figures exactly as typed.

3 ENTERING TIMES

- To enter a time in Excel, type the hour (using the 24-hour clock), a colon, then the minutes past the hour. Alternatively type the hour (using the 12-hour clock), a colon, the minutes past the hour, a space, and then either AM or PM.
- Into cell E12, type **15:45** and then press (Enter ↵).
- Excel displays the time in the cell exactly as you have typed it in.

9			
10		Last Updated	
11		Date	7-Jun-00
12		Time	15:45
13			
14	Proportion of our products that are		
15	Ice cream		
16	Sorbets		

9			
10		Last Updated	
11		Date	7-Jun-00
12		Time	15:45
13			
14	Proportion of our products that are		
15	Ice cream		
16	Sorbets		

4 ENTERING PERCENTAGES

- To enter a percentage, just type a number followed by the percentage sign. You can also convert a decimal number in a cell to a percentage by applying the **Percent Style** to a cell.
- Type **50%** into cell B15 and press (Enter ↵).
- Type **0.25** into cell B16 and press (Enter ↵).
- Click on B16 again, then click on the **Percent Style** button on the Formatting toolbar to convert the decimal to a percentage. Press (Enter ↵). Type **25%** into cell B17, and then save the workbook 🗋.

9			
10		Last Updated	
11		Date	7-Jun-00
12		Time	15:45
13			
14	Proportion of our products that are		
15	Ice cream	50%	
16	Sorbets		
17	Ice milk		

9			
10		Last Updated	
11		Date	7-Jun-00
12		Time	15:45
13			
14	Proportion of our products that are		
15	Ice cream	50%	
16	Sorbets	0.25	
17	Ice milk		
18			
19			
20			

253	**Saving and Naming**

FORMULAS AND CALCULATIONS

For even the simplest Excel worksheets, you will soon want to use formulas. A formula returns (calculates and displays) a value in a cell based on numbers you supply it with, arithmetic operators (such as plus or multiply), and cell references (the numerical values held in other worksheet cells). Much of the power of Excel derives from the use of cell references in formulas, because if you decide later on to change a value in a referenced cell, all formulas in the worksheet that depend on that reference are automatically recalculated.

1 MULTIPLYING TWO CELL VALUES

● If you want a cell to contain the result of multiplying the values of two other cells, you can type an = sign into the cell followed by the addresses of the two referenced cells, separated by the multiplication operator: *.

● In the ice cream sales worksheet, you want cell D3 to contain the revenue from Twizzlestick sales. This is the sales figure (cell B3) multiplied by the price per box (cell C3). So, select cell D3 and type: = **B3*C3**. Press [Enter ←].

● Select cell D3 again and look at the Formula bar. Note that there is a distinction between what D3 actually contains (a formula, as shown in the Formula bar) and what it displays (the value that is calculated by that formula).

	SUM	▼	X ✓ =	=B3*C3	
	A	B	C	D	E
1					
2	Product	Sales (boxes)	Price ($)	Sales Revenue	
3	Twizzlesticks	3467	$ 6.25	=B3*C3	
4	Chokky bars	893	$ 0.74		
5	Orange sorbet	98	$ 21.33		
6	Raspberry surprise	345	$ 12.75		
7			Total Revenue		
8					
9					
10		Last Updated			
11		Date	7-Jun-00		
12		Time	15:45		
13					
14	Proportion of our products that are				
15	Ice cream	50%			
16	Sorbets	25%			

	D3	▼	=	=B3*C3	
	A	B	C	D	E
1					
2	Product	Sales (boxes)	Price ($)	Sales Revenue	
3	Twizzlesticks	3467	$ 6.25	$ 21,668.75	
4	Chokky bars	893	$ 0.74		
5	Orange sorbet	98	$ 21.33		
6	Raspberry surprise	345	$ 12.75		
7			Total Revenue		
8					
9					
10		Last Updated			
11		Date	7-Jun-00		
12		Time	15:45		
13					
14	Proportion of our products that are				
15	Ice cream	50%			
16	Sorbets	25%			

2 FORMULAS USING THE MOUSE

- Instead of typing, you can use the mouse to help you construct formulas. Try this method for entering the formula: =B4*C4 into cell D4.
- Select cell D4 and type the = sign.
- Now click on cell B4. D4 now contains the expression: **=B4**.

	A	B	C	D	E
	SUM	▾	✕ ✓ =	=	
1					
2	Product	Sales (boxes)	Price ($)	Sales Revenue	
3	Twizzlesticks	3467	$ 6.25	$ 21,668.75	
4	Chokky bars	893	$ 0.74	=	
5	Orange sorbet	98	$ 21.33		
6	Raspberry surprise	345	$ 12.75		
7			Total Revenue		
8					

	A	B	C	D	E
	SUM	▾	✕ ✓ =	=B4	
1					
2	Product	Sales (boxes)	Price ($)	Sales Revenue	
3	Twizzlesticks	3467	$ 6.25	$ 21,668.75	
4	Chokky bars	893	$ 0.74	=B4	
5	Orange sorbet	98	$ 21.33		
6	Raspberry surprise	345	$ 12.75		
7			Total Revenue		
8					

- Type an asterisk (*) and then click on cell C4. Finally, press Enter.

	A	B	C	D	E
	SUM	▾	✕ ✓ =	=B4*C4	
1					
2	Product	Sales (boxes)	Price ($)	Sales Revenue	
3	Twizzlesticks	3467	$ 6.25	$ 21,668.75	
4	Chokky bars	893	$ 0.74	=B4*C4	
5	Orange sorbet	98	$ 21.33		
6	Raspberry surprise	345	$ 12.75		
7			Total Revenue		
8					

3 COMPLETING THE FORMULAS

- Now use either entry method to enter the formulas: **=B5*C5** into cell D5 and: **=B6*C6** into cell D6.

	A	B	C	D	E
	SUM	▾	✕ ✓ =	=B5*C5	
1					
2	Product	Sales (boxes)	Price ($)	Sales Revenue	
3	Twizzlesticks	3467	$ 6.25	$ 21,668.75	
4	Chokky bars	893	$ 0.74	$ 660.82	
5	Orange sorbet	98	$ 21.33	=B5*C5	
6	Raspberry surprise	345	$ 12.75		
7			Total Revenue		
8					

4 ADDING VALUES IN SEVERAL CELLS

● To add the values in several cells, you can type an addition formula. For example, to add together the sums in cells D3 to D6, you could use the formula: =D3+D4+D5+D6.

● However, when (as here) all the cells you want to add are adjacent in the same row or column, there is a quicker method – called AutoSum.

● In cell D7, you want to put the sum of the revenues generated by the individual products, held in cells D3 to D6. To do so, select cell D7, and then click the AutoSum button on the Standard toolbar.

● A flashing border appears around cells D3 to D6, and the term: =SUM(D3:D6) appears in cell D7 and in the formula bar. This indicates that a function (a special type of formula) called SUM, which adds the values in cells D3 to D6, is ready to be used in cell D7.

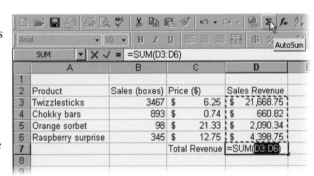

THE EXPONENTIAL OPERATOR

The exponential operator, ^, raises a value to a given power. For example, if you type: =A3^2 into a cell, Excel will take the value in cell A3 and square it. If you type: =A3^3, Excel will cube the value in cell A3. The exponential operator takes precedence over all other operators in Excel.

ARITHMETIC OPERATORS

The five arithmetic operators available are: + (addition), - (subtraction), * (multiplication), / (division), and ^ (raising to the power). These follow the standard order of operations, which can be overruled only by using brackets. For example, if you want to subtract A2 from 5, and then multiply the result by B2, you should type: =(5-A2)*B2.

● Press Enter↵, and the figure for total revenue appears in cell D7.

	A	B	C	D	E
	D8	▼	=		
1					
2	Product	Sales (boxes)	Price ($)	Sales Revenue	
3	Twizzlesticks	3467	$ 6.25	$ 21,668.75	
4	Chokky bars	893	$ 0.74	$ 660.82	
5	Orange sorbet	98	$ 21.33	$ 2,090.34	
6	Raspberry surprise	345	$ 12.75	$ 4,398.75	
7			Total Revenue	$ 28,818.66	
8					
9					

QUICK CALCULATIONS

Excel can be used for one-off calculations. If you want to perform a quick calculation and you don't have a calculator, you can use any cell in Excel instead. Suppose you want to add 23 to 31 and multiply the result by 27. Select a blank cell and type: =(23+31)*27, then press Enter↵. If you don't want to leave your calculation on display, you should then clear the cell 🗋.

SIMPLE FORMATTING

Even the most elementary worksheets may benefit from some basic formatting to help clarify which parts are headings and which are data, and to improve the visual attractiveness of the worksheet. The full range of Excel's formatting features could be the subject of a book in itself. The examples given below are some simple formatting ideas that can be applied with buttons on the Formatting toolbar.

1 EMPHASIZING HEADINGS

● It is common to distinguish column and row labels. One way of doing this is to emphasize them by using a bold, colored typeface.
● Select cells A2 to D2. Hold down the Ctrl key, and then click on cell B10.

	A	B	C	D	E
	B10	▼	= Last Updated		
1					
2	Product	Sales (boxes)	Price ($)	Sales Revenue	
3	Twizzlesticks	3467	$ 6.25	$ 21,668.75	
4	Chokky bars	893	$ 0.74	$ 660.82	
5	Orange sorbet	98	$ 21.33	$ 2,090.34	
6	Raspberry surprise	345	$ 12.75	$ 4,398.75	
7			Total Revenue	$ 28,818.66	
8					
9					
10		Last Updated			
11		Date	7-Jun-00		
12		Time	15:45		

🗋 | 305 | **Clearing Cells**

- Click the **Bold** button on the Formatting toolbar.
- Now click the arrow next to the **Font Color** button.
- Choose a shade of blue from the palette.
- Now select cells A3 to A6 and A15 to A17, and also make them bold, but using a different color.

Font Color button •

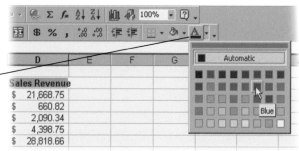

READY-MADE FORMATS

For some formatting ideas, select the whole table and choose the **AutoFormat** command from the **Format** menu. In the **AutoFormat** dialog box, browse through the options. If you like one, choose it and then click on **OK**.

2 ADDING A BORDER

- You can separate off distinct parts of a worksheet with a border. Here it would make sense to put a line under the main product sales data.
- Select cells B6 to D6.
- Click the small arrow next to the **Borders** button.
- Choose a thick bottom border from the palette.

TRANSFERRING FORMATS

You can copy a format from one cell to another without affecting the cell's contents. Select the cell whose format you want to copy, click the **Format Painter** button (a paintbrush) on the Standard toolbar, then click in the cell to which you want the copied format transferred.

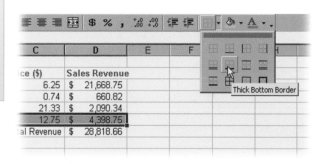

Fill Color button •

3 HIGHLIGHTING INFORMATION

● It is often worth highlighting important information with a background color.

● Select cell D7, which represents Fantasy Ices' revenue to date.

● Click the small down arrow to the right of the **Fill Color** button.

● Choose a light shade from the palette.

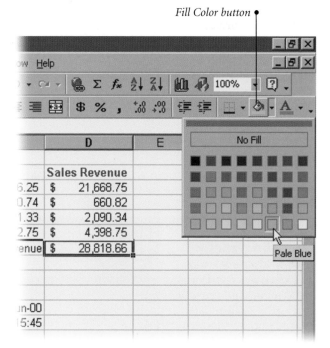

BUILDING WORKSHEETS

To build Excel worksheets fast and easily, you need to know about methods for copying data, creating simple data series, and adding new rows, columns, and cells to your worksheet.

COPYING DATA BY FILLING

Putting the same data into adjacent cells is a common Excel task. Instead of typing the data into every cell, you can type it once, and then copy it by using methods called **Fill** and **AutoFill**. To practice these techniques, here's an example, which consists of setting up an appointment diary for the directors of Fantasy Ices. Open the "fantasyices.xls" workbook, click on Sheet2 and rename this sheet **Diary**.

1 ENTER SOME TEXT LABELS
● Into cell A1, type **Morning Appointments July 31-August 4**. Type **Director** into cell A2, **Mr Twizz** into cell A4, and **Mrs Stick** into cell A11.

2 SELECT A RANGE OF CELLS TO FILL
● To perform a fill, select the cell(s) you want to copy, then extend the selection into the cells where you want the copied data to appear. In this case, you want to copy Mr Twizz into cells A5 to A8, so select the whole range A4 to A8.

NO MULTIPLE SELECTIONS

You cannot use Fill or AutoFill to copy data from a single cell (or range of cells) to multiple nonadjacent cells or ranges of cells. You can only fill data into groups of adjacent cells.

3 USE THE FILL COMMAND

● Choose **Fill** from the **Edit** menu. A submenu appears to the right of the **Fill** command. Choose **Down** from the **Fill** submenu.

● The range of cells from A4 to A8 now fills with the name of Mr Twizz.

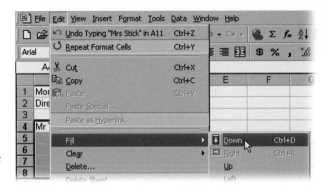

4 SELECT A CELL FOR AUTOFILL

● An alternative to **Fill** is **AutoFill**, which involves dragging the mouse rather than choosing a menu command.

● Select the cell or cells that you want to copy, in this example, cell A11 (Mrs Stick).

● At the bottom right-hand corner of the selected cell is a square called the fill handle. Move the mouse pointer over the fill handle until it becomes a cross. Now hold down the mouse button.

● Fill handle

FILLING A BLOCK OF CELLS

You cannot fill from a single cell into a block of cells (2 cells wide x 2 cells deep or bigger) in a single operation. Two operations are required to do this. First select the range into which data is to be copied, making sure that the cell containing the data to be copied is at one corner. Then choose a sequence of commands, such as **Fill Down** followed by **Fill Right**.

5 DEFINE THE FILL RANGE

● Move the mouse pointer around the worksheet. You will see that different ranges of adjacent cells are surrounded by a border. This is the range into which your cell selection will be copied. Drag the mouse until the border surrounds the range A11 to A15.

6 COMPLETE THE AUTOFILL

● Now release the mouse button. The label Mrs Stick is copied from cell A11 into cells A12 to A15.

FILLING IN ALL DIRECTIONS

The **Fill** command allows you to fill data into a range in any direction (down, right, left, and up). Choosing **Fill Down** in the submenu will copy the values in the cells on the top edge of the selected range into the rest of the range; choosing **Fill Right** will copy the values on the left-hand edge of the selected range into the rest of the range; and so on.

CREATING DATA SERIES

The AutoFill feature is one of Excel's "smart" features and can be used for more than just copying data into cell ranges. It can also be used to create data series across cell ranges, for example series of dates (Jan 1, Jan 2, Jan 3...), months (Jan, Feb, Mar...), days of the week (Mon, Tue, Wed...), and number series (1, 2, 3... or 5, 10, 15... etc). This can be time-saving when building certain types of worksheet.

1 CREATING A SERIES OF DAYS

● Into the Diary worksheet, type **Week Day** into cell B3, press Enter ↵, then type **Mon** (or **Monday**) into cell B4 and press Enter ↵ again.

• Now select cell B4 again, put your mouse pointer over the fill handle, and drag the mouse pointer so that the gray AutoFill border surrounds the whole range B4 to B8.

	A	B	C	D	E
1	Morning Appointments July 31 - August 4				
2	Director				
3		Week Day			
4	Mr Twizz	Mon			
5	Mr Twizz				
6	Mr Twizz				
7	Mr Twizz				
8	Mr Twizz				
9					
10		Fri			

• Release the mouse button. Instead of copying Mon into cells B5 to B8, AutoFill has filled these cells with the other days of the week (Tue, Wed, etc), which is what you want.

	A	B	C	D	E
1	Morning Appointments July 31 - August 4				
2	Director				
3		Week Day			
4	Mr Twizz	Mon			
5	Mr Twizz	Tue			
6	Mr Twizz	Wed			
7	Mr Twizz	Thu			
8	Mr Twizz	Fri			
9					
10					
11	Mrs Stick				

Don't want a series?

If you want to AutoFill a value like Jan, Tuesday, 9:00, or 12 Apr 2000, into a range of cells without producing a series, hold down the Ctrl key on the keyboard as you drag the fill handle. Doing this guarantees that you will get a simple fill instead of a series.

OTHER SERIES

You can also use AutoFill to produce series of months (Jan, Feb, Mar... , or January, February, March...), number series (for example, 1, 2, 3, 4... , or 10, 20, 30, 40...) and general series such as Period 1, Period 2, Period 3 etc. For all series except months, dates, days of the week, and hour series, you must type the first two items in the series that you want to create into adjacent cells, select them, and then drag the fill handle in order for the series to be incremented in the selected cells.

2 CREATING A SERIES OF DATES

● Type **Date** into cell C3 and 31 July 2000 into cell C4. Press Enter ↵.

● Select cell C4 again. Drag the fill handle to encompass the range C4 to C8.

● On releasing the mouse button, cells C5 to C8 fill with dates from 1 August to 4 August – again, exactly what you want.

	A	B	C	D	E	F	G
1	Morning Appointments July 31 - August 4						
2	Director						
3		Week Day	Date				
4	Mr Twizz	Mon	31 July 2000				
5	Mr Twizz	Tue					
6	Mr Twizz	Wed					
7	Mr Twizz	Thu					

	A	B	C	D	E	F	G
1	Morning Appointments July 31 - August 4						
2	Director						
3		Week Day	Date				
4	Mr Twizz	Mon	31-Jul-00				
5	Mr Twizz	Tue					
6	Mr Twizz	Wed					
7	Mr Twizz	Thu					
8	Mr Twizz	Fri					
9				4-Aug-00			
10							

3 CREATING A SERIES OF TIMES

● Sometimes you need to provide AutoFill with the first two values in a series in order to end up with the series that you want.

● Type **9:00 AM** into cell D3 and **9:30 AM** into cell E3, then select both cells.

● Drag the fill handle across to G3 and release.

● The time series is extended into F3 and G3.

	A	B	C	D	E	F	G
1	Morning Appointments July 31 - August 4						
2	Director						
3		Week Day	Date	9:00 AM	9:30 AM		
4	Mr Twizz	Mon	31-Jul-00				
5	Mr Twizz	Tue	1-Aug-00				
6	Mr Twizz	Wed	2-Aug-00				
7	Mr Twizz	Thu	3-Aug-00				

	=	9:00:00 AM					
B	C	D	E	F	G	H
ppointments July 31 - August 4						
Week Day	Date	9:00 AM	9:30 AM			
Mon	31-Jul-00					
Tue	1-Aug-00				10:30 AM	
Wed	2-Aug-00					

D3		=	9:00:00 AM						
	A	B	C	D	E	F	G	H	I	J
1	Morning Appointments July 31 - August 4									
2	Director									
3		Week Day	Date	9:00 AM	9:30 AM	10:00 AM	10:30 AM			
4	Mr Twizz	Mon	31-Jul-00							
5	Mr Twizz	Tue	1-Aug-00							
6	Mr Twizz	Wed	2-Aug-00							
7	Mr Twizz	Thu	3-Aug-00							
8	Mr Twizz	Fri	4-Aug-00							

COPYING AND PASTING

Copying and pasting is a technique used in many computer applications, not simply in Excel worksheets. All copy and paste operations work in the same way. You choose some data that you want to copy, and then use the **Copy** command. The original data stays where it is and the copy of the data is placed in a particular part of your computer's memory called the Clipboard. You then select where you would like the copied data to appear in your worksheet, and use the **Paste** command. The data is now copied from the Clipboard and placed in the chosen target area. You can repeat the **Paste** command to place the copied data over several different target areas if you wish. **Copy** and **Paste** commands can be carried out either via drop-down menus, toolbar buttons, or keyboard shortcuts.

1 COPYING A SINGLE CELL

● In your Fantasy Ices Diary worksheet, you want to set up three appointments for a Ms Black to meet with Mr Twizz.

● Type **Ms Black** into cell E4 and press Enter⏎.

● Select cell E4 again, and then choose **Copy** from the **Edit** menu.

● You will see a flashing outline appear around cell E4, indicating that its contents have been copied to the Clipboard.

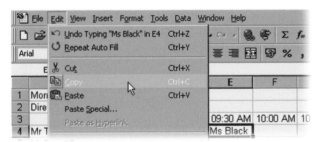

2 PASTING THE DATA

● Select cell E7 and then choose **Paste** from the **Edit** menu. Ms Black is pasted into cell E7.
● Select cell F8 and repeat the **Paste** command. Press the [Esc] key to complete the copy/paste operation.

KEYBOARD SHORTCUTS

There are keyboard shortcuts for the Copy command and Paste command. To copy, hold down the [Ctrl] key and press C. To paste, hold down the [Ctrl] key and press V. These shortcuts are used universally across all PC applications, so they are worth remembering!

Want to move, not copy?

If you want to move data in a worksheet, that is, you want to place it in a new location without leaving a copy in the original location, this can be carried out by an operation called cut and paste ⌐.

3 COPYING A BLOCK OF CELLS

● You now want to copy and paste the whole of Mr Twizz's diary to Mrs Stick's part of the diary. When pasting a block of data, you need only select the top left-hand cell of the target area for the paste.
● Select the block B3 to G8 and click the **Copy** button on the Standard toolbar.

4 PASTING THE COPIED BLOCK

● Select cell B10 – the top left-hand cell of your target area – and click the **Paste** button on the Standard toolbar.

● The copied data is pasted over the range B10 to G15. Your "fantasyices.xls" workbook can now be saved.

Pasted cells ●

MULTIPLE PASTES

To carry out multiple pastes after a **Copy** command, hold down the Ctrl key and then select, one by one, the various target cells for your pastes. You then simply choose **Paste** from the **Edit** menu. Alternatively, click the **Paste** button on the Standard toolbar.

Pasting Care

When copying and pasting a block of cells, if you try to select the whole target area for the paste but get the size wrong, Excel will come up with an error message, saying that the Copy and Paste areas don't match. It's generally better to select just the top left-hand cell of the target area. But always be careful when pasting blocks of cells – there is a risk of overpasting existing data in the worksheet, and you get no warning if this is about to happen.

COPYING BY DRAG AND DROP

Drag and drop is another very useful method for copying data from one cell or block of cells to another part of the worksheet. It is a quick method, because it is performed by dragging with the mouse rather than by choosing menu commands or toolbar buttons. However, it does require a little practice.

1 COPYING A SINGLE CELL

● In the Diary sheet of the "fantasyices.xls" workbook, you can practice some drags and drops after filling in some more dates for the directors of Fantasy Ices.

● Type **Dr Green** into cell D6. Position your mouse pointer over the bottom border of cell D6, and it turns into an arrow. Hold down the mouse button.

● Hold down the [Ctrl] key. A + sign appears next to the mouse pointer.

● Drag the mouse so that the mouse pointer moves down the worksheet. A gray rectangular outline, the same size as a cell, moves down the screen following the mouse pointer and the + sign. A yellow label with a cell address (like D8) on it also travels with the mouse pointer. This continually updates and indicates which cell the gray outline has reached.

	A	B	C	D	E
1	Morning Appointments July 31 - August 4				
2	Director				
3		Week Day	Date	9:00 AM	9:30 AM
4	Mr Twizz	Mon	31-Jul-00		Ms Black
5	Mr Twizz	Tue	1-Aug-00		
6	Mr Twizz	Wed	2-Aug-00	Dr Green	
7	Mr Twizz	Thu	3-Aug-00		Ms Black
8	Mr Twizz	Fri	4-Aug-00		
9					

	A	B	C	D	E
1	Morning Appointments July 31 - August 4				
2	Director				
3		Week Day	Date	9:00 AM	9:30 AM
4	Mr Twizz	Mon	31-Jul-00		Ms Black
5	Mr Twizz	Tue	1-Aug-00		
6	Mr Twizz	Wed	2-Aug-00	Dr Green	
7	Mr Twizz	Thu	3-Aug-00		Ms Black
8	Mr Twizz	Fri	4-Aug-00		
9					

	A	B	C	D	E
1	Morning Appointments July 31 - August 4				
2	Director				
3		Week Day	Date	09:00 AM	09:30 AM
4	Mr Twizz	Mon	31-Jul-00		Ms Black
5	Mr Twizz	Tue	01-Aug-00		
6	Mr Twizz	Wed	02-Aug-00	Dr Green	
7	Mr Twizz	Thu	03-Aug-00		Ms Black
8	Mr Twizz	Fri	04-Aug-00		
9					D8
10		Week Day	Date	09:00 AM	09:30 AM

● Drag until the gray outline reaches cell D13. Now for the "drop." Release the mouse button and finally the [Ctrl] key. Dr Green is copied to cell D13.

11	Mrs Stick	Mon	31-Jul-00		Ms Black	
12	Mrs Stick	Tue	1-Aug-00			
13	Mrs Stick	Wed	2-Aug-00	Dr Green		
14	Mrs Stick	Thu	3-Aug-00		Ms Black	
15	Mrs Stick	Fri	4-Aug-00			Ms Black
16						

2 COPYING A BLOCK OF CELLS

● You can drag and drop blocks of cells just as easily as single cells. Try this simple exercise.

● Select the range D4 to E6, and move the mouse pointer over the bottom border of the selection until you see the pointer turn into an arrow.

● Hold down the mouse button and the [Ctrl] key, and drag the mouse to the right until the gray rectangular outline surrounds the range F4 to G6. Then release the mouse button and [Ctrl] key.

● The dragged range gets pasted into F4 to G6.

	A	B	C	D	E	F
1	Morning Appointments July 31 - August 4					
2	Director					
3		Week Day	Date	09:00 AM	09:30 AM	10:00 AM	1(
4	Mr Twizz	Mon	31-Jul-00		Ms Black	
5	Mr Twizz	Tue	01-Aug-00			
6	Mr Twizz	Wed	02-Aug-00	Dr Green		
7	Mr Twizz	Thu	03-Aug-00		Ms Black	

	A	B	C	D	E	F
1	Morning Appointments July 31 - August 4					
2	Director					
3		Week Day	Date	09:00 AM	09:30 AM	10:00 AM	1(
4	Mr Twizz	Mon	31-Jul-00		Ms Black	
5	Mr Twizz	Tue	01-Aug-00			
6	Mr Twizz	Wed	02-Aug-00	Dr Green		
7	Mr Twizz	Thu	03-Aug-00		Ms Black F4:G6	

	B	C	D	E	F	G	H
	pointments July 31 - August 4						
	Week Day	Date	09:00 AM	09:30 AM	10:00 AM	10:30 AM	
	Mon	31-Jul-00		Ms Black		Ms Black	
	Tue	01-Aug-00					
	Wed	02-Aug-00	Dr Green		Dr Green		
	Thu	03-Aug-00		Ms Black			

Control to Copy

If you forget to hold down the [Ctrl] key during a drag and drop operation, you will find that you move the dragged data instead of copying it.

WHEN TO DRAG AND DROP

Drag and drop is just one way of copying data. The drag and drop technique in Excel is most useful for copying data over short distances on a worksheet. For copying data over longer distances, or from one worksheet to another, use the copy and paste technique. For copying from a cell to an adjacent cell (or cells), it is better to use **Fill** or **AutoFill**.

INSERTING NEW COLUMNS, ROWS, AND CELLS

It is in the nature of worksheets for them to grow and evolve over time, and it is common to extend them by adding new columns, rows, or individual cells as the need arises. When you do this, you have to shift some of the existing cells, together with their contents, to the right or further down in the worksheet in order to create room for the new cells. This usually causes no problems, although it does require some thought, especially when inserting individual cells or groups of cells.

1 INSERTING A COLUMN

● The company directors of Fantasy Ices want to make some 8:30 appointments to meet up with each other. This requires the creation of a new column in the Diary worksheet.

● Select column D by clicking on the column D header button. This is where you want the new column to appear.

● Choose **Columns** from the **Insert** menu.

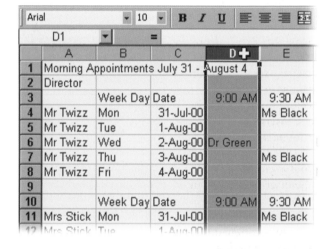

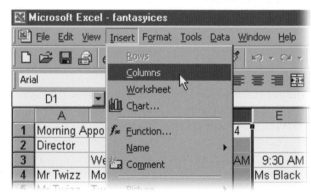

- A new blank column is inserted and the original contents of column D, and the contents of columns to the right of column D, are all automatically shifted one column to the right.
- Now type **8:30 AM** into cell D3 and copy this time to cell D10.
- Add some appropriate appointments to column D.

D1		▼	=	
A	B	C	D	E
1 Morning Appointments July 31 - August 4				
2 Director				
3		Week Day Date		9:00 AM
4 Mr Twizz	Mon	31-Jul-00		
5 Mr Twizz	Tue	1-Aug-00		
6 Mr Twizz	Wed	2-Aug-00		Dr Green
7 Mr Twizz	Thu	3-Aug-00		
8 Mr Twizz	Fri	4-Aug-00		

6 Mr Twizz	Wed	2-Aug-00	Mrs Stick	Dr Green
7 Mr Twizz	Thu	3-Aug-00	Mrs Stick	
8 Mr Twizz	Fri	4-Aug-00		
9				
10		Week Day Date	8:30 AM	9:00 AM
11 Mrs Stick	Mon	31-Jul-00		
12 Mrs Stick	Tue	1-Aug-00		
13 Mrs Stick	Wed	2-Aug-00	Mr Twizz	Dr Green

6 Mr Twizz	Wed	2-Aug-00		Dr Green
7 Mr Twizz	Thu	3-Aug-00		
8 Mr Twizz	Fri	4-Aug-00		
9				
10		Week Day Date	8:30 AM	9:00 AM
11 Mrs Stick	Mon	31-Jul-00		
12 Mrs Stick	Tue	1-Aug-00		
13 Mrs Stick	Wed	2-Aug-00		Dr Green
14 Mrs Stick	Thu	3-Aug-00		
15 Mrs Stick	Fri	4-Aug-00		
16				

CONTEXT SENSITIVE MENUS

Note that Excel's drop-down menus are context-sensitive. After you have selected a column in a worksheet, the **Insert Rows** command is not a feasible command, and so it is grayed out on the **Insert** menu. When a row or rows is selected, the **Insert Columns** command is similarly grayed out.

WHAT SHIFTS WHERE?

Remember that when you choose to insert a new column or columns, they are inserted at the left-hand side of the column(s) that you selected on the worksheet before choosing **Insert Columns**. When you insert some new row(s) they are inserted above the row(s) that you selected on the worksheet. There is no choice as to the direction in which columns or rows get shifted – this choice only appears when you insert one or more cells.

2 INSERTING TWO ROWS

● Mr Twizz wants to make some Saturday and Sunday appointments. This means adding two more rows to the worksheet.

● Select rows 9 and 10. This is where you want the new rows to appear.

● Choose **Rows** from the **Insert** menu.

● New blank rows are inserted and the original contents of rows 9, 10, 11 etc, are all automatically shifted two rows down.

● Select the range A8 to C8 and AutoFill these cells down to A10-C10. Enter some weekend appointments for Mr Twizz by typing **Mr Brown** into cells E9 and F10.

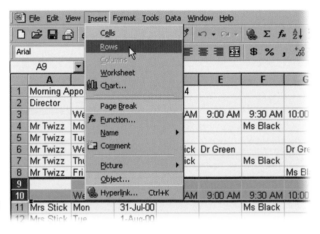

AutoFilled cells ●

3 INSERTING A FEW CELLS

● Mr Twizz wants to make some extra appointments for 9:15, but Mrs Stick doesn't need to. You want to add some individual cells, but not a whole row or column, to Mr Twizz's part of the worksheet.

● Select the range F3-F10.

● Choose **Cells** from the **Insert** menu.

● The **Insert** dialog box appears. To create room for your new cells, you have the choice of shifting the existing range F3-F10 (and all cells to the right) further to the right; or to shift F3-F10 (and all cells below) down. You want to shift the existing cells to the right, so just click on **OK**.

● Now type **9:15 AM** into cell F3, and fill in some 9:15 appointments with Ms Orange in cells F6 and F7 for Mr Twizz. Save your "fantasyices.xls" workbook.

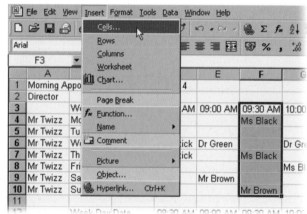

COPYING AND INSERTING

Copying and inserting consists of a combination of an Insert operation and a copy and paste operation. On occasions you will want to make a copy of a cell or a whole range of cells and place this copy on the worksheet but without pasting over and losing existing contents. So you need to create some extra room in the worksheet to take the copy. You could create this extra space with an Insert command, and then do a copy and paste. However, a copy and insert operation is quicker, as it achieves the same result with a smaller number of actions.

1 COPY/INSERT IN SEVERAL ROWS

- A new Director, Mr Bloggs, has joined Fantasy Ices. He needs a space for his own appointments in the Diary sheet of "fantasyices.xls," and his first appointments will be the same as Mr Twizz's.
- Select the rows you want to copy and insert – in this case, rows 3 to 11. Then click on the **Copy** button.
- Select a row where you would like the copied data to be inserted – in this case row 12.
- Choose **Copied Cells** from the Insert menu. The copied data is inserted into the worksheet.
- Now type **Mr Bloggs** into cell A13 and AutoFill down to cell A19.
Mr Bloggs now has his own section of the appointments diary.

COPY, DRAG, AND INSERT!

It is possible to copy, drag, and insert cells through a technique similar to copy, drag, and drop ⬁. To copy, drag, and insert, select the cell or cells to copy, and then hold down both ⏏ Ctrl and ⬆ Shift. Drag your selection to the insert/paste target area. You will see a gray outline shape follow the mouse pointer. If you want existing cells in the worksheet to move right when the insert happens, place this gray outline to the left of the target area. If you want existing cells to move down, place the gray outline above the target area. Then release the mouse button and both keyboard keys.

2 COPY/INSERT A SINGLE CELL

- At the other extreme, try copy/inserting a single cell. Dr Green needs an extra appointment with Mr Twizz at 9:30 AM on Thursday. This time slot is already taken up by Ms Black. No matter – with a copy/insert, Dr Green can have the 9:30 AM time slot and the appointment with Ms Black can be put back by half an hour.
- Select cell E6 and click on the **Copy** button.
- Click on cell G7 (the intended time slot) and choose **Copied Cells** from the **Insert** menu.
- When the **Insert Paste** dialog appears, choose **Shift cells right** and click on **OK**.
- Dr Green gets her 9:30 AM appointment with Mr Twizz and Ms Black's appointment is put back to 10:00 AM.

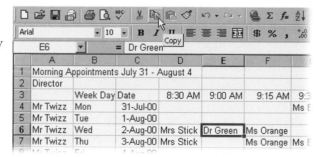

EDITING WORKSHEETS

This chapter is about editing existing worksheets. You can change the contents of cells, check spellings, move cells, add comments, remove cell contents, or delete the cells altogether.

CHANGING CELL CONTENTS

You can change the contents of a cell in its entirety or only part of the contents. For example, you can shorten a text label, or change the month but keep the original day. There is a single straightforward method for changing all of a cell's contents, and there are two distinct methods for making partial changes. These two methods are called "in-cell editing", and "editing in the formula bar." The examples given below are applied to the Sales worksheet of "fantasyices.xls."

1 CHANGING A TEXT LABEL

● The directors of Fantasy Ices have decided to relaunch Twizzlesticks under a new name.

● Select cell A3 – the cell that contains the Twizzlesticks label.

● Type the new name – **Kooltwists**. Press Enter ←┘. Note that the new label takes on the same format as the old label – when you change a cell's contents, it retains its format.

A3		▼	=	Twizzlesticks	
	A		B	C	Sal
1					
2	Product		Sales (boxes)	Price ($)	Sal
3	Twizzlesticks		3467	$ 6.25	$
4	Chokky bars		893	$ 0.74	$
5	Orange sorbet		98	$ 21.33	$
6	Raspberry surprise		345	$ 12.75	$
7				Total Revenue	$

A4		▼	=	Chokky bars	
	A		B	C	Sal
1					
2	Product		Sales (boxes)	Price ($)	Sal
3	Kooltwists		3467	$ 6.25	$
4	Chokky bars		893	$ 0.74	$
5	Orange sorbet		98	$ 21.33	$
6	Raspberry surprise		345	$ 12.75	$
7				Total Revenue	$
8					

2 ALTERING FORMULA VALUES

- There's an update required to the sales data for orange sorbets – that is, to the value held in cell B5.
- Select cell B5 and revise the number for the sales of boxes of orange sorbets.
- Press Enter←. Note that when you confirm the change to cell B5, the value in cell D5 (the sales revenue from orange sorbets) and D7 (total revenue) also change. This makes sense, but how has it happened?
- Click on cell D5 and look in the Formula bar. When there is a formula in the active cell, it shows in the Formula bar. Cell D5 contains the formula: **=B5*C5**. When you change any cell value referenced by a formula, Excel automatically updates the value in the cell containing that formula. Because you changed B5, Excel has automatically updated D5, which contains a formula referencing B5.
- Click on cell D7. It contains the formula: **=SUM(D3:D6)**. Because cell D5 (which is contained in the referenced range D3:D6) changed, the value in D7 updated as well.

B5 =145

	A	B	C	D
1				
2	Product	Sales (boxes)	Price ($)	Sales Revenue
3	Kooltwists	3467	$ 6.25	$ 21,668.75
4	Chokky bars	893	$ 0.74	$ 660.82
5	Orange sorbet	145	$ 21.33	$ 2,090.34
6	Raspberry surprise	345	$ 12.75	$ 4,398.75
7			Total Revenue	$ 28,818.66
8				
9				

B6 =345

	A	B	C	D
1				
2	Product	Sales (boxes)	Price ($)	Sales Revenue
3	Kooltwists	3467	$ 6.25	$ 21,668.75
4	Chokky bars	893	$ 0.74	$ 660.82
5	Orange sorbet	145	$ 21.33	$ 3,092.85
6	Raspberry surprise	345	$ 12.75	$ 4,398.75
7			Total Revenue	$ 29,821.17
8				
9				
10		Last Updated		

D5 =B5*C5

	A	B	C	D
1				
2	Product	Sales (boxes)	Price ($)	Sales Revenue
3	Kooltwists	3467	$ 6.25	$ 21,668.75
4	Chokky bars	893	$ 0.74	$ 660.82
5	Orange sorbet	145	$ 21.33	$ 3,092.85
6	Raspberry surprise	345	$ 12.75	$ 4,398.75
7			Total Revenue	$ 29,821.17
8				
9				
10		Last Updated		

D7 =SUM(D3:D6)

	A	B	C	D
1				
2	Product	Sales (boxes)	Price ($)	Sales Revenue
3	Kooltwists	3467	$ 6.25	$ 21,668.75
4	Chokky bars	893	$ 0.74	$ 660.82
5	Orange sorbet	145	$ 21.33	$ 3,092.85
6	Raspberry surprise	345	$ 12.75	$ 4,398.75
7			Total Revenue	$ 29,821.17
8				
9				
10		Last Updated		

3 IN-CELL EDITING OF TEXT LABELS

● Chokky bars are getting a name-change to plain "Chocolate bars." You can make this change by means of an in-cell edit.

● Double-click in the middle of cell A4. This prepares the cell for in-cell editing. The cell is ready to edit if you see an insertion point (small vertical bar) flashing between two letters in the cell.

● Click the mouse pointer before the first **k** in **Chokky**, then hold down the mouse button and drag the mouse to the right to highlight the string of letters **kky**. This is the part of the label that you want to replace. Now release the mouse button.

● Type **clate** and press Enter ↵ to leave **Choclate bars** (don't worry that you've introduced a deliberate spelling mistake! – you'll see why shortly).

● Now change **Raspberry surprise** to **Raspberry sundar** (again don't worry about the spelling mistake).

	Arial	10	**B** *I* <u>U</u>	
A4	✕ ✓ =	Chokky bars		

	A	B	C	
1				
2	Product	Sales (boxes)	Price ($)	Sal
3	Kooltwists	3467	$ 6.25	$
4	Chokky bars	893	$ 0.74	$
5	Orange sorbet	145	$ 21.33	$
6	Raspberry surprise	345	$ 12.75	$

	Arial	10	**B** *I* <u>U</u>	
	✕ ✓ =	Chokky bars		

	A	B	C	
1				
2	Product	Sales (boxes)	Price ($)	Sal
3	Kooltwists	3467	$ 6.25	$
4	Cho**kky** bars	893	$ 0.74	$
5	Orange sorbet	145	$ 21.33	$
6	Raspberry surprise	345	$ 12.75	$

A4	✕ ✓ =	Choclate bars		

	A	B	C	
1				
2	Product	Sales (boxes)	Price ($)	Sale
3	Kooltwists	3467	$ 6.25	$
4	Choclate bars	893	$ 0.74	$
5	Orange sorbet	145	$ 21.33	$
6	Raspberry surprise	345	$ 12.75	$
7			Total Revenue	$

A6	✕ ✓ =	Raspberry sundar		

	A	B	C	
1				
2	Product	Sales (boxes)	Price ($)	Sale
3	Kooltwists	3467	$ 6.25	$
4	Choclate bars	893	$ 0.74	$
5	Orange sorbet	145	$ 21.33	$
6	Raspberry sundar		$ 12.75	$
7			Total Revenue	$

4 EDITING IN THE FORMULA BAR

● Now click on cell C11, which contains the date 7 June 2000. You want to change this date to 15 August 2000.

● Place your mouse pointer in the Formula bar and you will see that it changes into an I-shaped cursor.

● Click to the right of the figure **7**, press down on the mouse button, and drag the pointer to the left to highlight the string of characters **6/7**. This is the part that you want to change. Now release the mouse button.

● Type **8/15** and finally press Enter⏎ .

On Second Thoughts...

If, while making a change to a cell, you decide not to make the change after all, you can abort the change by pressing the Esc key.

	A	B	C	D
1				
2	Product	Sales (boxes)	Price ($)	Sales Revenue
3	Kooltwists	3467	$ 6.25	$ 21,668.75
4	Choclate bars	893	$ 0.74	$ 660.82
5	Orange sorbet	145	$ 21.33	$ 3,092.85
6	Raspberry sundar	345	$ 12.75	$ 4,398.75
7			Total Revenue	$ 29,821.17
8				
9				
10		Last Updated		
11		Date	7-Jun-00	

Arial · 10 · **B** *I* U ≡ ≡ ≡

C11 = 6/7/2000

Formula Bar

	A	B	C
1			
2	Product	Sales (boxes)	Price ($)	Sale
3	Kooltwists	3467	$ 6.25	$
4	Choclate bars	893	$ 0.74	$
5	Orange sorbet	145	$ 21.33	$
6	Raspberry sundar	345	$ 12.75	$

Arial · 10 · **B** *I* U ≡ ≡ ≡

C11 ✕ ✓ = 6/7/2000

	A	B	C
1			
2	Product	Sales (boxes)	Price ($)	Sale
3	Kooltwists	3467	$ 6.25	$
4	Choclate bars	893	$ 0.74	$

Arial · 10 · **B** *I* U ≡ ≡ ≡

C11 ✕ ✓ = 8/15/2000

	A	B	C
1			
2	Product	Sales (boxes)	Price ($)	Sale
3	Kooltwists	3467	$ 6.25	$
4	Choclate bars	893	$ 0.74	$
5	Orange sorbet	145	$ 21.33	$
6	Raspberry sundar	345	$ 12.75	$
7			Total Revenue	$

CHECKING SPELLING

Excel provides a tool for checking the spelling of the text in your worksheets. The Spelling tool works by checking the spelling of each word against a built-in dictionary. When the Spelling tool finds a mistake, it offers you the choice of correcting the error or not, and in most cases will suggest the correct spelling. You have the opportunity to add specialist words, which Excel doesn't recognize, to your own custom dictionary so that the Spelling tool doesn't query them again.

1 STARTING THE SPELLING TOOL

● The Spelling tool checks each word in each cell, row by row, starting from the active cell. Unless a range of cells is selected when you check spelling, the tool checks the entire work-sheet, including both cell values and comments.

● To check the whole worksheet, select its top left-hand cell. In this case, select cell A1 of the Sales worksheets in "fantasyices.xls." Click the **Spelling** button on the Standard toolbar.

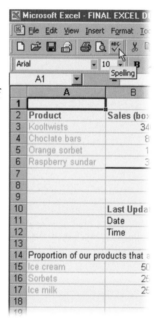

Habitual Misspeller

If there is a particular word that you habitually mistype or misspell, try putting it on an AutoCorrect list. This feature automatically corrects specified misspellings whenever you make them. To add to the AutoCorrect list, choose AutoCorrect from the Tools menu. Type your habitual misspell in the Replace: box, then the correct spelling in the With box, and click on OK.

DON'T EXPECT THE IMPOSSIBLE

Remember that the Spelling tool cannot pick up a typing error if the mistype gives rise to another, correctly spelled, word. For example, if you mistype "product" as "produce," the Spelling tool will not see this as an error! So you should do a visual check after using the Spelling tool.

2 ADDING TO YOUR DICTIONARY

● The Spelling tool displays the **Spelling** dialog box when a word is found that it doesn't recognize. If you want to add this word to your own custom dictionary so that it is not queried again, check that **CUSTOM.DIC** appears in the **Add words to** box, then click on the **Add** button.

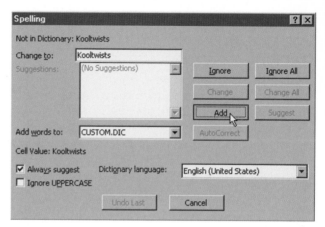

3 SPELLING TOOL SUGGESTIONS

● When the Spelling tool comes across **Choclate**, it suggests that this should be changed to **Chocolate**. You agree, so click on the **Change** button.

4 ACCEPTING A SPELLING

● When the Spelling tool comes across **sundar**, it provides various spelling suggestions of what you meant to type. In this case, click on **sundae** in the **Suggestions** box, and then click on the Change button.

● Once the Spelling tool has checked the entire sheet for misspellings, it comes up with a task completion message. Just click on **OK**.

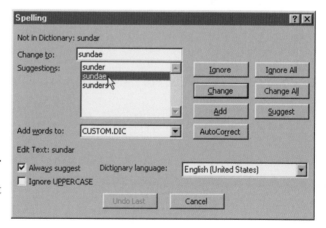

MOVING AND SWAPPING DATA

Moving data is similar to copying data, except that you leave no copy of the data behind in its original location. You can move data by cut and paste, or by drag and drop. These techniques are similar to copy and paste and copying by drag and drop. You can also carry out cut/inserts, which are similar to copy/inserts; but again they leave no copy of your original data on the worksheet.

MOVING BY CUT AND PASTE

● For a cut and paste, you first select a cell or cells that you want to move and then carry out a **Cut** command. You then choose a target area for the move and carry out a **Paste** command.

● In the Diary Sheet of your "fantasyices.xls" workbook, select cell E6 (Dr Green), and then click the **Cut** button on the Standard toolbar.

● An outline flashes around cell E6. Select cell E8 and click on the **Paste** button.

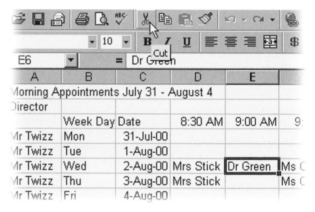

| 281 | Copying and Pasting | 284 | Copying by Drag and Drop | 290 | Copying and Inserting |

● Dr Green appears in cell
E8 and disappears from E6.
The data has moved from
E6 to E8.

B	C	D	E	F
pointments July 31 - August 4				
Week Day	Date	8:30 AM	9:00 AM	9:15 AM	9:
Mon	31-Jul-00				Ms
Tue	1-Aug-00				
Wed	2-Aug-00	Mrs Stick		Ms Orange	
Thu	3-Aug-00	Mrs Stick		Ms Orange	Dr (
Fri	4-Aug-00		Dr Green		
Sat	5-Aug-00		Mr Brown		

MOVING BY DRAG AND DROP

● Moving by drag and
drop is identical to copying
by drag and drop, except
that you don't need to hold
down the Ctrl key.

● Select cells F6 and F7
(which both contain Ms
Orange). Place the mouse
pointer over the bottom
border of F7 and see that it
turns into an arrow.

● Hold down the mouse
button and drag the mouse
to the left. Once you have
positioned the gray outline
over cells E6 and E7, release
the mouse button.

● The data in cells F6 and
F7 moves across.

SWAPPING ROWS AND COLUMNS

To swap two adjacent
columns, click the right-
hand column and click on
the **Cut** button. Now click
the left-hand column and
choose **Cut Cells** from the
Insert menu. To swap two
adjacent rows, select and
cut the lower row, then
select the upper row and
choose **Cut Cells** from the
Insert menu.

CUTTING AND INSERTING

● When you cut and insert, the cut data is removed from one part of the worksheet and placed into new cell(s) inserted elsewhere in the worksheet. Normally, you have to specify where existing cells should move to accommodate the new cells.

● Select cell G4 (Ms Black). Click on the **Cut** button.

● Select cell E9 and choose **Cut Cells** from the **Insert** menu on the Menu bar.

● In the **Insert Paste** dialog box, choose **Shift cells right**.

● Ms Black moves from cell G4 to cell E9. Other cells in row 9 are shifted to the right to accommodate the new insertion.

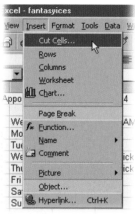

How Does Moving Affect Formulas?

Special repercussions arise from moving (or copying) formulas, cells containing formulas, or cells referenced by formulas within a worksheet. However, Excel generally arranges for formulas to continue working wherever they are moved, or wherever data referenced by the formulas is moved.

KEYBOARD SHORTCUT

There is a quick keyboard shortcut for the Cut command. Hold down the Ctrl key and then press the x key. Remember that Ctrl plus C can be used for the Copy command, and Ctrl plus v for the Paste command.

SWAPPING CELLS BY CUTTING AND INSERTING

● If you cut some data and then attempt to insert it elsewhere in the same row or column, Excel manages the operation differently from other cut/insert operations. Instead of creating new cells, it moves the actual cells containing the data, and you are given no choice as to the direction in which other cells should be shifted. The positions of the moved and displaced cells are swapped, which is usually what you want to happen.

● In your Sales worksheet, you want to swap the data in rows 5 (Orange sorbet) and 4 (Chocolate bars). First select the range of cells A5 to D5, and click on the **Cut** button.

● Now select cells A4 to D4 and choose **Cut Cells** from the **Insert** menu.

● The cells that were previously A5 to D5 are moved to A4 to D4, and the cells that were previously A4 to D4 automatically drop down to occupy A5 to D5.

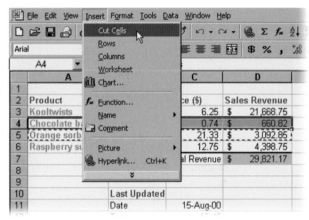

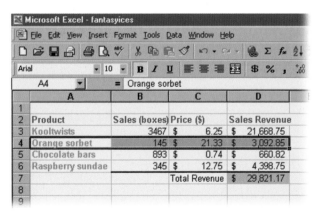

ADDING AND EDITING COMMENTS

So far, you have seen that a cell can contain text, numerical values, and formulas. A cell also has a format associated with it and every cell has a name. A further property that can be associated with a cell is a comment. This is like a note attached to the cell. You can easily add comments to cells and they can be displayed, changed, edited, or deleted at any time in the future.

1 ADDING A COMMENT

● Select a cell to which you would like to add a comment. For this example, select cell A15 in the Sales sheet of the "fantasyices.xls" workbook. Choose **Comment** from the **Insert** menu.

● A pale-yellow comment box appears, joined by a short arrow to the cell it refers to. At the top of the box, Microsoft Excel automatically inserts the name of the licensed user, which it assumes is the "commentator." Below this is a flashing insertion point.

SHORTCUT MENUS

Note that the context-sensitive shortcut menu that appears when you right-click a cell contains several commonly used actions, including Copy, Paste, and Insert. Also Cut and Clear Contents as well as Insert Comment or Edit Comment.

298 Moving by Cut and Paste

306 Clearing Cell Contents

- Type your comment.
- If you are someone different from the recorded licensed user and you wish to register this, double-click on the person's name to highlight it. Then type your own name in its place.
- To close the comment, click on a blank cell outside the comment box.

13		
14	Proportion of our prod	**Dick Twizz:**
15	Ice cream	I think we can classify
16	Sorbets	the chocolate bars as ice
17	Ice milk	cream, for now at least.|
18		
19		
20		

13		
14	Proportion of our prod	Dick Twizz:
15	Ice cream	I think we can classify
16	Sorbets	the chocolate bars as ice
17	Ice milk	cream, for now at least.
18		
19		
20		

2 DISPLAY AND EDIT COMMENTS

- Cells with comments attached have a small red triangle at their top right-hand corners.
- Move the mouse pointer over cell A15, and the comment is displayed automatically.
- To edit the comment, move the mouse pointer over the cell and click the right mouse button. A shortcut menu appears. Choose **Edit Comment** from the shortcut menu.
- You can now type in some more text or edit the existing text.

4	Orange sorb		Insert...		$	21.33	$
5	Chocolate ba		Delete...		$	0.74	$
6	Raspberry su		Clear Contents		$	12.75	$
7					Total Revenue	$	
8			Edit Comment				
9			Delete Comment				
10			Show Comment				
11						15-Aug-00	
12			Format Cells...			15:45	
13			Pick From List...				
14	Proportion of c		Hyperlink...				
15	Ice cream						
16	Sorbets			25%			
17	Ice milk						

13		
14	Proportion of our prod	the chocolate bars as ice
15	Ice cream	cream, for now at least.
16	Sorbets	Even though they
17	Ice milk	contain only about 35
18		percent ice|
19		
20		

3 RESIZING A COMMENT BOX

● If the amount of text in a comment box becomes too long for the box, you can resize the box.

● Place your mouse pointer over the bottom right-hand corner of the comment attached to cell A15. You will see it turn into a double-headed arrow.

● Hold down the left mouse button and drag the corner of the comment box to resize it. You will see an outline preview of the new box size.

● Release the mouse button once you are happy with the new size of the box.

Double-headed arrow ●

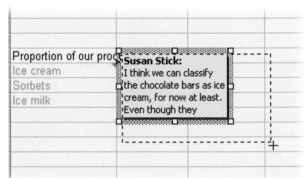

LOTS OF COMMENTS

To display all comments on a worksheet at the same time, choose **Options** from the **Tools** menu and click on the **View** tab at the top of the dialog box. Choose **Comment & indicator**, and then click on **OK**. Change the option back to **Comment indicator only** to hide comments.

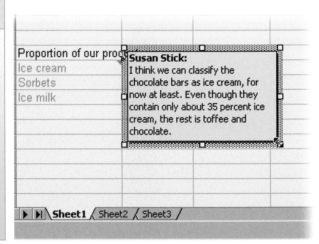

CLEARING CELLS

Occasionally you'll want to remove some worksheet data. You can either clear or delete relevant cells. Of these, clearing is the less drastic maneuver. When you clear a cell, you remove some (or all) of the items associated with the cell without removing the cell itself. You have to choose whether you want to remove the cell's contents, its format, comments attached to the cell, or all of these at once.

1 CLEARING A FORMAT

● You can clear the format from a cell without changing its contents (values or formulas it contains). The cell then reverts to a "general" format – the standard format that all cells have before they are given any special format.

● In the Sales worksheet, choose cell B10, which reads "Last Updated."

● Choose **Clear** from the **Edit** menu, and **Formats** from the submenu.

● Cell B10 reverts to a standard format.

Clearing a Comment
To clear a comment (but not content or format) from a cell, right-click the cell and choose **Delete Comment** from the pop-up menu.

2 CLEARING CELL CONTENTS

● It is common practice to clear cell contents, but you must remember that clearing contents alone does not remove formats and comments.

● Select cells A15 and B15 in the Sales worksheet.

● With the mouse pointer over cell B15, click the right mouse button and a pop-up shortcut menu appears. Choose **Clear Contents**.

● The cells' contents have been removed, but the little red triangle indicates that there is still a comment attached to cell A15.

● Cell A15 has also retained its special format. Type **Ice cream** back into the cell and the continuing presence of both the comment and special format becomes apparent.

CLEARING BY FILLING

An alternative method for clearing cells is to use the Fill Handle to duplicate empty, blank cells over the area you wish to clear. This method clears the contents and formats but not the comments.

3 CLEARING ALL FROM CELLS

● If you want to clear out a cell completely, returning it to a pristine state, use the Clear All command.

● Select the range A14 to B17 in the Sales worksheet.

● Choose **Clear** from the **Edit** menu and then choose **All** from the submenu.

● Everything – contents, formats, and comments – has now been removed.

CLEARING WITH THE KEYBOARD

You can clear contents (not formats and comments) from a cell, or a range of cells, by selecting the cell(s) and then hitting the ← Bksp or Del. Never try to clear a cell by typing a space into it (using the keyboard spacebar). The cell may look empty, but it actually contains a space character that could cause problems later on.

DELETING COLUMNS, ROWS, AND CELLS

Deleting columns, rows, and cells means removing the actual cells from the worksheet and not just the cell contents. Just as nature abhors a vacuum, similarly Excel cannot tolerate "holes" in worksheets. So when cells, rows, or columns are deleted, other cells in the worksheet have to be shifted in order to plug the gap. Deletions are thus the diametric opposite of insertions ⌐.

1 DELETING A COLUMN

● Try practicing some deletions on the Diary worksheet you have created in the "fantasyices.xls" workbook.

● Mr Twizz and Mrs Stick decide they don't want to meet up for any 8:30 appointments after all. Select column D, and then choose **Delete** from the **Edit** menu.

● Column D is deleted, and all columns to the right of column D shift one column to the left.

2 DELETING A FEW ROWS

Mr Bloggs leaves, so he no longer requires space in the Diary worksheet.

● Select rows 12 to 20, click on the right mouse button, and choose **Delete** from the pop-up menu.

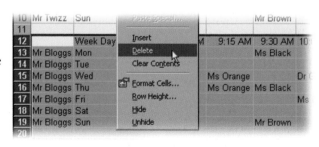

286 Inserting New Columns, Rows, and Cells

● Rows 12 to 20 disappear, and the rows below row 20 move up to fill the gap that the deletion created.

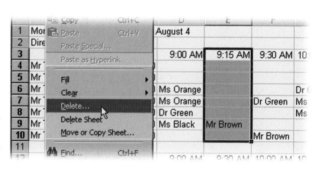

3 DELETING SOME CELLS

● Mr Twizz decides to cancel his 9:15 appointments. Select cells E3 to E10, and then choose **Delete** from the **Edit** menu.
● A dialog box appears asking whether you want to shift cells left or shift cells up. Choose **Shift cells left** and click on **OK**.
● Cells E3 to E10 are removed, and cells to the right are shifted left.

SURE YOU WANT TO DELETE?

Before deleting cells, ask yourself whether you really just want to clear them ⬚. Deleting cells removes the cells from the worksheet and moves other worksheet cells. If all you want to do is to "blank out" some cells, use the Clear command instead.

305 **Clearing Cells**

USING THE INTERNET

IN THIS SECTION YOU WILL FIND a simple introduction to exploring the internet through your PC and making the most of what the internet has to offer. Step-by-step chapters contain explanations of everything from launching Internet Explorer and understanding the toolbars to navigating between Web pages and using Outlook Express to send and receive email. This section takes you through basic and advanced searching techniques, explaining how to use different search commands to find what you are looking for on the World Wide Web; it also shows you how to bookmark your favorite sites and how to personalize Internet Explorer to suit your needs. The final chapter deals with the email program Outlook Express, showing you how to compose and send a message, and how to receive, read, organize, and reply to incoming mail.

THE WORLD WIDE WEB

The World Wide Web, commonly known as "the Web," is the largest and fastest growing area of the internet. This chapter tells you how it works and what you can do on the Web.

WHAT IS THE WEB?

The World Wide Web is a vast information resource that exists around the world on hundreds of thousands of computers called Web servers. These contain websites that can vary in content from a single page to many thousands of pages that are electronically linked to each other. The total number of pages now available on the World Wide Web is numbered in billions. These pages add up to a global library of information that you can access and navigate by using your computer.

HOW THE WEB WORKS

The World Wide Web consists of countless pages all connected via the global communications network provided by the internet. The connections are made by hypertext links, or "hyperlinks," which are addresses embedded in the Web pages. These links may connect to pages on the same website, or to a computer on the other side of the planet.

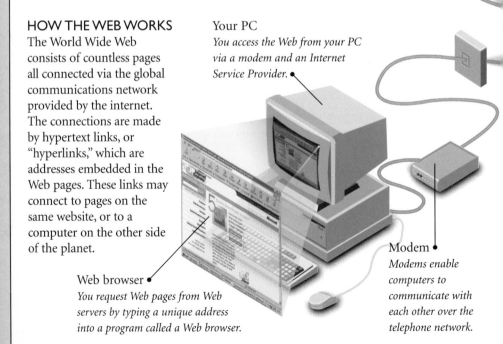

Your PC
You access the Web from your PC via a modem and an Internet Service Provider.

Web browser
You request Web pages from Web servers by typing a unique address into a program called a Web browser.

Modem
Modems enable computers to communicate with each other over the telephone network.

HOW DO YOU ACCESS THE WEB?

To access the Web you need a personal computer connected to a modem – an electronic device that translates the computer's digital signals into the analog signals that can pass along telephone lines. You also need an account with an Internet Service Provider (ISP), which operates powerful computers permanently connected to the internet, and is your gateway to the Web. Through your modem and your ISP, you can explore what is available on the Web by using a program called a Web browser.

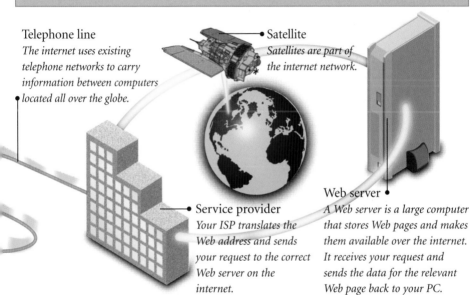

Telephone line
The internet uses existing telephone networks to carry information between computers located all over the globe.

Satellite
Satellites are part of the internet network.

Service provider
Your ISP translates the Web address and sends your request to the correct Web server on the internet.

Web server
A Web server is a large computer that stores Web pages and makes them available over the internet. It receives your request and sends the data for the relevant Web page back to your PC.

ISN'T THE WEB THE SAME AS THE INTERNET?

Many people use the terms "World Wide Web" and "internet" to mean the same thing, but they are different. The internet is a global network of interconnected computers that communicate with each other via the existing telecommunications networks. The Web uses the internet network to access and link websites. As well as providing the essential infrastructure over which the World Wide Web is able to operate, the internet offers a variety of other forms of communications and resources, including email, newsgroups, and discussion groups. If the internet is like a system of roads linking places together, then requests for Web pages, and the data from Web pages, are just two of the many kinds of traffic that travel on this road system.

WHAT'S ON THE WEB?

The pages of the World Wide Web offer information on just about every topic you care to think of. Whether your interests include current affairs, astrophysics, golf, or Antarctic flora and fauna, somewhere there is certain to be a website devoted to that topic. The Web has always been the home of academic information, but in recent years it has also become an information base for public sector bodies, government departments and, most noticeably, commercial organizations.

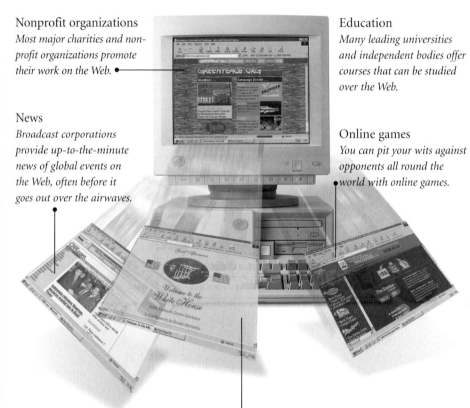

Nonprofit organizations
Most major charities and non-profit organizations promote their work on the Web.

News
Broadcast corporations provide up-to-the-minute news of global events on the Web, often before it goes out over the airwaves.

Education
Many leading universities and independent bodies offer courses that can be studied over the Web.

Online games
You can pit your wits against opponents all round the world with online games.

Commercial organizations
You can buy anything over the Web, from books and clothes to your weekly groceries.

Research
Libraries, universities, public and commercial bodies, and individuals all publish information on the Web.

Government bodies
To email the President or contact your local council, you will almost certainly find the right address on a website.

Hobbyists
Individuals create their own websites on topics they are interested in, but amateur information is not always reliable.

What's on a Web Page?

When the Web started, Web pages contained only text and very basic formatting, and they offered very little in the way of design. Today's Web pages are a world away from those early pioneers and many sites now aspire to be multimedia extravaganzas. A Web page is likely to incorporate sophisticated graphics and include video clips, sound sequences, and interactive animations. You may even be able to play miniature software programs knows as "applets" on the page.

Download files
Web pages can contain files that you transfer to your own computer to view or install.

Programs
While you are viewing a site, a program can run independently within the Web page.

Graphics
A well-designed website can be a showcase for the skills of the graphic designer.

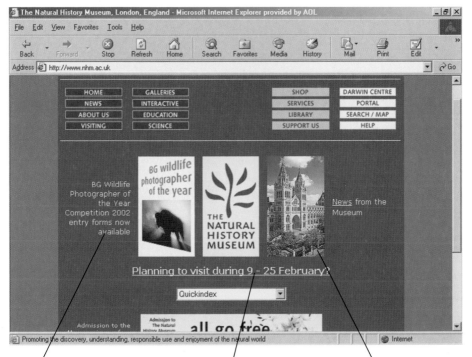

Text •
Text within a page can be copied, pasted, and saved to your hard disk.

Hypertext links 📄 •
Use hypertext links, or "hyperlinks," to go directly to other relevant sites.

Multimedia files
These can be sound, video, or interactive animations.

• Photographs
Images on a Web page can also act as hyperlinks.

331 **Recognizing Hypertext Links**

WHAT IS A WEB BROWSER?

A Web browser is a piece of software installed on your PC that lets you look at (or "browse") different websites. The most widely used Web browsers are Netscape Navigator and Microsoft Internet Explorer. Navigator was the first to arrive and quickly became the most popular browser on the market. Microsoft then created its own browser, called Internet Explorer, and ever since there has been a strong rivalry between the two, but both are excellent browsers. You can have both of them installed on your PC, and which one you use is a matter of personal preference.

WHICH PROGRAM?

The examples shown in this book use Internet Explorer, but the pages should look almost the same using Netscape Navigator. New versions of these browsers are released from time to time. For example, Internet Explorer 5 replaced version 4, adding new features. It is best to use the most recent release of either browser providing your PC has sufficient memory and speed to support it.

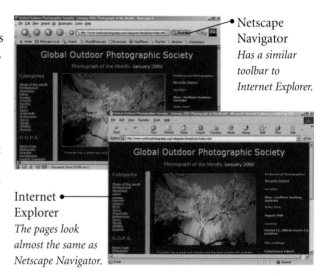

Netscape Navigator
Has a similar toolbar to Internet Explorer.

Internet Explorer
The pages look almost the same as Netscape Navigator.

MORE ABOUT BROWSERS

Most websites look the same regardless of which browser you use. But you might notice small changes if you use both. This is because HTML (the programming language for Web pages, called the Hypertext Markup Language) describes how a page appears, and different browsers may interpret these instructions differently. Also, Netscape Navigator and Internet Explorer support some tags that are unofficial features of HTML designed to give users a reason to use that particular browser. But these features are not widely used – most websites stick to using "official" HTML, so that all browsers can read the page correctly.

UNDERSTANDING WEB ADDRESSES

Web addresses are known as URLs. This stands for Universal (sometimes Uniform) Resource Locator. URLs are made up of two distinct parts: a protocol and a domain name. The protocol, the first part of the URL, tells the Web browser what type of site it is contacting – a website, a file transfer site, or a secure website, for example. In this case the protocol is http, standing for Hypertext Transfer Protocol, the standard for Web communications. The second part, the domain name, is like a street address – it tells the Web browser where to go to find the site.

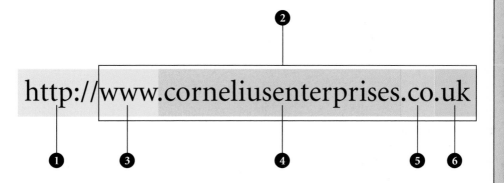

THE DIFFERENT PARTS OF A WEB ADDRESS

1 Protocol

Most Web addresses begin with http://. This stands for Hypertext Transmission Protocol. This protocol is used to transfer ordinary Web pages over the internet. Other protocols you are likely to encounter are ftp:// (file transfer protocol) and https://. This protocol is used on "secure" websites, for sending and receiving sensitive information.

2 Domain Name

The domain name has several parts and is mapped to an Internet Protocol (IP) address.

3 www

The vast majority of Web addresses have www (standing for World Wide Web) as the first part of the domain name.

4 Host

This part of the domain name is a name chosen by the owner of the website and can be, for example, a company name.

5 Type of site

This part of the domain tells you what type of site the website is. For example, .co or .com stand for commercial sites; .gov for government organizations; .org for non-profit organizations; and .edu or .ac for educational sites.

6 Country

Websites other than US sites also have a country code. UK denotes a website based in the United Kingdom.

INTERNET EXPLORER

Internet Explorer is one of the most popular Web-browsing programs, offering all the facilities that you need to browse the Web and become part of the online community.

WHAT CAN EXPLORER DO?

Internet Explorer comes as a standard part of Windows software and was probably already installed on your computer when it arrived. Explorer is more than just a Web-browsing program: it is a suite of programs offering a variety of Internet-related activities: from browsing the Web and composing and sending email, to taking the plunge and publishing your own Web pages. Outlook Express is the name of the email program that comes with Explorer,

and FrontPage is Explorer's home Web-publishing program. Both these programs are the subject of their own books in the *DK Essential Computers* series, but a brief description is given here to help give you an idea of how the three programs are inter-related and what each can do.

The last chapter of this section shows you how to use the basic features of Outlook Express ⬧ to compose, send, receive, and read email messages.

WHAT IS EXPLORER?
Internet Explorer is the Web-browsing program that enables you to connect to websites and view them, surf the Web using hypertext links, and download files and programs from the Internet to your own computer. By default, its email features operate through Outlook Express, and its Edit feature is directly linked to Microsoft FrontPage.

◢
376 **Outlook Express**

OUTLOOK EXPRESS

Outlook Express is an email program that enables you to perform all the activities necessary to send and receive email, manage your own online address book, and exchange files and information with friends over the Internet.

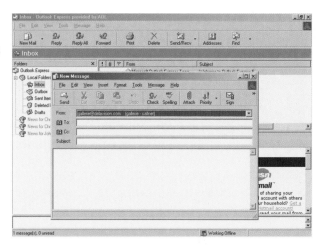

FRONTPAGE

The time may come when you want to create your own Web pages. FrontPage helps you to do just that. It provides a Web-page editor that enables you to build Web pages, with only a minimal understanding of HTML. You can then publish them live on the Web using your own computer as a Web server.

INSTALLING OTHER COMPONENTS

If Outlook Express or FrontPage are not on your computer, you can install them from your Windows or Internet Explorer CD-ROM. If you cannot locate your disks, another option open to you is to download a new version of Internet Explorer from the Microsoft website and reinstall the entire program on your computer, making sure that you elect to install these additional programs during the installation process. Click the Microsoft button on the Links bar to go to Microsoft's website.

LAUNCHING INTERNET EXPLORER

You can launch Internet Explorer directly from your computer's desktop by clicking on the shortcut icon or from the Windows Start menu by following the instructions shown opposite. Before you can actually connect to a website using Explorer you will need to connect to your Internet Service Provider. It does not matter whether you do this before or after starting Explorer. When Explorer starts running, it checks to see if it can find an active Internet connection. If it cannot detect a connection it will usually locate and launch the connection software belonging to your Internet Service Provider to create a connection. Alternatively, you can launch your service provider at any time.

CONNECT TO YOUR SERVICE PROVIDER

● If you are using a dial-up connection, double-click on your Service Provider's desktop shortcut icon to open its sign-on dialog box.
● In the sign-on box, type your user name and password if they are required.
● Click once on the **Sign on** button to dial your service provider.

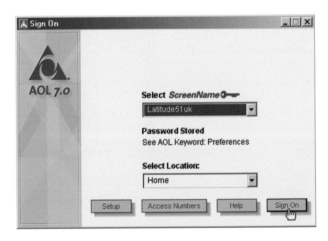

WHAT IS A DIAL-UP ACCOUNT?

With a dial-up account you have a log-in name and a password that you choose yourself. You use your modem to make a connection to your service provider's system and through this you are linked to the internet.

1 USING THE START MENU

● Click on **Start** on the Windows Taskbar to bring up the main menu.

● When **Programs** is highlighted and the pop-up programs menu appears, move across to highlight **Internet Explorer**.

● Click on **Internet Explorer** and the Explorer window opens □.

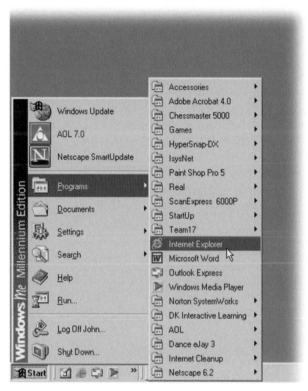

2 USING A SHORTCUT

● First, locate the Internet Explorer shortcut. This is a blue, graphically styled "e" with Internet Explorer written beneath it.

● When you have found it, position the mouse over the **e** and double-click to launch the Explorer program.

● The Explorer window appears □.

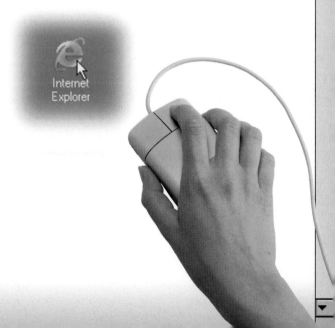

THE EXPLORER WINDOW

The Explorer main browser window opens automatically when you start Internet Explorer. It offers a selection of different toolbars, including a standard menu bar, an area for viewing Web pages and a status bar at the foot of the window. The status bar displays information relating to the transfer of pages and connectivity.

THE EXPLORER WINDOW

1 Title bar
The Title bar shows the title of the current Web page. It also tells you whether you are connected to the Internet or are working offline.
2 Menu bar
This shows the main menus that give you access to all Explorer's features.
3 Standard buttons
This toolbar contains all the main features you need to navigate around the Web.
4 Address bar □
This is where you type the addresses of websites that you want to visit.
5 Links bar
This toolbar provides a selection of links to your preferred websites.
6 Main browsing window
This area is where the websites that you visit will be displayed.

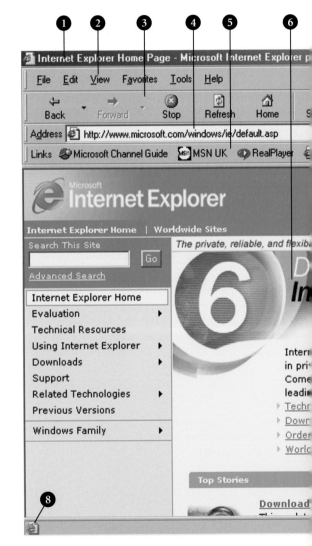

⌐
328 **Using the Address Field**

CROWDED TOOLBAR?

You can hide the labels on the Standard toolbar to make room for more buttons. Right-click on the toolbar and click **Customize** in the menu. In the **Text options** box of the **Customize** window, click the arrow and select **No text labels**. Click on **Close**.

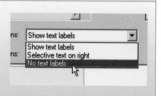

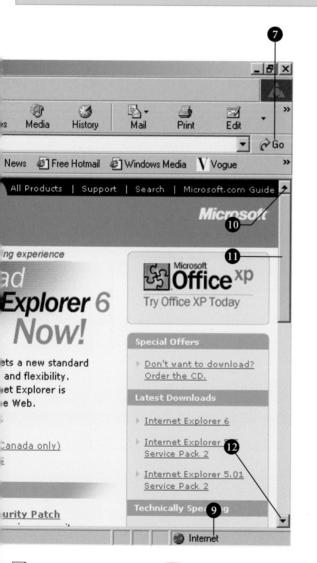

THE EXPLORER WINDOW

7 Go button ▯
After typing the address of a website, using this button will request the page.

8 Status bar
This bar has information relating to the activity being carried out. For example, **Done** *will indicate that a requested Web page has been transferred to your Web browser, or, if you click on a hyperlink ▯, the URL of that link will be displayed.*

9 Connectivity icon
When you are working online, this icon is displayed.

10 Scroll-up arrow
Click on this arrow to move up the current Web page.

11 Scroll bar box
Drag this box in the scroll bar to see other parts of the current page quickly.

12 Scroll-down arrow
Click on this arrow to move down the current Web page.

THE EXPLORER TOOLBAR

It is perfectly possible to use Internet Explorer using only the features provided on the standard buttons toolbar. This toolbar is at the top of the Explorer window and comprises a row of graphically styled buttons. These buttons are shortcuts to features that will help you find your way round the Web quickly, so it is worth spending time familiarizing yourself with the toolbar and learning what each symbol means. Each item on the toolbar is also in the main menus.

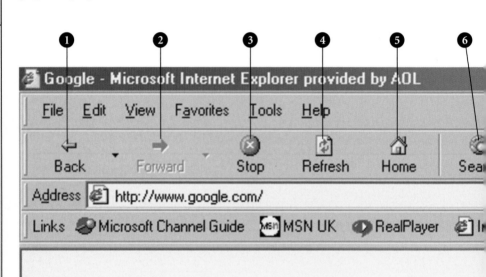

THE STANDARD TOOLBAR

1 Back
Takes you to the previous page you were on.
2 Forward
Displays the page on screen before using the Back button.
3 Stop
Stops a page downloading.

4 Refresh
Refreshes the current page to show the latest version.
5 Home
Loads the default home page.
6 Search
Opens the Search panel in the Explorer window. This gives you

access to features that help you connect to search engines.
7 Favorites
Opens the Favorites panel in the Explorer window, which allows you to create, access, and manage your favorite sites on the Web.

333 **Navigating Back and Forth**

338 **Searching with Explorer**

350 **The Favorites Panel**

CUSTOMIZING A TOOLBAR

You might want to move the toolbars. To move the Links toolbar, place the cursor over the "handle," hold down the mouse button, the cursor becomes a double-headed arrow, then "drag" the bar to the preferred location.

ScreenTips

If you forget what any of the buttons on the toolbar do, all you have to do is click on the button and wait for a few seconds. A box appears with the button's name.

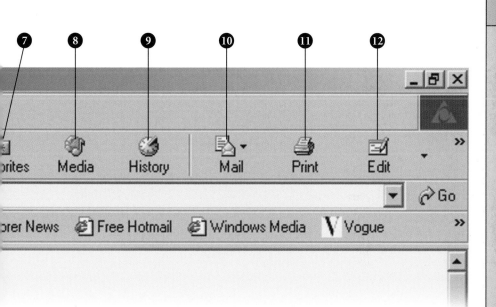

THE STANDARD TOOLBAR

8 Media
Find and play media files.
9 History
Opens the History panel that provides a list of websites that you have previously visited, and by clicking one you can automatically connect to it.

10 Mail
Provides options related to email including opening a message and pasting the address of the current page into a new message.
11 Print
Prints the current page.

12 Edit
Allows you to edit the code of the current Web page, either in text form or using a Web page editor, such as FrontPage. Save any changes on your hard disk, but they will not affect the Web page itself.

335 **Opening the History Panel**

SAVING CONTENT

It is not possible for you to create or alter Web pages using the Internet Explorer browser. However, there will be many occasions when you come across screens containing information that you want to save, review later on, or to edit for your own personal use. Internet Explorer enables you to save text, images, and other files and programs onto your hard disk. Open a Web page that you would like to save for later use, and try some of the techniques described here.

1 SAVING A WEB PAGE

● To save an entire Web page to your hard disk, click on **File** in the Menu bar and select **Save As**.
● In the **Save Web Page** dialog box, type the file name and click on **Save**.

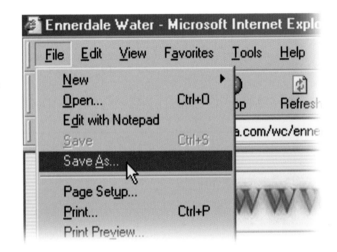

2 SAVING IMAGES

● Place the mouse cursor on the image that you want to save. Click the right mouse button to display a pop-up menu.

● Select **Save Picture As** and click with the left mouse button.

● In the **Save Picture** dialog box, navigate to the folder where you would like to save the file.

● Type a name in the **File name** box and click on the **Save** button.

DOWNLOADING FROM WEB PAGES

Many Web pages contain files such as sound or video files, PDF files (Portable Document Files that can be viewed using Acrobat Reader), or computer programs. It is usually possible to save these files onto your hard disk. To save a file, follow Step 2 above and on the pop-up menu choose **Save Target As**. You will need the software to view or play the files that you save.

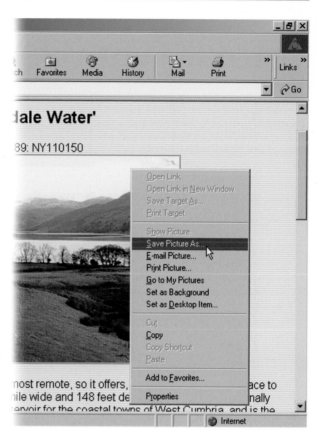

MOVING BETWEEN PAGES

Browsing, or "surfing," the Web is simply a process of opening a
Web page in your browser, identifying the "hot" elements on
that page and using them to move to another page.

USING THE ADDRESS FIELD

When you connect to your Service
Provider ⌂ and start Internet
Explorer, your default home page ◻
automatically opens in the browser
window ⌂. This page is likely to be a
Microsoft page or the home page of your
service provider. While it may contain
useful information for new users, soon

you will want to strike out and visit a site
of your choice, perhaps your company's
website or an international news site. You
do this by telling your computer the
address of the site you wish to visit. Find
the addresses of several sites you would
like to visit and try accessing them
following the instructions below.

1 CLEARING THE ADDRESS BAR

● Before you can type the
address of a site you must
first clear the current
contents of the address bar.
Position the mouse cursor
anywhere in the address
field and click once.
● The contents of the
address bar are highlighted.
● Press the ← Bksp key to
delete the contents.

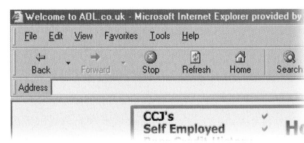

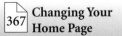

2 TYPING THE ADDRESS

● You will notice that there is now a flashing insertion point in the address bar, ready for you to begin typing. Type the address as it appears, taking care to copy exactly all the punctuation and spelling.

3 CONNECTING TO A SITE

● Once you have typed the address, move the mouse cursor over the **Go** button, to the right of the address bar, and click once. Alternatively, you can also press the Enter ↵ key.

● Wait for a few moments while your computer contacts the remote computer you are calling. You can follow the progress of this call by watching the information in the Status bar at the foot of the browser window. Once the connection has been made, you will see the information in your browser window begin to change. When the Status bar says **Done**, the page has been fully downloaded to your computer.

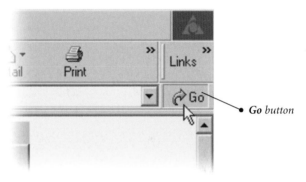

● *Go button*

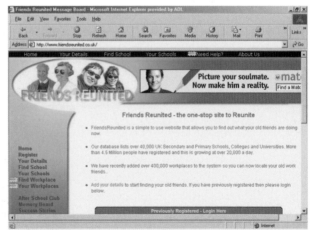

4 EDITING AN ADDRESS

● If you mistype the address, don't worry. Just as you can with a word processor, you can simply edit your mistakes.

● Position the mouse cursor after the character you wish to change and click the mouse button once. This will highlight the entire address, as in Step 1.

● Click again and the cursor will change to a flashing cursor ready for you to type any changes using the keyboard.

● When the address is correct, either click on the **Go** button or press Enter ⏎ .

HAVING TROUBLE CONNECTING?

 The page cannot be displayed

The page you are looking for is currently unavailable. The Web site might be experiencing technical difficulties, or you may need to adjust your browser settings.

There is a wide variety of reasons why you may experience difficulty connecting to a site. Servers sometimes go down and cannot be accessed. If you cannot get connected for this reason wait before trying again, but the wait can be anything from a few seconds to several hours. Another reason may be that you have mistyped the address. Check that the spelling and the punctuation are correct, and that no extra characters have crept in. Any slight discrepancy will prevent a connection.

FOLLOWING LINKS BETWEEN PAGES

Links are the very essence of the World Wide Web, and it is by following them that you can move from page to page without typing a new address each time. Links have several different guises, and learning to recognize their various forms will help you get the most from the Web. Hypertext links are the most common form and are displayed as text on the page, but graphic buttons and other images are increasingly used as a way of encouraging you to move to another page. Dorling Kindersley's website uses both types of links. Try identifying each of the types of links described here and following them using the instructions below.

RECOGNIZING HYPERTEXT LINKS

These are the most common and easily identified link. They are usually underlined and shown in a different color.
- Move the mouse cursor over the underlined text.
- If the cursor changes to a hand, the text is "hot."
- Click the mouse button once to follow that link.

VISITED LINKS

As you follow hypertext links within a single website you may start to notice two colors of links on the Web pages. This is because the links you have visited usually change color as a way of helping you keep track of where you have and have not been.

USING A NEW WINDOW

When you are browsing the Web, it can be useful to open a page in a new window so that you have two or more browser windows open at the same time. You can continue to explore one page while another is being downloaded. To open any link in a new window, place the mouse cursor over the link, right-click the mouse and choose **Open Link in New Window** from the pop-up menu that appears.

RECOGNIZING NAVIGATION BUTTONS

Many websites use graphically styled buttons as the main way of navigating around the site. These buttons often appear at the top, bottom, or side of a page.

- Move the mouse cursor over the different buttons.
- Wherever the cursor changes to a hand there is a link from that image. The button usually changes color as well.
- Click the mouse button once when you want to follow a particular link.

Navigation buttons •

RECOGNIZING IMAGE LINKS

Some of the more design-conscious websites use graphically styled button, which may not obviously appear to be links. These images may or may not have text labels to act as signpost, which can offer a more exploratory and intuitive approach to surfing. Again, the way to discover such links is to move the mouse cursor over the images and see if it changes to a hand.

Navigating Back and Forth

Following links is simple once you know how, but before long you may find that you have completely moved away from where you started, and are not sure how to get back. You may also have encountered a few interesting pages on the way but failed to note their addresses. How do you return to find them again? Internet Explorer provides several features that enable you to move between the pages you have visited. Open any Web page and follow between six and ten different links, then practice navigating using some of the techniques described below.

BACKWARDS AND FORWARDS PAGE BY PAGE

● Moving back is the most common operation you'll perform. To move back to the previous page you visited, place the cursor over the **Back** button on the toolbar and click once. Repeat the process to move back through several pages.

● To move forward to a page you were on before

you pressed **Back**, place the cursor over the **Forward** button and click once.

Repeat the process to move forward to the most recent page you opened.

USING THE BACK MENU

● To move back to any page you have visited in the current session, position the mouse cursor over the arrow to the right of the **Back** button and click once. Select the page you wish to return to from the drop-down menu that appears.

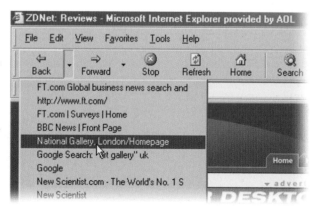

USING THE FORWARD MENU

● To move forward to any page that you accessed in the current session before you used the **Back** feature, position the mouse pointer over the arrow to the right of the **Forward** button and click once.

● Select the page you wish to return to from the drop-down menu that appears.

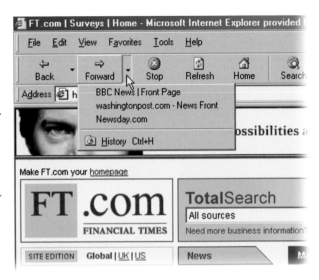

USING THE ADDRESS MENU

Explorer makes its own list of sites you visit regularly or access specifically by typing the address.

● You can access any of the listed sites by positioning the mouse over the arrow at the end of the address bar and clicking once. A drop-down menu appears.

● Use the scroll bar to see the full list. Position the mouse cursor over the address of interest and click once to promote that address into the address bar. If a connection is not made automatically, click **Go** or press the [Enter ↵] key to make the connection.

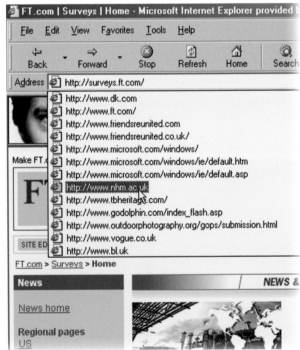

USING THE GO TO MENU

The **Go To** menu provides a list of all the sites you have visited in the current session.

● To access this menu, click on **View** in the Menu bar and select **Go To**. The list of sites appears in the lowest section of the drop-down submenu.

● Position the mouse cursor over the site you wish to access and left-click once.

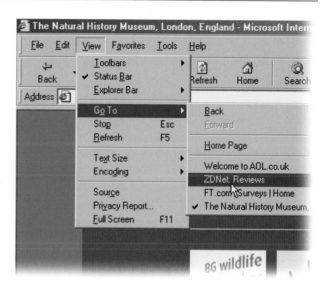

USING THE BROWSING HISTORY

Another means of accessing websites that you have already visited is to use Internet Explorer's History feature. This maintains a record of all the websites that you have visited during the current session as well as over the last few days or weeks. You can specify how many days you would like

Explorer to keep items in its History, and you can also clear all items from this memory whenever you wish to start afresh. Once you have visited a few websites, open the History panel and try returning to a site you visited earlier by following these instructions.

OPENING THE HISTORY PANEL

● To see a list of all the items stored in History, position the mouse cursor over the **History** button on the main toolbar and click once. The History panel will open inside the Explorer window.

OPEN A PAGE IN THE LIST

- Position the mouse cursor over any page in the list so that it turns into a hand.
- Click once to open the page you want in the main browser window.

Sorting the History

You can sort the History pages by clicking the small arrow to the right of the **View** button in the History bar. A drop-down menu appears from which you can select to sort by date, site, the most visited, or in the order the pages have been visited today.

CHANGING THE LENGTH OF TIME SITES REMAIN IN HISTORY

- Click on the **Tools** menu and select **Internet Options**. The **Internet Options** dialog box opens showing the General settings.

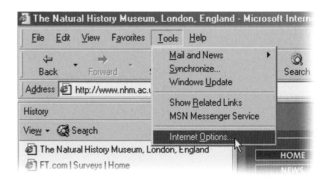

● At the bottom of this box is the **History** subsection. To change the number of days for which History will remember sites, position the mouse cursor in the box to the right of **Days to keep pages in history**, and double-click to select the number in the box.

● When it is highlighted, type the required number of days. Click on the **OK** button at the foot of the dialog box.

CLEARING THE HISTORY

● Open the **Internet Options** box as described opposite. Position the mouse cursor over the **Clear History** button in the History panel and then click the **OK** button to close the box.

CLOSING THE HISTORY PANEL

● Position the mouse cursor over the **X** on the History bar and click once.

SEARCHING THE WEB

The Web has a variety of sophisticated search tools, called search engines, which exist purely to help you find your way around the billions of pages stored on computers worldwide.

SEARCHING WITH EXPLORER

Explorer has a Search panel that enables you to search for websites, companies, email addresses, and other information according to keywords or phrases that you type. Connect to your Internet Service Provider, then try searching with the Search panel, following the procedures illustrated here.

USING THE SEARCH PANEL

● Position the mouse cursor over the **Search** button on the toolbar and click once. The Search panel will open to the left of the main window.

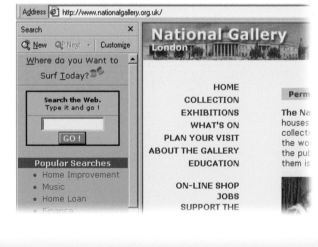

● Click the mouse in the search box and type your keyword(s). Position the mouse cursor over the **Go!** button and click once to start your search.

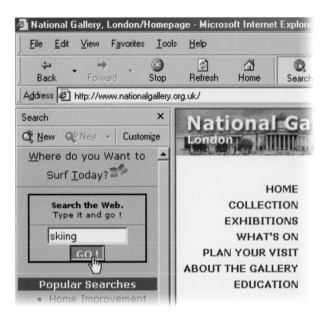

● The results will appear in the main window after a few seconds. Use the scroll bar on the extreme right of the results window to browse the full list.

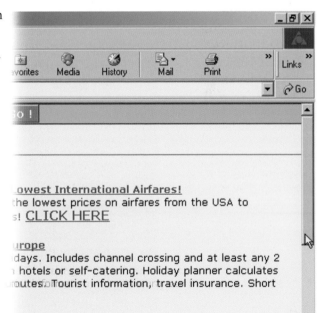

● Position the mouse cursor over the title or hyperlink of any site in the list and click once to open that page.
● The page appears in the main browser window.

CUSTOMIZE YOUR SEARCHES

● Internet Explorer provides several ways in which you can search the internet in the way that suits you.
● Begin by clicking on the **Customize** button at top right in the Search panel.

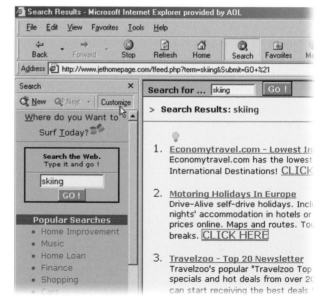

● The **Customize Search
Settings** dialog box opens.
● Click on **Use Search
Assistant**.

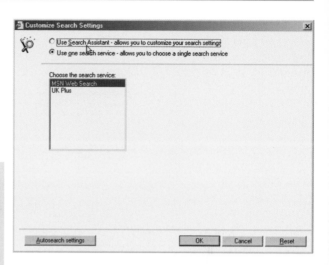

Ending a download
If you begin to down-
load a page that you've
found via a search, you
may soon decide that
it's not what you're
interested in. A quick
way to end a download
is to press the [Esc] key.

● The contents of the
Customize Search Settings
dialog box changes. You
might want to change the
default search provider
from MSN Web Search to
UK Plus. This will make
the search results more
UK-oriented.
● To do this, highlight **UK
Plus** below **Find a Web
page** and click on the "up"
button below the search
engine list.
● UK Plus is now
promoted to be the default
search engine when you use
the Search panel to
perform searches.

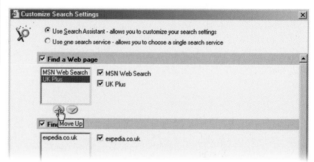

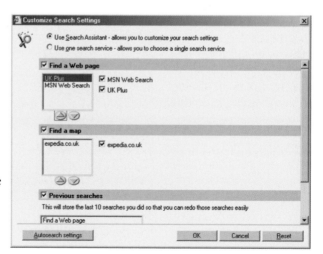

● Click on the OK button when you have finished customizing the search options.

THE POPULAR SEARCHES OPTION

● Select one of the categories in the Search panel by clicking on it.

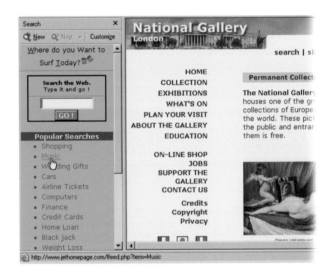

● The search results appear in the main browser window.

● Use the scroll bar at the right of the window to view the results, or to scroll to the bottom of the list where you can click on **More Results** to display the next page of relevant sites.

7. **Books, Music, Movies, Video Games, and More!!!!**
Get great deals on wide selection of books, music, movies, video games, electronics and much more!!!! You won't want to miss this opportunity. CLICK HERE

8. **anewShop.com's Guide to Online Music Shops**
Reviews, price comparisons, and quick links to popular online music merchants. Find out the latest deals and specials. CLICK HERE

9. **Get 12 CDs For the Price Of 1!**
Get 12 CDs for the price of 1 when you join BMG Music Service! From rock to classical, easy listening to metal, country to jazz, R&B to alternative -- BMG Music Service has something for everyone. Join and start picking your FREE CDs today! CLICK HERE

10. **Get CD s, Reviews, Magazines, Even 11 CD s Free!**
Get CD's FAST – rock, classical, jazz, & more – plus detailed music reviews & risk-free music magazine trials! Buy new, buy used, even get *12 for the price of 1* with BMG music via affiliate Adam's SmileZone CLICK HERE

PERFORMING AN AUTOSEARCH

Explorer also allows you to perform an autosearch directly from the Address Bar  without opening the Search panel.

● Position the mouse cursor in the address bar and click once to highlight the text already there.

● Type the word or phrase you wish to search for. Press the [Enter ←] key to execute the search, and wait for the results to appear in the main window.

● Any matches will be displayed as a list of hyperlinks 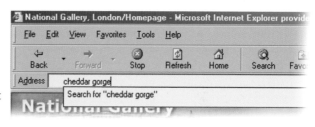, which you can click on to view the sites in the main Explorer window.

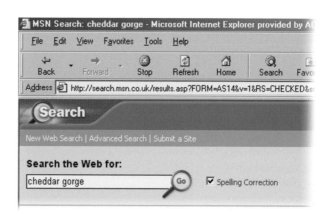

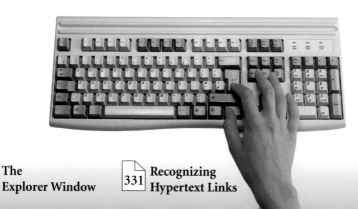

322 | The Explorer Window

331 | Recognizing Hypertext Links

CHOOSING A SEARCH TOOL

The Web has a host of search sites you can use, each drawing on its own database of information. Explorer's Search Assistant accesses several different search engines, but if your search is obscure, you may have to cast your net a bit wider. There are many other search tools that you can try, some of which specialize in certain types of information, such as email addresses or newsgroups. To search effectively, it pays to match your search tool to the type of information you want to find, and to understand the nature of your search. Are you looking for all sites related to a particular subject, or do you seek a specific person or company, for example?

WEB DIRECTORIES

Web directories are lists of subject categories and subcategories that you can browse through looking for websites. Using a directory is rather like looking up a telephone number in the yellow pages. It gives you all the entries in a particular category, but in order to find the information, you have to know where to look for it. Consequently, directories are most helpful when you are looking for general information by subject or by an activity.

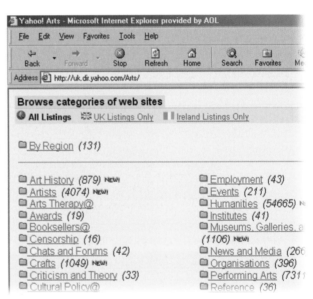

DIRECTORY ADDRESSES

Here are the addresses of some of the more popular Web directories:

Zeal . . . . www.zeal.com
Yahoo! . . . . www.yahoo.com
Lycos . . . . www.lycos.co.uk
UK250 . . . . www.uk250.co.uk

SEARCH ENGINES

Here are the addresses of some of the more popular search engines:

www.altavista.com   askjeeves.com
www.dogpile.com   infoseek.go.com
www.excite.com   looksmart.co.uk
www.hotbot.com   webcrawler.com

SEARCH ENGINES

Search engines offer more powerful searching facilities than Web directories, and will search the Web according to the information you give them by using keywords and other information including language and country. The search engines match your search criteria to Web pages that are listed in their index, and return a list of "hits," or matches, with your search criteria. The most relevant matches are listed first. You can then view the matched sites by following hyperlinks ⬚. The AltaVista search engine has a huge database and offers multilingual searches. Results are usually returned within a matter of seconds.

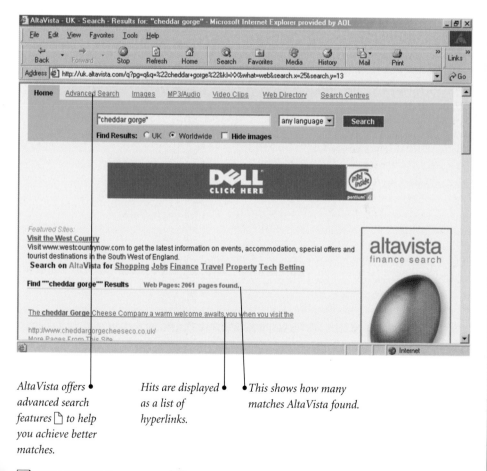

AltaVista offers advanced search features ⬚ to help you achieve better matches.

Hits are displayed as a list of hyperlinks.

This shows how many matches AltaVista found.

331 **Recognizing Hypertext Links**

349 **Refine Your Search**

SEARCHING TIPS

There are no hard and fast rules about Web searching, and it can be one of the most frustrating activities. Even with all the millions of websites to choose from, many people complain of not being able to find anything on the Web. There are many reasons it can be difficult: there is no universal index of websites; sites tend to be registered by developers rather than editors, so the information given to the

databases is not always very helpful; and each search engine logs different information and operates in a slightly different way from its counterparts. So, although there are some general tips and guidelines that will help you search more effectively, you will find that there is no substitute for taking the time to explore the specific hints and instructions offered on each individual search site.

READ THE INSTRUCTIONS

Most of the search engines contain instructions on how to search. Spend some time reading these. They can usually be accessed via a hyperlink 📄 or help button found on the search engine's home page.
● The NorthernLight search engine: (**www.northernlight.com**) has simple, clear instructions that are accessed by clicking Help on the home page.

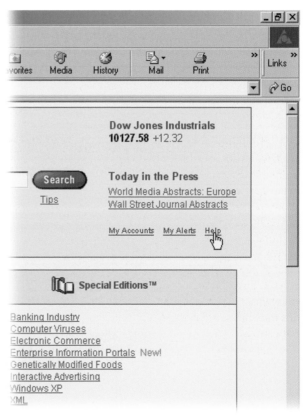

● The instructions tell you that you can also ask questions, such as "What is the capital of Sweden?"

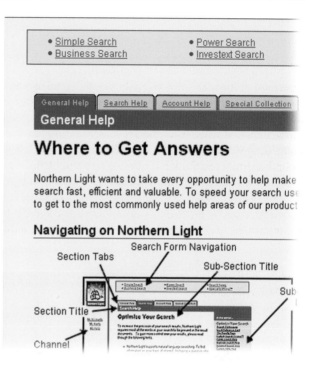

Try again...
If you have no luck with one search engine or directory, try running the same search on an alternative engine; they use different databases of websites.

USE MULTIPLE KEYWORDS

Using more than one keyword makes a search more specific. If seeking novels by a particular author, for example, the keywords "books" and "faulks" are more likely to produce useful results than using either word by itself. Separate different keywords with spaces.

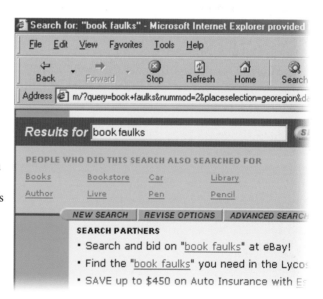

SEARCH FOR EXACT PHRASES

When using two keywords, the search engine finds sites that contain both keywords. A search for White House is as likely to find sites about white-painted houses as well as the presidential residence. Putting quotation marks around "White House" tells the engine to look for that exact phrase.

SEARCHING FOR PEOPLE

With the ever-increasing popularity of email, being able to find people on the Internet is becoming as important as finding websites. There are several excellent people finding directories that list e-mail addresses and residential listings.

InfoSpace . . . . www.infospace.com
AnyWho . . . . www.anywho.com
Switchboard . . . . www.switchboard.com
WhoWhere? . . . . www.whowhere.com
Yahoo!: People Search . . . . www.people.yahoo.com

USE LOGICAL OPERATORS

Most search engines understand logical expressions, such as AND, OR, or NOT. They help to narrow down a search. When used between one or more keywords, these expressions have the following meanings: NEAR looks for pages where the adjacent keywords occur close together; AND looks for pages where instances of both words occur; OR looks for pages where there are instances of either keyword; NOT looks for pages where there are instances of the word preceding NOT, but not the word following it.

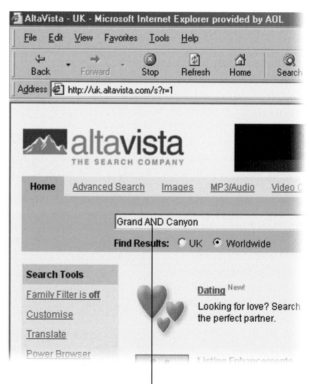

● Logical operators are placed between keywords when searching.

REFINE YOUR SEARCH

Many search engines allow you to refine your search using advanced search criteria. You may be able to specify the language, country, and type of media you are looking for. The exact criteria will vary from engine to engine, so it is best to try out several sites to find the one that best suits you.

● On the Lycos home page, you can refine your search at the bottom of a page of hits.

SET YOUR SEARCH PREFERENCES

Many of the large search engines enable you to customize their search pages so that you do not have to select your search options each time you use that search engine. Once you have found an advanced search formula that works, you can tell the search engine to remember the preferences for you.

● On some sites you can access the customize page from the **My** button on the home page. You can choose a user name and password, and you then have the option to select your preferred search criteria.

This is an example of how the customize page can be accessed from the My button on the home page.

BOOKMARK YOUR FAVORITE SEARCH TOOLS

If you become a regular Internet user you are likely to return to at least one of the search engines on a regular basis. It is useful to bookmark your favorite □ search sites so that you are able to access them quickly whenever you wish.

FAVORITES

Internet Explorer provides a way for you to create a digital bookmark for any site as a "favorite," which adds it to a special list that you can access quickly and easily whenever you wish.

THE FAVORITES PANEL

One of the features of Internet Explorer is a window that you can have open all the time on the left-hand side of the main browser window. It is called the Favorites panel, and from this panel you can access and organize your collection of favorites.

Explorer provides some suggested favorite places to get you started. Once you have connected to the Internet, you can try accessing some favorites using the Favorites panel and some of the other methods described in this chapter.

OPENING THE FAVORITES PANEL

● Position the mouse cursor over the **Favorites** button on the main toolbar and click once.
● The Favorites panel will open on screen in the left-hand side of the main Explorer window.

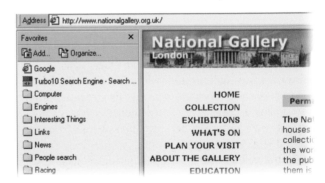

OPENING A FAVORITE SITE

● In the Favorites panel, position the mouse cursor over the site that you wish to open. When the cursor turns into a hand, click once to open that site in the main window.

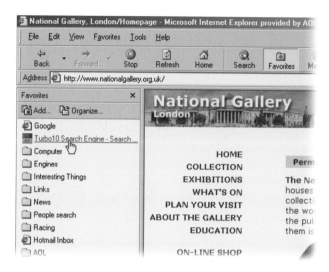

CLOSING THE FAVORITES PANEL

● When you have finished using your favorites, you can close the Favorites panel by positioning the mouse cursor over the **X** in the Favorites bar and clicking once. The main browser window expands to fill the available space.

Close button ●

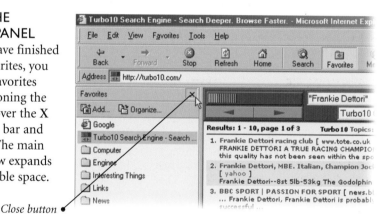

OPENING A FAVORITE USING THE FAVORITES MENU

You can also access your favorites directly from the Favorites menu. The advantage of using the menu instead of the panel is that you have a larger window area in which to view the Web pages you select. To open a favorite using this method, position the mouse cursor over the Favorites menu and click once. A drop-down menu will appear, listing all your current favorites. Move the mouse cursor over the one of interest (submenus appear next to folders). When it becomes highlighted click the mouse once to open it.

CREATING YOUR OWN FAVORITES

As your experience of finding your way around the World Wide Web increases, it is inevitable that you will accumulate a selection of sites that you refer to more than any others: your preferred search engine 🗋, news providers, your bank, particular companies, and sites offering a little light relief, for example. These sites are the perfect candidates to be your favorite places. Adding one of these sites to your favorites is very simple and can be done by using the Favorites panel or via the Favorites menu, depending on how you prefer to use your browser. Connect to the Internet and open a site that you would like to add to your favorite places. Then follow the instructions below, using whichever method you prefer.

1 CREATING USING FAVORITES PANEL

● Position the mouse cursor over the **Favorites** button on the main toolbar and click once to display the Favorites panel on-screen.
● In the Favorites panel, position the mouse cursor over the **Add** button and click once. Now go to Step 3.

Add button ●

Keyboard favorites
Once you are familiar with creating your own favorites, you'll feel confident about using the keyboard shortcut to creating a favorite, which is to hold down the Ctrl key and press D.

345 Search engines

2 CREATING USING FAVORITES MENU

● Alternatively, position the mouse cursor over **Favorites** on the Menu bar and click once to activate the Favorites menu.

● Position the cursor over **Add to Favorites** and, when it becomes highlighted, click once.

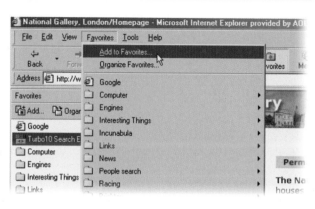

3 NAMING A FAVORITE

● The **Add Favorite** dialog box now opens and the name of the favorite you have just created will be shown in the **Name** box. If you would like to change the name, position the mouse cursor after the text in the Name box and click once. A flashing insertion point will appear. Press the ← Bksp key and hold it down until all the text has been deleted.

● Now type your preferred name for this favorite. The chosen name is only a label to help you identify the site. It does not alter the address of the website.

● If you wish to store the favorite in a particular folder go to Step 4, otherwise click on **OK**.

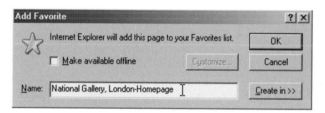

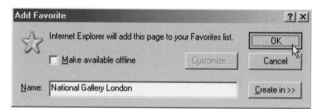

4 FILING A FAVORITE

● In the Add Favorite box, click the **Create in**>> button to open the Favorites directory. Navigate to the folder you wish to store the favorite in. Double-click on the folder to open it and single-click on a folder to select it.

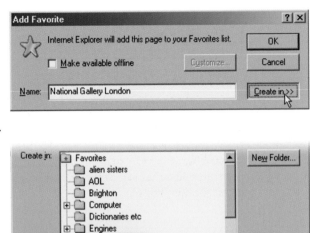

● When you have selected the folder, position the cursor over the **OK** button at the top-right and click once to save the favorite in the chosen folder.

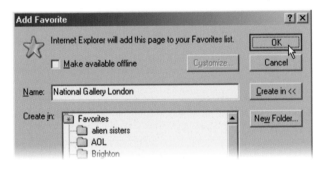

MAKING FAVORITES AVAILABLE OFFLINE

If you access some of your favorite places frequently, you can make them available for offline browsing. This means that the page will be saved locally on your computer and you will not need to connect to your service provider every time you want to see it. This may save your phone bills, but it will also mean that if the site is updated often you may not have the latest information. To make a page available for viewing offline, position the cursor over the favorite and right-click. Place the mouse cursor over **Choose Make Available Offline** from the pop-up menu and left-click.

ORGANIZING YOUR FAVORITES

You will find that your list of favorites grows very quickly, and you may find it helpful to create a structured filing system for them so that you can easily find the things you are looking for. You can do this with folders in much the same way that you organize any other files that you store on your computer. Because the Web is changing all the time, you may also find occasions when you go to a favorite only to discover that it no longer exists. It is easy to delete a defunct favorite from the list. All these functions can be managed from the Organize Favorites box. This box can be accessed from the Favorites menu or the Favorites panel.

1 ORGANIZING IN FAVORITES PANEL

● Position the cursor over the **Favorites** button on the main toolbar and click once.

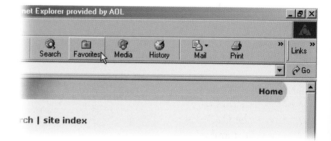

● Position the cursor over the **Organize** button in the Favorites panel and click once.

● The **Organize Favorites** box will open.

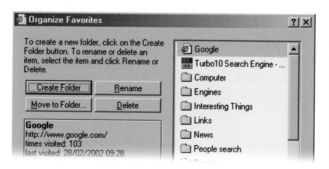

2 ORGANIZING IN FAVORITES MENU

● Alternatively, position the mouse cursor over **Favorites** on the Menu bar and click once.
● Position the mouse cursor over **Organize Favorites** and click once.
● The **Organize Favorites** box opens.

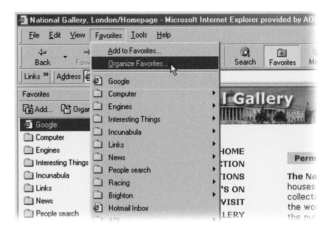

CREATING A NEW FOLDER

● To create a new folder on the top level simply click the **Create Folder** button. A new folder will appear in the list on the right.
● Type the name of the folder and then press the $\boxed{\text{Enter} \hookleftarrow}$ key.
● To create a folder within another folder, click on the folder in the list on the right so that it becomes highlighted.

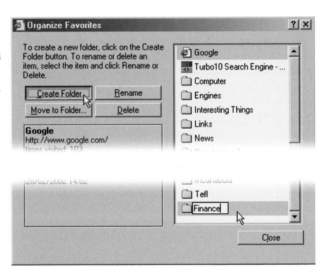

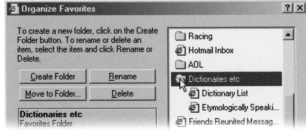

● Now click the **Create Folder** button. Then type the name of the new folder.

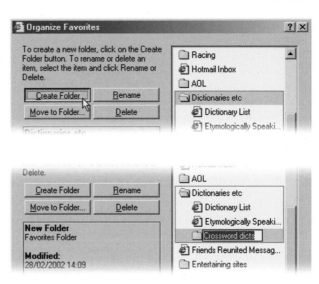

MOVING A FAVORITE

● To move a favorite from one folder to another, click on the favorite in the list on the right so that it is highlighted.
● Click the **Move to Folder** button. The **Browse for Folder** window opens.

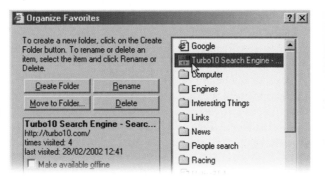

Drag and drop

If you can see the location to which you want to move a favorite, you can place the cursor over it, hold down the mouse button and "drag" it to the new location where it can be "dropped."

- Navigate to the folder that you wish to store the favorite in, and single-click on the folder to select it.
- When you have selected the folder, click on the **OK** button to move the favorite to the selected folder.

DELETING A FAVORITE

- To delete a favorite, click on the favorite in the list on the right so that it is highlighted.
- Position the cursor over the **Delete** button and click once. The favorite will be removed from the Favorites list.

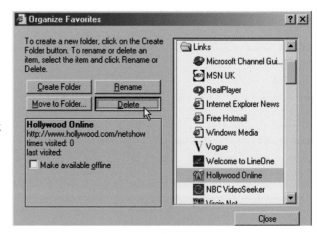

ADDING A FAVORITE TO THE LINKS BAR

To add a favorite site to the Links bar while it's on-screen, place the cursor over the Internet Explorer icon at the beginning of the address and hold down the left mouse button. Drag to the Links bar and find a location where the cursor changes to a vertical bar and release the mouse button. Your site now appears in the Links bar.

RENAMING A FAVORITE

- To rename a favorite, click on the favorite in the list on the right so that it is highlighted.
- Click on the **Rename** button. The name of the favorite becomes highlighted in a box so that you can edit it.
- Type in the new name and press the [Enter ←] key. You will see the name change in the list.

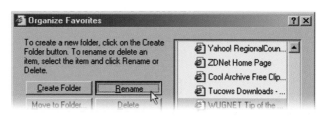

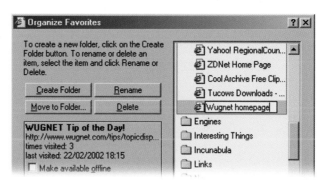

CLOSING THE ORGANIZE BOX

- When you have finished, close the **Organize Favorites** box by clicking on the Close button.

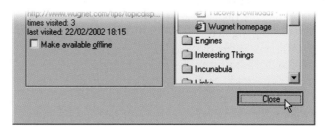

USING THE RIGHT MOUSE BUTTON

With the Favorites panel open in the browser window, you can perform several of the activities shown here, such as deleting and renaming, directly from the panel by using the right mouse button. Position the mouse cursor over any favorite and click the right mouse button once. You will see a pop-up menu with **Delete** and **Rename** as options. Move the mouse cursor over the desired option and click the left mouse button to activate it. If you choose **Delete**, you will be asked to confirm the action. Click **Yes** to proceed. If you select **Rename**, a text box that you can edit will appear. Type the new name and press the [Enter ←] key when you have finished.

PERSONALIZING

Internet Explorer is configured using Microsoft's default settings. However, it is possible to personalize the way Internet Explorer looks and works to suit your own preferences.

THE INTERNET OPTIONS WINDOW

The Internet Options window is where you can change Explorer's default settings. It allows you to change aspects such as display settings, security features, connection details, content control, storage of Internet files by the cache (an area of temporary memory on your hard disk) and other features. There are also major changes you can make when you have more experience. Most of the settings referred to in this chapter can be changed using the Internet Options window.

OPENING INTERNET OPTIONS WINDOW FROM THE MENU
● Click on **Tools** on the Menu bar to open the Tools menu. Move down to **Internet Options** on the menu and click once to open the **Internet Options** window.

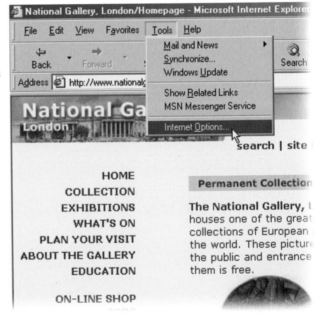

USING THE RIGHT MOUSE BUTTON

● Alternatively, position the mouse cursor over the Explorer icon on the desktop. Click the right mouse button, highlight **Properties** from the pop-up menu that appears, and click the left mouse button to open the **Internet Options** window.

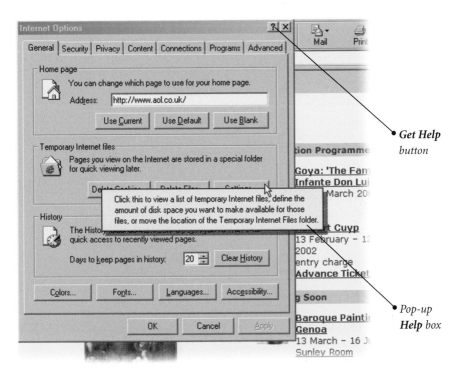

● *Get Help*
button

● *Pop-up*
Help box

HELP WITH INTERNET OPTIONS

● If you are not sure what an Internet Option does, you can get help by clicking on the question mark at top right of the **Internet Options** window. A question mark is attached to the cursor, which you can then move to the option you need help with and then click once. A Help box pops up telling you about that option.

SAVING YOUR OPTIONS

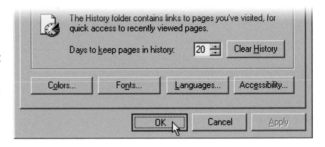

● When you have made any changes to the Internet Options, click on the **OK** button to save the changes. Click **Cancel** if you do not want to save the changes.

CHANGING THE DISPLAY SETTINGS

Web designers often specify the color, size and font for text, the color of links, and background color as part of an integral design of their sites. If you cannot read the text easily, you can override the default settings of the page. The downside is that the look of Web pages may be adversely affected. Text may not flow neatly around images, and some images may appear transparent or fuzzy when viewed against a background color that they were not designed for. However, you can choose to use your preferred settings all the time, or only when a design has not been specified.

CHANGING FONT SIZE FROM THE MENU

You can increase or decrease the size of the text used on Web pages.

● Click on **View** in the Menu bar and highlight **Text Size**. A submenu appears,

● Move the cursor over your preferred option and click with the left mouse button.

● The setting you choose will remain in force until you change it again.

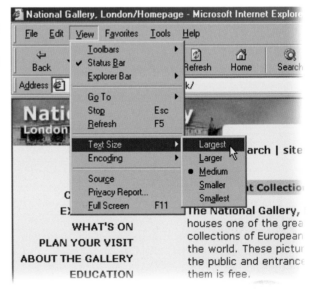

CHOOSING THE TYPEFACE

Under the General tab of Internet Options you can choose which font, or typeface, you would like Internet Explorer to use. The font you choose will be used when a typeface has not been specified in a Web page as part of its design. To choose a font, first open the Internet Options window , place the cursor over the General tab, click once to bring it to the front, and follow these instructions.

● Click the **Fonts** button at the foot of the window to open the **Fonts** box.
● In the **Fonts** dialog box, use the scroll bars to find your preferred font, place the cursor over it and click to select it, then click the **OK** button to select it and return to Internet Options.
● Save your options  to apply the new settings.

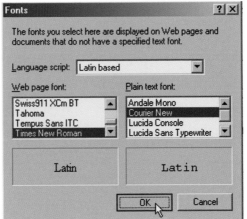

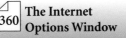

| 360 | The Internet Options Window |
| 362 | Saving Your Options |

CHOOSING HYPERLINK COLORS

You can specify the colors that display normal text, and for unvisited and visited hyperlinks 🗋. You can also choose a "hover" color. If you choose a hover color, a hyperlink changes to that color when you roll the cursor over that link.

SETTING A COLOR

● Whether you want to set a text, hyperlink, or a background color, begin by opening the Internet Options window 🗋 and click on the **General** tab to bring it to the front if it is not already displayed.

● Click the **Colors** button at the foot of the window to open the **Colors** dialog box.

● In the **Colors** dialog box, if there is a check mark in the **Use Windows colors** check box, click in that box to remove the check mark.

● Click the color box next to either **Text** or **Background**, depending on which of the two settings you want to change.

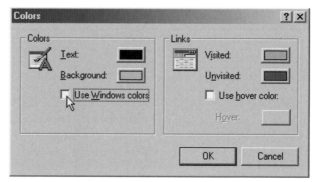

331 **Recognizing Hypertext links**

360 **The Internet Options Window**

● The color palette opens, click on your preferred color then click on **OK**.

● When you want to return to the default text color, simply click in the **Use Window colors** check box to place a check mark in the box.

● Change the **Visited** and **Unvisited** hyperlink colors by following the same process in the **Links** panel.

● To set a hover color, click the mouse in the **Use hover color** check box and then click on the color button next to **Hover**. Select your preferred color from the color palette as before.

● Click on the **OK** button at the bottom to leave the Color dialog box, then save your options to apply the changes.

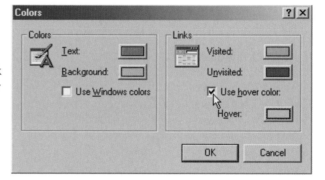

OVERRIDING PAGE DISPLAY SETTINGS

The font and color settings that you choose are only used if a Web page does not specify these options in its design, but with Web developers becoming ever more design conscious, most now tend to specify fonts, font sizes, and colors. If you would prefer to use your settings all the time when using the Web, you can elect to override the design style of the page using Explorer's Accessibility options. These Accessibility options are found under the General tab of the Internet Options. You can choose to override Web page font, background color, and font point size settings, or only a selection of these features. First, open the Internet Options window ⌐ and click the mouse over the General tab to bring it to the front.

● Click on the **Accessibility** button at the bottom of the window to open the **Accessibility** dialog box.
● Place the cursor over the check box next to the option that you want to set, and click to place a check mark in the box. Then click on **OK** to close the **Accessibility** box.
● Save your options ⌐ to apply the changes.

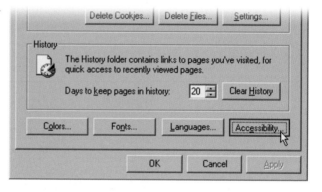

CHANGING YOUR HOME PAGE

The home page is the page that opens each time you start Internet Explorer. When you first install Explorer, the home page is usually configured to open Microsoft's website. There may well be information of interest to you on Microsoft's site, but it is more likely to be of only occasional interest. The ideal home page would be a page that you will want to open each time you connect. It might be a useful jumping off point or source of information you require regularly. The page you choose will depend mainly on how you use the Web. Among the possible contenders as your home page might be your favorite search engine, news site, share tracker, bookstore, game site, chat site, your Internet Service Provider, or email access on the Web. Changing the home page is simple and can be done from the General tab in the Internet Options window.

● In the **Home Page** section of the Internet Options dialog box, double-click the mouse in the **Address** field to highlight the address of your current home page, and type the address of your new home page.
● You can click on **Use Current** if you want to set your home page as the Web page that is currently displayed behind the Internet Options dialog box.
● Save your options to apply the changes. This page now appears when you start Internet Explorer or when you click the **Home** button on the toolbar.

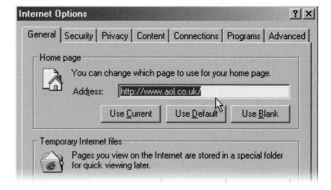

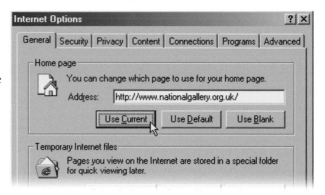

MANAGING THE CACHE

The cache is an area of temporary memory on your hard disk where Explorer stores temporary internet files. These are transferred to your computer when you request a Web page. They display the Web page and include the image, text, and multimedia files. Explorer stores these files so that time can be saved by loading the page from the hard disk if you revisit the page. You may want to clear the cache to save space, you may want to open a page from the cache, or tell Explorer how often to compare a cached page to one on the Web. These instructions show you how.

CLEARING THE CACHE

● You access the cache by first opening the Internet options window and clicking the **General** tab.
● Click on the **Delete Files** button in the **Temporary Internet files** section to clear the cache of these temporary internet files.

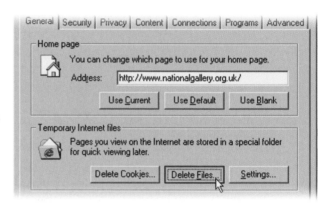

● The **Delete Files** confirm box opens. Simply click on the **OK** button.

OPENING THE CACHE SETTINGS

● Click on the **Settings** button to open the **Settings** dialog box.

● The dialog box options determine how often Explorer checks the cache.

● Choose **Every visit to the page** if you want to make sure you always have the most recent version of a Web page.

● Click the **View Files** button to see a list of files stored in the cache. You can open any of these files in Explorer by double-clicking on them.

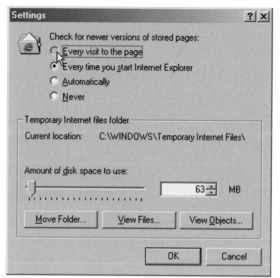

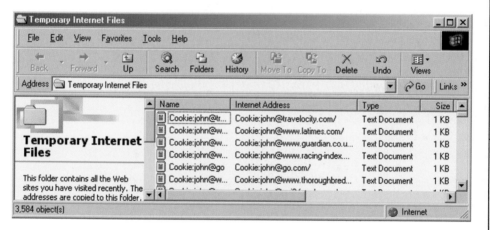

● Click **OK** to leave the **Settings** box. Save your options to apply the changes you have made.

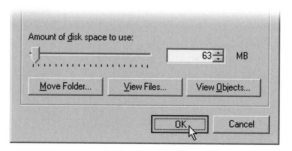

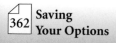

Saving Your Options

362

HANDLING MULTIMEDIA FILES

If you are using the Internet with a slow modem connection, you may decide not to download images and other multimedia files because they slow down the speed at which a Web page is downloaded to your computer. Explorer lets you specify which types of files to turn off in the Advanced section of Internet Options.

● Open the Internet Options window and click on the **Advanced** tab to bring it to the front.
● Use the scroll bar to scroll down until the Multimedia icon is at the top of the window.
● If you want to disable any multimedia files, and they are already checked, click in the check box next to the relevant options from **Play animations, Play Sounds, Play videos**, and **Show pictures**.
● Save your options to apply the changes.

MULTIMEDIA PLUG-INS

Internet Explorer 5 comes with three multimedia "plug-in" programs pre-installed: Shockwave, Flash, and RealPlayer. These plug-ins enable you to view most of the animations, sound files, and videos used on the Internet. If a Web page requires a different plug-in, you will be prompted to install it. This is usually just a process of downloading the software and installing it, then returning to the Web page to see what it has to offer.

360 **The Internet Options Window**

362 **Saving Your Options**

CHOOSING PROGRAMS

Explorer provides its own email and newsreading facilities, in the shape of the Outlook Express program, but if you already have email or newsreading programs installed on your computer, your can opt to use those programs instead of Outlook Express. By setting your program preferences, you are able to access your other programs directly when you choose email or News from Explorer's Tools menu. Follow these instructions to set up the available program options. First, open the Internet Options dialog box and click the Programs tab.

● Choose your preferred option for each of these program types by clicking the arrows to view a list of programs to choose from. Select a program by highlighting it and clicking on it.

● Click **OK** to save your chosen options.

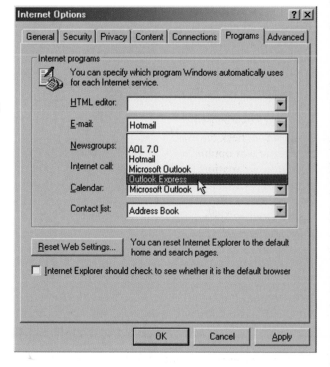

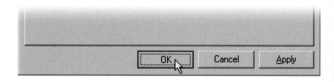

SETTING UP SECURITY

With the global expansion of electronic commerce, and money changing hands over the internet around the clock, online security is an important issue, but one that can only be touched on here. Internet Explorer provides several types of security settings. It allows you to set the level of risk that you are prepared to take when receiving data over the internet. For example, how likely is the data to harm your computer with a virus? It also offers control over the type of content you receive; and it has features that enable you to identify secure and trusted websites. This is particularly important since the advent of online shopping.

SETTING THE ZONE AND LEVEL

The Internet Option **Security** tab enables you to categorize particular websites into various zones, such as trusted or restricted, and set the level of security you would like to operate across each zone, such as high or low security risk. You may want to set up this security for "secure" websites where you can shop or send confidential information. To set up the security for a zone, follow this sequence:

● Highlight the relevant icon in the top panel by clicking on it.

● Click on the **Sites** button to add a site to that zone (this option is only available for the Trusted and Restricted zones).

● The **Trusted sites** dialog box opens. Type the address of the website you would like to add in the **Add this webSite to the zone** field, then click **OK**.

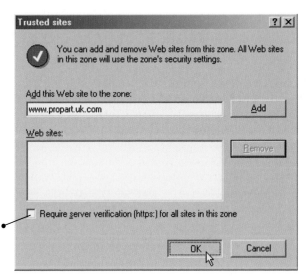

Check this box if you want this zone to include "secure" websites, that are prefixed by **https://** *only.*

● Use the mouse to drag the **Security level** slider to the desired position (you will see the name of the level change as you move the slider).
● Click **OK** to save your changes or repeat the sequence for another site.

Security level slider

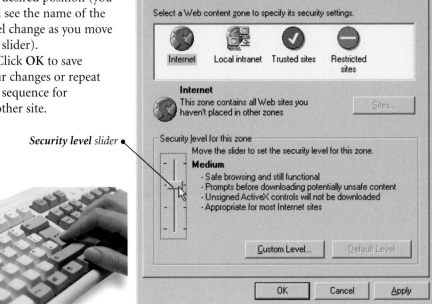

CONTROLLING CONTENT

As well as being the home to millions of interesting sites, the Web is also fertile ground for pornography and many other forms of unauthorized, offensive, and illegal information. To prevent your Web browser from being used to view sites that contain this kind of material, you can use Explorer's Content Advisor features. These enable you to censor sites that feature bad language, nudity, sex, and violence.

● First, open the Internet Options window and click the **Content** tab.
● In the **Content Advisor** dialog box, click on the **Enable** button.

● On the **Ratings** tab, click on the type of content that you want to control in the **Select a category** window.

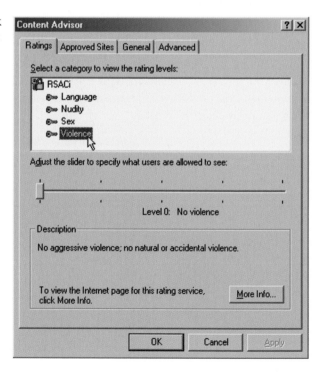

● Drag the slider across to the desired level of access (you will see information about the levels as you move the slider).

● Repeat this process for each of the content types you want to control.

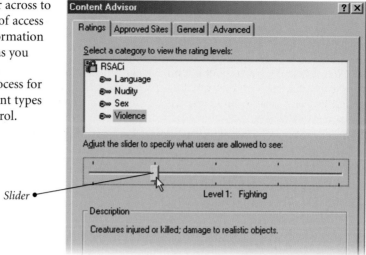

Slider

● Click on the **OK** button.

● Type your password in both fields of the **Create Supervisor Password** box. (Remember to make a note of this somewhere safe!) Now click on **OK**.

● Your content security is now set up and only you, as the holder of the password, can alter the settings.

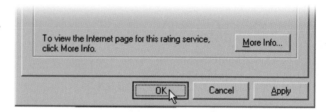

OUTLOOK EXPRESS

Outlook Express is part of Microsoft's Internet Explorer web browser suite of programs. It offers all the features you need to be able to send and receive electronic mail over the internet.

WHAT OUTLOOK EXPRESS CAN DO

Outlook Express provides a gateway to the world of electronic mail. It allows you to send ⌐ and receive ⌐ electronic mail messages, and it provides facilities for you to record and store all your email addresses and personal contact details, in the form of an electronic address book.

Outlook Express has the additional benefit that if there are other people who wish to use your computer to receive their own email, you can create multiple user identities so that their email and contact details can be kept separately and privately from your own.

EMAIL

Email is the main activity provided by Outlook Express. It provides a user-friendly interface that makes it easy to compose, send, and receive email messages directly from the main window. Email messages can contain text, pictures, hypertext links to websites, and even self-contained file attachments.

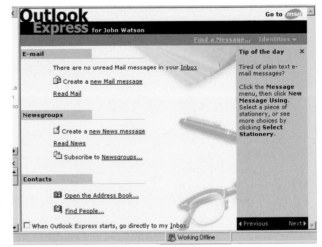

381 Sending Messages

382 Checking for Mail

LAUNCHING OUTLOOK EXPRESS

Outlook Express can be started, or "launched" from either the Windows Start menu, directly from the desktop (if the Outlook Express shortcut has been placed on the desktop), or from within Microsoft's Internet Explorer program itself. Follow the steps to launch the program using any of these methods.

FROM THE DESKTOP

To launch Outlook Express from the desktop:

● Locate the Outlook Express shortcut icon. This has the appearance of an envelope with two blue arrows encircling it, and the words "Outlook Express" are written beneath it.

● Position the mouse pointer over the Outlook Express icon and double-click the left mouse button to launch the program.

THE OUTLOOK EXPRESS PANEL

Once the program has started up, the Outlook Express window appears showing the Outlook Express panel on the left. This panel has shortcuts to some features of the program, such as creating new email messages and opening the Address Book.

The Outlook Express window

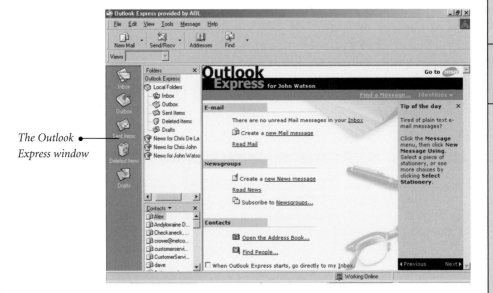

THE MESSAGE WINDOW

Email messages are composed in the Message Window, which is accessed by clicking the New Mail button on the toolbar. An email message is made up of several parts. The message "header" contains the sender, the recipient(s), and the subject of the message. The message "body" contains the message itself. A message may also contain other elements such as file attachments. These pages show the message window and how to use it to compose an email.

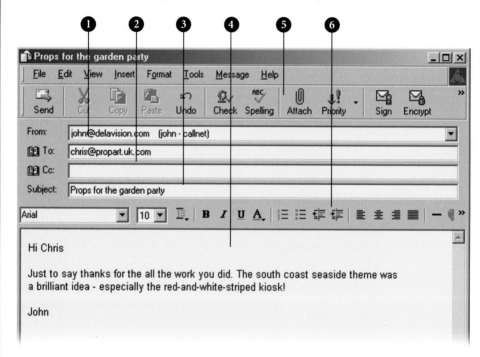

THE MESSAGE WINDOW

1 The To: field
This contains the address of the recipient

2 The Cc: field
This contains the addresses of other recipients of the message

3 The Subject: field
This contains the subject of the message

4 The message body
This is where the text is entered

5 The Toolbar
This contains the main activities you will carry out

6 The Formatting Toolbar
This allows you to word-process your messages

COMPOSING A MESSAGE

Composing a message can involve a number of different steps, which depend, for example, on whether you wish to include extra files, how many recipients there are, or whether you intend to send the message immediately. This section shows the basic process of composing an email and refers you to other sections where you will find information on how to carry out the other options.

COMPOSING A NEW MESSAGE

● Select a mail folder, such as the Inbox or Outbox, by clicking it in the Folder list or Folder bar.

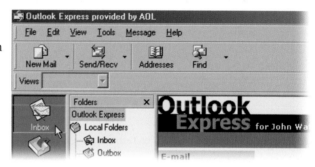

● Click the New Mail button on the toolbar. This opens a new Outlook Express message window.
● Click the mouse in the message body area of the window and type the text of your message.

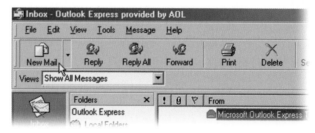

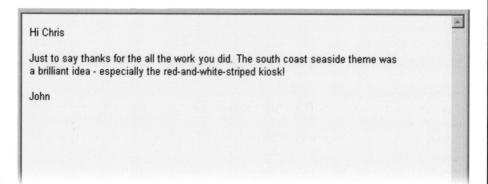

Hi Chris

Just to say thanks for the all the work you did. The south coast seaside theme was a brilliant idea - especially the red-and-white-striped kiosk!

John

ADDRESSING A MESSAGE

You can send a message to only one person, or simultaneously to as many people as you want by including all their email addresses in the address or the Cc: fields. Type the addresses exactly, otherwise they will not be delivered.

1 TYPING THE ADDRESS

● Place the cursor in the Address field and type the recipient's email address. Follow the capitalization and punctuation exactly.

2 USING CARBON COPIES

● You can send a "carbon copy" of an email to one or more people at the same time by typing their address(es) in the **Cc:** field.

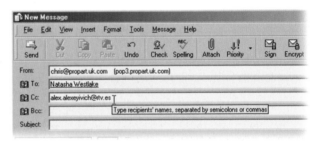

3 MULTIPLE RECIPIENTS

If you wish to include more than one address in either the Address or the Cc: field, first click in either field.

● Type the first email address, taking care to type it exactly.

● Type a semicolon or a comma, then a space, and then the next address. Repeat this step for each new address.

SENDING MESSAGES

Outlook Express offers several options when sending: you can send a message at once or send it later. For example, you can use Send Options to keep copies of messages, or to record automatically the addresses of people who write to you.

1 THE MESSAGE WINDOW

● To send a message you have finished composing, click the Send button on the toolbar. If you are online, it will be sent immediately. If you are offline, the message will be automatically stored in the Outbox ready for sending when you go online.

2 SENDING LATER

If you have finished a message, but do not want to send it immediately, you can store it to be sent later.

● Click on File in the Menu bar and select Send Later. The message is saved in the Outbox ready for sending when you go online to send your messages.

CHECKING FOR MAIL

When you launch 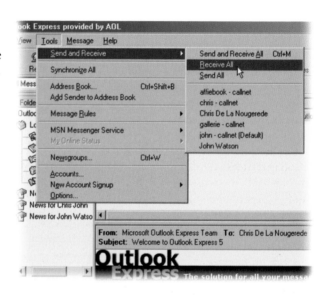 Outlook Express and go online, the program checks your mail server for incoming mail and downloads new messages into your Inbox so that you can read them. There are several methods that you can use to check for new mail while you are online.

To try them out, first open the Inbox by clicking the Inbox button or folder in either the Outlook bar or the Folders list. When you want to receive mail you will need to go online. If you try to collect mail while offline, you will be prompted to connect to your service provider.

USING THE MENU

● Click on the **Tools** in the Menu bar and choose **Send and Receive**. From the submenu that appears, choose either **Send and Receive All** or **Receive All**, depending on whether or not you wish to send messages at the same time as checking for new ones.

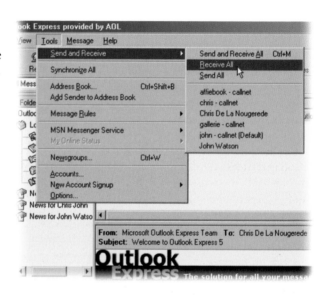

USING THE SEND/ RECV BUTTON

● Click the **Send/Recv** button on the main toolbar. New messages appear in the message list and any mail waiting in your outbox is sent.

READING INCOMING MESSAGES

All your incoming email arrives by default in a message folder called the Inbox. The Inbox can be accessed either from the Outlook bar or the Folders list. It stores and lists all your incoming messages. You may notice that some messages in the Inbox appear in a bold typeface. These are new, or "unread," messages. When you want to read these messages all you have to do is to click the Inbox folder, then select the message you want to read in the message list. As usual, there are several ways in which you can read your incoming mail. To try them out, first open the Inbox by clicking on the Inbox icon on the Outlook bar.

OPENING A MESSAGE

● In the Inbox message list, choose which message you want to read and then double-click the message.

● Alternatively, you can select the message by clicking it once with the mouse, and then press the ⌊Enter ⏎⌋ key to open the message. A message window opens displaying the contents of the message. If the message is too long to fit in the window, use the scroll bars at the side to scroll down through the text.

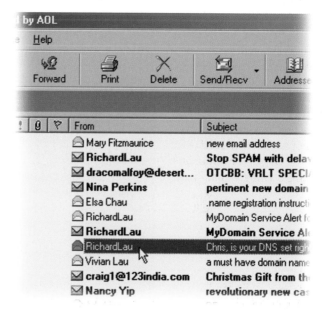

THE NEW MAIL ICON

It is easy to tell when new messages arrive because a New Mail icon appears on the Windows taskbar. This has the appearance of an envelope. To be able to view the messages, you must go to your Inbox in the main Outlook Express window.

RESPONDING TO MESSAGES

There are several ways in which you may wish to respond to incoming email. You may want to reply to the sender directly, to all the recipients of the message, or to forward the message on to someone else, perhaps including a brief note of your own. You may want to print the message, or you may not want to respond at all, but just move the message to a new folder so that you can keep it for reference. Outlook provides for all of these eventualities. Many of these activities can be carried out from the message window. To practice them, first open the message.

1 REPLYING TO THE SENDER

● To reply to the sender, click the **Reply** button on the toolbar. A message window opens with the contents of the sender's message included, and his or her email address inserted in the **To:** field. Type your response and send it in the normal way.

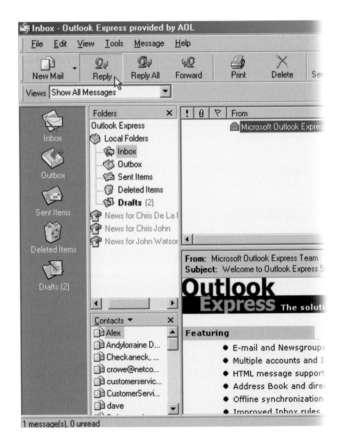

2 REPLYING TO ALL

● To reply to the sender of the message as well as all the other people to whom the message was circulated, click the **Reply All** button on the toolbar.

● A message window will open with the contents of the sender's message included, and all the recipients' addresses listed in the address fields.

● Compose your response and then send it in the normal way.

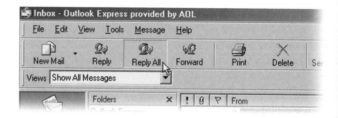

3 FORWARDING MESSAGES

● To forward a message to one or more people, click the Forward button on the toolbar. A message window will open with the contents of the sender's message included, but the address field will be blank.

● If you want to add remarks of your own, click the mouse at the top of the typing area and type your message in that area.

● Address the message 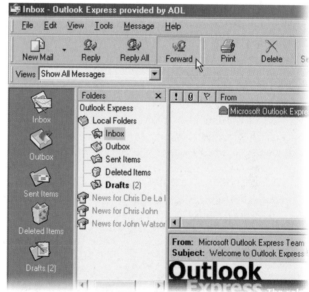 to the recipients and send it in the usual way.

4 PRINTING THE MESSAGE

● To print the message, click the Print button on the toolbar. Choose from the print options and then click the OK button.

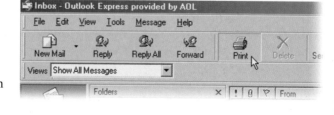

MANAGING YOUR EMAIL MESSAGES

There is more to email than just receiving and reading, and composing and sending messages. If you become an active email correspondent, before long your Inbox (and Sent Messages folder) will become so full as to be overflowing. Many people find it useful to create new mail folders into which they can move messages to be kept. Messages that you do not want have to be deleted on a regular basis to save valuable space on the hard disk. This section shows how to perform the basic activities that will help you manage your email messages effectively.

1 DELETING MESSAGES

To delete a message from the message list, click on the message file and then press the [Del] key on the keyboard or the Delete button on the toolbar. The message is removed from the message list and transferred to the Deleted Items folder.

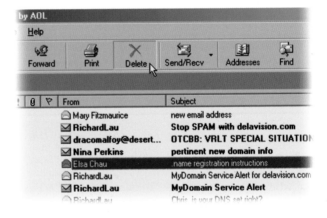

2 CREATING A NEW FOLDER

● Position the mouse on one of the folders in the Folders list and right-click the mouse once. From the pop-up menu choose **New Folder**. The **Create Folder** dialog box opens.

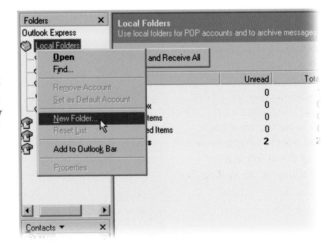

- Click the mouse in the **Folder Name** field and type the name of the folder.
- In the Folders list below click the mouse on the folder in which you would like to create the new folder. The folder becomes highlighted.
- Click the **OK** button to create the folder. The new folder will now appear in the Folders list.

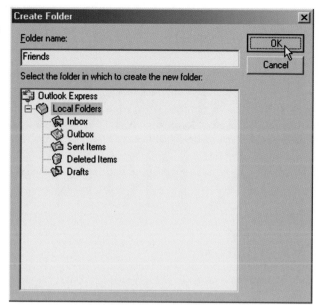

3 MOVING TO OTHER FOLDERS

- To move a message from one folder to another, ensure that the Folders list and the Message window are visible.
- Place the mouse pointer over the message you want to move and hold down the mouse button.
- Drag the mouse pointer until it is over the folder into which you would like to move the message. Release the mouse button and the message is relocated in the new folder.

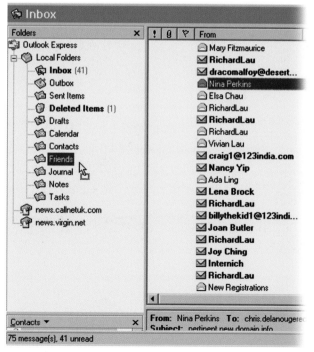

SCANNERS & PRINTERS

EVEN THE MOST NOVICE OF PC USERS, or those on a tight budget, now have the chance to scan images into a computer, manipulate them into their own designs, and print out the results in color at near-photographic quality. With cheap and easy-to-use scanners and inkjet printers, the creative possibilities are endless. Yet the whole process can seem daunting to the uninitiated.

This section provides straightforward guidance on all aspects of scanning and printing, taking you through the whole process, from choosing and installing the hardware, to scanning, correcting, and printing your images. By the end of the section, you will have received a thorough grounding in using these two vital pieces of PC hardware, and will be ready to let your imagination run wild.

THE HARDWARE

A scanner and printer are probably the first things you should consider buying in addition to the computer itself. If you are lucky, they may have even been included in your PC package.

DISCOVERING THE POSSIBILITIES

Your PC really isn't proving its worth if you haven't yet discovered the possibilities open to you by adding a scanner and color printer to the setup. Being able to transfer images into your computer opens up an exciting new world of creativity, as the PC is a very powerful tool when it comes to manipulating and editing them.

THE HOME PC SETUP
With the right peripherals, your PC can become a truly creative workstation.

Your computer is used to treat the images in any way you like; and with the right software you can manipulate your pictures beyond recognition.

Pictures and photographs enter your computer via the scanner and are saved on your hard drive.

MANIPULATING YOUR IMAGES

At first you will just be thrilled to see your pictures and photographs appear on your monitor screen. You might apply them to your Windows Me desktop as a "wallpaper," or simply treat your color printer as a copier, and make duplicates of photographs for your friends. The next step is to create your own designs for cards, invitations, or magazine pages by inserting scanned images into desktop publishing (DTP) and word processing programs.

From here the really exciting stuff begins. With graphics and image editing software, you can manipulate your images, perhaps combining two or three pictures into a montage. Have you ever wanted to be pictured standing on an exotic beach? Now you can, without ever going there!

Your printer can add to the creativity, too. Many have the facility to print long banners, or transfers that you can apply to T-shirts. The possibilities really are endless – you just need plenty of imagination.

PERIPHERALS

An external piece of hardware that is connected to your computer (such as a scanner or printer) is known as a peripheral. Peripherals are connected via cables to ports at the back of your computer, and require software "drivers" that are installed on to your computer's hard drive in order to operate.

The printer can output your modified image in minutes, usually at near-photographic quality. You can reduce or enlarge your designs, and print as many copies as you like.

WHAT DOES A SCANNER DO?

A scanner is used to transfer pictures, patterns, and images from printed material or photographs into your computer. A lamp passes over the item you are scanning, transferring the information back to the PC as digital data through a light sensitive chip called a CCD (see box below).

A DESKTOP REFLECTIVE SCANNER

The lid of the scanner is closed during a scan to prevent external light from entering the scanner and affecting the quality of the scan.

The item that you want to scan is placed faced down on the glass of the scanner, also known as the scanner bed.

The scanner lamp passes over the picture, reflecting light back into the CCD chip. The scan is then converted into digital data and displayed on your PC.

Rulers and guides are printed around the scanner bed to help position items accurately.

Some scanners have a button that launches the scanning software, or even performs the scan itself.

THE CCD CHIP

Most of the technology involved in scanning the image is centered around the CCD chip *(charge-coupled device)*. Put simply, the sensors on the CCD measure the light being reflected from your picture by the three primary colors (red, green, and blue). This is enough information for your image to appear in full color by the time it reaches your computer.

WHAT DOES A PRINTER DO?

Without a printer, you are unable to output any images and designs from your computer. While there are several different types available, as a home PC user you are most likely to own a color inkjet printer. These printers transfer dots of ink onto the paper by firing it from a cartridge through small nozzles or crystals contained in a print-head. Although you may see the picture you have printed in full glorious technicolor, in actual fact the printer – like the scanner – has only used a small range of different colors to recreate the image, overlapping the various inks to provide millions of colors.

A COLOR INKJET PRINTER

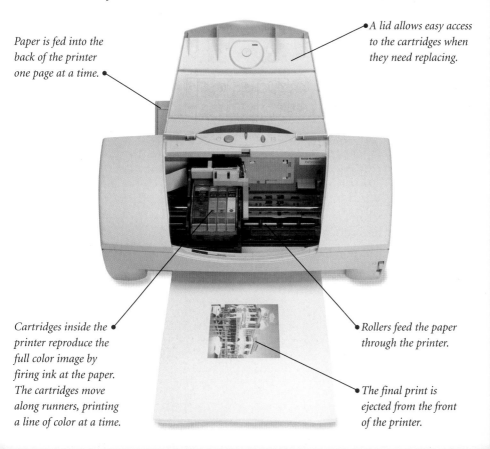

Paper is fed into the back of the printer one page at a time.

A lid allows easy access to the cartridges when they need replacing.

Cartridges inside the printer reproduce the full color image by firing ink at the paper. The cartridges move along runners, printing a line of color at a time.

Rollers feed the paper through the printer.

The final print is ejected from the front of the printer.

THE RIGHT PURCHASE

It is important to consider carefully what you will be using your scanner and printer for, and the results you expect from them, before making a decision at the computer store.

DIFFERENT TYPES OF SCANNER

On the face of it, most of the scanners you see in the computer store will look very similar. The differences are primarily hidden in the technology, with some scanners offering far higher resolution than others ⬧. An important physical difference to be aware of, however, is that most scanners only scan reflective material (items that reflect light from their surface, such as photographs). There are some scanners available that can also scan transparent items (objects through which the light passes, such as slides and photographic negatives).

FLATBED REFLECTIVE SCANNERS

The most common type of scanner is one that scans reflective material such as printed pictures and photographs. There is a huge range to choose from and most are quite compact in size.

ALL-IN-ONE

There are some printers available that can also scan, fax, and copy all in one ⬧. If convenience and space-saving are your goals, then this might be the solution. However, don't expect them to offer the same range of functions or quality as a scanner that is dedicated to the task.

Reflective
The Visioneer 6100 USB scanner.

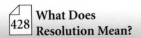

428 What Does Resolution Mean?

397 Black and White Laser Printers

USING A DIGITAL CAMERA INSTEAD OF A SCANNER

A scanner is simply a means of turning graphic information into a digital file and getting it into your computer. If you have a digital camera, this, in effect, performs a very similar task. Assess your needs and think about using your camera to transfer simple graphics or low-quality pictures on to your PC – you may not need a scanner at all. For example, you could very easily photograph a piece of artwork, such as a hand-drawn logo, and then retouch it or trace it in a graphics program.

FLATBED SCANNERS WITH A TRANSPARENCY HOOD

If you want to scan transparencies and photographic slides into your computer, you will need a scanner with a transparency hood. The hood contains a second lamp that replaces the usual flat lid covering the scanner bed.

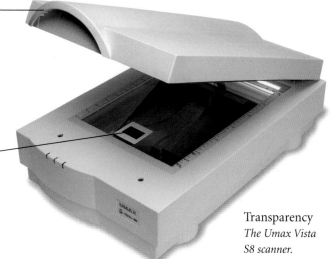

In addition to the standard lamp in the bottom of the scanner, the transparency hood also contains a lamp so that light can pass through the slide or transparency.

Transparencies and slides are positioned on the scanner glass like a conventional picture. Depending on your scanning software, you can sometimes scan many into your computer at once.

Transparency
The Umax Vista S8 scanner.

DRUM SCANNERS

Drum scanners are way beyond the budget, and needs, of the average PC user. However, if you ever require a particularly good quality scan for a professional job then you can send your picture to a bureau. They will use a drum scanner (so-called because the picture is attached to a rotating cylindrical drum) and provide you with a high resolution image on disk.

DIFFERENT TYPES OF PRINTER

Dot matrix printers, which used long rolls of perforated paper and offered very poor print quality, are now rarely seen; and although there are other good quality printers around – dye sublimation printers, for example – their use is usually restricted to professional proofing. For the average user, printer choice has now really fallen between inkjet printers and laser printers, and you will see an abundance of these available at the computer store.

COLOR INKJET PRINTERS

These have fast become the most suitable printer for the home user. The cost of the printer and the quality of the prints themselves seems dispropor-tionate, as most inkjets are capable of near-photographic quality yet many cost very little to buy.

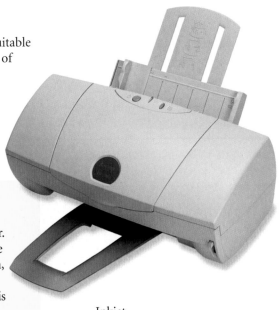

What does Bubble Jet mean?
You may see the term "Bubble Jet" used in relation to an inkjet printer. Don't let this confuse you – Bubble Jet is simply a trademark of Canon, and although the technology may differ slightly, a Bubble Jet printer is still an inkjet printer.

Inkjet
The Canon BJC3000 Bubble Jet printer.

INK CARTRIDGES

Color inkjet printers use replaceable ink cartridges that usually contain three inks – yellow, magenta, and cyan, and sometimes also black. If you have a lot of pages to print that consist of only text, then some models provide the option of replacing the color cartridge with one that contains only black ink.

BLACK AND WHITE LASER PRINTERS

Although more expensive than color inkjets, laser printers provide high-quality, black-and-white prints that are particularly suited to lengthy text documents. Because they print at a very fast rate, they are also especially useful if you want to print multiple copies. The most common models take 8½ x 11in (A4) paper, however there are also some available that can take both 8½ x 11in and 11 x 17in (A3).

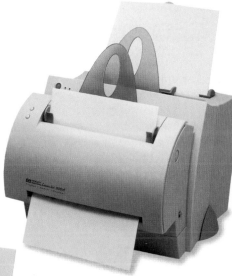

Laser

A lot of laser printers aimed at the home and small business user, like the Hewlett Packard HP1100A (above) and 3150 (left) LaserJet printers, serve a multitude of tasks. As well as print, they can also scan black and white images and act as a fax machine. In addition, these models can operate independently from the computer as photocopiers.

TONER CARTRIDGES

Like photocopiers, laser printers use a cartridge containing heat-sensitive black toner. The toner in a cartridge goes a very long way and should provide a few thousand prints before it needs replacing.

CHOOSING A SCANNER AND PRINTER

There is a scanner and printer available to suit every need and budget. However, with so much choice, you should carefully consider what results you expect before buying. Unlike printers, the availability of different types of desktop scanner is limited, so choice is really dictated by the technical specification of each one. Your choice of printer falls realistically between a color inkjet printer or a black-and-white laser printer, and you need to be familiar with their advantages and disadvantages. Generally speaking, an inkjet printer will provide the most flexibility and, most importantly, color. The choice of color inkjets can still be overwhelming though, with the price range being vast, so look carefully at the functions each one offers.

THINGS TO CONSIDER WHEN BUYING A SCANNER

RESOLUTION
Probably the most crucial aspect of choosing a scanner is the resolution that it offers ⬚. Resolution affects the final quality of your scanned image, so you need to assess what you need and compare your requirements to the scanners on offer. Look for a scanner that offers at least 600 x 1200dpi resolution (you may also see 300 x 600dpi on offer – which is lower – and 1200 x 2400dpi, which is higher).

COLOR DEPTH
Color depth affects the color of your image and is measured in bits. The higher bit-depth your scanner boasts, the better represented the color will be in the final scan. Look for a scanner with 36-bit color depth.

WHAT YOU ARE SCANNING
Remember that if you want to scan photographic slides into your computer, then the scanner you choose will need a transparency hood ⬚. Unfortunately, however, this facility comes with a higher price.

SOFTWARE
Take extra care to study what software is provided with each scanner. This can vary dramatically from model to model, but even the most basic scanners should come with a simple scanning program. You don't have to pay very much more, however, to find scanners that are bundled with image editing software as well, sometimes even scaled-down versions of professional packages. These are invaluable if you want to start retouching your images and correcting them to improve their quality ⬚. Another useful application to find included is optical character recognition software, which scans text into your computer as an editable document ⬚.

⬚ 428	**What Does Resolution Mean?**	⬚ 395	**Transparency Hood**
⬚ 434	**Improving Your Scan**	⬚ 433	**Optical Cha Recognitior**

THINGS TO CONSIDER WHEN BUYING A PRINTER

PRINT QUALITY

Although laser printers have always offered the best quality prints (you should expect a minimum of 300dpi–600dpi), inkjets are improving rapidly. Photographic quality is now common-place on even the budget models, and you should expect a resolution of 600dpi–1200dpi on the inkjet printer that you buy.

COLOR OR BLACK AND WHITE?

This is simple. Unless you really do need to output many black and white documents (in which case a laser printer may suit you better), buy a color inkjet for maximum flexibility.

SPEED

Inkjets can be notoriously slow, especially if your computer doesn't have much processing power 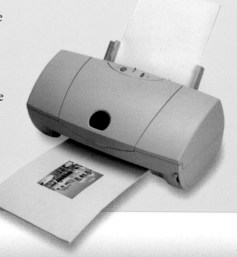, but this is a small price to pay for photo quality prints. Unfortunately, an inkjet can be just as slow even when it only has one color to print. For printing many pages of black text, a laser printer will be more suitable – the speed of printing is unsurpassed when it comes to desktop printers.

PAPER SIZE

Affordable inkjet printers accommodate 8½ x 11in (A4) paper, although some offer the facility to print banners on a roll. Although laser printers are also commonly 8½ x 11in, there are models available with two trays – one for 8½ x 11in, one for 11 x 17in (A3).

RUNNING COSTS

Although inkjets have fairly high running costs when you take into consideration the price of replacement ink cartridges and the special paper required, for short runs and infrequent printing they are perfect. Laser printers provide many more prints from their toner cartridges and use standard copy paper that is cheap to buy.

SIZE

Inkjet printers are particularly compact, as the component parts, including the ink cartridge, are small. Also, the paper is usually fed into the printer from above, sometimes one sheet at a time. Laser printers have to accommodate a reasonably large toner cartridge and sometimes a removable paper tray, usually situated at the bottom of the printer where you can stack many sheets of paper. Therefore, a laser printer will take up more desk space – far more if you opt for an 11 x 17in (A3) model.

COMPATIBILITY

Before rushing out to purchase any scanner or printer,
you will need to determine what can feasibly be connected
and used with your own computer.

CABLE CONNECTIONS AND PORTS

If you have recently bought a home computer package that included a scanner and printer, as well as all the cables required to connect everything, you should not encounter any compatibility problems. However, not all scanners and printers are compatible with every PC on the market, and this issue can become even more complicated if you are trying to connect a new scanner or printer to an old PC, or attaching many different external hardware devices.

WHAT CONNECTION DO I HAVE?
Before choosing a scanner or printer, you need to determine exactly what connection sockets (known as ports) are available at the back of your computer, so that you can purchase devices that are compatible. The three main types of connection are parallel, SCSI, and USB. Each has its advantages concerning the rate of data transfer, but some also have many disadvantages when it comes to ease of installation.

SCSI computer cable and port.

SCSI PORTS
SCSI *(Small Computer System Interface)* devices require a card to be inserted into the inside of your computer that incorporates the SCSI port. SCSI ports provide a fast rate of data transfer, but also create the most work when it comes to installation. Unless your PC already has a SCSI port, you will have to start tinkering about inside your computer to install one, so SCSI is probably best left alone.

PARALLEL PORTS

Most computers have a parallel port, which has been the standard for connecting a printer to a PC for some time. Installation of parallel devices is reasonably straightforward, but the down side is that using a parallel scanner along with a parallel printer can create a few compatibility problems. The printer shown also has a USB port (see below).

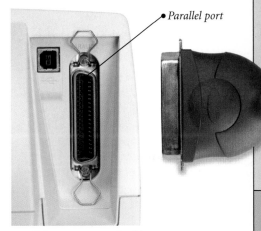

Parallel port

Parallel printer port and cable.

USB PORTS

On the other hand, USB *(Universal Serial Bus)* ports have started to become the new standard on modern computers, and both parallel and SCSI ports are being superceded by USB technology. USB provides huge advantages in connecting peripherals to your computer as, in theory, devices that you connect are "plug and play." In other words, you can plug in the device and start using it with minimum fuss. The message here is that if you are buying a new PC package, look for USB compatibility throughout all of your devices. **We will be concentrating on connecting USB devices in this book.**

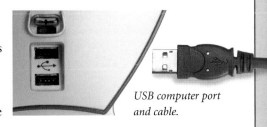

USB computer port and cable.

USB peripheral port and cable.

USB HUBS

The main advantage of USB, apart from the ease in which you can simply "plug-and-play," is the number of different peripherals you can connect to your PC in a chain. However unlikely it may be for you to need such versatility, you are actually able to connect up to 127 USB devices to your computer. Normally, you would only expect to connect half a dozen at most, but to keep things neat you may want to consider investing in a USB hub. This device sits next to your computer and plugs into one of the USB ports. The hub itself is basically a multiadaptor containing a number of USB ports that enable you to plug all your peripherals into a port of their own. This keeps the cable connections accessible on your desk, rather than behind the computer.

HARDWARE REQUIREMENTS

The whole issue of your PC's processing power, and its suitability for your external devices, can soon spiral down into indecipherable technical jargon. However, if you have recently bought a new PC, it will most probably have enough power to operate your scanner and printer, and allow you to run a few top-end graphics and photo retouching programs as well. If you are concerned, perhaps because you are still running an old PC with a slow processor, then just check on a couple of things before attempting to attach a new scanner and printer. The hardware checklist on this page gives a list of ideal requirements.

CHECKING YOUR SYSTEM SPEC

If you have kept the packaging from your computer, the chances are that there will be a sticker on the box listing specifications like processor speed, RAM, and hard drive capacity. However, if you have upgraded your computer, these details may now be inaccurate. If you have no written details available, you can obtain some of the information by right-clicking on the icons for **My Computer** and the hard drive (C:) and selecting **Properties**.

HARDWARE CHECKLIST

By ensuring that your PC has the following recommended minimum specifications, you should not have any difficulty using a scanner and printer. You will also have enough disk space and processing power to use image editing software and save high resolution scans.

- 300MHz processor
- 32Mb of RAM
- 3Gb of hard drive space
- 24-bit graphics card
- Color monitor
- Two free USB ⬒ ports or a USB hub ⬒.

PRINTER CONSIDERATIONS

Inkjet printers use the PC's memory to process the print job. Therefore, the more memory you have available on your PC, the less likely you are to have a problem with painfully slow printing. It also means that printing won't interfere with other tasks you want to perform on your computer in the meantime. Laser printers usually have their own memory built-in to control the printing, but GDI laser printers – also sometimes called Windows printers – are able to use the computer's memory in the same way that an inkjet printer does.

⬒ 401 **USB Ports**

⬒ 401 **USB Hubs**

CHANGING THE MONITOR SETTINGS

● To ensure your scanned images appear at a good quality onscreen, you should optimize your monitor settings.

● Click on the **Start** button, and select **Control Panel** from the **Settings** menu.

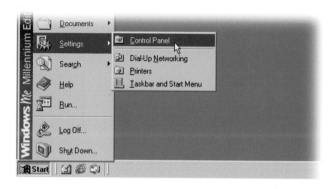

● In the **Control Panel** window, double-click on the **Display** icon.

● The **Display Properties** window will appear.

● In the **Colors** panel, select the highest possible setting (usually **24-bit** or **32-bit**). A lower setting can produce a poor quality image onscreen.

● Click on **OK**.

What is the monitor resolution?

A monitor always displays an image at 72dpi, meaning there are 72 dots, or pixels, of information in every inch of the screen.

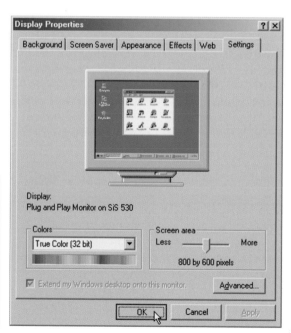

INSTALLING A SCANNER

Before you can start scanning any images, you need to ensure that your computer recognizes the scanner, and that you have installed the software required to operate it.

UNPACKING YOUR NEW SCANNER

It is worth taking time during the whole installation process to ensure that everything goes according to plan. Although the process should be straightforward enough, a simple error early on can result in spending a frustrating couple of hours trying to work out why your scanner isn't working. We are going to take you through the whole process, starting at the beginning with unpacking the scanner from its box. This may seem trivial, but there are a few important points here that are fundamental to the installation process.

Before you start...
It is important to check that everything that should have been supplied with your scanner is in the box. There should be a power cord, a cable to connect the scanner to the computer, a CD-ROM or disk containing software and drivers, and an installation/user manual. If any of these is missing, it will be impossible to install your scanner.

1 REMOVING THE PACKAGING
● Take care when handling your scanner. Although scanners are fairly sturdy, they contain glass and a lamp so they demand some respect!
● There is likely to be some kind of label or other device securing the scanner lid. Begin by removing this and any other residual packaging.

2 UNLOCKING THE SCANNER

• The scanner's moving parts are held in place during transit by a locking mechanism. This varies depending on the make and model, but there should be a switch, bolt/nut, or screw that is usually located on the underside of the scanner.

• Release the mechanism. Keep any screws or bolts in a safe place as you should replace them whenever you transport your scanner in the future.

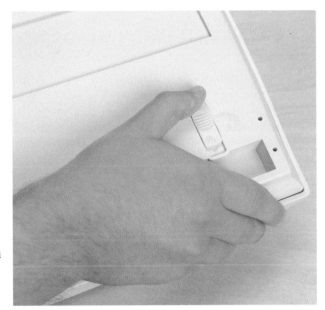

3 LOCATING THE SCANNER

• Place the scanner on a flat, level surface within easy reach of your PC.

• Check that the cables will reach both the power supply and the back of the computer.

CONNECTING THE SCANNER CABLES

The majority of modern scanners and printers come with USB connections 🗎. USB is designed to make the connection and installation of these external devices relatively straightforward. As you are more than likely to be using this form of connection, the following steps, and those in the next chapter, concentrate on installing hardware with USB support. If your computer does not support USB, and is reliant on a parallel or SCSI connection 🗎, then things can be slightly more complicated and you should refer to the installation manuals that came with your scanner.

1 CONNECTING THE USB CABLE

● First, connect the USB cable to the port at the rear of the scanner.
● Important: don't connect the other end of the cable to the computer just yet.

2 CONNECTING THE POWER

● Next, connect the power cord into the jack on the scanner.
● Connect the other end of the cable to an outlet and ensure that both the power and the scanner are turned on.

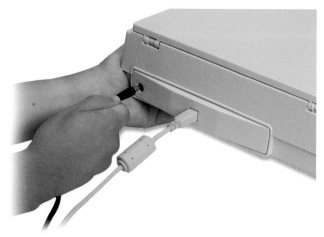

🗎 **401** USB Ports

🗎 **400** What Connection Do I have?

Scanner Installation

Installing the scanner and software is always best done in conjunction with the manual supplied, as there are always differences between manufacturers. The following sequence is therefore intended as an example only, although the steps that we take you through should be very close to those you will encounter for any scanner. The scanner and program that we have chosen (Visioneer PaperPort) requires the software to be installed before the scanner. For an example of installing hardware before software, turn to the printer installation 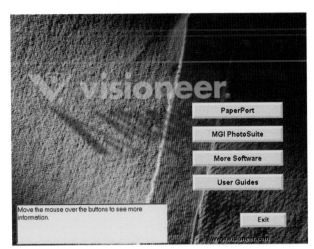.

1 LAUNCHING THE CD-ROM

- Insert the CD-ROM that was supplied with the scanner into your computer's CD drive.
- The disk should start to run automatically and an introductory screen will appear.

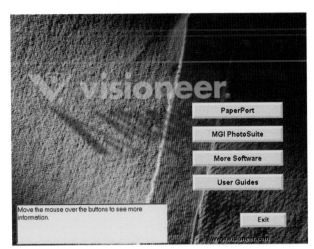

- If this doesn't happen, double-click on the **My Computer** icon on the desktop and launch the disk by double-clicking on the (**D:**) drive icon in the **My Computer** window.

415 **Printer Installation**

2 INSTALLING THE SOFTWARE

● For now, only install the software required to make the scanner work. This should include the hardware drivers and the TWAIN drivers 📄. Our scanner has been supplied with software called PaperPort.

● Click on **Install PaperPort.** You may notice other pieces of software on the disk, such as retouching programs. Ignore these for now as you can install them at a later date if you wish.

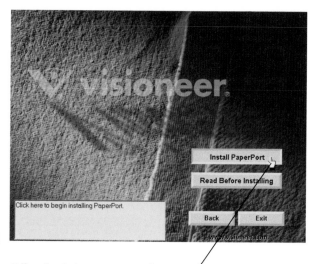

Follow the choices onscreen until you are given the option to install the software

● You may see some progress bars appear while the installation process begins.

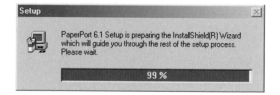

3 REGISTERING THE PRODUCT

● At some point during the installation you will need to read and accept a license agreement.

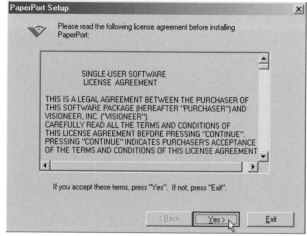

● You will also have to
register the product in
your name.
● Enter the relevant details,
and then click **Next**.

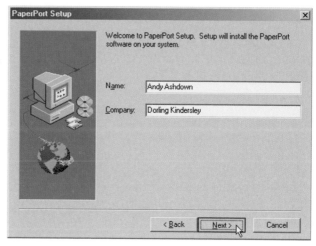

4 SELECTING A LOCATION

● When prompted, select
the location where you
want the software to be
installed on your computer.
These fields are usually
filled in automatically and
direct the software to the
default Programs folder.
● Click on **Next**.

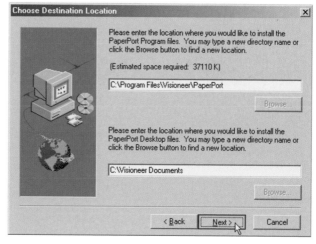

● A progress bar should
appear to indicate that the
files are being copied from
the disk to your hard drive.

5 CONNECTING THE SCANNER

● At this point in our installation process, Windows prompts us to connect the scanner to the computer.

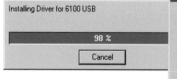

Installing Driver for 6100 USB

98 %

Cancel

Connect your scanner.

Please connect your Visioneer USB scanner now. If you plugged the scanner in prior to installing the software unplug the scanner and plug it back in. Refer to the Installation Guide that came with your scanner for setup instructions. Please press the OK button when done.

OK

● Plug the USB cable from the scanner into the USB port on your computer.

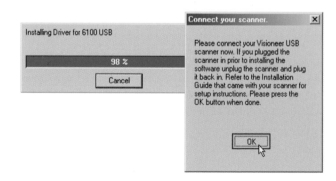

● *Locate an available USB port on the back of your computer*

● As soon as you plug the cable into the USB port, Windows will announce that it has found new hardware and is in the process of loading the relevant software for the scanner.

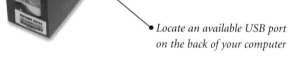

New Hardware Found

Visioneer 6100 USB Scanner

Windows has found new hardware and is locating the software for it.

● Once the installation process is complete press the **OK** button.

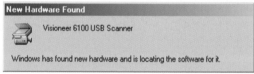

Installing Driver for 6100 USB

98 %

Cancel

Connect your scanner.

Please connect your Visioneer USB scanner now. If you plugged the scanner in prior to installing the software unplug the scanner and plug it back in. Refer to the Installation Guide that came with your scanner for setup instructions. Please press the OK button when done.

OK

- Windows Me will confirm that the installation was successful and ask you to restart your computer.
- You will not be able to use the new software until the computer has restarted, so click on the **Finish** button.
- Your computer should automatically shut down and boot up again. If it fails to do so, refer to Restarting Your Computer below.

Choose to restart your computer

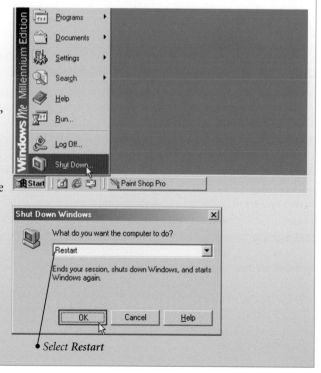

RESTARTING YOUR COMPUTER

It is usually necessary to restart your computer before you can use newly installed software. If the installation process does not provide you with the option, or it doesn't work, you can do it manually. Exit the installer CD and quit any other programs. Click on the **Start** button on the desktop, and choose **Shut Down** from the menu. In the **Shut Down Windows** window, click the downward pointing arrow. Choose **Restart** from the drop down list and click on **OK**. Your computer will turn off, then boot up again.

Select Restart

Setting Up the Scanning Software

Before you can use the scanner, you will need to set up the software so that it recognizes the scanner you are using. The following steps apply whether you are using software supplied with your scanner, as below, or accessing the scanner through an image editing program ⌐⌐, although in that case the process may differ slightly.

1 OPENING THE SOFTWARE

● Click on the **Start** button and open the **Programs** menu.
● Your newly installed software should be available under this menu, or the installation process may have automatically created a shortcut on the desktop.

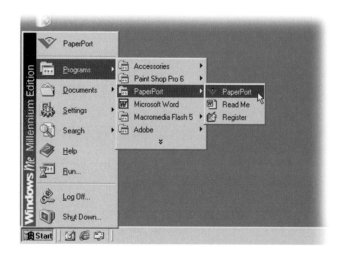

2 SELECTING THE SOURCE

● The scanning software will open.
● We will go into more detail on how to use the software later, so don't try to do anything just yet. For now, all we want to do is ensure that the software can locate the scanner.
● Click on **File** and choose **Select Source** from the drop-down menu.

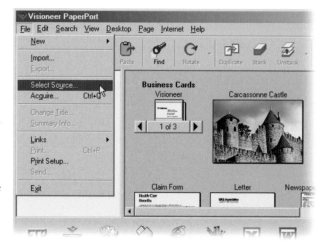

434 **Image Editing Software**

● The **Select Source** window will open and your new scanner should be listed.
● Highlight it and click on **Select**.
● This process should only have to be done once – from now on the software will remember the source.

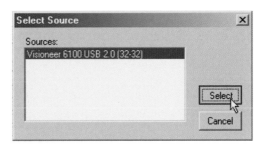

● Close the program by clicking on **File** and selecting **Exit** from the drop-down menu.

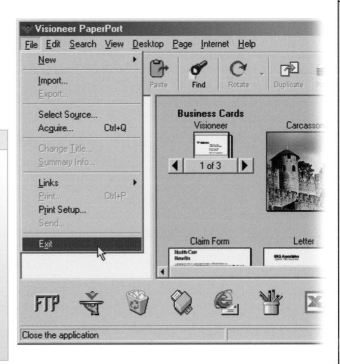

TWAIN DRIVERS

A TWAIN (*Technology Without An Interesting Name*) driver is the link between the scanner and your software, providing the interface that you need to perform a scan ⌐. It can be accessed through most image editing programs once you have selected the source.

INSTALLING A PRINTER

The installation process for a USB printer should be no more complicated than for a USB scanner. However, this chapter deals with a couple of techniques just in case you encounter problems.

CONNECTING THE PRINTER CABLES

As discussed in a previous chapter 📄, we are concentrating on installing hardware with USB compatibility. If your printer does not have a USB port and relies on a parallel connection instead, refer to your instruction manual.

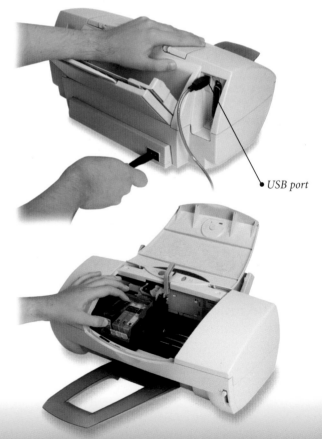

1 CONNECTING THE CABLES
● Connect the USB and power cables to the ports at the back of your printer, then connect the power cord to an outlet and ensure the power is turned on.
● As with the scanner, don't plug the USB cable into the computer until you begin the installation process.
● Switch on the printer.

● USB port

2 INSERTING THE INK CARTRIDGE
● Depending on your printer, you may also need to insert the ink cartridge at this stage. Refer to the manual that came with your printer for advice.

📄 402 USB Ports

PRINTER INSTALLATION

This example demonstrates an installation using a Lexmark Inkjet printer. Here, we are installing the printer before the software but, as before, use the steps just as a guide and refer to the manual supplied. The next example (page 418) demonstrates a printer being installed in a different way. Refer to both examples, along with your manual, before you begin to decide which method is relevant to you – both may be relevant.

1 ADDING NEW HARDWARE

● Plug the USB cable from the printer into the USB port on your computer.
● When you insert the cable, Windows recognizes that you have connected new hardware and opens the **Add New Hardware Wizard**. If the Wizard does not launch, click on the **Start** button and select **Control Panel** from the **Settings** menu. Double-click on the **Add New Hardware** icon.
● Insert the CD-ROM into your computer.
● Click in the radio button to ask Windows to search for the best driver for your hardware device.
● Click on **Next**.
● Windows performs an automatic search for the software relating to your computer.

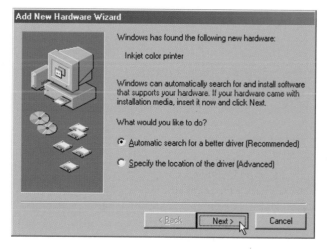

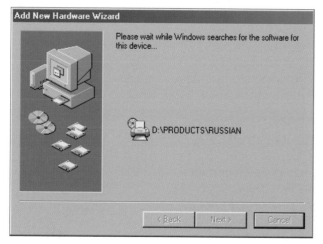

2 LOCATING THE CORRECT DRIVER

● The Select Other Driver window opens. It contains a listing of driver descriptions for your printer. Scroll down the list and select your printer, also check that the language in the Location list, matches your language.

● Click ok when you are ready.

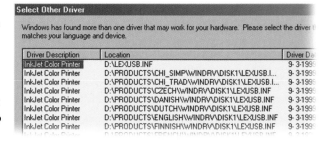

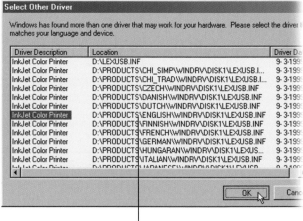

Select the driver that matches your language

● The driver software will be installed onto your computer.

● When Windows has completed the installation, click on the **Finish** button.

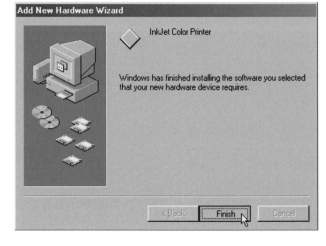

3 INSTALLING FROM THE CD-ROM

● Next, the CD-ROM may automatically run so that you can continue to install further software relevant to your printer.

● Read and accept the license agreement when it appears.

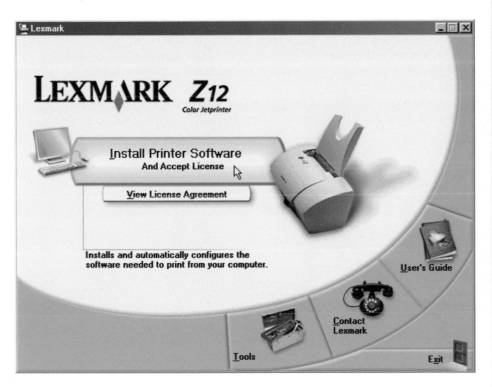

● When the CD-ROM provides the option, choose to install the software.

● A progress bar will appear to indicate that the files are being copied to your computer.

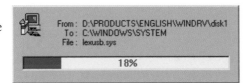

From : D:\PRODUCTS\ENGLISH\WINDRV\disk1
To : C:\WINDOWS\SYSTEM
File : lexusb.sys

18%

● When installation is complete, quit the CD-ROM by clicking on **OK** and restart your computer □.

411 **Restarting Your Computer**

USING THE ADD PRINTER WIZARD

If the previous installation example using the manufacturer's CD-ROM worked correctly, the following steps should have been implemented automatically and your printer will be ready to use. However, if you find that something didn't quite go to plan you may have to carry out this task as well. The following sequence can also be used as a completely alternative installation technique to the previous example, and you may want to follow this route if the CD-ROM installer is not available, or if it does not seem to be installing the printer drivers correctly. Here, we are installing a Lexmark inkjet printer using the Windows Me Add Printer Wizard.

1 OPENING THE PRINTERS

● Click on the **Start** button at the bottom left of the taskbar and choose **Printers** from the **Settings** menu.
● The **Printers** window will open.

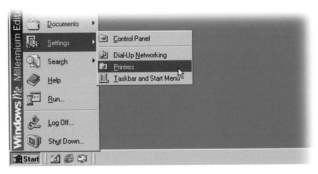

2 OPENING THE WIZARD

● If you see an icon for your printer already located in this window, then you can go straight to step 6 as the necessary software has already been installed.
● If there is no icon, double-click on the **Add Printer** icon to launch the **Add Printer Wizard**.
● To begin installing your printer using the Wizard, click on **Next**.

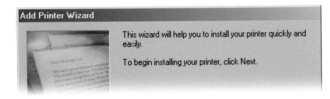

3 SELECTING THE CONNECTION

- The Wizard will ask you how your printer is connected.
- We will assume that you are connecting the printer directly to your computer, rather than on a network of many computers, so select the radio button next to **Local printer** and click on **Next**.

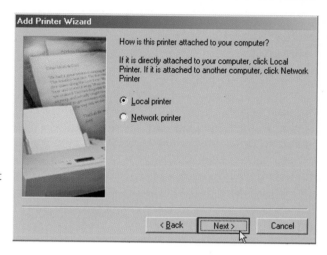

4 SELECTING YOUR PRINTER

- Ignore the printer selection and click on **Have Disk**.
- Insert the CD-ROM into your computer.

If you didn't have an installer disk with your printer, you may be able to find your printer listed here

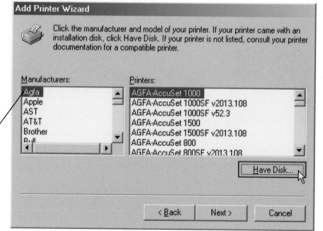

- Select the CD-ROM by clicking on the down arrow underneath **Copy manufacturer's files from**, and highlighting the relevant drive (usually the D: drive).
- Click on **OK**.

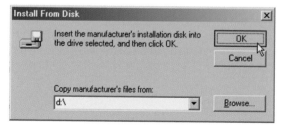

- Select the make and model of your printer and click on **Next**.

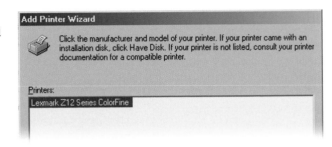

5 SELECTING THE CORRECT PORT

- You will now be asked to select the port that your printer is attached to.
- Identify the port from the list and select it. It should be obvious which port to select and it may even be labeled with some kind of reference to a printer, possibly even the make and model.
- Click on **Next**.

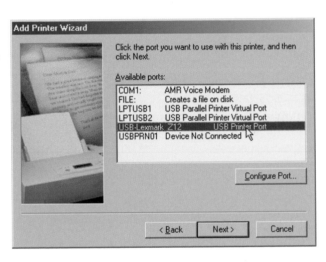

- The final screen will ask you to confirm the name of the printer.
- This field will be filled in automatically and there's no real need to change it.
- Click the radio button next to **Yes** to make all your programs use this printer. Then click on **Finish** to complete the installation.

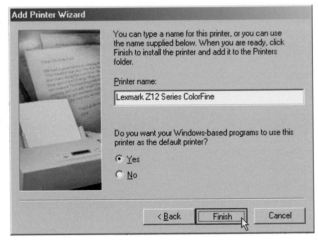

6 CHECKING THE PROPERTIES

● You will now see that an icon for your new printer has been added in the **Printers** window.

● To confirm that everything has installed correctly, highlight the icon and click the right mouse button.

● Select **Properties** from the bottom of the pop-up menu and a window displaying the properties for the printer will open.

● Click on the **Details** tab at the top of the window.

● Ensure that your printer is listed and that it is printing to the correct port (check this against the port you selected in Step 5).

● If the port is not selected, click on the down arrow and highlight the correct port in the list.

● Click on **OK** when you have finished.

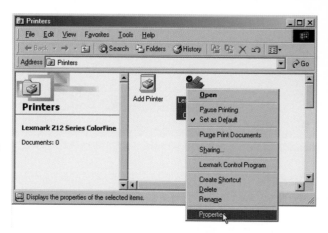

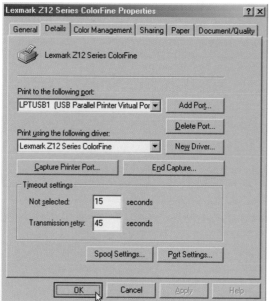

TEST PRINTS

At the end of the installation process your printer software should provide you with the option to perform a test print, which you should do to check that everything is working correctly. If the software does not launch automatically, you should be able to locate the software for your printer by clicking on the **Start** button and opening the **Programs** menu.

SCANNING AN IMAGE

Scanning a picture into your computer is really very simple,
but you need to understand some basic terms and settings to
ensure you get the best results from your scanner.

USING THE SCANNING SOFTWARE

At this point, you could quite easily place a picture on your scanner, launch the software, and press the scan button. The chances are that an image would indeed appear on the screen, and to the untrained eye the quality of the scan would seem to be sufficient. So what's the problem? Well it's not quite as simple as all that – your computer needs to be given some directions for it to provide you with a scanned image that truly meets your needs. The software that was supplied with your scanner will vary depending on the make and quality of the product you bought, but the basic look and operation of each one is similar to the example shown here.

1 LAUNCHING THE SOFTWARE
● Click on the **Start** button on the desktop and select the scanning software from the **Programs** menu.

Alternatively...
You can also launch the scanning software from within image editing programs. To gain access to the scanning interface, click on **File** followed by **Import > TWAIN > Acquire....**

2 LAUNCHING THE INTERFACE

● Depending on your software, you may have to click on **TWAIN** or **Acquire** when the program opens to open the scanning interface.

● The program will launch, and a screen similar to the one below will appear.

● *This software has some predefined settings ready for you to use, so you don't have to worry about providing information about mode and resolution unless you wish to redefine these.*

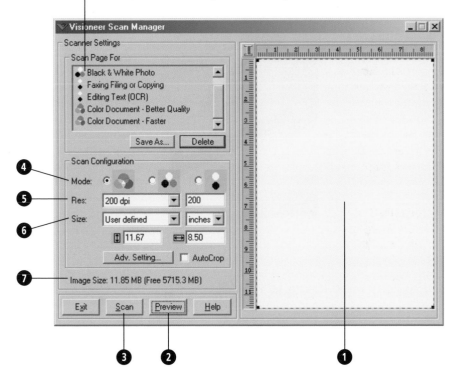

THE SCANNING INTERFACE

❶ The item you are scanning appears here once you perform a prescan (or preview)

❷ Preview

❸ Scan

❹ Mode

❺ Resolution

❻ Size

❼ Image Size shows how large the file size will be once the item is scanned

PERFORMING A PRESCAN

Unless you are scanning a particularly large picture, scanning the entire area of the scanner bed would result in an image that had a lot of unnecessary space around the edges, which in turn would increase its file size. To scan a more specific area, you need to preview the image by performing a prescan.

1 POSITIONING THE PICTURE

• Position the picture that you are going to scan face down on the scanner bed.

• There are often some rulers or guides around the edges of the glass to help you position the item accurately. Generally, the top of the picture should be nearest to you.

• Close the scanner lid.

Keeping the scanner bed clean

It is important to clean the glass plate on your scanner regularly. Even the smallest specks of dust and dirt will be picked up by the scanner and will appear on your image. Use a special glass cleaner and a soft cloth to remove any grime.

2 PREVIEWING THE IMAGE

• Ignoring the other settings, click on **Preview**.

• You will hear the scanner operate and it will perform a quick pass over your picture, which will appear in the preview screen.

• A prescan is exactly what it suggests – the scanner has not yet done a proper scan or passed any information about the image to your computer.

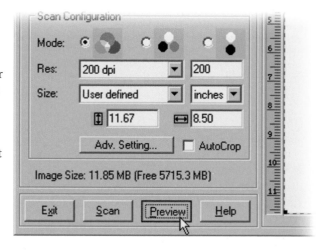

SELECTING THE SCAN AREA

Now that you can see the contents of your scanner bed accurately, you can tell whether your picture is positioned correctly, or whether any of the image is being cut off at the sides. If you do need to make any adjustments to the positioning of your picture, do so and perform another prescan ⌐. Next, you need to select only the area of the preview that you want to scan.

1 DRAWING A MARQUEE

* The preview area of the screen represents the entire surface of the scanner bed.
* You can tell the scanner which part of the preview to scan properly by drawing a marquee (a square made up of flashing dotted lines) around the relevant area.
* Either there will be an existing marquee onscreen, or you will have to draw one by clicking in one corner of the preview and dragging the cursor across to the opposite corner.

The preview scan •

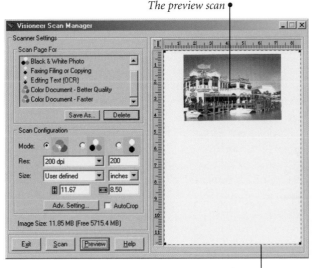

If the marquee is not flashing, click on it once to select it •

2 ADJUSTING THE MARQUEE

* To adjust the marquee so that it is exactly positioned around the image you want to scan, position your cursor over the top corner of the marquee.
* The cursor will turn into a double-headed arrow.

● With the double-headed cursor showing, hold down the left mouse button and drag the corner of the marquee to the top corner of your image.

● Repeat the process with the bottom corner, so that the marquee surrounds your image.
● If you would like your image to have a border, then simply allow a little room around the edges when you adjust the marquee.

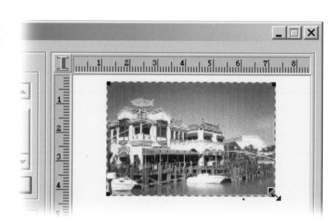

MOVING AN ENTIRE MARQUEE

To move the entire marquee, place the cursor inside it and the cursor changes to a four-way arrow. Hold down the left mouse button and drag the marquee to enclose the area of the image that you want to be scanned.

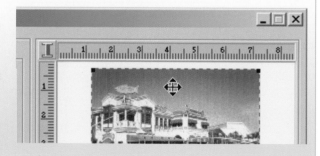

SELECTING THE CORRECT MODE

You are likely to see the following modes available within your scanning software, and you should scan with the correct mode depending on how you are going to use your image. Your scanner may have a preset mode that you can change.

THE DIFFERENT MODES EXPLAINED

RGB COLOR
RGB stands for red, green, and blue. All images that are scanned in this mode are made up of these three colors. All computer monitors use RGB, so RGB should be used for images that will be displayed onscreen, such as web graphics. RGB can also usually be used for images that are printed on a color inkjet printer.

CMYK COLOR
CMYK stands for cyan, magenta, yellow, and black, so images that are scanned in this mode are made up of these four colors. Any color image that is going to be printed on a printing press must be saved in the CMYK mode. If your scanner does not scan in CMYK then you will need to convert the image afterward in an image editing program.

GRAYSCALE BLACK AND WHITE
This mode creates black and white images with tones of gray.

LINEART BLACK AND WHITE
Lineart does not use color or tones of gray. Because an image scanned in lineart mode will simply appear as a solid black graphic on a white background (or vice versa), it will not require a lot of information and, as a result, will have a small file size. Therefore you can afford to scan lineart images at the maximum resolution possible to obtain a good quality image.

SELECTING THE SCANNING MODE
● Select the correct mode by clicking once in the radio button next to your preferred mode.

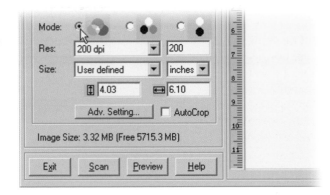

CHOOSING THE CORRECT RESOLUTION

Resolution is possibly the most important aspect of scanning an image, and yet it is also the one area that most people don't understand. The resolution that you scan at directly affects the quality, file size, and usability of the image you are scanning.

WHAT DOES RESOLUTION MEAN? You will see the resolution setting in your scanning software referred to as dpi. This stands for dots per inch. Basically, if an image is scanned at 100% size at 100dpi then it will contain 100 dots, or pixels, of information in every inch. The same image scanned at 100% size at 600dpi will contain 6 times the amount of information in an inch. A low resolution means that the image contains less information overall, and will be of a poorer quality than that of an image scanned at a high resolution.

1 SELECTING THE RESOLUTION

● The default resolution setting in our software is 200dpi, which would result in a good quality scan, suitable for output through an inkjet printer.
● However, as an example, we are going to increase the resolution slightly so that the image would be suitable for a commercial print process ⬚.
● Click on the down arrow next to the resolution box to see a selection of other resolutions.
● In this case we are going to select 300dpi by highlighting it.

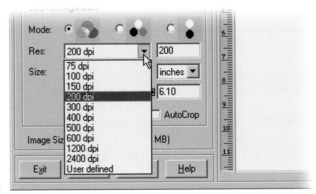

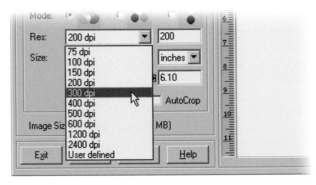

⬚ 429 **What Resolution Should I Scan At?**

2 ENTERING A SPECIFIC VALUE

- If your software doesn't provide a list of optional resolutions, or if you want to enter a more specific value, highlight the text in the resolution field by dragging the cursor over the current value with the mouse button held down.
- Type in your new resolution value.

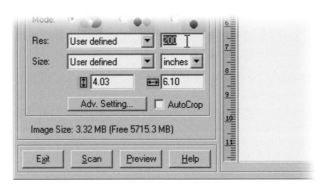

Type the resolution value here

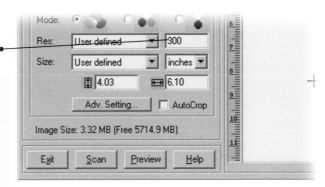

Selecting size

Your software may give you the option to scan the image at a larger or smaller size, which you would usually do by entering a percentage value (e.g. 200% size). If you want to print an image larger than its original size, you will need either to increase the physical size of the image in this way, *or* adjust the resolution to compensate. For example, if you wanted to print the image in our example (which we are scanning at 100% at 300dpi) at twice its original size, it would need to be scanned at 600dpi.

WHAT RESOLUTION SHOULD I SCAN AT?

The following examples give some ideal resolutions for scanning images according to their final use. The resolutions given are based on the image being used at 100% (the same size as the original) or less. Remember either to increase the resolution or scan the image at a larger size if you are going to make the scan bigger before it is printed.

- Images and graphics for use on a web page: **72dpi**
- A color or grayscale picture for outputting to a color printer: **150dpi to 200dpi**
- A color or grayscale picture to be printed on a commercial printing press: **300dpi**
- A lineart black and white image to be used for any purpose: **1200dpi**

SCANNING THE PICTURE

After selecting the scan area, the mode, and the resolution, the final step in turning your picture into a digital file on your computer is for the scanner to carry out a scan using the information and settings that you have provided it with.

1 STARTING THE SCAN

● Click on the **Scan** button.

● A progress bar will appear onscreen while the scanner is working.
● If for any reason you want to stop the scan, click on the **Cancel** button.

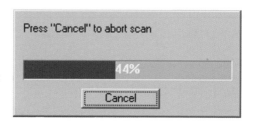

CONSIDER THE LEGAL ISSUES BEFORE YOU SCAN

Remember that to reproduce another person's work without their specific consent is breaking copyright law. If you are planning to scan a photo, drawing, or image from any source other than your own (from a book or magazine, for example) and then use it in any commercial sense (such as in a brochure or poster) then you must gain written permission from the owner of the image before doing so. For example, the copyright owner of any photograph is usually the person who took the picture. If permission is granted, it usually comes at a price and you will have to pay the copyright owner what is known as a royalty fee for the privilege. Scanning such things as money, postage stamps, and corporation trademarks is illegal and out of the question.

2 SAVING THE IMAGE

● The way in which the scanned image will appear onscreen depends on how your software works.

● The software we are using automatically saves images into its own clipboard, from which you can open them by double clicking on their icon.

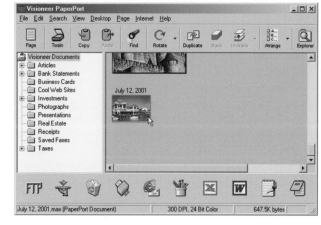

● You may have to name and save the image manually to a desired location on your computer by selecting **Save As** from the **File** menu.

● If you want to perform any further scans, simply return to the scanning interface 🗋.

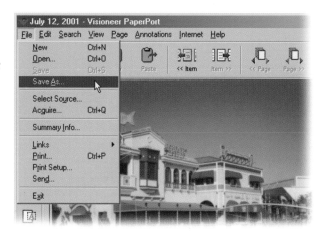

FILE FORMATS

When you save images, consider their final use and select an appropriate file format (or *type*) from the **Save as type** drop-down menu in the **Save As** window. The following two examples are the most commonly used and are available in most scanning and image editing software.

● **JPEG** *(Joint Photographic Experts Group):* Compresses the file but loses detail from the image. This makes it ideal for use in web graphics and email.

● **TIFF** *(Tagged Image File Format):* Retains detail in the image and is widely recognized. Use this format for images that you are going to print.

SCANNING AN OBJECT

You are not limited to scanning flat, two-dimensional pictures into your computer. Within reason, you can also use your scanner to create an image of real three-dimensional objects – just like taking a photograph. Obviously there is a limit to what you can place on to the scanner bed, but you can get some very impressive results from most small items. To get the best possible quality, you need to restrict the amount of external light that naturally enters the scanner from around the object.

1 POSITIONING THE OBJECT

● Place the item that you want to scan on the scanner bed, in this case a toy car.
● The height of the object may mean that the scanner lid will not close properly, and additional light will enter the scanning area. This will decrease the quality of your scan.
● To reduce this intrusion of light, place something around the sides of the scanner. Some books, for example, would be ideal.

2 PREVIEWING THE OBJECT

● Prescan and scan your object in the usual way, just as if it were a picture ▯.

3 SCANNING THE OBJECT

● The final scan will be of a reasonable quality, but it will be necessary to do some corrective work to the image to improve it ⌐|.

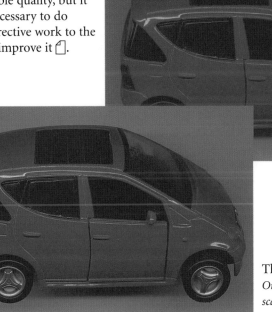

The Final Image
Once corrected, the quality of a scanned object – such as this toy car – can be remarkably high.

Don't stop there...
If it will fit on the scanner bed, then the chances are that you will get a perfectly good result from any item. Try scanning fabric or wood for example. Beware though – the glass plate on your scanner can easily get scratched, so position heavy or sharp objects carefully.

OPTICAL CHARACTER RECOGNITION

Your scanner can be very versatile, and there are many features at your disposal in addition to simply scanning pictures and objects. Optical Character Recognition (OCR) software enables you to scan printed text into your computer, which, rather than becoming an image file, is saved as an editable text file. The software recognizes each individual character and, although it provides the occasional minor error, it pieces together a document that can be treated like any other text file, in Microsoft Word for example. The main advantage of this is the time saved by not having to key in text that already exists.

⌐ Improving
434 Your Scan

IMPROVING YOUR SCAN

No matter how good your scanner is, the quality of your image can usually be greatly improved by applying some minor corrective tweaks using image editing software.

IMAGE EDITING SOFTWARE

Your picture is now scanned into your computer, but that isn't necessarily the end of the story. Your image probably requires some minor adjustment to ensure that it's looking its best when you come to use it. The software packages that come supplied with some scanners can actually have some advanced image editing functions built-in. However, to really get the most out of your scanned images, you should think about using a retouching program designed for the job.

PAINT SHOP PRO

Paint Shop Pro™ is a relatively inexpensive image editing program with some quite advanced features, and we will be using this program here. However, there are many software packages available that can do the same things. If you are using a different program, use the steps outlined here as a guide and look for the same options within the menus of your own image editing software.

OPENING THE IMAGE
- Launch Paint Shop Pro and select **Open** from the **File** menu.

- Locate and highlight your scanned file, and click on the **Open** button to open the image.

ADJUSTING BRIGHTNESS AND CONTRAST

Scanned images can often look a little dull compared with the original picture. It is a good idea, therefore, to get into the habit of adding a bit of life to every picture that you scan. You can do this by using the **Brightness/Contrast** command.

1 BRIGHTNESS/ CONTRAST

● Click on **Colors** and select **Adjust**, followed by **Brightness/Contrast** from the submenu.

For more advanced correction options…

Instead of choosing **Brightness/Contrast** to correct your image, you can also make more subtle changes by using some of the other functions. Click on **Colors** and select **Adjust**. Experiment by adjusting your image using **Highlight/ Midtone/Shadow** and **Hue/Saturation/ Lightness**.

THE BRIGHTNESS/CONTRAST COMMAND

Adjusting brightness and contrast is one of the easiest ways to correct an image. The brightness function controls how light or how dark your image appears, and the contrast function alters the degree of shading. When you apply a change with either command, the highlights, midtones, and shadows in the entire image are all affected at once. For this reason, the command is ideal for the home user who, generally, only needs to make changes suitable for low resolution output. If you were adjusting the image for professional use, you would be advised to use more advanced functions.

2 SELECTING AUTO PROOF

- The **Brightness/Contrast** window will open.
- Click the **Auto Proof** arrow. This will automatically update the preview image in the background, as you make adjustments, so you can see the overall effect of the changes that you make.
- These changes won't actually be implemented until you finally close the **Brightness/Contrast** window.

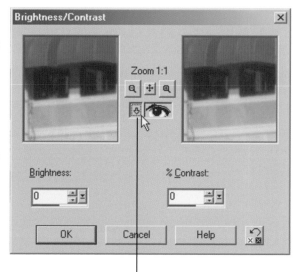

Ensure that you click on the Auto Proof arrow

3 CHANGING THE PREVIEW AREA

- The preview boxes in the window also display close-ups of the existing image (in the left-hand box) and the effect of any adjustments that you make (in the right-hand box).
- When you first open the **Brightness/Contrast** window, the close-up is automatically set to the center of the image. However, this is not necessarily the best part of the image to use for previewing your adjustments.
- Position the cursor over the left-hand panel so that a hand appears.

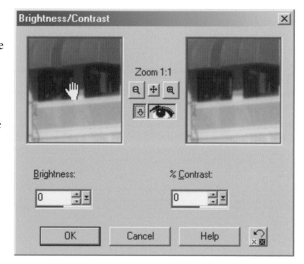

● Click and hold the mouse button and drag the image preview to an area with sufficient detail.

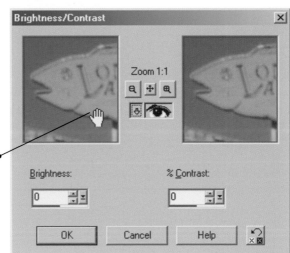

Reposition the preview where you can see more detail in the picture

4 ADJUSTING THE BRIGHTNESS

● Assess whether your image needs to be lighter or darker (scanned images tend to need lightening).

● To adjust the brightness, click on the upward pointing arrow.

● To brighten the image, click on the upward pointing arrow. To darken it, click on the downward pointing arrow.

● You will see the change take place to the preview images. Only minor adjustment is usually required, as too much will lose detail from your image.

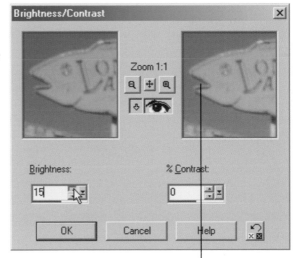

The brightness of the image will change in the right-hand preview box

5 ADJUSTING THE CONTRAST

● Now do the same with the **Contrast.**

● Click on the slider bar and drag it to the left or right until you are happy with the adjustment.

View the change in contrast in the right-hand preview box

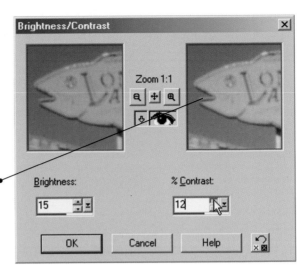

● Click on the up or down arrows until you are happy with the adjustment.

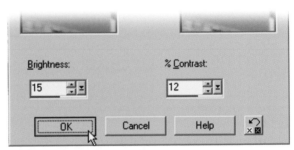

● Your picture will be updated with the changes that you made.

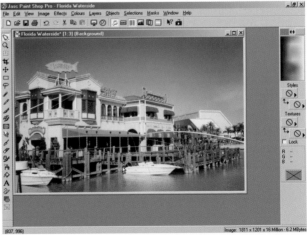

SHARPENING THE IMAGE

Blurring is a common problem in scanned images. Even if at first glance the picture seems fine, you will be surprised at just how much of an improvement can be made by a subtle adjustment to the sharpness. Sharpening the image can also help to compensate for any blurring that results from inkjet printing.

1 SELECTING UNSHARP MASK

- Click on **Effects** and select **Sharpen**, followed by **Unsharp Mask** from the drop-down menu.

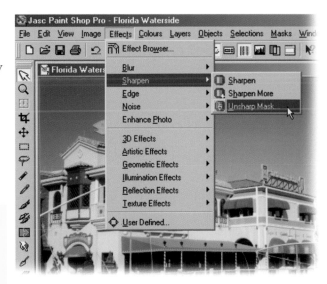

Using the Sharpen and Sharpen More functions

You will also find these two commands available in the **Sharpen** menu alongside **Unsharp Mask**. They apply an overall adjustment to the image, which helps to focus blurred edges; but while they may provide enough of a sharpening effect to improve your image, they do not offer the same level of control as **Unsharp Mask**.

THE UNSHARP MASK COMMAND

When you apply **Unsharp Mask**, the contrast of the pixels that make up the image is increased, so that there is more difference between adjoining pixels – thus sharpening the image. You adjust the sharpness of the image by entering values into three fields: Radius, Strength, and Clipping. To fully explain how these work in conjunction with one another is unnecessary here, and experimentation is really the key until you achieve the desired result. You will only need to make minor adjustments, as too much will make the image look unnatural.

2 ADJUSTING THE SHARPNESS

● As before, position the preview so that it displays an area of the image with sufficient detail, and turn on the **Auto Proof** function so that you can see the overall effect on your picture.

● By clicking on the up and down arrows next to the radius, strength, and clipping fields, you can increase or decrease the sharpening effect. As before, only minor adjustment will be necessary.

● When you are satisfied that you have improved the image sufficiently, click on **OK**.

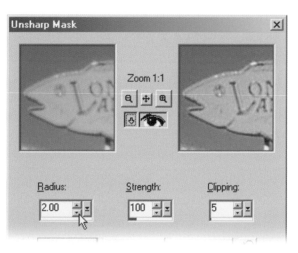

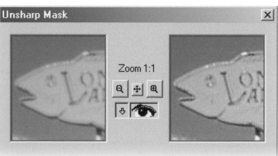

● Your corrected image will be displayed onscreen.

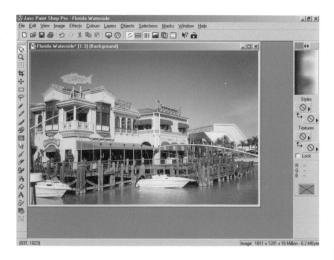

CROPPING THE IMAGE

It may be that you are not happy with the overall shape of your image, or you may want to lose part of a picture that you wish wasn't in shot – a person or building, for example. Cropping your picture simply means cutting off unwanted information from around the edges. This also helps to reduce the file size.

1 SELECTING THE CROPPING TOOL

● Select the cropping tool from the toolbar on the left of your screen.

The cropping tool ●

2 POSITIONING THE CROP

● When you place the cursor over the image window it will take on the shape of the cropping tool.
● Position the cursor at the point you would like to be the top left corner of your picture.

This position will become the top left corner of your picture when it is cropped

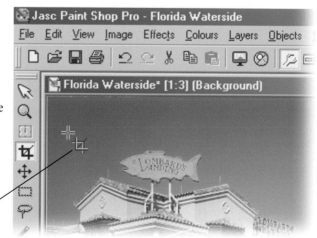

● While holding down the mouse button, drag a rectangle over the image until you reach the point that you would like to be the bottom right corner of your picture.

● Everything outside the rectangle will be deleted when you confirm the crop, so ensure that the selected area is precisely the part of the image that you want.

This position will become the bottom right corner of your picture when it is cropped ●

3 ADJUSTING THE CROP

● Release the mouse button when you are happy with the shape of the rectangle.

● If you want to begin again, click once outside the rectangle so that it disappears.

● You can move the existing rectangle to another position by placing the cursor inside it and holding down the mouse button while you drag the rectangle to a new position.

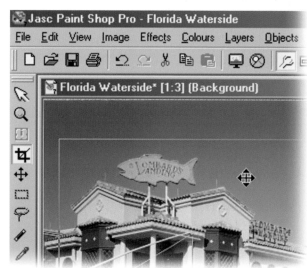

4 CROPPING THE IMAGE

- When you are satisfied with the area you have selected, double-click inside the rectangle.
- Your picture will be cropped to its new shape.

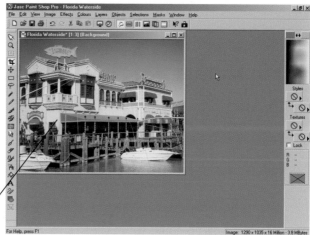

The picture is cropped to size •

SAVING THE CORRECTED IMAGE

After you have completed the corrective work on your image, it is wise to save the document as a second file, keeping the original untouched. Then, if for any reason you are not happy with the final result when you print the corrected picture, at least you will be able to return to the original and try again. Instead of selecting **Save**, choose **Save As** from the **File** menu. In the **Save As** window, name the document so that it is clearly marked as the corrected image (for example add **Retouched** to the end of the original name), then click **Save**.

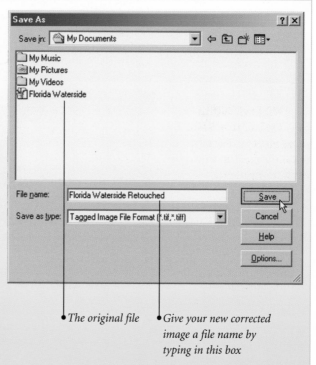

• *The original file*

• *Give your new corrected image a file name by typing in this box*

PRINTING YOUR IMAGE

Your designs are not doing you justice when they are trapped inside a computer screen. Having a color print that you can touch and hold adds real value to your work.

THE PAGE SETUP

The following sequence shows you simply how to print the scanned image that we corrected in the previous chapter. Don't forget, however, that this really is the thin end of the wedge – once you become more ambitious with your scanned images, you will want to start using them in conjunction with desktop publishing software to create your own designs. Or perhaps you will be using a graphics program to create illustrations and montages from a series of scanned pictures. Whatever you are printing, the first task is to check the **Page Setup**, which dictates how large your image will print and where it will appear on the paper.

1 OPENING THE PAGE SETUP

● With your document open, click on **File** and select **Page Setup** from the drop-down menu.

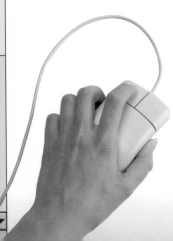

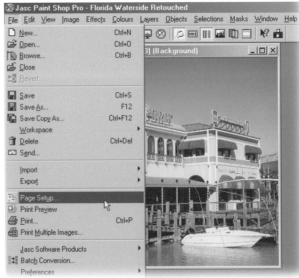

2 SELECTING THE PAPER SIZE

● The **Page Setup** window will open.

● Click on the down arrow next to **Size** and highlight the paper size that you are using with your printer. This is most likely to be 8½ x 11in (A4).

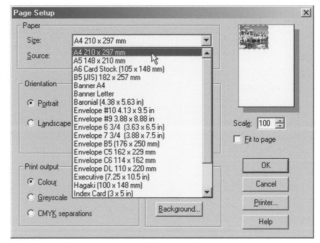

3 CHANGING THE ORIENTATION

● If you want your document to print so that the image appears on the paper horizontally, click in the **Landscape** radio button so that a bullet appears.

● The preview in the top right of the window will change to show you how your document will appear when it is printed.

Checking this box ensures that your image prints in the center of the paper

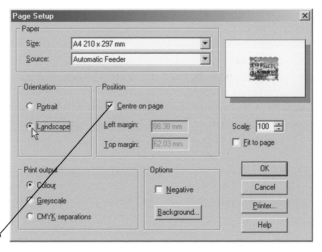

Printing from other programs

Although the sequence shown demonstrates printing an image from Paint Shop Pro, the process is virtually identical no matter what program you are using. You will find the same settings and options under the **Page Setup** and **Print** menus in any software package, even though they may look slightly different.

4 CHOOSING OTHER OPTIONS

● Refer to the annotation below to decide whether you want to activate any other options.

● When you have finished, click on the **OK** button.

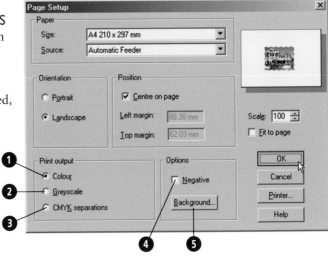

OTHER PAGE SETUP OPTIONS

① Prints image in color
② Prints image as grayscale (black and white)
③ Prints four grayscale separations: one page

each for cyan, magenta, yellow, and black
④ Prints the image in its reverse colors
⑤ Click here to select a

background color to "frame" your image
⑥ Enlarges or reduces the image to print as large as possible on the paper

5 VIEWING A PRINT PREVIEW

● If you want to see a final preview of how your document is going to print, select **Print Preview** from the **File** menu.

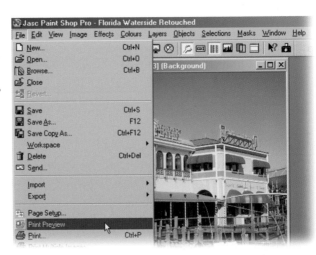

● To return to your image, click on the **Close** button to close the preview.

The Close button •

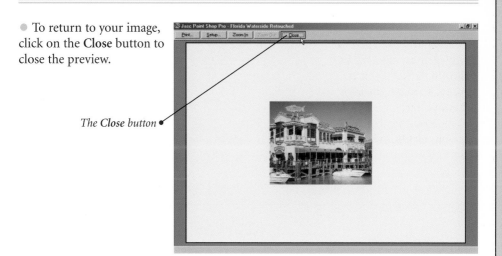

SETTING THE PRINT OPTIONS

The following settings concern the printer itself, and how it outputs your image. The options that you choose here will have a bearing on the final quality of your printed image, so make sure everything is correct before starting the print process.

1 OPENING THE PRINT SETUP

● Click on **File** and select **Print** from the drop-down menu.

2 OPENING THE PRINT PROPERTIES

● The **Print** window will open.

● Click on the **Properties** button.

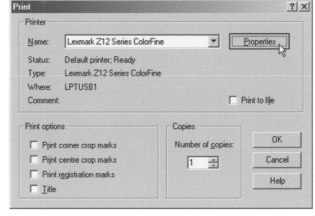

3 SELECTING THE PAPER TYPE

● The window that opens now will display options for your own particular printer. Again, the appearance may be slightly different depending on the printer that you have, but the same options should be available.

● Click on the **Document/Quality** tab at the top of the box and select the type of paper that you are using ▢.

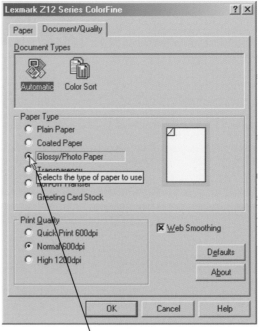

• *Make your choice of paper from the list*

SELECTING PAPER

Selecting the correct paper to use with your inkjet printer is an important issue. Although the printer itself does require compatible paper, the main issue is the quality of the print itself. You will not be able to achieve a photo quality print on conventional paper as it will absorb too much of the ink and the image will have a slightly "soft" appearance. You will need to invest in some photo quality inkjet paper to achieve the best results. As this paper can be quite expensive, it is worth reserving the use of it to your final, edited images only, and use standard matt inkjet paper for everything else. In addition to photo quality paper, the range of materials that you can put through an inkjet printer is ever expanding. You can also purchase glossy film for even higher quality prints, transparency film for use with overhead projectors, and card for greetings.

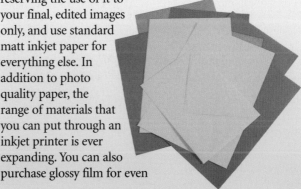

4 SELECTING THE PRINT QUALITY

● Select the resolution at which you want to output your document by clicking in the radio button next to the relevant option under **Print Quality** (remember to choose a quality that fits the resolution of your image 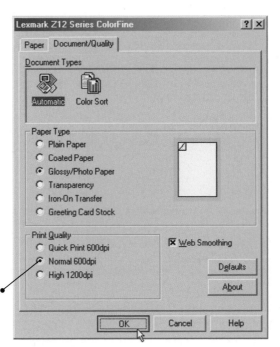).
● Click on the **OK** button to close the window.

600dpi will provide a good quality print that doesn't take too long to process

Choosing the Correct Resolution

5 PRINTING THE DOCUMENT

● Refer to the annotation below to decide whether you want to activate any more options.

● When you have finished, click on the OK button to start the printing process.

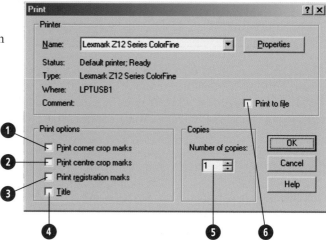

OTHER PRINT OPTIONS

❶ Prints lines to indicate the edge of the image

❷ Prints lines to indicate the center of the image

❸ Prints marks in exactly the same place on every page so that separations can be matched

❹ Prints the document name on the page

❺ Prints duplicate copies of your document

❻ Sends the print file to your hard disk, rather than the printer itself

● A status screen may now appear to tell you how the printing is progressing.

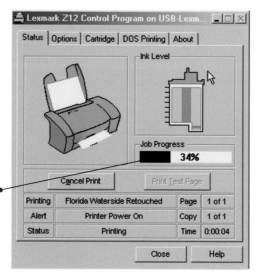

*This **Job Progress** panel shows that 34% of the job has been processed*

CHECKING THE PRINT STATUS

If your printer software does not provide its own print status window, you can use Windows Me to see how your job is progressing. The Windows Me Printers function allows you to view the progress of all the documents you have sent to the printer, and through it you can pause, restart, or cancel them if you wish.

1 OPENING THE PRINTERS
● While your print job is processing, click on the **Start** menu on the desktop and select **Settings,** followed by **Printers** from the drop-down menu.

2 OPENING THE STATUS WINDOW
● The **Printers** window will open.
● Double click on your printer's icon.

RESOLUTION AFFECTS PRINT SPEED

You may start to feel frustrated at the length of time it is taking for your document to come out of the printer. However, don't be tempted to pause or cancel the printing process unless you are sure there is a genuine problem. Many inkjet printers take a long time to process and print documents, especially those that are being printed at a high resolution ⌐⌐.

428 | Choosing the Correct Resolution

3 PAUSE THE PRINTING

● The status window for your printer will open, displaying a list of the print jobs that are currently being processed.

● Highlight the document that is currently being printed by clicking on it.

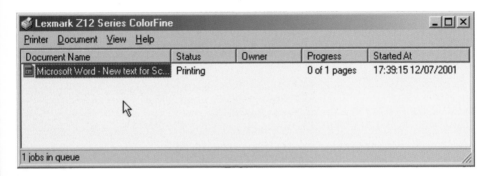

● With the file highlighted, click on the **Document** menu and select **Pause Printing**.
● Your document will temporarily stop being processed.

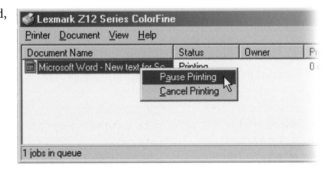

4 RESUME THE PRINTING

● To start your print job processing once more, select **Pause Printing** again.

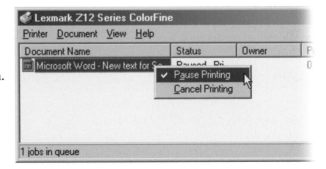

● You can continue viewing the progress of your print job until your document finally leaves the printer, or you can continue working normally.

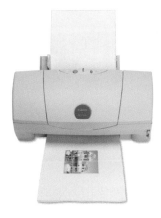

CLEARING PAPER JAMS

Although it does not happen often, occasionally paper will jam inside your printer – either because the paper that you are using is incompatible, or because the paper is not feeding through the printer correctly. Freeing the paper is relatively easy, but don't try to force it, as this could damage the mechanisms inside your printer. Instead, gently pull the paper through the rollers. If the paper really won't give, simply turning the printer off and on again may inspire the printer to spit your page out. Depending on how much of your document has processed, you may have to send your document to print again after you have freed the paper jam. Look in the print status window to see whether the document is still listed and whether or not it is processing.

5 CANCEL THE PRINTING

● If you want to stop your document from being printed altogether, highlight the file in the window and select **Cancel Printing** from the **Document** menu.

I want to cancel all my print jobs
If there are many documents listed in the status window and you want to cancel them all – maybe because the first document printed incorrectly – select **Purge Print Documents** from the **Printer** menu. This will cancel all print jobs and they will disappear from the window.

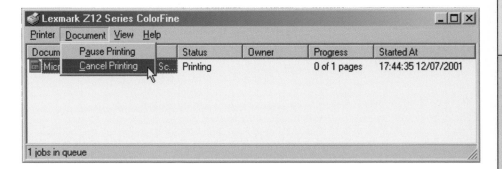

COMPUTER TROUBLESHOOTING

THE PERSONAL COMPUTER HAS changed our lives in so many ways, allowing us to look after our home finances, produce highly designed documents, and spend hours surfing the internet. But most users assume that a PC can manage its own affairs despite our bad habits, poor practices, and sometimes thoughtless use of such a highly technical and complex machine. The aim of this section is to help you optimize some performance aspects of your PC and to avoid common problems. You will discover how to maintain your hard drive, keep it clean by defragmenting the files, check for viruses, and delete old files that clutter up and slow down your PC, as well as finding out how to prepare for emergencies that may arise.

ABOUT YOUR PC

In a competition for causing heartache, frustration, and sometimes physical violence, the PC would be in the running for first prize; but it doesn't have to be this way.

LOOKING AFTER YOUR PC

Most of us don't realize (or ignore) how much we abuse the machines we depend on. However, with a little knowledge and a small amount of time, the sometimes tense relationship you have with your computer can be made easier.

RECURRING TASKS

Most computer users follow an endless round of activities including installing and uninstalling software, downloading a new version, moving files, making a copy, deleting the old version, and inevitably

Although a crash-free computer can't be guaranteed 100%, you can help to reduce the possibility of future problems occurring.

forgetting where a particular file is saved.

Every computer is subject to these events and, over time, they may result in bad files, duplicate files, unused files, and any amount of unnecessary data clogging up, and slowing down, the performance levels of your machine.

Although the PC is built to cope with an astonishing amount of data, there comes a time when you need to assess exactly what you do and don't need, and carry out a major cleanup of your system. This book introduces a number of simple methods to tidy up your computer.

> **MAKING A STARTUP DISK!**
>
> Later in this book there is a section explaining how to protect yourself if your computer will not start up 📁. A startup disk takes only moments to create and will prove to be an invaluable asset when the time comes to use it.

Startup Disk
January

📄 **About**
494 **Startup Disks**

Copying files

download

installing

moving & deleting

Your computer has to deal with a colossal amount of data and keep track of its movements.

HELP IS AT HAND

For a PC to operate correctly, there are hundreds of components, as well as the software, that must all work together. Inevitably, performance problems do occur as a result of glitches, and these may either be trivial or, rarely, terminal. The actions you take to resolve a problem when one occurs may have an effect, but sometimes they are inappropriate. For example, restarting your computer can clear a fault, but if your machine is running slowly, restarting your PC is unlikely to solve the problem. Part of the answer lies in knowing what is available

to help you. Among the software on your computer, there are tools for preventive maintenance to help stop faults from developing, and others to rectify problems when they do occur. For example, later in this section we will show you how to clean your PC's hard drives of unwanted files. We will then delve deeper and explain how to use utilities such as ScanDisk and Disk Defragmenter to examine, clean up, and repair broken and damaged files on the hard drive. These are simple, but effective, procedures and techniques to keep your PC in working order.

THE WORKING PC

If you are new to computers, you may be uncertain about the meanings of the terms that are used to describe the different elements that make a PC work. Here we explain the differences between peripherals, software, and hardware.

Peripherals

A peripheral is a piece of equipment that is used for either input (such as a keyboard or scanner) or output (such as a printer, monitor, or external modem) and can be connected to your computer. Most peripherals require a piece of software to make them run. This is known as a driver and is supplied along with the peripheral. Upgrades to the drivers can sometimes be downloaded from the internet.

Software

Software comes in many shapes and sizes and is usually supplied on a CD-ROM, unless of course you are downloading it from the internet •

Hardware

Computer hardware consists of all the physical elements of the system, including the main PC unit, monitor, keyboard, mouse, and any additional peripherals.

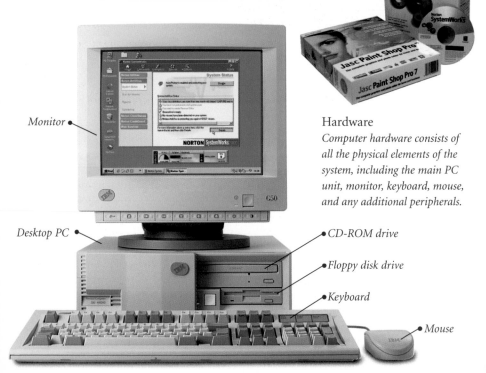

Monitor •

Desktop PC •

• CD-ROM drive

• Floppy disk drive

• Keyboard

• Mouse

Rear of CD-ROM drive and internal cabling

CD-ROM drive drawer

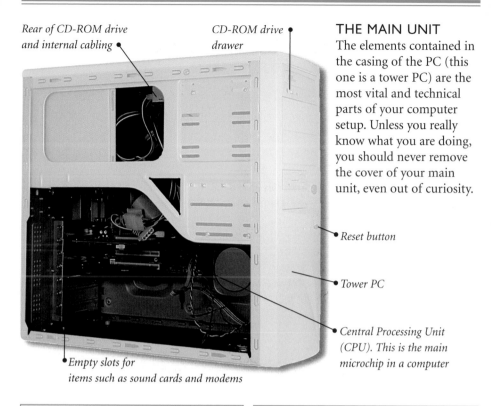

THE MAIN UNIT

The elements contained in the casing of the PC (this one is a tower PC) are the most vital and technical parts of your computer setup. Unless you really know what you are doing, you should never remove the cover of your main unit, even out of curiosity.

Reset button

Tower PC

Central Processing Unit (CPU). This is the main microchip in a computer

Empty slots for items such as sound cards and modems

HARDWARE

Hardware is made up of the parts of your computer that you can see and touch. The keyboard, mouse, scanner, printer, modem, and monitor are all hardware, as is the PC system box, which may be either a tower unit or a desktop unit. The PC system box houses the microchips, the related circuitry that make the input and output peripherals work, as well as the drives, including the hard disk drive, which store all your software. It is also the component to which all the peripherals are connected. The PC is adaptable and can be easily upgraded.

SOFTWARE

Your computer needs software, or programs, for the hardware to function, and for you to do anything useful with your computer. Software comes in many forms – from simple utilities to immense computer games. Most software is now supplied on CD-ROM.

Computers have more speed and capacity than ten years ago and software developers make the most of these developments by pushing the hardware faster and harder. Programs have outgrown floppy disks as a means of storing them, and now software is supplied on higher capacity CD-ROMs.

BASIC TROUBLESHOOTING

In this chapter, we will deal with fast recovery from problems, isolating and identifying problems, closing a crashed program, and removing unnecessary software and dead shortcuts.

BASIC RECOVERY STEPS

When troubleshooting, remember that computers are completely logical and that there is always a rational reason why a problem has occurred. Correctly identifying the reason and finding a solution will be easier if you work step-by-step. However, try one or more of these basic recovery steps first when you next become aware that your computer is beginning to malfunction.

QUIT AND RESTART
● Quit the program and restart the computer to reload the operating software. Minor problems, especially temporary memory problems, can be solved in this way.

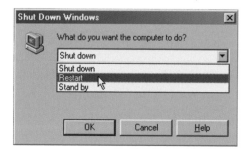

SAVE AS AND REOPEN
● Save your work under a different name and location by using the **Save As** option, quit the program, restart it, and open the new version of your work.

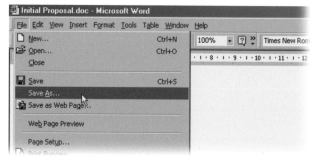

REINSTALLING
● If your software has
become corrupted,
reinstalling it from the
original disks may often
resolve the problem.

*The Microsoft Office
install options include a
Repair Office function*

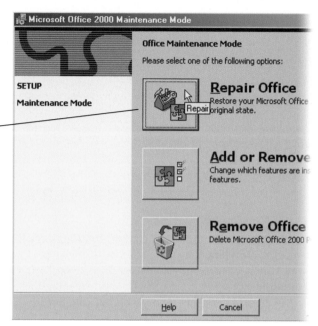

DISK REPAIR UTILITY
● Use a disk repair utility,
such as Norton Utilities,
that scans and repairs your
hard drive and carries out
other system maintenance.

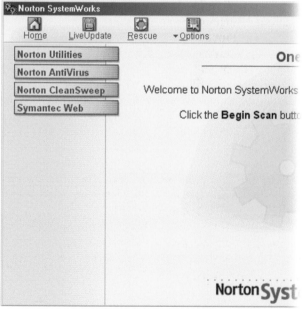

ISOLATING A PROBLEM

The preceding steps should help you to recover from an emergency, but to find out what went wrong, you may need to move on to problem isolation. A distinction to draw is between hardware and software problems. Most systems consist of only a few major components: monitor, printer, hard drive, CD-ROM drive, and the system box, and each can be isolated to identify a problem. As far as software is concerned, every computer is different, but they can share characteristic problems, the cause of which can be identified by isolating suspect applications.

HARDWARE ISOLATION

● A simple example is that if you have no display on the monitor, check the power lights on both the computer and the monitor. If the computer light is on but the monitor light is off, check the monitor for burning smells, have a look at all the cables, particularly the power cords, and listen for a high-pitched whine or squealing sound. All of these (apart from the cables) are symptoms of a failed monitor.

Do not open the monitor

Never take the back off a monitor. Opening the casing of a monitor exposes you to dangerously high voltages from 10,000 to 50,000 volts, even when the monitor is disconnected. You are endangering your personal safety by attempting to repair a monitor. Limit activities to identifying the symptoms before seeking professional help.

SWAPPING COMPONENTS

If your hardware problem has symptoms that are less obvious, it may be possible to isolate the problem by swapping a peripheral with another model of the same type. If the problem continues with a replacement peripheral, try swapping the cables. If that cures the problem, you have isolated the cause to a fault in the original cable. If not, the problem lies with the system box, which will probably need professional attention.

If you have no display, and yet the computer is switched on and running, the monitor or its power supply has failed.

WINDOWS ME HELP SYSTEM

There are times when even the most proficient PC user will bump into a problem that cannot be easily answered without a little assistance. Micosoft **Help and Support** is an invaluable resource for solving the most basic of "how to" scenarios, to complex networking problems. Chances are that if you have a problem, you will find a solution here. There are also some useful troubleshooting guides and even links to the internet for on-line assistance.

OPEN HELP AND SUPPORT

● To open the main **Help and Support** window, click on the **Start** button and then on **Help**.

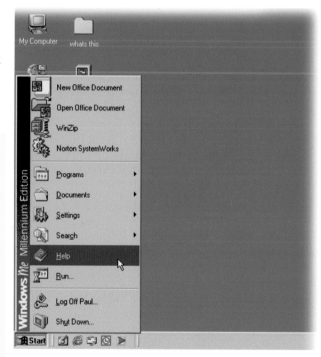

At Startup..

When your PC first starts up, it puts itself through a checking process, making sure that everything is working correctly and determining which hardware devices are installed. It also works out whether you are booting the PC from its own hard disk, or a CD-ROM (if you were having problems, you may want to boot from the Windows Me CD-ROM – see the section on using a startup disk ⌐).

494 **About Startup Disks**

● The main Microsoft **Help and Support** window opens. This introductory page offers you a guide to basic computing with Windows Me, including how to use the internet, printing, scanning, and playing games.

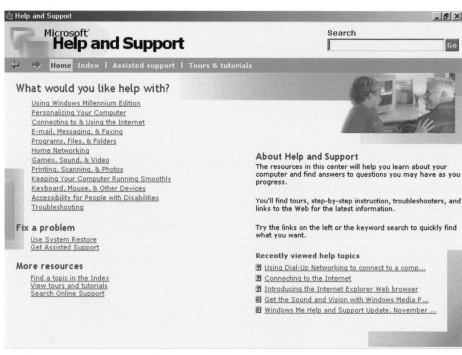

● To get the necessary help, click on the appropriate hyperlinked text.

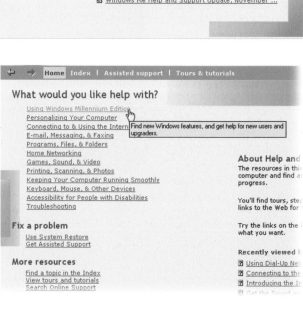

What is a hyperlink?
A hyperlink can be an image, table, or text that links to another item once it is clicked on.

- Near the top of the window, you will find an index that links to all the items contained within **Help and Support**. You can also click on **Assisted support**, which has its own links to the internet, or **Tours & tutorials**.

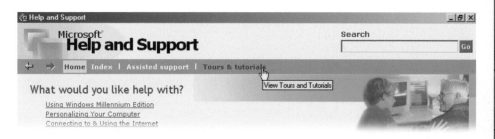

- At the top right of the window, you will find a **Search** panel. Type in a key word to discover more about a particular topic.

- For this example, type in the word **clock** and then click on the **Go** button.
- The results of the search are displayed on the right-hand side of the window.

Click here for more information on how to search

You searched for *clock*

Help & Information:

- ⓘ Changing the elapsed time before hard disk turns off
- ⓘ Changing the elapsed time before computer goes on standby or hibernate
- ⓘ Changing your computer's time
- ⓘ Changing your computer's time zone
- ⓘ Changing the way your computer displays the time

🖨 **Print**   **Change View**

Click one of the links on the left.

● In this example, we have clicked on the link that says **Changing your computer's time.** You will see that

Windows Me's instructions on how to do this appears in the right-hand side of the window.

● *The topic is displayed on the right-hand side of the window.*

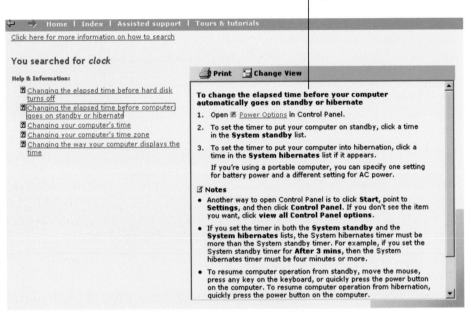

● The search result can be either printed by clicking on the **Print** button, or viewed in its own window by clicking on the **Change View** button.

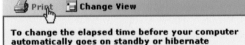

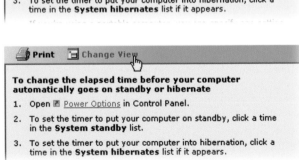

To change the screen back to how it looked originally, click on the **Change View** button again

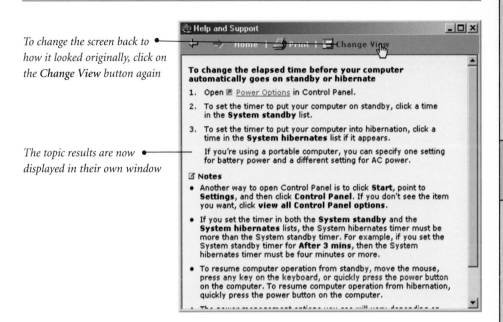

The topic results are now displayed in their own window

● If you find that you have delved rather deeply into the help system, simply click on the **Home** button.

TROUBLESHOOTING WEBSITES

http://www.troubleshooters.com
This site is a great starting point for any troubleshooting or debugging task.

http://wombat.doc.ic.ac.uk
This site is a free online dictionary of computing.

www.fhsu.edu/cis/es/howto.html
Links to a number of troubleshooting and technical queries sites.

http://zdnet.com/sr/columns/glass
A site that welcomes technical queries by email.

www.techadvice.com/tech/C/ComputerTS.htm
A site with preprepared questions and answers in text format, with a number of links to other web pages and websites to refer to if you can't find what you're looking for here.

CLOSING A CRASHED PROGRAM

Making a diagnosis of why your computer is not functioning correctly is not always an easy task, and there are numerous reasons why your machine may have failed. Faults sometimes rectify themselves without an obvious reason, but from time to time your computer will need some help to free itself from a problem.

WHEN YOUR PC FREEZES
One of the most common problems to occur with a PC is when everything "freezes" or "locks up" while you are using an application, and the mouse and keyboard will not respond. This is rarely the fault of the hardware – the problem usually lies with the software in use.

1 FREEZES AND LOCKUPS
● First, give your PC a moment to sort itself out. Never hastily turn the PC off as this can lead to further problems.

2 USING CONTROL, ALT, AND DELETE
● After waiting a while, try to close the locked-up application by using the key combination of: Ctrl + Alt + Del.
● Holding down these keys simultaneously should display the **Close Program** dialog box.

3 CLOSE PROGRAM DIALOG BOX

● This box shows all the applications that are currently running on your system, and next to the locked-up application there should be a message that reads: **Not Responding**.

● Click on the name of the application in the dialog box, and click on the **End Task** button.

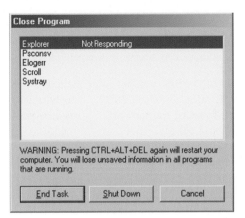

4 END TASK OR SHUTDOWN

● If the software still refuses to close immediately, wait a few moments before pressing Ctrl + Alt + Del again, which should reboot your machine. If the computer still won't respond, then you will have to press the reset button on the front of your PC, if you have one. If you don't have a reset button, then you will need to turn the machine off, wait for 15 seconds, and then turn it on again in the conventional way.

Off button ●

Reset button ●

REMOVING UNNECESSARY FILES

The performance of your PC can be slowed down by the accumulation of unnecessary files. Deleting files one at a time can be a lengthy business. Here, we explain how to locate a folder containing these files and how to delete them.

1 SELECT WINDOWS EXPLORER

● The files that are to be deleted are temporary files stored in a folder called **Temp** within the **Windows** folder. These files are left in the **Temp** folder when your computer crashes, and can safely be deleted.

● To find them, begin by clicking on the **Start** button, select **Programs**, and then **Windows Explorer**.

2 FINDING TEMPORARY FILES

● Click on the plus (+) sign next to **My Computer**, then **Local Disk** and finally the **Windows** folder, scroll down to the **Temp** folder and click on it.

● Its contents are displayed in the right-hand panel.

*The **Temp** folder is contained within the **Windows** folder* ●

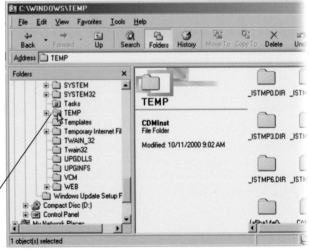

3 SORTING FILES BY TYPE

● Firstly, click on the **View** drop-down-menu and select **Details** from the list.

● Next, scroll along the window and click on the **Type** column header to list the files by type, then scroll down to see the start of the TMP files.

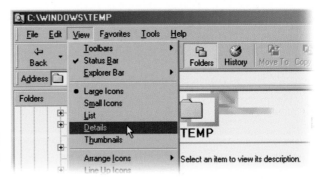

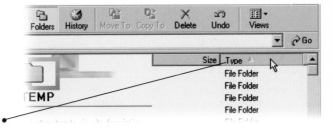

*The **Type** column header* ●──────

4 SELECTING THE TMP FILES

● Click on the first **TMP** file, scroll down to display the last **TMP** file and, while holding down the Shift key, click on the last **TMP** file to select them all.

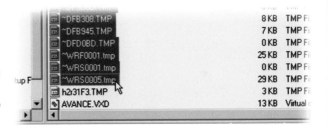

5 SELECTING THE DELETE OPTION

● Click on **File** in the menu bar and select **Delete**.

● An alert box asks you to confirm that the files are to be deleted. Click on **Yes**, and the files are deleted.

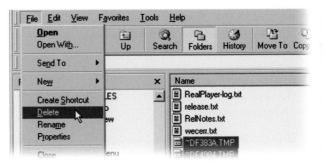

CLEANING UTILITIES

Many problems can be prevented by keeping your hard disk well organized. Windows provides three tools for this task, and commercial cleanup software is also readily available.

USING SCANDISK

ScanDisk can check for damaged files and make sure that your hard disk is correctly storing information. It can also be set up to correct any problems automatically. ScanDisk also looks for files and folders that have invalid file names, dates, and times, and corrects these problems more thoroughly and quickly than is possible by using manual methods.

First aid for files
ScanDisk checks for damage and carries out repairs.

1 OPENING SCANDISK
● Click on the **Start** button, then select: **Programs, Accessories, System Tools**, and finally **ScanDisk**.

2 THOROUGH OR STANDARD?

● When the **ScanDisk** dialog box opens, select the hard drive, **Local Disk (C:)**, as the drive to be scanned.
● As this may be a first-time scan, click on the **Thorough** radio button to select that type of scan.
● Click in the **Automatically fix errors** check box.

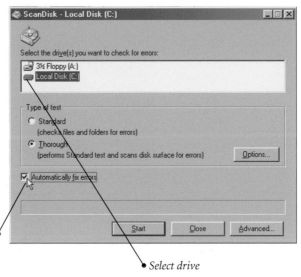

Automatically fix ● *errors check box*

● *Select drive*

3 OTHER CHOICES

● Once you have selected the **Thorough** test, the **Options** button becomes available. Clicking on this button opens the **Surface Scan Options** dialog box, which provides scanning options. The standard test, which scans the system and data areas, is performed by default. ScanDisk can then look for any physical damage to your computer. You can also choose which specific areas of your disk are to be scanned. Click on OK to return to the main **ScanDisk** window.

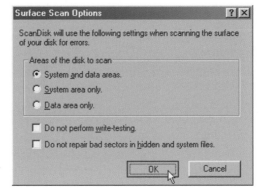

ADVANCED OPTIONS

By clicking on the **Advanced** button in the **Scandisk** dialog box, you can access options that include tests to deal with lost file fragments and invalid files. There is also the opportunity to create a log file so that you can see what has been fixed and what file problems have been found.

4 BEGINNING THE SCAN

● Once you are satisfied with your selections, begin the scan by clicking on the **Start** button in the **ScanDisk** dialog.

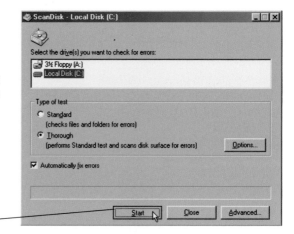

Click on Start

● ScanDisk runs through its scanning operation, checking disks and folders, as well as the physical surface of the hard drive. The **Checking folders** bar at the foot of the dialog box provides feedback on the program's progress.

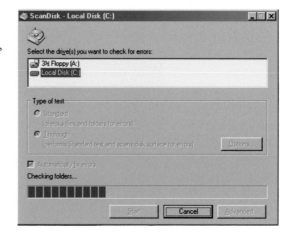

5 THE SCANDISK RESULTS

● The scanning and fixing of your disk will take some time. If you have chosen to scan one disk at a time, click **Close** when the first one has finished, and you can then choose the next disk to be scanned.

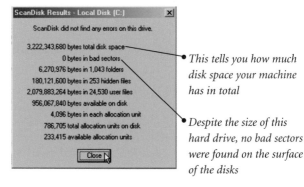

This tells you how much disk space your machine has in total

Despite the size of this hard drive, no bad sectors were found on the surface of the disks

Using Disk Cleanup

Windows also contains a piece of software called Disk Cleanup. This program offers options to select files to search for and possibly delete, which creates more free disk space. This is a safe method if you are uncertain about deleting files.

1 OPENING DISK CLEANUP

● Click on the **Start** button, then select **Programs, Accessories, System Tools**, and finally **Disk Cleanup**.

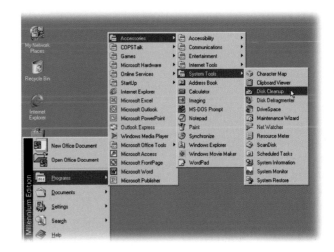

2 SELECTING THE DRIVE

● Disk Cleanup asks you which drive you would like to clean. With the majority of computers the hard drive is (**C:**), and this is the drive to be cleaned.

3 FREE SPACE

● Disk Cleanup then calculates how much free space it can create for you.

4 DESCRIPTION DIALOG

● In the next dialog box, Disk Cleanup tells you exactly how much space it can free up by deleting unnecessary files, such as temporary internet files, offline web pages, downloaded program files, the Recycle Bin (this means emptying files from the bin, not deleting it!), and other temporary files.

● Select the file types that you want Disk Cleanup to delete by clicking once in each of the check boxes next to them. It is best to accept each of Disk Cleanup's recommended file types.

● Once you have selected the items that you want to clean up, click on OK.

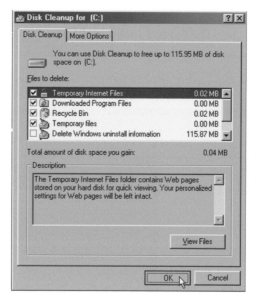

CLEANUP ROUTINES

If you are a fairly frequent user, you could establish a weekly cleaning schedule. Once you have carried out the first thorough clean as described in this section, the process can be quickly carried out.

5 BEGINNING THE CLEANUP

● As a final step before starting, a confirmation panel opens. Click on Yes.

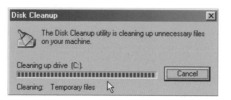

6 FINISHING THE CLEANUP

● After working through the selected options, Disk Cleanup shuts down automatically and you are returned to the Desktop.

USING DISK DEFRAGMENTER

Through normal use, files on a hard disk are broken up and scattered instead of being placed together. This is known as fragmentation and means that the computer has to work harder to gather all the information it needs to perform the required tasks. Disk Defragmenter reconstructs the fragmented files, meaning that they will load faster as the computer does not have to spend time looking for them. Disk Defragmenter also reorganizes files by putting those that are most frequently used at the start of your hard drive to speed up the working process.

HOW DOES FRAGMENTATION HAPPEN?

Fragmentation is not something that you can physically see or be aware of at the time it occurs. The two panels below illustrate how fragmentation occurs. The process has been simplified to provide a basic representation, although in reality disk fragmentation is very complex and depends on a large number of variables.

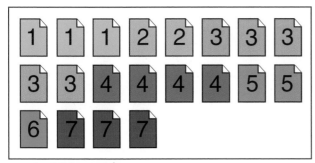

Your hard disk – week one.

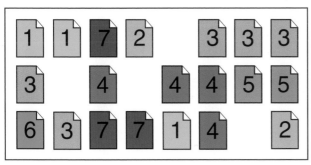

Your hard disk – week three; the files have started to be fragmented.

THE FRAGMENTATION PROCESS

In week one, the files show no fragmentation. However, by week three, there is evidence of fragmentation. This may be due to old software being uninstalled, work being carried out on existing documents, or scanning and saving new images. If a file is opened, added to, and saved, the enlarged file may be split up and placed wherever there is room. After a while, the file structure becomes severely fractured. Defragmenting not only cleans up the drive, it can also increase the performance of your hard disk by up to 10%.

1 BEGINNING THE OPERATION

● Click on the **Start** button and select: **Programs, Accessories, System Tools,** and finally **Disk Defragmenter.**

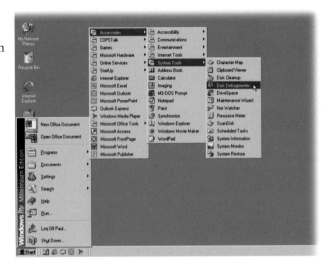

2 SELECTING THE DRIVE

● Disk Defragmenter asks which drive to defragment. You may choose to do more than one, but **Drive C** is selected here, which is the same drive that Disk Cleanup refers to as HD1 (C:).
● Click on **OK.**

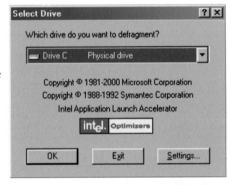

The Screen Saver
It is advisable to turn off your screen saver while running Disk Defragmenter 🗋. Every time the screen saver turns itself on, Disk Defragmenter is forced to start the defragmentation process again.

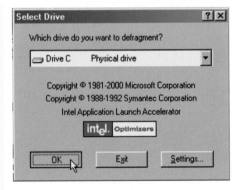

481 **Turning Off Your Screen Saver**

3 STARTING DEFRAGMENTING

● The defragmentation process starts. Microsoft Windows provides an animated graphic to accompany the process, which takes some time.

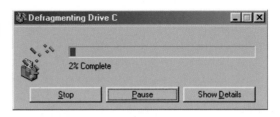

The Show Details button ●

4 CLICKING ON SHOW DETAILS

● Clicking on the **Show** **Details** button will give you a diagrammatic represen-tation of the processes that are taking place. It may take a while for something to happen here.

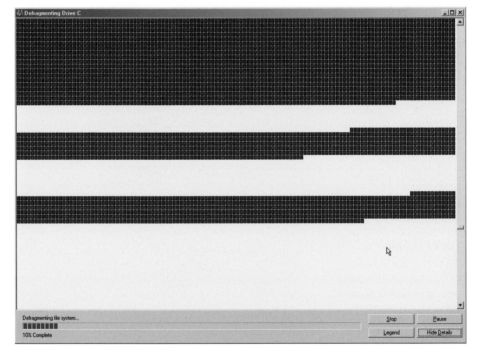

• To see an explanation of what the graphics mean, click on the **Legend** button.

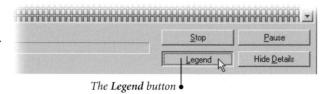

*The **Legend** button* •

5 THE DEFRAG LEGEND PANEL

• The **Defrag Legend** panel shows what the different colored rectangles represent in the main window.

• They are divided into the locations where the files belong; the files that are being read, written, or have been optimized; and free and damaged areas of the hard drive.

• You may close this panel at any time without interrupting the defragmentation process.

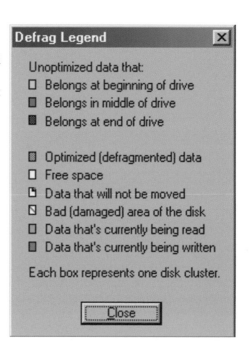

*The **Defrag Legend** panel shows, by using colored blocks, a listing of the different file types, what is happening to them, and explains where they belong.*

6 PAUSING THE PROCESS

• If you need to monitor the process, but have to leave your computer, you can pause Disk Defragmenter at any time.

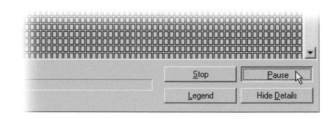

● Having clicked on **Pause**, the **Pause** button becomes a **Resume** button, which you can click when you are ready to proceed.

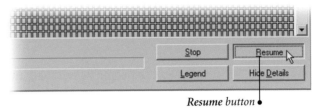

Resume button ●

7 SELECTING OTHER SETTINGS

● When you first start Disk Defragmenter, you can click on the **Settings** button for further options.

● The default settings in the **Disk Defragmenter Settings** dialog box are optimized for best results, and it is easiest to leave these settings unchanged.
● Click on **OK** when you are ready.

TURNING OFF YOUR SCREEN SAVER

First, right-click on the Desktop. In the pop-up menu, click on **Properties** at the foot of the menu. The **Display Properties** dialog box opens. Click on the **Screen Saver** tab at the top of the box. In the center of the box is a drop-down menu below the words **Screen Saver**. Click on the down-arrow to the right, scroll through the list until (**None**) is highlighted, and click on it. Click on **Apply** and then on **OK**. To reset the screen saver, select one from the **Screen Saver** drop-down menu, click on **Apply** and then on **OK**.

MAKING BACKUPS

Computers fail for many reasons, and when they do it's important that you have a copy of your work, applications, and, more importantly, your operating system.

WHAT DOES BACKING UP MEAN?

Making a backup, in its simplest form, involves copying all the information held on your computer from your hard drive to removable, portable media, such as a disk or magnetic tape, that can be removed from the computer and stored.

BACKUP MEDIA

The best way to recover from a major accident is to have a comprehensive backup on disk or tape. If the computer is stolen or irretrievably damaged, you should be able to rebuild your data from the backup disks. The main types of removable media suitable for the home PC backup are: Zip and Jaz disks, DAT tapes, CD-R (Compact Disk Recordable), and DVD. Although DAT and DVD are suitable backup devices for the office, they may be larger than necessary for the home user. A CD writer is relatively cheap, and blank CDs in bulk cost less than blank audio tapes. Zip and Jaz drives are also relatively inexpensive. Floppy disks are less suitable for backing up because of their limited capacity. A Zip disk can hold almost 100 times the data of a floppy disk, and a CD can hold up to 740 times as much.

When choosing a backup medium, you should take into account the cost of the drive and the disks, and the storage capacity that each type offers.

MICROSOFT BACKUP

Microsoft Backup is part of Windows Me and easily allows you to make a backup of your work onto any form of media: Zip or Jaz drives, CD-ROM, or removable hard drive. It also allows you to compress the files as they are copied. The compression process means that files take up less space on your storage tape or drive.

1 FINDING BACKUP

● Microsoft Backup can be found by clicking on the **Start** button, then selecting **Programs, Accessories, System Tools**, and then **Backup**.
● Insert a blank disk into your floppy disk drive.

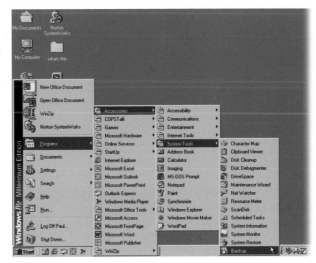

INSTALLING MICROSOFT BACKUP FROM THE WINDOWS ME CD

To install Microsoft Backup from the Windows Me CD, insert the CD into the drive and click the **Add/Remove Software** button when the options appear. In the next window, choose the **Windows Setup** tab. In this window, scroll down to find **System** **Tools**. Double-click on **System Tools** to open that window. **Backup** will probably be at the top of a list in that window. Ensure that this box is checked and click on **OK**. In the next window, click on **Apply** and Microsoft Backup will be installed on your computer.

FLOPPY DISKS

On the next few pages, we will be using a floppy disk to back up a file, mainly because almost everyone will have a floppy drive. However, as has already been mentioned, we do not recommend using a floppy disk to make backups of files as their capacity is very limited.

2 THE MAIN SCREEN

● Two windows appear: the main backup screen explains what a backup is, and asks what you would like to do. Here, we want to create a new backup, so click on that radio button and then on **OK**.

Click on this radio button to create a new backup

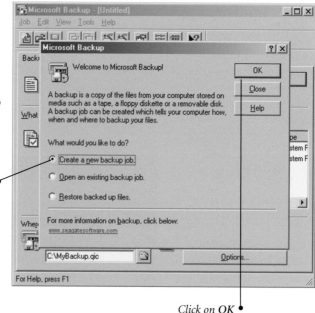

Click on OK

3 THE BACKUP WIZARD

● The next screen to appear is the **Backup Wizard**. If you have a large capacity backup medium, such as a CD writer, then you can back up the entire contents of your computer by using the first option. In this example, a single file is to be backed up onto a floppy disk.

● Select the second option of selecting the files to be backed up by clicking on its radio button, then click on **Next**.

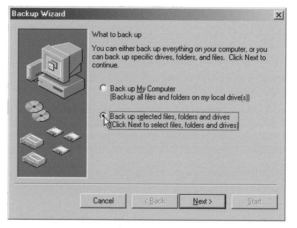

4 LOCATING THE FILES

● As only selected items have been chosen to be backed up, they need to be found on the computer. Beneath **What to back up**, click on the plus signs to open folders. In this case, the **C:** drive has been selected, followed by the **My Documents** folder, and then the **My Pictures** folder.

● Double-click the folder, and the image file **Flowers** is listed on the right. As this is the file to be backed up, place a checkmark in the box next to it. Then click on **Start**.

Click on the plus signs to open each folder; once the folder is open the plus signs become minus signs

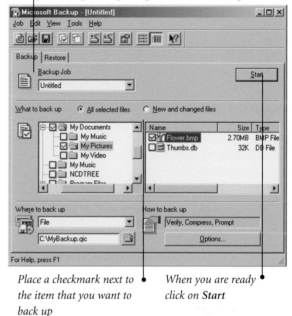

Place a checkmark next to the item that you want to back up

*When you are ready click on **Start***

5 SELECTED FILES

● For the next step, choose to back up **All selected files** and click on **Next**.

*Choose **All selected files***

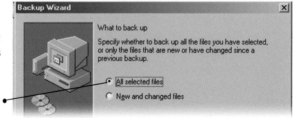

6 WHERE TO BACK UP?

● We need to tell the Wizard where to back up the files. If the floppy drive is already shown, click on **Next**. If it is not, click on the **Folder** button to bring up the **Where to back up** dialog box.

The Folder button

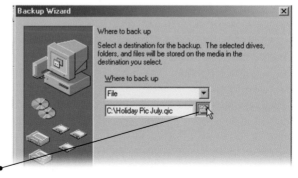

7 SELECTING THE DRIVE

● The **Where to back up** dialog box opens.
● Select your floppy drive (usually the A: drive) using the pull-down menu.

The floppy drive ●

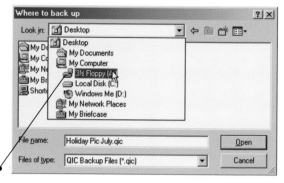

● Click on the **Open** button.

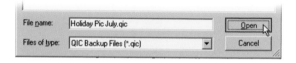

8 NAMING THE FILE

● You are returned to the **Backup Wizard** window.
● Click on the **Next** button.

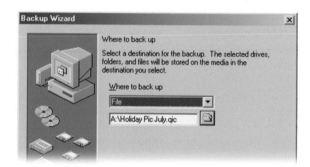

9 CHECKING AND CORRECTING

● Select both of the options in this dialog box. The first one checks to make sure that the file has been copied over correctly, the second option compresses the file.
● Click on the **Next** button.

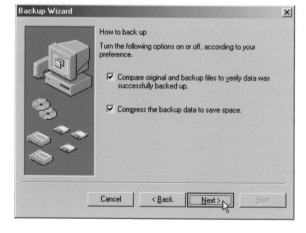

10 CHOOSING A NAME

● Using the drop-down menu, select a name for the backup, in this instance we have chosen to use the date. You can type your own choice of name.

● Click on the **Start** button.

Drop-down menu ●

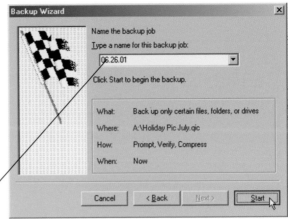

Backup Wizard

Name the backup job

Type a name for this backup job:

06.26.01

Click Start to begin the backup.

What:	Back up only certain files, folders, or drives
Where:	A:\Holiday Pic July.qic
How:	Prompt, Verify, Compress
When:	Now

Cancel   < Back   Next >   Start

11 THE PROGRESS WINDOW

● The **Backup Wizard** now presents you with a dialog box that shows the progress of the backup operation. As we only have one file to back up, the whole process is completed very quickly.

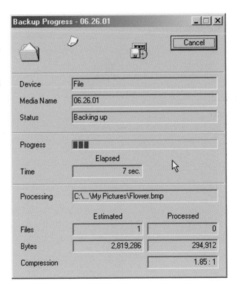

Backup Progress - 06.26.01

Cancel

Device	File
Media Name	06.26.01
Status	Backing up

Progress

Elapsed

Time   7 sec.

Processing   C:\...\My Pictures\Flower.bmp

	Estimated	Processed
Files	1	0
Bytes	2,819,286	294,912
Compression		1.85 : 1

12 FINISHING THE TASK

● An alert panel appears confirming that the backup is finished. Click on **OK** once more to exit the program, then close the main backup window.

Microsoft Backup

⚠ Operation completed.

OK

VIRUSES

We are all susceptible to computer viruses that can come to us as a result of downloading software from the internet, or passing from computer to computer by disk or email.

THE RISKS OF A VIRUS

A computer virus is a program or piece of code that can attach itself to programs on your computer. Some viruses can be considered almost harmless, perhaps throwing up joke messages; but some can delete a few or all of the files on the hard drive, causing a complete system failure known as a crash. A system failure may render your PC completely inoperable – unable even to boot up.

HOW DOES A VIRUS OCCUR?

A computer virus will have been written by someone. Most viruses start as small programs that lie hidden, attached to an application on your computer, until they are activated by running the application. The virus looks for another program to infect. It then changes each program so that it, too, contains a copy of the virus and waits for the next unsuspecting victim. Viruses are created in different ways, that is, they can infect and affect different parts of your computer. For example, a program virus will infect program files. A program file will have a file ending (or extension) such as .COM (command file) or .EXE (executable file). An executable file is the kind of file that you would use to open an application by double-clicking on it. Program viruses are common because they are easier to write.

HOW DOES A VIRUS GET ONTO MY MACHINE?

There are many potential sources that may contain a virus. A borrowed piece of software or a zip or floppy disk may contain a virus. Other ways in which a virus can infect a computer include downloading files from the internet, from a private bulletin board, or by opening an infected email. Viruses used to be conveyed from computer to computer only by executable program files. However, newer viruses, known as "macro" viruses, can exist in any document created by applications, such as Microsoft Word, which use a macro language.

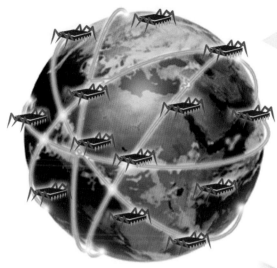

1 *The virus is designed and created by a programmer, who will probably start the trail of destruction by means of mass emailing. The emails may have file attachments that contain the virus.*

2 *The emails are received and the attachments are opened by the recipients. The virus contaminates the person's computer.*

4 *Once again, the mail is opened and the virus attaches itself to the new computer. The unsuspecting culprit may email his friends or give copies of the file and the virus now begins to take effect.*

3 *The file attachment may be passed to a friend via floppy disk or again by email. The virus then spreads.*

The virus is not selective. Once it has been passed to your system via a floppy disk, downloaded on a piece of software from the internet, or from an email, it will be only a matter of time before it triggers itself and begins to infect your computer.

WHAT DOES A VIRUS CONTAIN?

Replication engine: A successful virus makes copies of itself that move on to other computers.
Protection: A virus protects itself from detection by amending sectors on the hard drive to conceal its presence.
Trigger: The event that activates the virus may be a date and time that is read by the virus from the system clock, or by an action being repeated a certain number of times by the user.
Payload: This is the damage that the virus has been set to cause, which may or may not include loss of data.

VIRUS DEFINITIONS

Boot sector viruses: These are spread when there is an infected floppy disk, bootable or not, in the disk drive when a computer is booted. The virus is copied to the hard drive where it moves the original boot sector to another part of the disk and takes over the computer's operations.

Program viruses: These attach themselves to program files. Running them loads the virus into memory where it replicates.

Macro viruses: These viruses infect files created by applications that use a macro language, such as Microsoft Word. The virus issues commands that are accepted, understood, and executed as valid macros by the application.

Multipartite viruses: These combine the features of boot sector viruses and program viruses. They are able to move in either direction between the boot sector and applications on the hard drive.

SOME KNOWN VIRUSES

AMBULANCE

Ambulance has also been known as RedX and Red Cross. It infects command files (these are invisible files that make your computer work). It is a rare virus that displays a moving ambulance and plays a siren sound.

AVALON

Again, Avalon infects command files, but it also infects executable files. This virus has a trigger that is set to work on the 31st of any month. It can render the drive useless and nonbootable.

ZELU

Zelu infects all files but is also a rare virus. It is known as a Trojan horse and is not strictly a virus, although it has the same effect. The file is normally called Y2K.EXE and pretends to be a year 2000 compatibility checker. After software containing the virus has been installed and is run, the virus flashes file names across the bottom of the screen pretending to check them, but in reality it is overwriting and destroying them. You are then informed that you have been fooled and hit with a virus. As we are in the third millennium, this virus is no longer a real threat.

PARITY BOOT

This virus is fairly common. Once on your system, it checks every hour to see if it has infected a floppy disk. If it hasn't, then it displays a message on your screen that says "Parity Check," and causes your computer to crash.

VBS/NEWLOVE.A

This virus lodges itself in the Windows folder when it is first run following infection of your hard drive. It adopts a file name from the Recent Documents folder, or creates a random file name. The virus sends copies of itself to all entries in the address book by using Outlook Express. All drives connected to the computer are searched, and files are replaced by copies of the virus; the extension .VBS is added to the file name.

ANTIVIRUS SOFTWARE

There are a number of antivirus applications available, and some are available free over the internet. However, these tend to detect only the more common viruses. If you require software that is more comprehensive and able to detect the rarer viruses, it is advisable to use an industry-standard virus detector.

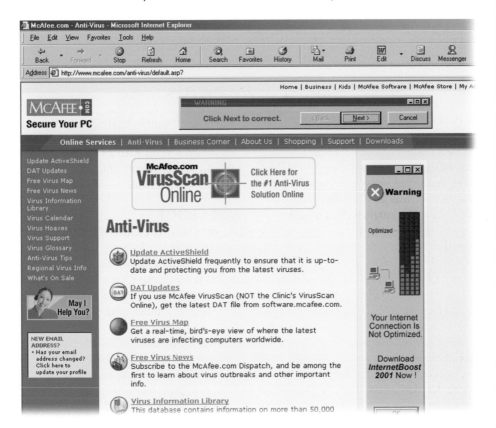

MORE FROM MCAFEE

McAfee's website, **www.mcafee.com**, invites you to download and upgrade antivirus software, much of which is offered on a two-week, free trial period. The site also provides opportunities to report viruses, to browse through their database of 50,000 known viruses, and to view a virus glossary of terms and virus definitions. The virus calendar gives the trigger dates of virus payloads. Also available is a database of hoax viruses.

NORTON ANTIVIRUS

Norton AntiVirus is one of the most popular and well-known antivirus software packages available. Norton offers virtually unrivaled protection, a very user-friendly interface, and simple updating that is available over the internet.

EASILY UPDATABLE

Norton AntiVirus is a utility available within the Norton SystemWorks suite. It gives protection while you are surfing the internet or retrieving information from floppy disks. It can even be set up to scan incoming emails and their attachments.

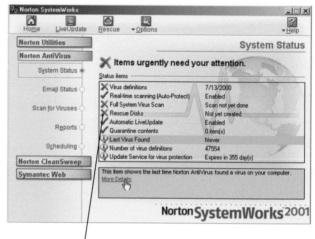

System Status
System Status determines exactly what measures you should take to protect your PC.

● Once you have clicked on the **More Details** link, the **System Status Details** dialog box opens and tells you how long ago it was since a virus was found on your computer. Click on **OK** to close the window.

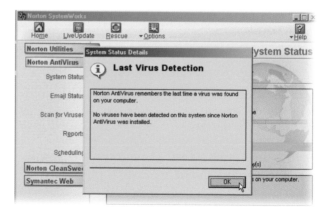

● Click on an item in the list (in this instance we have clicked on **Virus Definitions**), and then on **More Items**, which appears at the bottom of the panel.

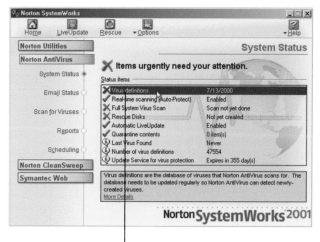

Select the items that you
wish to update.

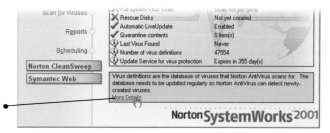

Click on the **More Details**
text link.

● You are once again presented with the **Systems Status Details** window. This time however, you are offered the chance to update your virus definitions, these will be downloaded from the internet and will protect you against the newest viruses. Click the **Yes** button to start the process.

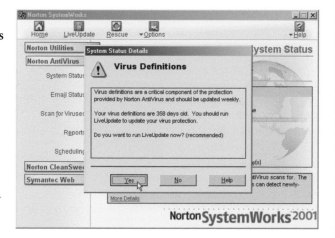

ABOUT STARTUP DISKS

One of the most important accessories for your computer setup, and probably the one that is most overlooked as far as looking after your PC is concerned, is a startup disk.

WITH SAFETY IN MIND

There is a small chance that one day your hard drive will fail, for one of several possible reasons, and your PC will be unable to start on its own. It is therefore very important that you create a startup disk that can be used to boot your computer because with a failed hard drive, a startup disk will be your only resource. By following a few easy instructions, you can avoid considerable problems, loss of time, and possible loss of data. Once created, do not forget where the disk is.

WHAT IS A STARTUP DISK?

A computer may fail to start if the system files become corrupted. There can be many reasons for this happening. For example, you may be unlucky enough to have your hard drive infected by a virus, or you may have installed some new software incorrectly, causing a software conflict.

A startup disk is created on a standard 3½-inch floppy disk. With a startup disk, your computer will boot from that rather than from the hard drive. Not only will it start your computer, it also allows you to run some diagnostic programs to fix problems if necessary. It is best to use a new disk for this task, but if you are going to use an old disk, it first needs to be reformatted. Reformatting a disk erases its contents, so make sure that the disk does not contain anything that you will need to refer to in the future.

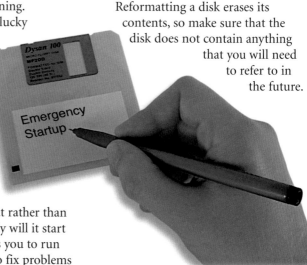

FORMATTING A FLOPPY DISK

Although you can easily erase items from a floppy disk, it can become fragmented over time and can contain all kinds of hidden litter, which could even corrupt the disk. It is therefore a good move, especially when creating something as important as a startup disk, to reformat an old disk.

1 INSERTING THE FLOPPY DISK

● Take a floppy disk and insert it into the floppy disk drive.

2 OPENING MY COMPUTER

● Double-click on the **My Computer** icon on the Desktop.

3 THE FLOPPY DISK ICON

● The **My Computer** window opens. If you need to copy any files from the floppy disk, do so now. If you don't need anything from the disk, click on the 3½ **Floppy** (A:) icon.

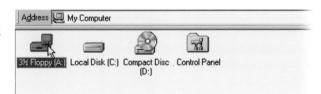

4 SELECTING FORMAT

● Click on **File** in the menu bar and select **Format** from the drop-down menu.

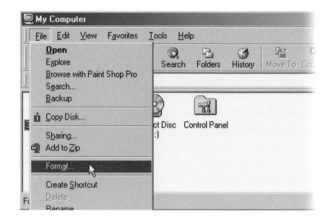

5 SELECTING THE TYPE OF FORMAT

● The **Format - 3½ Floppy (A:)** dialog box opens. Click on the **Full** radio button for a full format.

Click on Full ●

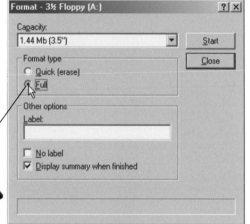

● Click on the **Start** button to begin the process.

Click on Start ●

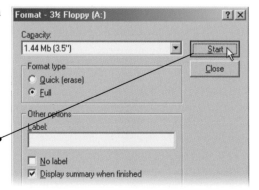

6 INITIALIZE AND FORMAT

● Windows goes through an initialization process and then begins to format the disk. A bar shows how far the formatting has progressed.

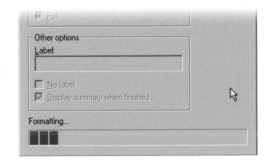

7 FORMAT RESULTS

● At the end of the process, the **Format Results** box is displayed. This shows how much free space is available on the newly formatted disk. Click on **Close**, then close any other windows. Eject the floppy disk from the drive and keep it in a safe place.

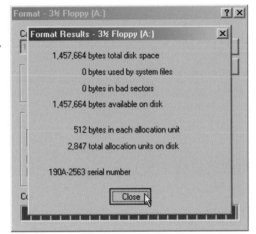

KEEPING THOSE DISKS SAFE

The best thing to do with a new startup disk is to label it clearly and store it with the original system disks, CDs, printer drivers, and Windows software. In this way, you will always know where to find the disk in an emergency.

MAKING A STARTUP DISK

Now we have a newly formatted disk, it can be made into a startup disk. This process will probably take a maximum of 10 minutes to complete, and should only require one floppy disk. You may need your Windows Me CD available.

1 FIRST STEPS

● To begin the process of making a startup disk, click on the **Start** button, select **Settings** from the pop-up menu, then **Control Panel.**

● From the **Control Menu**, double click on **Add/Remove Programs**

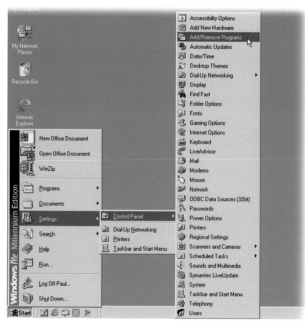

2 THE ADD/REMOVE PROGRAMS PANEL

● The **Add/Remove Programs Properties** dialog box opens. Click on the **Startup Disk** tab.

3 CREATING THE STARTUP DISK

● The **Startup Disk** tab gives you brief details about a startup disk. Click on the **Create Disk** button.

● Windows may ask you to insert the Windows Me CD. Click on **OK** when you've done so.

● Windows begins to prepare the necessary startup files to copy onto the disk.

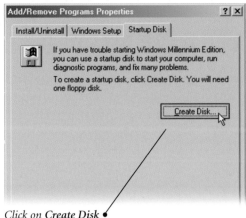

*Click on **Create Disk***

6 INSERTING THE DISK

● When Windows is ready, the **Insert Disk** dialog box appears asking you to insert a disk. Click on **OK** when you have inserted the newly formatted floppy disk into the drive.

7 COPYING FILES AND DATA

● Windows continues the process by loading all the necessary files and data onto the floppy disk.

● When the process has been completed, click on **OK** and take the floppy disk out of the drive.

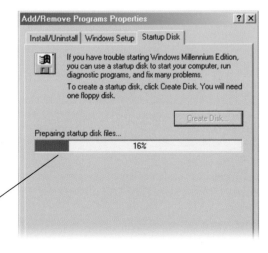

Windows runs through its procedure and continues preparing the startup disk files

EMERGENCY MEASURES

In this chapter, we will discuss some emergency measures that can be applied, using your startup disk, in the event that your computer does not operate properly or will not start at all.

USING SYSTEM RESTORE

System Restore is new to Windows Me and gives you the opportunity to return your PC to a state in which it was working in a satisfactory manner, therefore undoing things that may have caused problems. For instance, you may have installed a new piece of software that has damaged the way your monitor driver operates, corrupting it in some way. System Restore will try to return your computer to a stage before the install.

You can create your own restore points or you can use those already on your PC. The latter are known as System Checkpoints, and they are created when new software is installed.

1 USING SYSTEM CHECKPOINTS
• First, go to the **Start** menu, and then choose **Programs, Accessories, Systems Tools**, and, finally, **System Restore**.

Restore the restore...
If you perform a restore and are not happy with the results, you can always revert back to the stage from which you performed the restore!

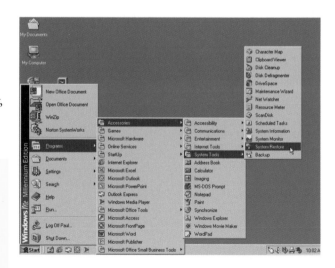

2 CHOOSING A RESTORE POINT

● You have two choices here. The first is to restore your PC to a time that has been determined by your computer or you can create your own restore point.

● If you have a problem with your PC at the moment, select the **Restore my computer to an earlier time** button and then click on **Next**.

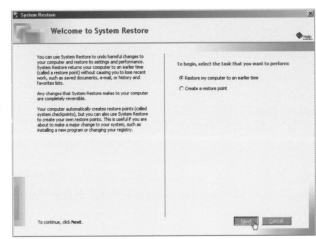

3 CHOOSING A DATE

● A calendar appears. In this example, no restore points have been created by the user – only System Checkpoints are available. These are shown as slightly bolder numbers in the calendar.

● To restore your PC to one of theses dates, click on the number and then the **Next** button.

● Before you continue, you will be asked to make sure that you do not have any applications open at this time. When you are ready, click on the **Next** button.

● Your computer begins the restore routine, which may take a while. Your computer will then automatically restart.

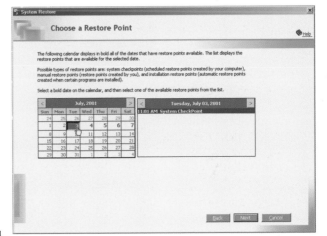

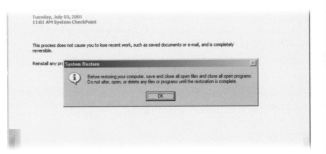

CREATING YOUR OWN RESTORE POINT

You can create a restore point on your PC at any time. However, the best time is probably when you are happy that everything is operating smoothly, or perhaps before you are about to perform a large install of some new software, something that may damage the smooth running of your computer.

1 FROM THE BEGINNING

- First, go to the **Start** menu, and then choose **Programs, Accessories, Systems Tools,** and, finally, **System Restore.**

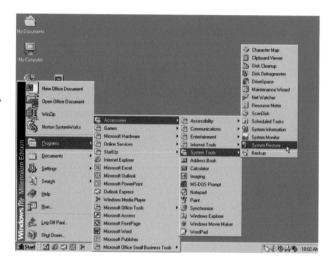

2 CREATING A RESTORE POINT

- In the main window select the **Create a restore point** button and then click on the **Next** button.

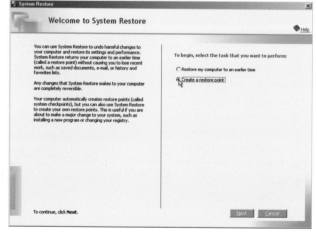

3 NAMING THE RESTORE POINT

● The next window opens and a cursor flashes in a text panel. Give your restore point a name, for example, **My first restore point**.

● When you have finished, click on the **Next** button.

● The restore point is created and you are asked to confirm your restore point name. If you are not happy with it, then click the **Back** button and rename it.

● If you are happy with the name, click on the **OK** button.

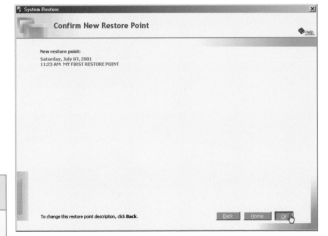

MICROSOFT UPDATE

It is worth using the Microsoft Update feature on your PC, as frequent software updates are available for items such as System Restore. Bugs are fixed and new functionality added to make the software smoother and easier to use.

BOOT FROM THE STARTUP DISK

Using the restore function shown on the previous pages is all very well if the problem that you encountered can be solved in that manner, however, if your hard drive fails, the consequences can range from an emergency boot to disk replacement. As you have made a startup disk, you may be able to at least start the computer and restore some data even if you haven't made a backup.

1 READY TO BEGIN?
● First, turn your computer off completely using the power switch on the front.

NO GUARANTEES

There is never any fail-safe way of making your machine crash-proof. You may find, for example, that even when you do manage to boot from the startup disk, your machine is not working well. This could be a hardware problem and you should consult your local supplier. On the other hand, you may be fortunate and only need to run a repair utility to restore your hard drive.

2 INSERTING THE STARTUP DISK
● Put your startup floppy disk into the disk drive and then turn your machine on.

3 INSERT THE WINDOWS CD
● Once your machine is starting up, open the CD drawer and insert your Windows Me CD.

4 NOW WHAT HAPPENS?

● You may be alarmed at the images that your PC now displays onscreen as you watch, but there's no need to worry, as this is standard practice. Your PC is only going through a routine of checking that it has all the files that it needs.

● Your PC boots up in what is known as MS-DOS mode (using the startup floppy disk), which is the long-established operating system that is still used as the backbone of Windows.

• In the Microsoft Windows Me Startup Menu, you are offered four options:
1. Help
2. Start computer with CD-ROM support.
3. Start computer without CD-ROM support.
4. Minimal Boot.

At this prompt, the Startup Menu allows you to start your system, possibly with CD-ROM support.

```
Microsoft Windows Me Startup Menu
=============================
1. Help
2. Start computer with CD-ROM support
3. Start computer without CD-ROM support
4. Minimal boot
Enter a choice: 1          Time remaining: 24
```

● Using the cursor keys, select option number 2; **Start computer with CD-ROM support** and then press the enter key.

5 UP AND RUNNING

● Your computer will now start with CD-ROM support, and the startup disk will find the appropriate software for your CD-ROM drive.

ON-SCREEEN PROMPTS

On screen prompts take you through the tasks that will try to correct the problems that caused your PC to die. There are no guarantees that the problem won't occur again. You may have irreparable damage to your hard disk, in which case, you should consult a qualified technician.

GLOSSARY

APPLICATION
Another term for a piece of software, usually a program.

ARCHIVE
A file, which is usually compressed, containing back up copies of your work.

ATTACHMENT
Almost any type of file can be sent within an email by "attaching" it to a message that you send.

BACK UP
To create copies of your work on an external device, such as a floppy disk, in case you lose documents or your computer develops a fault.

BOOLEAN MODIFIERS
Words that help you to modify the terms of a key word search.

CCD
Charge Coupled Device. A light-sensitive chip contained within a scanner that converts a scanned image into digital data.

CD-ROM
Compact Disk – Read Only Memory. A disk containing data such as games and programs. Data can only be read from the disk, not written to it.

CMYK
Cyan, Magenta, Yellow, and Black (Key). Printers use inks in these four colors, overlapping them to create full-color images.

COLOR DEPTH
The quality and level of color in a digital image, measured in bits.

COMPRESSION
The act of reducing the size of a file by using software to "compact" it into an archive.

CRASH
The term applied when a computer suddenly stops working during a routine operation.

DEFRAGMENTING
The process of reassembling and arranging badly distributed files on a hard drive.

DESKTOP
The screen that appears once Windows Me has started up, which displays the taskbar and, among others, icons for My Computer, My Documents, and the Recycle Bin.

DIALOG BOX
A rectangle that appears on the screen and prompts you for a reply, usually with buttons, e.g. OK or Cancel.

DOCUMENT
A file containing user data, such as text written in Word.

DOWNLOAD
The process of file-transfer from a remote computer to your own computer.

DPI
Dots Per Inch. The units commonly used to express the resolution of an image.

DRIVER
A piece of software that enables the computer to communicate with attached hardware, such as a scanner or printer.

EMAIL (ELECTRONIC MAIL)
A system for sending messages between computers that are linked over a network.

FILE
A discrete collection of data stored on your computer.

FILE NAME EXTENSION
Three letters added to the end of a file name that indicate what type of file the document is, e.g. .txt (a text file).

FILE PROPERTIES
Information about a file, such as its size and creation date, and attributes that determine what actions can be carried out on the file and how it behaves.

FLOPPY DISK
A removable disk that allows you to store and transport small files between computers.

FOLDER
A folder stores files and other folders, to keep files organized.

FONT
The typeface in which text appears onscreen and when it is printed out.

FORMULA
In Excel, an expression entered into a cell that calculates the value of that cell from a combination of constants, arithmetic operators, and (often) the values of other cells.

FREEWARE
Software that can be freely used and distributed, but the author retains copyright.

FUNCTION
In Excel, a defined operation or set of operations that can be performed on one or more selected cell values, cell addresses, or other data.

GIF (GRAPHICS INTERCHANGE FORMAT)
A widely used file format for web-based images.

GRAYSCALE
An image that is made up entirely of black, white, and tones of gray.

HARD DRIVE
The physical device on your computer where programs and files are stored.

HARDWARE
Hardware is the part of a computer that you can physically see or touch.

HTML (HYPERTEXT MARK-UP LANGUAGE)
The formatting language used to create web pages. HTML specifies how a page should look on screen.

HYPERLINKS
A "hot" part of a web page (e.g., text, image, table etc.) that links to another part of the same document or another document on the Internet.

HYPERTEXT
Text that contains links to other parts of a document, or to documents held on another computer. Hypertext links on web pages are usually highlighted or underlined.

ICON
A graphic symbol, attached to a file that indicates its type or the program it was created in.

IMAGE EDITING
The process of altering an image on the computer, either to improve its quality or to apply a special effect.

INKJET PRINTER
A type of color printer that fires small dots of ink from a cartridge onto the paper. The detail that can be achieved is so fine that almost photographic quality can be produced.

INSERTION POINT
A blinking upright line on the screen. As you type, text appears at the insertion point

INSTALLING
The process of "loading" an item of software onto a hard drive. See also uninstalling.

INTERNET
The network of interconnected computers that communicate with one another.

INTERNET SERVICE PROVIDER (ISP)
A business that provides a gateway to the internet.

JPEG
Joint Photographic Experts Group. A compressed file format, ideally used for low resolution images that don't contain a lot of detail, such as web graphics.

LASER PRINTER
A kind of printer that uses heat-sensitive toner to output high quality black and white prints at high speed.

LINEART
An image that is made up of black and white only, with no tones of gray.

MODEM
A device used to connect a computer to the internet via a telephone line.

NETWORK
A collection of computers that are linked together.

NEWSGROUPS
Internet discussion groups on specific topics, where people can post information or contribute to public debates.

NEWSREADER
Software that enables you to access and use newsgroups. Outlook Express has newsreader capabilities.

PARALLEL PORT
A port supplied on most computers, usually used for connecting printers.

PATH
The address of a file on a computer system.

PERIPHERAL
Any hardware device that is connected to your computer.

PIXELS
The individual color or grayscale dots that make up an image on a computer screen.

PLUG-IN
A program that adds features to a web browser so that it can handle files containing, for example, 3D and multimedia elements.

PORT
The socket on the back of a computer, or other piece of hardware, into which you connect the cables.

PROGRAM
A software package that allows you to perform a specific task on your computer (also known as an application).

PROTOCOL
A set of rules that two computers must follow when they communicate.

RADIO BUTTON
Small onscreen button within an application that visibly turns on and off when clicked with a mouse.

RECYCLE BIN
The location on your desktop where deleted files are stored. Files remain here until the Recycle Bin is emptied.

RESOLUTION
The density of the dots that make up an image, measured in pixels or dpi.

RESTORE
To return data from the Recycle Bin to its original location.

RGB
Red, Green, and Blue. An image displayed on a computer screen is created from a combination of these three colors.

RULER
Indicators at the top and left of the screen, with marks in inches or centimeters like a real ruler. Rulers also show the indents and margins of the text.

SCAN
The digital image file that is created by a scanner and saved on your computer.

SCROLL
To scroll is to move up or down the document.

SCROLL BARS
Bars at the foot and the right of the screen that can be used to scroll around the document.

SCSI PORT
Small Computer System Interface. A port that provides fast file transfer, and allows many hardware devices to be connected in a chain.

SELECT
Highlighting files or folders to enable you to perform certain activities on them.

SERVER
Any computer that allows users to connect to it and share its information and resources.

SHAREWARE
Software that is made freely available for use on a try-before-you-buy basis.

SHORTCUT
A link to a document, folder, or program located elsewhere on your computer that, when you double-click on it, takes you directly to the original.

SOFTWARE
A computer needs software to function. Software ranges from simple utilities to immense computer games.

STATUS BAR
The small panel at the foot of an open window that displays information about the items located there.

TASKBAR
The gray panel at the bottom of the desktop screen that contains the Start button, along with quick-access buttons to open programs and windows.

TIFF
Tagged Image File Format. A file format that retains a high level of information in an image, therefore suited to images that contain a lot of detail.

UNINSTALLING
The process of removing an item of software from the hard drive by deleting all its files.

USB PORT
Universal Serial Bus. A type of port that allows for very simple installation of hardware devices to your computer

USENET
A network of computer systems that carry internet discussion groups called newsgroups.

VIRUS
A program or piece of computer code deliberately created and distributed to destroy or disorganize data on other computer systems.

WEB BROWSER
A program used for viewing and accessing information on the web.

WEBSITE
A collection of web pages that are linked together, and possibly to other websites, by hyperlinks.

WINDOW
A panel displaying the contents of a folder or disk drive.

WIZARD
Interactive sequences that ask you questions and then set up a new file for you.

WORLD WIDE WEB (WWW, W3, THE WEB)
The collection of websites on the Internet.

INDEX

ACKNOWLEDGMENTS

Dorling Kindersley would like to thank the following:
Paul Mattock of APM, Brighton, for commissioned photography.
Indexing Specialists, Hove.

Canon Inc.; Hewlett-Packard Company; Jasc Software, Inc. for permission to reproduce screen shots of Paint Shop Pro™ (Copyright © 1997-2001 Jasc Software, Inc. All rights reserved); Lexmark International, Inc.; Microsoft Corporation for permission to reproduce screens from within Microsoft® Windows® Me, Microsoft® Notepad, Microsoft® Paint, Imaging for Windows®, Microsoft® Wordpad, Microsoft® Windows® Explorer, Microsoft® Outlook Express, Microsoft® Internet Explorer, Microsoft® Windows® Media Player, Microsoft® Word 2000, Microsoft® Excel 2000; Scansoft Inc.; Symantec Corporation for permission to reproduce screens from within Norton SystemWorks 2000; Umax Systems GmbH; Visioneer, Inc.; WHSmith.co.uk; WinZip Computing, Inc. for permission to reproduce screen shots of WinZip (Copyright 1991-2001, WinZip Computing, Inc.).

altavista.com; aol.co.uk; askjeeves.com; bigfoot.com; deja.com; copernic.com; directhit.com; dmoz.org; dogpile.com; download.cnet.com; excite.com; fortunecity.com; friendsreunited.co.uk; ft.com; godolphin.com; google.com; groups.google.com; hotbot.yahoo.com; infoseek.com; jethomepage.com; looksmart.com; lycos.com (© 2000 Lycos, Inc.); McAfee.com; metacrawler.com; msn.com; mus.com; nasa.gov; nationalgallery.org.uk; netscape.com; nhm.ac.uk; northernlight.com; outdoorphotography.org; shop.com; smartpages.com; sproutman.com; tucows.com; turbo10.com; winfiles.com; zone.com